A critical reader of the Romantic Grand Tour

A critical reader of the Romantic Grand Tour

TRISTES PLAISIRS

CHLOE CHARD

Manchester
University Press

Copyright © Chloe Chard 2014

The right of Chloe Chard to be identified as the author of this work has been asserted by her in accordance with the Copyright, Designs and Patents Act 1988.

Published by Manchester University Press
Oxford Road, Manchester M13 9PL
www.manchesteruniversitypress.co.uk

British Library Cataloguing-in-Publication Data
A catalogue record for this book is available from the British Library

ISBN   978 0 7190 4498 4   hardback

ISBN   978 0 7190 4499 1   paperback

First published 2014

The publisher has no responsibility for the persistence or accuracy of URLs for any external or third-party internet websites referred to in this book, and does not guarantee that any content on such websites is, or will remain, accurate or appropriate.

Typeset 9.5pt Stone Serif by
Servis Filmsetting Ltd, Stockport, Cheshire

For Vincent

Contents

List of figures — viii
Preface — x

Introduction: 'sun-beams bring death' — 1
   I: Triste plaisir — 5
   II: The tropes of travel: how to avoid languor in language — 23

1. Pleasure — 39
   I: The foreign and the familiar — 39
   II: Tourism: the management of pleasure — 58

2. Rising and sinking in sublime places — 75

3. Danger and destabilization — 110
   I: Indolent delicious reverie — 110
   II: Disease, debilitation and delusions of revival — 120
   III: Banditti — 137

4. Art, unease and life — 159
   I: Odd spectators — 160
   II: Sculpture studios: socialising with works of art — 189

5. Gastronomy, gusto and the geography of the haunted — 215

Bibliography — 242
Index — 254

List of figures

1. Henry Tresham, *The Ascent of Vesuvius* (1785-90), watercolour over graphite. Yale Center for British Art, Paul Mellon Collection (B1977.14.6296) — page 108
2. *Diana and Her Nymphs*, after Domenichino, engraved by Giovanni Franco Venturini. Victoria and Albert Museum, V&A Images/Victoria and Albert Museum, London (21136) — 135
3. 'Peasants in Search of Banditti', in Maria Graham, *Three Months Passed in the Mountains East of Rome, during the Year 1819*. Drawn by 'C.L.E.' and engraved by I. Clark — 151
4. 'Station of the Brigands near Guadagnola', in Maria Graham, *Three Months Passed in the Mountains East of Rome*. Drawn by 'C.L.E.' and engraved by I. Clark — 152
5. 'The APOLLO BELVEDERE', plate XI in Joseph Spence, *Polymetis*, engraved by L.P. Boitard. Research Library, The Getty Research Institute, Los Angeles (85-B5725) — 165
6. Antonio Canova, *The Three Graces*, front view, engraved by Domenico Marchetti, in *Recueil de statues, groupes, bustes, mausolées, colosses et monumens de tout genre, exécutés par Canova, dessinés et gravés sous les yeux de l'auteur*. Research Library, The Getty Research Institute, Los Angeles (91-F0) — 167
7. Antonio Canova, *The Three Graces*, back view, engraved by Domenico Marchetti, in *Recueil de statues, groupes, bustes, mausolées, colosses et monumens de tout genre*. Research Library, The Getty Research Institute, Los Angeles (91-F0) — 168
8. 'The FARNESE HERCULES', plate XVI in Joseph Spence, *Polymetis*, engraved by L.P. Boitard. Research Library, The Getty Research Institute, Los Angeles (85-B5725) — 172
9. Thomas Rowlandson (attributed), 'Don Luigi meets Donna Anna in the Museum', Plate VII, Lewis Engelbach, *Naples and the Campagna Felice*. Research Library, The Getty Research Institute, Los Angeles (2566-911) — 175

List of figures   ix

10. Detail from 'Ancient Greek Paintings, from Herculaneum', Plate VI: II of in Lewis Engelbach, *Naples and the Campagna Felice*. Research Library, The Getty Research Institute, Los Angeles (2566-911) 176
11. H.D.C. Martens, *Pope Leo XII Visits Thorvaldsen's Studios near the Piazza Barberini, Rome, on St Luke's Day, October 18th 1826* (1830) Thorvaldsens Museum, Copenhagen 190
12. Antonio Canova, *Venere Vincitrice*, front view, engraved by Domenico Marchetti, in *Recueil de statues, groupes, bustes, mausolées, colosses et monumens de tout genre*. Research Library, The Getty Research Institute, Los Angeles (91-F0) 194
13. Antonio Canova, *Venere Vincitrice*, back view, drawn by Luigi Durantini and engraved by Angelo Bertini, in *Recueil de statues, groupes, bustes, mausolées, colosses et monumens de tout genre*. ©The British Library Board (Tab.488.c.) 195
14. Antonio Canova, *Naiad* (also known, more specifically, as *Chloris*), front view, drawn by G. Tognoli and engraved by Angelo Bertini, in *Recueil de statues, groupes, bustes, mausolées, colosses et monumens de tout genre*. ©The British Library Board (Tab.488.c.) 206
15. Antonio Canova, *Naiad* (also known as *Chloris*), back view, drawn by G. Tognoli and engraved by Domenico Marchetti, in *Recueil de statues, groupes, bustes, mausolées, colosses et monumens de tout genre*. ©The British Library Board (Tab.488.c.) 207
16. *Hermaphrodite*, in Domenico de Rossi, *Raccolta di statue antiche e moderne*, illustrated by Pavolo Alessandro Maffei, Plate LXXVIII, engraved by Claude Randon. ©The British Library Board (688.i.9.) 208

Preface

This book was suggested to me in 1992 by Anita Roy, then commissioning editor at Manchester University Press, as one that would allow readers access to texts that were usually unavailable except in rare book libraries. A number of such texts can now be read on various websites, but are not usually accompanied by introductory material that might explain why anyone except specialists in travel – or cultural historians engaged in scholarly detective work – should find much intellectual or imaginative allure in them.

In compiling *Tristes Plaisirs*, therefore, I have provided longer introductions than are usual within the genre of the travel anthology, in order to draw attention to some of the more strange, disconcerting and labile strategies through which travel writings map out a relation between self, word and world. I have shied away from the usual tendency of anthologists to throw an air of dull predictability over the Grand Tour, by working their way through a sequence of established themes and sights (Italian marital irregularities, nuns, St Peter's, Vesuvius . . .). Some of these objects of commentary do in fact assume a role in the chapters that follow, but I have aimed to select passages that consider them in an unexpected and sidelong manner – often by elaborating on the very diverse forms of emotional and aesthetic response that they excite.

In annotating these excerpts from travel books, I have attempted to limit the proliferation of notes: I have not duplicated information that is given – or implied – in the passage itself, or in my commentary on it, and I have not supplied dates or details for well known artists, writers and other public figures. I have avoided providing translations for those foreign expressions where the meaning is obvious to any English speaker (except in odd cases where several snippets from foreign languages are used in swift succession, and omitting translations of one or two might cause confusion).

My work on one particular text that plays a part in this book – Hester Piozzi's *Observations and Reflections* – was initially directed towards a scholarly edition of the entire work, to be published in the series 'The

Literature of Travel, Exploration and Empire', published by Cassell. I was supported in my research for this edition by a Visiting Fellowship at the Centre for Cross-Cultural Research, at the Australian National University, Canberra (where the series was conceived and edited), and a Study Abroad Fellowship from the Leverhulme Trust. After the publisher twice changed hands, the series came to an end, and the contract for my book was cancelled. My continued sense of the interest of this travel book has prompted me to include four passages from it in the current selection.

In addition to the support for my work already mentioned, I should like to express my gratitude to the Getty Research Institute, Los Angeles, where I spent a year as a Getty Scholar in residence, and the Paul Mellon Centre for Studies in British Art, who awarded me the Paul Mellon Rome Fellowship the British School at Rome for four months. Several library fellowships also played a part in my work on *Tristes Plaisirs*: at McMaster University Library, the Yale Centre for British Art, the Huntington Library and the William Andrews Clark Library. I had a chance to test out the interest and usefulness of some of the material in this book for undergraduates when teaching the imaginative geography of the Grand Tour during a year as a Bye-Fellow at Newnham College, Cambridge.

I should also like to acknowledge a grant from the Authors' Foundation (Society of Authors, London), and a Carlyle Membership from the London Library, which has allowed me to continue to use the Library's collections.

This book has benefited from conversations with many friends, including Mary Beard, Rosemary Bechler, Gabi Dolff-Bonekämper, James Greene, Anthony Howell, Helen Langdon and Claire Lyons. For advice on specific points, I am indebted to Georgina Born, Alex Drace-Francis, Katharine Kittredge, Esther Langdon, Kenneth Lapatin, Maria Loh, Jean-Clément Martin, Roberta Panzanelli, Pasquale Pasquino, David A. Powell, Ian Patterson, Isabelle Remy, Nicholas Thomas, Josephine Tomalin and Eileen White. Particular thanks are due to Karen Gunterman, my research assistant during my year at the Getty Research Institute. Malcolm Baker, Tim Knox, Todd Longstaffe-Gowan and Jonathan Marsden supplied crucial help with picture research.

At Manchester University Press, I am grateful to Anita Roy for commissioning the book and to Matthew Frost for seeing it through much of its development.

Large parts of this book were drafted at the homes of friends in various parts of the world, who generously provided refuges that allowed me to concentrate on writing. I should especially like to thank Rosie and Nat Chard, Marigold Hodgkinson and Winslow Foot, Michael Hollington, Claire Lyons and Joost van Oss, Brigid O'Connor, Marcella Ruble and Alan Harris, and Lisa Wood and Adrian Binks.

The person to whom I owe most, in this as in all enterprises that I have valued, is Vincent Woropay, who added immense delight and imaginative vision to my travels, and whose loss makes me all the more profoundly conscious that travelling is a 'triste plaisir'.

Introduction

'SUN-BEAMS BRING DEATH'

> When the point of arrival is settled in advance, it exercises a general attraction, we desire it, it emits signs. Thus, in the countryside, the city glows.
> Michel Butor, 'Travel and Writing' (1974)

> 'Oh S,' said E, 'the sights are worse than the journeys.'
> Sybille Bedford, *A Visit to Don Otavio* (1953)

> Localities are often treated like persons.
> Sigmund Freud, *The Interpretation of Dreams* (1900)

Sydney, Lady Morgan, in her travel book *Italy* (1821), offers an account of Naples that provides a useful starting-point for considering approaches to travel – and strategies for translating travel and topography into forms of language – at a time when travelling on the Grand Tour can be described as doubly destabilized. On the one hand, assumptions about travel, over the late eighteenth and early nineteenth centuries, are displaced or thrown into question. On the other hand, travellers frequently describe themselves as hovering on the brink of various forms of destabilization and danger. Morgan, in this extract from her book, touches on physical danger (as represented by deadly sunbeams, 'burning vapours' and the destructive power of volcanic eruptions), but also notes the perils of restlessness and fatigue that travel entails. Her visit to Herculaneum, moreover, supplies a frisson of horror and terror, of a kind offered by the Gothic novels of the 1790s: the traveller visits the dimly lit depths of the partially excavated city, and considers their effect upon 'the mind of the nervous and fanciful':

Lady Morgan [Sydney Morgan, née Owenson], *Italy*, 2 vols (London: Henry Colbum, 1821), vol. 2, pp. 335–9

Naples is the ordinary termination of the stranger's pilgrimage to Italy. The memory, overloaded by the numerous remembrances committed to its keeping – the mind worn by the reiterated calls made on its perceptions – novelty exhausted, curiosity blunted, all dispose even the most ardent traveller to a repose, the indulgence of which has become both morally and physically necessary. More churches to visit, more palaces to see, more monuments to study, would become a duty, and cease to be an amusement; and it is a relief, rather than a disappointment, to learn that Naples contains few if any of these objects, worthy to arrest that attention on which Florence and Rome have already so deeply drawn. The antiquities of Naples, and its environs, are its sites, its buried cities, and classic ports; its historical recollections are the perpetuated horrors of a foreign despotism, registered in its Moorish, Spanish and Arabic architecture: but its great, its distinguishing feature is the singular and sublime character stamped on its region by Nature! In this point of view Naples stands alone; taking her perilous position on the brink of destruction, reposing her luxurious villas on the edge of a crater, and raising her proud towers on the shifting surface of an eternally active volcano. Such fatal but inevitable engines rarely allure the proximity of man; they are found lording the desolation where human interests end, amidst the ice deserts of Kamtschatka, the altitudes of the Andes, the outskirts of the world; but the gay, brilliant, fantastic city, which pours its restless, busy, bustling population at the foot of Vesuvius, with an electric fluid for its atmosphere, and rivers of flame, and showers of ashes, for its ordinary phenomena – such a city is well worth visiting, though it had not one attraction besides that of its awful and uncertain site. Here the plain of to-day is the mountain of to-morrow*; and Nature performs her greatest operations with all her rude materials round her, within the view of man, and the precincts of his daily neighbourhood. Here she is seen revealing her processes of creation, changing, combining, exhausting, renewing, and recreating, but never destroying! – her means and modes exposed to every eye – but what her object and her end? the most prying of her creatures, man, has never yet, and never may discover!

In Rome, and its surrounding deserts, every thing depicts the death of Nature. In Naples, and its environs, all evinces her vigour and activity – an activity that preys upon itself, a feverish vitality that consumes while it brightens. The air is fire, the soil a furnace. Sun-beams bring death† as they fall! and the earth, when struck, sends up burning vapours!‡ Every where

---

* The Monte Nuovo (at a short distance from Naples). In the night of the 29th of September, 1588, after a violent trembling of the earth, a terrible volcanic explosion took place, and after three days awful fermentation of the elements, the hill now called Monte Nuovo, arose out of the plain. During this sublime but terrific operation, showers of cinders fell to the distance of twenty-four miles, and the spacious hospital of the Tripergola, was swallowed in the abyss, with many private dwellings. See Marc-Antonio de' Falconi, Degl' incendj di Pozzuoli.

† The *Coup de Soleil*.

‡ The moment the surface of the Solfatara (the Forum Vulcani of Strabo) is struck, a column of hot vapour rises, as if by the touch of an enchanter. One almost expects to see the

the ruins of time and man are mingled with the fragments of an overwrought creation; and the amphitheatres of Augustus and Pompey, the villa of Cicero, and the altars of Caligula, identified by prostrated masses of sculptured marbles, lie scattered amidst the extinct volcanoes of Pozzuoli.*
In the environs of Naples there lies subject-matter for the antiquarian, the painter, the naturalist, and the philosopher! Its coasts are bathed by the sea of Homer! its lakes and its hills afford the topography of Virgil.† Its vineyards bloom over caves where the Cumean Sibyl composed her oracles; and every cliff and headland is a history, the register of a crime, or the land-mark of an adventure which had made the immortality of him who recorded, or him who performed them.‡

From the multiplicity of objects which present themselves worthy of description and tempting to describe, it is difficult to reject one, and vanity to attempt any. The painters, historians, antiquarians, and travellers of modern times have left nothing new to tell – nothing untouched to delineate. Naples has been a fertile, and is now an exhausted subject: to view its volcanoes and reach its classic shores, the north of Italy has been rapidly and carelessly run over, its histories unsearched, and its monuments unexamined; and to the traveller of the present day nothing is left, but cautiously and briefly to obtrude upon the reader some object of overwhelming importance, whose impression is deep-seated, and whose description, if not new, may at least not be languid.

After days and nights given to the coasts and land scenery of Naples,

---

Genius of Brimstone gradually incorporating and rising out of them. Its soil, of many-coloured sulphurs, affords a new aspect of nature.

* Pozzuoli, the most ancient historical site in Italy, (and in the height of Roman glory, characterized by its grandeur and magnificence,) contains the ruins of the Temples of Serapis, of Diana, and many other monuments. The villa Puteolana of Cicero, and his stadium, are sites rather than monuments, visited and disputed over by wrangling antiquarians. Caligula, in his mad passage over the bridge of boats, paused in the Temple of Neptune, in Pozzuoli, to offer propitiatory sacrifices. Here too Caesar, on his way to give battle to Antony, sacrificed to the winds, to Neptune, and the sea.

† The road from the town of Pozzuoli leads between the Via Cumana and the *Monte Nuovo* to the Lake Avernus; and all the scenery of the eleventh book of the Odyssey, and of the Æneid, spreads beneath the eye; – but when we visited its *Cimmerian* shores, they were glowing in sunshine; sites that awed the spirits of Hercules and Ulysses, now looked invitingly gay; and the terrible Avernus of antiquity resembled the carp and tench lake of an English park. Still the superb ruins of the Thermæ and Temple of Apollo strewn near it, meet the dreams of the imagination; and a subterranean passage, with its classic name of the Sibyl's grotto, realized one at least of its poetic visions; even though a little Christian chapel dedicated to St. Januarius rose in the centre.

‡ The scene of the terrible tragedy of which Agrippina was the heroine lay on the beautiful coast of Baiæ; – the monument or sepulchre, called Sepolcro di Agrippina, lies on the shore between the picturesque Castello di Baiæ and the headland of Misenum. The whole of these shores look as if they were etched and painted – the drawing and colouring equally exquisite: they were not very accessible; but they well repay the fatigue and trouble of visiting them. The sea-pieces of Salvator Rosa are recalled at every step.

to Pozzuoli and Baiæ, to the lovely ascents of Posilipo and the lava shores of Portici, the objects which struck us most were those which strike all! – Vesuvius and Pompeii, the grotto of Posilipo, and the burnt wastes of the Solfatara. From Naples to Pompeii, the route along the bay includes not only one of the loveliest of the many lovely views of this region; but most of the principal objects for which the naturalist and antiquarian visit this extraordinary region – Herculaneum, Portici, Vesuvius. A long suburban line of buildings – some shattered and miserable (the abodes of the people), others spacious but deserted (the villas of the nobles), leads to the royal palaces of Portici, by the village of Resina – the first stage in this journey of wonders, at which taste or curiosity is induced to stop; for the streets of Resina cover the buried ruins of Herculaneum. A mass of formless buildings, inhabited by dingy, dirty beings, are sunk to the right of the road, where the visitor descends from his carriage, and is met by the grim gaunt guide of Herculaneum, who having distributed a candle to each of the party, and furnished himself with many, proceeds by a cavernous aperture in the earth to descend the sloping surface between its black and gloomy walls, over which so many centuries have passed. A descent of eighty palms (for it is said that seven layers of lava lie between the soil of Herculaneum and of Resina) leads to the subterranean defile, where there is so little to see, and so much to sadden.

The terror lest the lights should be extinguished in this dense dark tomb, increased by the caution with which the experienced guide multiplies illumination, by sticking a candle here and there against the lava walls, as he proceeds, as land-marks to return by – the dim glimmer of these distant lights, as the winding of the narrow labyrinth is followed, with a thousand horrors conjured up by the impressions of darkness, leave on the mind of the nervous and fanciful but one dominant feeling – the desire of returning to day-light and fresh air. Little indeed is to be seen in the depths of Herculaneum but the ruins of the amphitheatre, round whose orchestra the guide leads his protégés*; but the whole is so partially excavated, and the darkness so impenetrable, that the view is indistinct, and the impression carried away incomplete. The monuments are indeed so buried in the lava, (which must have fallen in liquid floods, pouring into every space,) that the

---

* It is scarcely necessary to observe, that, in 1726, an accidental excavation made by the Prince d'Elbeuf, who was building a villa at Resina, occasioned the discovery of *Herculaneum*, buried by an eruption of Vesuvius in the year 79; whose ashes are said to have fallen in Egypt. In the course of the excavation by Charles the Third, father to the present King, a portico, two temples, a magnificent theatre, and several private houses were discovered; but to the disgrace of that government, whose exchequer was inadequate to pay spies and pensioned favourites, those great works were stopped, and the excavations already made filled up; so that nothing now remains but the proscenium and some other parts of the great amphitheatre.

most accurate idea which can be formed of this terribly preserved city, is that given by fossil forms impacted in their matrices. In one place we saw the impression of a comic mask in the lava; and other objects were pointed out by the guides, to which *one* of the party, at least, gave more faith than examination. The sound of the carriage-wheels over our heads, as we reascended, driving through Resina, and the first ray of daylight, awakened the pleasantest sensations to which this visit to Herculaneum gave birth. Every reflection connected with it is terrible; and yet the villages built over it swarm with inhabitants, who may, every time Vesuvius explodes, expect the same fate as the great city beneath has experienced.

I: *Triste plaisir*

Restlessness

Morgan, embarking upon her account of Naples, emphasizes the restless desire to move onwards that propels the traveller towards the warm South: 'to view its volcanoes and reach its classic shores, the north of Italy has been rapidly and carelessly run over, its histories unsearched, and its monuments unexamined.' The theme of restlessness recurs in travel writing of this period. Germaine de Staël, in her novel *Corinne, ou l'Italie* (1807) – a work repeatedly invoked in travel narratives of this period – describes travel as 'un triste plaisir' ('a sad pleasure'), and speaks of 'cet empressement, cette hâte pour arriver là où personne ne vous attend, cette agitation dont la curiosité est la seule cause' ('this hurry, this haste to arrive somewhere where no one awaits you, this agitation that stems merely from curiosity').[1] Henry Matthews, in his *Diary of an Invalid* (1820), dwells on the more positive and therapeutic aspects of such haste and agitation: 'When the mind is full of fret and fever, the best remedy is to put the body in motion, which, by establishing an equilibrium between the two, may perhaps restore something like tranquillity to the whole system.'[2] Chateaubriand, musing on the life of a sailor in his *Itinéraire de Paris à Jérusalem, et de Jérusalem à Paris* (1811), presents constant travel as a powerful metaphor for a plot of desire in which, he maintains, humans are inexorably caught up: a plot in which we constantly pursue objects of longing, for which our desire dissolves the moment that we attain them:

---

[1] Madame de Staël, *Corinne, ou l'Italie*, edited by Claudine Herrmann, 2 vols (Paris: Éditions des Femmes, 1979), vol. 1, p. 25.
[2] Henry Matthews, *Diary of an Invalid*, second edition (London: John Murray, 1820), p. 167.

> Il y a dans la vie du marin quelque chose d'aventureux qui nous plaît et qui nous attache. Ce passage continuel du calme à l'orage, ce changement rapide des terres et des cieux, tiennent éveillée l'imagination du navigateur. Il est lui-même, dans ses destinées, l'image de l'homme ici-bas: toujours se promettant de rester au port, et toujours déployant ses voiles; cherchant des îles enchantées où il n'arrive presque jamais, et dans lesquelles il s'ennuie s'il y touche; ne parlant que de repos, et n'aimant que les tempêtes.[3]
>
> There is in the life of the sailor something adventurous that pleases us and to which we feel attached. This continual passage from calm to storm, this rapid change of lands and skies, keep the imagination of the navigator awakened. He is himself, in his destinies, the image of man here below: always promising himself that he will stay in port, and always unfurling his sails; seeking enchanted islands at which he hardly ever arrives, and in which he grows bored if he does touch upon them; speaking only of rest, and loving only storms.

Other writings emphasize the allure of the warm South, in particular, in drawing the traveller onwards – as Morgan does, when she cites Naples as the city that induces such haste. Anna Jameson, describing the journey southwards from Rome in her *Diary of an Ennuyée* (1826), traces the power of the 'enchanted land' before her to dissipate even the most extreme despondency. Quoting the passage from *Corinne* already cited, she initially associates the sadness of travel not with restlessness but with 'languid passiveness':

> I left Rome this morning exceedingly depressed. Madame de Staël may well call travelling *un triste plaisir:* my depression did not arise from the feeling that I left behind me any thing or any person to regret, but from mixed and melancholy emotions, and partly perhaps from that weakness which makes my hand tremble while I write – which has bound down my mind, and all its best powers, and all its faculties of enjoyment, to a languid passiveness, making me feel at every moment, I am not what I was, or ought to be, or might have been.[4]

The delights of the South, however, exercise an enchantment that seems partially to dissipate such languor:

> 2. – Our journey to-day has been long, but delightfully diversified and abounding in classical beauty and interest. I scarce know what to say, now that I open my little book to record my own sensations: they are so many, so various, so painful, so delicious – my senses and my imagination have been so enchanted, my heart so very heavy – where shall I begin?
>
> In some of the scenes of to-day – at Terracina particularly, there was beauty beyond what I ever beheld or imagined: the scenery of Switzerland is of a different character, and on a different scale: it is beyond comparison grander, more gigantic, more overpowering, but it is not so poetical. Switzerland is not Italy – is

---

[3] [François René de] Chateaubriand, *Itinéraire de Paris à Jérusalem, et de Jérusalem à Paris*, edited by Émile Malakis, 2 vols (Baltimore and London: Johns Hopkins University Press, [1811] 1941), vol. 2, p. 210.

[4] [Anna Jameson,] *Diary of an Ennuyée*, second edition (London: Henry Colburn, 1826), p. 206.

not the enchanting *south*. This soft balmy air, these myrtles, orange groves, palm trees; these cloudless skies, this bright blue sea, and sunny hills, all breathe of an enchanted land: 'a land of Faery.'[5]

Fatigue

In Morgan's narrative, however, 'even the most ardent traveller' arrives in Naples too tired, for the moment, to spurn the prospect of 'repose'. The reasons for seeking out that city – and, yet more clearly, those for pausing there – are, she suggests, the various forms of fatigue induced by the traversal of Italy.

> More churches to visit, more palaces to see, more monuments to study, would become a duty, and cease to be an amusement; and it is a relief, rather than a disappointment, to learn that Naples contains few if any of these objects, worthy to arrest that attention on which Florence and Rome have already so deeply drawn.

The attraction of the warm South, then, is located in part in its symbolic role (and, in terms of early nineteenth-century perceptions, its practical role) as a topography beyond the domain of 'duty'.[6] Naples satisfies an urgent need for 'a repose, the indulgence of which has become both morally and physically necessary'.

The question of fatigue is noted by many travellers, Charles Dupaty, in his *Lettres sur L'Italie* (1788), proclaims, after viewing paintings at the Palazzo Sera, in Genoa: 'Il n'y a pas de termes dans aucune langue pour les copier', and adds: 'J'ai besoin que le sommeil vienne fermer mes yeux: ils sont fatigués d'admirer' ('There are no expressions in any language strong enough to describe them. I really want repose, and wish for Morpheus to close my eyes: they are fatigued with admiring').[7] Anna Jameson, in Venice, is similarly afflicted by weariness: 'I am fatigued, and my head aches; – my imagination is yet dazzled: – my eyes are tired of admiring, my mind is tired of thinking, and my heart with feeling – Now for

---

[5] [Jameson,] *Diary of an Ennuyée*, pp. 208–9.

[6] Naples is routinely defined by travellers as a city in which there are few works of art to see. Joseph Forsyth comments on the palace of Capo di Monte, in *Remarks on Antiquities, Arts, and Letters during an Excursion in Italy in the Years 1802 and 1803*, first edition (London: T. Cadell and W. Davies, 1813), p. 295: 'Most of the pictures serve as mere upholstery. Indeed, the keeper himself felt shame for his stores, and condemned by a "non guardi" ["don't look"] whole rooms to neglect.' All further references to this text are to this edition, unless otherwise stated. Works endorsed by the taste of the time are obviously less numerous in the city than at Rome, but the denial that there is much art in Naples can also be seen as a means of implying that the overwhelming proliferation of paintings and sculptures in Rome (as discussed below) has left the traveller unable to assimilate many more of them.

[7] [Charles Marguerite Jean Baptiste Mercier Dupaty,] *Lettres sur l'Italie, en 1785*, 2 vols (Rome and Paris: de Senne, 1788), vol. 1, pp. 30–1; *Sentimental Letters on Italy*, translated by J. Povoleri, 2 vols (London: J. Crowder and J. Bew, 1789), vol. 1, p. 27.

repose.'⁸ Such fatigue is explored repeatedly and elaborately by Stendhal. In *Promenades dans Rome* (1830), he describes himself and his companions returning each evening 'horriblement fatigués' ('horribly tired') after viewing the sights of the Eternal City; at one point, he counsels the reader as to how to avoid the weariness induced by visual satiety:

> En sortant de Saint-Pierre, voyez l'architecture du mur extérieur de l'église, au couchant, derrière la sacristie. Après quoi passez à un objet absolument different, allez aux jardins Borghèse ou à la villa Lante. Faute de cette méthode, vous vous fatiguerez étonnamment et arriverez plus vite au *dégoût de l'admiration*. C'est le seul sentiment que le voyageur ait à redouter ici.⁹
>
> As you leave St Peter's, go and see the architecture of the outer wall of the church, on the west, behind the sacristy. After which, move on to a completely different object: go to the Borghese gardens or the Villa Lante. Unless you follow this method, you will grow amazingly weary and you will more quickly find yourself *disgusted with admiring*. This is the one feeling that the traveller has to dread here.

Stendhal reaffirms, at intervals, that he and his companions are, at least to begin with, ruthlessly selective in what they view: after the nymph in the foreground of Domenichino's *Diana and Her Nymphs*, at the Palazzo Borghese (see Figure 2), has 'séduit tous les cœurs' ('seduced every heart'), he notes, 'nous avons passé fièrement les yeux baissés devant les autres tableaux' ('we strode on proudly, with lowered eyes, before the other paintings'). On an earlier visit to this same collection, they make the 'vraiment noble' gesture of paying a whole scudo – 5 francs and 38 centimes, the traveller tells us – to the *custode*, before devoting themselves to a few choice works; 'touché de notre génerosité' ('touched by our generosity'), the man gratefully tries to force them to see the rest of the collection. 'Nous nous sommes enfuis' ('We fled'), Stendhal concludes.¹⁰

Rome – the setting in which Stendhal so strongly emphasizes the need to keep fatigue at bay – is repeatedly defined by other travellers, too, as exceptionally exhausting. One precondition for this view of the city is that it is seen as the point on the itinerary at which the traveller encounters the greatest proliferation of sights – the objects worthy of arresting the traveller's attention that Morgan finds so gratifyingly thin on the ground in Naples. Charles Nicolas Cochin, in his *Voyage d'Italie* (1758), explains simply: 'Je n'ai pu faire aucune note sur les belles choses qu'on voit à Rome, à cause de leur quantité, qui est en quelque façon innombrable' ('I have been unable to make any mention of the beauti-

---

⁸ [Jameson,] *Diary of an Ennuyée*, p. 70.
⁹ Stendhal [Henri Beyle], *Promenades dans Rome*, in *Voyages en Italie*, edited by V. del Litto (Paris: Gallimard, [1830] 1973), pp. 593–1291; p. 604, p. 622; *Diana and Her Nymphs* is now in the Villa Borghese rather than the Palazzo. See also, for example, p. 629: 'nous étions fatigués d'admirer' ('we were weary of admiring').
¹⁰ Stendhal, *Promenades dans Rome*, p. 635, p. 629.

ful things that are to be seen in Rome, because of their quantity, which is in a sense incalculable').[11] Rome is also a city in which more is at stake than elsewhere, since it occupies a crucial role in a narrative that closely determines the range and limits of what can be said about European travel from the late sixteenth century until at least the 1830s: the narrative of the Grand Tour.

The Tour, it is worth noting at this point, is usually defined by cultural historians as a practice of travel. The concern of the present book, however, is not with a practice but with a discourse of European travel, which adopts as a point of reference the approach to travelling associated with the Grand Tour. This discourse is viewed here as a set of concepts, assumptions, arguments, theoretical options and rhetorical strategies, which determine the range and limits of what can be said or written about European travels that entail a journey southwards across the Alps.[12] As a practice, the Tour is generally considered as part of the education of a gentleman, adopted first by the British gentry and aristocracy and then by other northern Europeans, and by men and women of the middle classes; it is sometimes defined with reference to a particular itinerary through Italy, and sometimes seen as sufficiently flexible to include almost any European destination.[13] Within the discourse of European travel, the concept of the Grand Tour as a culturally and socially privileged way of travelling allows a speaking subject to claim specific forms of authority in commenting on certain specific domains of objects. Some of these forms of authority depend upon an identification with a British, male, patrician figure: it is assumed, in travel writings, that the traveller can speak as one enjoying the prestige that such a figure would enjoy, no matter what identity he or she actually claims.

The concept of the Tour also supplies the crucial precondition that makes it possible for the traveller to map out an imaginative topography

---

[11] Charles Nicolas Cochin, *Voyage d'Italie: ou, recueil des notes sur les ouvrages de peinture et de sculpture, qu'on voit dans les principales villes d'Italie*, 3 vols (Paris: 'Ch. Ant. Jombert', 1758), vol. 1, p. 103. Cochin's account of why he has decided not to embark on a catalogue of the works to be seen in Rome occupies one short page; he then moves on to Tivoli.

[12] Different approaches to the Grand Tour among recent scholars have produced some divergences of emphasis: as Nicholas Thomas points out in his entry for 'Grand Tour' in Iain McCalman (general editor), *An Oxford Companion to the Romantic Age: British Culture 1776–1832* (Oxford: Oxford University Press, 1999), p. 533: 'It has frequently been presumed that promiscuity and good living were the most prominent elements of the Grand Tour experiences of men; and transgression and licence were indeed preoccupations of travellers themselves. It is, however, easy to neglect the political and aesthetic reflection prompted by travel.'

[13] For a work that presents the Grand Tour as strongly British, masculine and patrician in character, see Bruce Redford, *Dilettanti: The Antic and the Antique in Eighteenth-Century England* (Los Angeles: The J. Paul Getty Museum and the Getty Research Institute, 2008).

of Europe, structured around a symbolic opposition between the warm South and the cold North. The topography of the warm South is flexible: on the one hand, the whole of Italy is the land of the South; on the other, Italy itself divides into a northern region and a southern one, which begins as the traveller reaches Rome.

The precise itinerary followed by different travellers, when moving from North to South, varies considerably, but the Eternal City is a destination that all travellers, it is taken for granted in travel books, must desire to reach, whether or not they actually attain it. Sir James Edward Smith, borrowing the formulations of Conyers Middleton's *Letter from Rome* (1729), emphasizes as strongly as possible the importance of the city to the Tour:

> 'Twas the sentiment of an ingenious traveller, that of all the places he had seen or should see, it was by far the most delightful; – that a voyage to Italy might properly enough be compared to the common stages of the journey of life. At our first setting out through France, the pleasures that we find, like those of our youth, are of the gay fluttering kind, which grow by degrees, as we advance towards Italy, more solid, manly, and rational, but attain not their full perfection till we reach Rome; from which point we no sooner turn homewards, than they begin again gradually to decline; and though sustained for a while in some degree of vigour, through the other stages and cities of Italy, yet dwindle at last into weariness and fatigue, and a desire to be at home.[14]

Rome, then, demands not only a resolute commitment to sightseeing, but also a high seriousness: a capacity for 'solid, manly, and rational' pleasures. Naples, in contrast, offers pleasures that require no rational preparation or effort, but simply take possession of the traveller. James Galiffe, in *Italy and its Inhabitants* (1820), adopts a physiological terminology to convey a receptiveness to pleasure that goes beyond the control of the will; noting the incomparable character of multiple features of both nature and culture, he comments:

> All this completely overpowers the faculties at first, and produces a sort of intoxication, which opens every pore to new and indescribable impressions. It is really as if one had previously been only half alive, and as if new senses were developed which had hither[to] lain dormant and unconscious. There is besides a positive pleasure even in breathing the air of Naples, and it is impossible not to yield to a sensual delight in the mere feeling of existence.[15]

Anna Jameson sums up the difference between instinctual and rational pleasure by observing: 'One leaves Naples as a man parts with an enchant-

---

[14] *Memoir and Correspondence of the Late Sir James Edward Smith, M.D.*, edited by Lady [Pleasance] Smith, 2 vols (London: Longman, Rees, Orme, Brown, Green and Longman, 1832), vol. 1, pp. 224–5; letter dated 'April 9, 1787'. Smith himself did not turn back at Rome, but went on to Naples.

[15] James Galiffe, *Italy and its Inhabitants: An Account of a Tour in that Country in 1816 and 1817*, 2 vols (London: John Murray, 1820), vol. 2, p. 59.

ing mistress, and Rome as we would bid adieu to an old and dear-loved friend.'[16] John Chetwode Eustace, in his *Tour through Italy* (1813–19), ponders the matter at greater length, introducing it through a cluster of negatives that suggest a more tortuous effort of cogitation:

> I know not whether the traveller is not more struck with the appearance of Rome on his return from Naples, than he was on his first entrance. Not to speak of the grandeur of the objects that meet his eye, even at the gate, and are certainly well calculated to make a strong impression, it has been justly observed that the stir, the animation, the gaiety that pervade the streets of Naples, still fresh in his recollection, contrast singularly with the silence and solemnity that seem to reign undisturbed over all the quarters of Rome. The effect of this contrast is increased by the different style of building, the solidity and magnitude of Roman edifices, and the huge masses of ruin that rise occasionally to view, like monuments of a superior race of beings. We seem in our journey to have passed over not miles but ages, and arrived at a mansion where the agitations of the *present* are absorbed in the contemplation of the *past*, and the passions of this world are lost in the interests of that which is to succeed it. Rome is not therefore like Naples, the seat of mirth and dissipation; of public amusement, or even of private conviviality. The *severe majesty* that seems to preside as the genius of the place, proscribes frivolity, and inspires loftiness of thought and gravity of deportment. It imposes even on scenes of relaxation a certain restraint, that without infringing on the ease of conversation, and the confidence of familiar intercourse, gives a serious bias to the mind, and disposes it imperceptibly to reflection.
>
> But if in Rome, we seek in vain for the lighter amusements, such as balls, routs, and operas; we are supplied with other entertainments of a much higher, and to a man of solid judgment, of a much more satisfactory nature. Not to speak of the arts and sciences, that seem to expand all their treasures, and to court our observation at every step, he who delights to range in thought over the past, and converse with the great of ancient times, will here find an inexhaustible fund of occupation in every street and the memory of some noble achievement or illustrious person meeting him at every turn.[17]

Many other travel writings construct implicit elisions between the demands that the sights of Rome make upon travellers and the various forms of authority that the objects of viewing embody: the authority of the ancients, that of the masters of 'modern excellence' in art and – a form of authority readily rejected by Protestant northerners, but nonetheless one that is seen as insistently asserting itself in disconcerting ways – that of the Roman Catholic Church. (Stendhal claims to be in a bad mood for two days as a result of being severely reproved in the church of San Andrea della Valle for – supposedly – conversing about the Domenichino frescos in too loud a voice.)[18]

---

[16] [Jameson,] *Diary of an Ennuyée*, p. 308.
[17] John Chetwode Eustace, *A Tour through Italy, Exhibiting a View of its Scenery, its Antiquities, and its Monuments; Particularly as they are Objects of Classical Interest and Elucidation*, 3 vols (London: J. Mawman, 1813–19), vol. 2, pp. 66–7.
[18] Stendhal, *Promenades dans Rome*, pp. 891–2.

Naples, on the other hand, is almost invariably invested with animation; while commentaries on the city note the paradoxical combination of vivacity and languor there, oppositions between Naples and Rome usually select the liveliness of the former city as the most striking point of contrast to Roman seriousness and sobriety. For Morgan, that liveliness stems primarily from the vitality of the natural world: 'In Rome, and its surrounding deserts, every thing depicts the death of Nature. In Naples, and its environs, all evinces her vigour and activity.' Galiffe sets up the contrast in an especially dramatic way, by emphasizing the 'overpowering lassitude' and 'constant lowness of spirits' induced by 'the unwholesome summer air' in Rome. He carries out his sightseeing tours 'in a sort of slumber', and then finds that 'when I tried, in the evening, to review and digest what I had seen and heard in the course of the day, I had only that confused recollection of circumstances which one experiences on awaking, and trying to put together the uncertain fragments of a dream.' He sums up:

> At Naples, I felt life animating me so forcibly, that it seemed to act as a substantive and separate power: at Rome, I almost forgot that I existed; and every motion seemed rather the effect of a mechanical impulse, than an effort of my will.[19]

Pleasure and danger

When Morgan declares that 'Naples is the ordinary termination of the stranger's pilgrimage to Italy', then, her adjustment of the established itinerary of the Tour, as mapped out by Sir James Edward Smith, unleashes an implicit reflection on the nature of the pleasures that the Tour may incorporate. The assumption that travellers will want to travel on from Rome to Naples is common by the early nineteenth century, but Naples, whether visited or not, represents a topographical excess – a destination that demands a degree of adventurousness beyond what is strictly required in order for the traveller to speak with the authority of a participant in the Grand Tour, but that realizes more completely the most fundamental aim of the Tour: to move southwards. As such, the city is invested not only with intense pleasure but also with danger: to traverse the area between Rome and Naples, travellers are at pains to point out, they must risk the perils of banditti and of malaria. (William Hazlitt, in one of the passages in Chapter 3, explains his desire to travel on from Rome to Naples and his reluctant decision not to do so, as a vision of attack by banditti assails him.) Once there, the prospect of enervation (explored in other passages in the chapter) is both gratifying and unsettling.

---

[19] Galiffe, *Italy and its Inhabitants*, vol. 2, p. 351, pp. 351–2, p. 352.

Travel writing of this period devotes enormous attention to the dynamics of the relation between pleasure and danger. The writings from which the extracts here are taken all assume – just as earlier travel writings do – that the Grand Tour is a practice of travel in which the aim of the traveller – however aware of the ease with which purposefulness may be thrown off course – is to appropriate the topography of the foreign as a source of pleasure and benefit. The precise strategies through which the traveller is expected to derive pleasure and benefit from the foreign, however, undergo various changes, all of which depend upon a new definition of what travel entails. Throughout the course of the Grand Tour, travelling is seen as an occasion for gathering knowledge of the world and finding ways of ordering that knowledge – even though it is recognized, smilingly or censoriously, that this enterprise can easily go wrong, and that young English milordi who fail to rise to the opportunities that the Tour offers them may in fact find themselves 'poxed and pillaged' by predatory locals.[20] At the end of the eighteenth century, this concept of travel is supplemented, and partially displaced, by a concept of travel as an adventure of the self, which entails crossing behavioural and symbolic boundaries at the same time that the traveller traverses geographical limits. This venturing self is impelled not only by curiosity – the desire for knowledge – but by multifarious other forms of desire, which become entangled with the pursuit of knowledge in a range of different and sometimes unpredictable ways.[21]

Travel as an adventure of this kind offers the hope of self-exploration and self-realization, but also poses a threat to identity and stability: the restlessness that is so often touched upon in travel writings of the period is one of many forms of danger and destabilization that are seen as assailing the traveller. Pleasure, far from merging seamlessly with benefit, may also contribute to the overwhelming intensity of the experience of alterity, and so exercise a radically unsettling influence. The frisson of flirting with danger becomes one of the primary pleasures of the encounter with

---

[20] See Tobias Smollett, *Travels through France and Italy*, edited by Frank Felsenstein (Oxford: Oxford University Press, 1981); first published in 1766, p. 241: in Rome, commenting on the 'raw boys, whom Britain seemed to have poured forth on purpose to bring her national character into contempt', Smollett remarks: 'One engages in play with an infamous gamester, and is stripped perhaps in the very first partie: another is poxed and pillaged by an antiquated cantatrice: a third is bubbled by a knavish antiquarian; and a fourth is laid under contribution by a dealer in pictures.'

[21] On the complexities of curiosity, see Barbara M. Benedict, *Curiosity: A Cultural History of Early Modern Inquiry* (Chicago and London: University of Chicago Press, 2001), Nigel Leask, *Curiosity and the Aesthetics of Travel Writing, 1770–1840: 'from an antique land'* (Oxford: Oxford University Press, 2002) and Nicholas Thomas, 'Licensed Curiosity: Cook's Pacific Voyages', in *The Cultures of Collecting*, edited by John Elsner and Roger Cardinal (London: Reaktion Books, 1994), pp. 116–36.

the other. (Sydney Morgan obliquely evokes this concept in one of the passages in Chapter 2, in which English travellers laugh and flirt beside the crater of Vesuvius.)

The plot of crossing boundaries and encountering danger confers on geographical boundaries an especially dramatic role, as sites where narratives of danger can be expected to unfold. The Alps – the great boundary between the cold North and the warm South – generate plots of destabilization that become metaphorically entangled with the sublime – an experience that is also understood as incorporating moments of exceeding limits and feeling destabilized (so, too, is sexual or romantic adventure, which now ceases to be considered as a mere aberration from the traveller's main enterprise, and becomes caught up in the diverse quests of the traveller as a subject of desire).

In response to this approach to travel, another is formulated: a much more cautious approach, that can be termed *tourism*. The touristic approach recognizes that travel is essentially transgressive – that it entails crossing boundaries and exceeding limits – but aims to keep at bay the destabilizing and perilous consequences of such transgression. Tourism, then, does not set itself in opposition to the task of extracting pleasure from the foreign; it simply maps out a more carefully limited form of hedonism, in which it is acknowledged that managing pleasure also entails an attentive management of danger.[22]

Fatigue, however, assumes a paradoxical role within the management of pleasure and danger. A common strategy by which traveller-narrators affirm their commitment to keeping danger at bay is that of insisting that their experience of the foreign is, for the most part, limited to encounters with art, architecture and nature, rather than with human beings. (Jameson, in one of the passages in Chapter 1, explains the efficacy of this strategy, in excluding aspects of day-to-day life that distress other travellers.) Sightseeing itself – the very activity that is defined as safe from such threats to the traveller's composure – nonetheless threatens to unleash perils of its own: the traveller feels overwhelmed by the sheer quantity

---

[22] The term *tourist* is used from the late eighteenth century onwards (the first example cited by the *Oxford English Dictionary* is dated 1780), but often suggests primarily someone making a tour – a definition that merges easily with the contemporary usage of the term, and so makes it difficult to fix the period of transition between the two. Forsyth, at Tivoli, remarks: 'On returning to the Sibilla-Inn we found tourists like ourselves, on asses like our own, caricatured on the walls by English draughtsmen'; *Remarks on Antiquities, Arts, and Letters*, p. 274.

Byron, however, in a letter of to John Murray (11 September 1820), dismisses a travel writer whom he considers a superficial observer of Italy as 'a trashy tourist'; *Byron's Letters and Journals*, edited by Leslie A. Marchand, 13 vols (London: Murray, 1973–94), vol. 7, p. 175.

of the sights to be viewed, and by the need to prove equal to the task of assimilating them.

Whether sightseeing is self-protective or overwhelmingly exhausting, however, not only Rome, but Italy in general, is seen as offering exceptional numbers of sights and wonders: Morgan suggests that the traveller who has traversed the northern and central parts of the country will have had little opportunity to rest from the duties of the sightseer. Italy is also defined as a country in which sights of a destabilizing character proliferate: repositories of cultural memory – such as ruins and antiquities – that define the topography as a haunted one, in which pleasure is inseparable from a sense of loss. In Thomas Love Peacock's satirical novel *Nightmare Abbey* (1818), Scythrop, the character who represents Shelley, enlarges on the element of distress within the melancholy pleasure that is routinely seen as the most obvious response to ruins:

> It is indeed, much the same as if a lover should dig up the buried form of his mistress, and gaze upon relics which are any thing but herself, to wander among a few mouldy ruins, that are only imperfect indexes to lost volumes of glory, and meet at every step the more melancholy ruins of human nature – a degenerate race of stupid and shrivelled slaves, grovelling in the lowest depths of servility and superstition.[23]

The pleasures that the traveller pursues, in other words, are implicitly recognized as the objects of desires that may prove disturbing or discomfiting. Chateaubriand's plot of pleasure infinitely deferred is only one of the narratives of desire that defines any straightforward satisfaction in encounters with the foreign as utterly elusive.

The Tour feminized and effeminated

More complex and equivocal plots are generated by the promise or threat of enervation in the warm South. The dangers of enervation are often indicated metonymically by references to Hannibal and his army effeminated in Capua: James Johnson, in *Change of Air* (1831), sees the warm South as 'a climate which unmanned not only the conquering Romans but the conquerors of Rome'.[24]

Effemination of the enervated variety is, in fact, only one of a wide range of concepts of gender that become entangled in plots of destabilization.

---

[23] Thomas Love Peacock, *'Nightmare Abbey'; 'Crotchet Castle'*, edited by Raymond Wright (Penguin: Harmondsworth, 1969), p. 98.
[24] James Johnson, *Change of Air; or, the Pursuit of Health; an Autumnal Excursion through France, Switzerland and Italy, in the Year 1829*, third edition (London: S. Highley, 1831), p. 293.

Participation in the Grand Tour, it has already been suggested, entails an identification with a male, patrician figure from the British Isles.²⁵ Anna Jameson, for example, in her observation that 'one leaves Naples as a man parts with an enchanting mistress', identifies with a masculine experience of desire, and obliquely evokes the return to a domain of duty and responsibility that awaits the male patrician back home, and forces him to renounce pleasure and enchantment.

On the other hand, traveller-narrators chart a whole network of forces that pull them in apparently contrary directions, as far as gender is concerned. During the eighteenth century, the feminizing effect of travel comes to be defined not as an aberration from an ideal standard of virtue and taste, but – to a limited extent – as a necessary product of the polish and sophistication conferred by viewing works of art, mingling in foreign society and acquiring a wider experience of the world. Excessive identification with a rough-hewn version of masculinity is mocked, in some writings, as evidence of a failure in acquiring such polish. John Armstrong, writing under the pseudonym of Lancelot Temple in his *Short Ramble through Some Parts of France and Italy* (1771), invokes an imagined group of spectators who object to the beauty of the *Apollo Belvedere*, and, in doing so, reveal themselves as crudely resistant to the feminizing refinement conferred by a familiarity with art and aesthetic matters: 'I have heard sensible people say that a man has nothing to do with beauty . . . That a man is handsome enough if he does not frighten his Horse, is a coarse kind of Proverb.'²⁶

The authority derived from speaking as a 'man of taste', moreover – an authority claimed by any traveller, male or female, who aspires to comment on art – is defined in equivocal ways; the exercise of taste readily merges with a feminized acquisitive acumen. As Denise Gigante has suggested: 'Although the British Man of Taste was gendered male, he asserted

---

[25] For a definition of travel on the Grand Tour as a confirmation of masculinity in an earlier travel book, see, for example Richard Lassels, *The Voyage of Italy; or, A Compleat Journey through Italy*, edited by S. W[ilson], 2 parts (Paris: V. du Moutier, 1670), Part 1, unpaginated preface: 'Traveling preserves my yong nobleman from surfeiting of his parents, and weanes him from the dangerous fondness of his mother. It teacheth him wholesome hardship . . . And what generous mother will not say to her son with that ancient? *Malo tibi malè esse, quam molliter:* I had rather thou shouldst be sick, then soft.'

[26] Lancelot Temple [John Armstrong], [A] *Short Ramble through Some Parts of France and Italy* (London: T. Cadell, 1771), pp. 35–6.

Changes in the strategies through which the 'polishing' effects of art are defined during the eighteenth century, in relation to the dangers of effeminate luxury and sensuality, are charted by John Barrell in 'The Dangerous Goddess: Masculinity, Prestige and the Aesthetic in Early Eighteenth-Century Britain', in *The Birth of Pandora and the Division of Knowledge* (Basingstoke: Macmillan, 1992), pp. 63–87.

himself (in practice at least) as a consumer, navigating the middle-class divide between aesthetic taste and material desires.'[27]

At the same time, traveller-narrators, from around the middle of the eighteenth century onwards, adopt a rhetoric of emotional responsiveness, and define such responsiveness as feminized, yet also compatible with manly sincerity, simplicity and restraint. Expressions of emotion only compromise the traveller's authority if they are open to the suspicion of pretension and affectation. (One of the most direct portrayals of pretentiousness as a feminized aberration from manly good sense is the Marquis of Normanby's assertion that 'travel . . . is the hot-bed of affectation; if there be a seed, a germ of it in the disposition, travel will force it to the light, and it is for this reason that womankind are so rarely improved by seeing foreign countries, and return in general so much more affected and ridiculous'.)[28]

Fantasies of effemination in the warm South, then, are caught up in a web of uncertainties as to what varieties of experience or forms of language can be seen as feminine, feminized, effeminate, masculine, manly, or too insistently male.[29] Such uncertainties have often been noted by cultural historians concerned with romanticism (or Romanticism), as a set of themes and preoccupations – and a series of beliefs about language, the self and the world – that are discernible from around the late eighteenth century onwards. Julie Ellison, in *Delicate Subjects*, provides an elegant summary of romantic equivocations over gender:

> In romantic texts gender ideology becomes apparent in the theme of love and in the importance of affect or mood. For it is the language of mood – to speak from within the wishful thinking of romantic poetry, poetics, and hermeneutics – that is interpreted by love's cognitive faculty, divination. The key terms of romantic poetics – the sublime, the haunted, the grotesque, the sentimental, the ironic, memory, desire, imagination – are accompanied by the desire to be understood intuitively.
>
> Intuition is marked as a feminine quality, just as most objects of romantic longing are, including childhood, nature, and the demonic. The invention of the romantic subject as the hero of desire is therefore wholly bound up with the feminine. At the same time, romantic writers suspect that desire may be a form of power, understanding a form of science, and woman a form of sabotage. Objects of desire are lost or violated in ambivalent allegories of the domestic and the maternal. Ultimately, the feminine becomes, first, wholly figurative or non-referential and then invisible.[30]

---

[27] Denise Gigante, *Taste: A Literary History* (New Haven and London: Yale University Press, 2005), p. 14.

[28] [Constantine Henry Phipps,] Marquis of Normanby, 'The Boy Connoisseur', in *The English in Italy*, 3 vols (London: Saunders and Otley, 1825), vol. 2, pp. 71–81; p. 72; the traveller continues: 'Mankind still is far from proof.'

[29] This last category is neatly exemplified by the commentary on the *Apollo Belvedere* in Temple, *Short Ramble*, just quoted (pp. 35–6).

[30] Julie Ellison, *Delicate Subjects: Romanticism, Gender, and the Ethics of Understanding* (Ithaca and London: Cornell University Press, 1990), pp. 10–11.

Travel writings of the late eighteenth and early nineteenth centuries constantly make play with these equivocations, and with the categories caught up in them: much of the present book is concerned with the sublime and the ironic (Chapter 2), memory, the haunted and nature (all-pervasive), the Gothic (which makes an intermittent appearance), and the sentimental (a constant source of irony).

Pedantry and poetry

By the early nineteenth century, large numbers of travel books are published that name a female author on the title page. (Before the last few decades of the eighteenth century, such books are very rare.) Women are recognized as participants in the Grand Tour from at least the middle of the eighteenth century onwards; they are nonetheless readily classified as participants of a slightly anomalous kind. Joseph Forsyth, in his *Remarks on Antiquities, Arts, and Letters during an Excursion in Italy* (1813), cites the presence of women in the more alarming regions of Vesuvius as a sign that the lure of danger and the promise of heroic adventure are in abeyance: 'Vesuvius is now an exhausted subject. Its fire and smoke, its glory and terrors, are vanished for the present. Ladies, as I read in the Hermit's Album, go down to the bottom of the crater.'[31]

At the same time, traveller-narrators writing as women pronounce on all the usual domains of objects included in published travel books, speaking with an authority derived from their claim to have visited the places that they describe in person and to have responded to these objects. (The first half of Chapter 4 is concerned with the roles that female spectators – whether travellers or locals – are assigned in commentary on art.) As beings who are assumed to possess especially strong intuitive powers, moreover, female travellers are often invested with a particular authority to appropriate the topography of the haunted without lapsing into the fault of pedantry – one of the forms in which the rhetorical vice of affectation is seen as manifesting itself. In a footnote to the extract above, Morgan emphasizes that the passage 'with its classic name of the Sibyl's grotto' realizes one of the 'poetic visions' of the imagination; her choice of 'poetic visions' over the pedantic trappings of scholarship is proclaimed more acerbically at another point in her narrative, when she directly mocks two classicizing tours of Italy (Joseph Addison's *Remarks on Several Parts of Italy*, published in 1705, and Eustace's *Tour through Italy*) for supplying conventionalized invocations of past glories for 'imitative tourists'. At Reggio ('or, in the language of the antiquarian, REGIUM LEPIDI,

---

[31] Forsyth, *Remarks on Antiquities, Arts, and Letters*, p. 320.

FORUM LEPIDI'), she argues, with reference to her own Anglo-Irish background, that two obscure Irish towns – 'Much-injured *Maughirow!*' and 'Neglected *Magherafelt!*' – might be considered equally deserving of interest, were it not for 'the fatality of a geographical position':

> Did your ruins now strew, and your mire now defile, an *Italian* Dukedom, instead of an Irish district, the learned would pause over your hovels, and your very pigs would be objects of classic interest; you would be considered as an historic feature in the land; and escaping from the mute inglorious destiny that now awaits you, your glories would be reiterated by the Addisons and Eustaces of future ages, and your fame would be given to the deathless echoes of imitative tourists.[32]

Eustace, in fact, comes to supply a metonym for dry pedantry, to be rejected by all travellers, male or female, who aspire to 'poetic visions'. Shelley, in a letter to Peacock from Rome in 1819, declares: 'I have said what I feel without entering into any critical discussions of the ruins of Rome, & the mere outside of this inexhaustible mine of thought & feeling – Hobhouse, Eustace, & Forsyth will tell all the shew-knowledge about it – "the common stuff of the earth".'[33] Jameson consigns Eustace to the category of a writer devoted to empty verbosity, and unequal to personal responsiveness:

> I discovered to-day (and it is no slight pleasure to make a discovery for one's self,) the passage which formed the communication between the Coliseum and the Palace of the Cæsars, and in which the Emperor Commodus was assassinated . . . If I had time I might moralize here, and make an eloquent tirade *à la Eustace* about imperial monsters and so forth – but in fact I *did* think while I stood in the damp and gloomy corridor, that it was a fitting death for Commodus to die by the giddy playfulness of a child, and the machinations of an abandoned woman.[34]

Rome and Naples, unsurprisingly, become closely entangled in this interplay between pedantry and poetry. Rome, so often seen as a city demanding 'solid, manly, and rational' efforts at understanding (to borrow the terms used by Sir James Edward Smith), is less easily seen as lending itself to an intuitive, feminized grasp of antiquity. In Naples and the South, in particular, where antiquity is often described as mediated by nature and even revived by the vitality of the natural world, the haunted character of the terrain is often presented as demanding an intuitive rather than a scholarly response.

---

[32] Morgan, *Italy*, vol. 1, p. 274. For a further account of suspicions of pedantry in the early nineteenth century, see my essay 'Scholarship and Sensibility: Anna Jameson and Sydney Morgan in Siren land', in *Women, Scholarship and Criticism: Gender and Knowledge c. 1790–1900*, edited by Joan Bellamy, Anne Laurence and Gill Perry (Manchester and New York: Manchester University Press, 2000), pp. 58–75; pp. 63–8.

[33] *The Letters of Percy Bysshe Shelley*, edited by Frederick L. Jones, 2 vols (Oxford: Oxford University Press, 1964), vol. 2, p. 89.

[34] [Jameson,] *Diary of an Ennuyée*, p. 186.

The especially intense drama generated by the interplay between the two cities supplies one of the reasons why the present book focuses, to a large extent, upon writings about the Italian peninsula from Rome southwards. Rome is the city in which travellers become caught up in complex dramas as they determine their own relation to the authority of the past; Naples is the setting that promises the greatest imaginable pleasure. It would be possible to assemble a critical reader of late eighteenth-century and early nineteenth-century travel writing with a very different emphasis: to focus, for example, on the proliferation of anecdotes of Gothic, semi-feudal life, set in the northern and central Italian city-states, to consider descriptions of popular festivals, and the life of the people, throughout the Italian peninsula, or to chart the beginnings of the change in taste that led travellers, when considering Italian painting, to devote a new attention to the works of the precursors of Raphael, as encountered, above all, in Tuscany and Umbria.[35] Narratives of pleasure, transgression and danger, however, are assigned their moments of greatest drama first upon the Alps – the great natural boundary between the cold North and the warm South, as described in several of the passages in Chapter 2 and then, secondly, in the traversal of the dangerous liminal space between Rome and Naples – considered in most of the passages in Chapter 3. A longing for the warm South is registered when the traveller looks down onto Italy from an Alpine elevation; it is registered yet more strongly as he or she approaches Naples.

Process, incompletion and vitality

Another precondition for the fascination with Naples and the warm South at this time is the ease with which nature in the South provides instances of process and incompletion – two more of the recurrent

---

[35] Stendhal's *Rome, Naples et Florence* (edited by Pierre Brunel; Paris: Gallimard, 1987; first published 1818, and, in revised form, in 1826) ends with a narrative that dramatizes the turbulence of Italian passions (pp. 411–13). Forsyth tells the same story in the second edition of *Remarks on Antiquities, Arts, and Letters* (London: John Murray, 1816), pp. 196–7. See also, for example, the story told by William Hazlitt in his *Notes of a Journey through France and Italy* (London: Hunt and Clarke, 1826), pp. 315–18, citing Stendhal's *De l'amour* as his source.

Stephen Bann, in 'Le peuple romain' (*Maestà di Roma: d'Ingres à Degas; les artistes français à Rome*, exhibition catalogue, Rome, Electa, 2003, pp. 244–8), notes the general movement of academic painters to Italy in the nineteenth century, in search of the local colour vaunted by romantic writers (p. 245).

For an account of the change in taste, see Francis Haskell, *Rediscoveries in Art: Some Aspects of Taste, Fashion and Collecting in England and France* (London: Phaidon, 1976); the most striking literary treatment of the change is Edith Wharton's 'False Dawn (The 'Forties')', in *Old New York* (New York: Simon and Schuster, 1995; first published in 1924), pp. 7–80.

themes of the period – and metaphors for process within the discussion of other domains of objects.³⁶ At the start of her account of Naples, Morgan notes the astonishing 'vigour and activity' of Nature: 'an activity that preys upon itself, a feverish vitality that consumes while it brightens'. The perils of the region, explained more fully in a footnote, are evoked in a dramatically compressed form: 'Sun-beams bring death as they fall! and the earth, when struck, sends up burning vapours!' The restlessness that drives Morgan onwards from Rome propels her from a region marked by 'the death of Nature' to scenes in which 'every where the ruins of time and man are mingled with the fragments of an overwrought creation'.

The unsettling character of Naples, then, is located, here, in its disorderly incompleteness: Nature 'is seen revealing her processes of creation, changing, combining, exhausting, renewing, and recreating, but never destroying!' In the genre of the first-person travel narrative, process is not necessarily a dangerous and destabilizing force, but it always threatens or promises to disorder established conventions of observing. The phenomena of the natural world are not the only source of 'changing, combining, exhausting, renewing, and recreating': the upheavals of the Napoleonic wars and the uncertainty of Italy's political future after 1815 provide endless occasions for speculation (not only in the South, of course, but throughout the Italian peninsula). The power of such upheavals to intervene even in the sedate rituals of the sightseer is poignantly emphasized in Forsyth's *Remarks*, when the traveller concludes his chapter on his 'Journey to Turin' with the brief paragraph:

> I arrived at Turin on the 25th of May, 1803. The next day I was arrested as a British Subject, and I am now passing the TENTH YEAR OF MY CAPTIVITY.³⁷

---

36 On the fascination with incompleteness, together with fragmentation and ruin (and also infinity), see Thomas McFarland, *Romanticism and the Forms of Ruin: Wordsworth, Coleridge, and Modalities of Fragmentation* (Princeton: Princeton University Press, 1981), pp. 11–34.
37 Forsyth, *Remarks on Antiquities, Arts, and Letters*, p. 387. Forsyth mentions 'my long captivity' in the 'Advertisement' to this edition (p. vi). Some copies of the second edition include a preface by the traveller's brother, Isaac Forsyth, who explains that, during Joseph Forsyth's imprisonment, 'the anxiety which he incessantly felt to be delivered from restraint, absorbed every other consideration, and prevented the application of his mind to any fixed subject, or to composition of any kind'. Seeing other *détenus* released 'in consequence of appearing before the public in the character of authors', he is nonetheless 'induced to prepare the notes he had made while on his tour in Italy, and publish them in England'. This bid for freedom fails, and he is released only in April 1813, after the English and their allies enter Paris. Observing him sink into 'a weakness of nerve, and a lassitude of mind', his relations send him on a tour of the Scottish Highlands, where 'the objects of grandeur and sublimity which presented themselves . . . and the wonders of Staffa, delighted and interested him exceedingly, and he returned home apparently invigorated

Anna Jameson, in one of the passages in Chapter 1, proclaims a fascination with the possibilities of political change in Italy at the same time that she denies any desire 'to sweep up the leavings of the "fearless" Lady Morgan'.[38] She also touches on process, incompletion and vitality when she moves on from this topic to the art of improvisation, in which performers compose verses on the spot, often to music, whether in the relatively exclusive settings of *accademie* (usually translated as 'concerts') or, in the case of more humble *improvvisatori*, on the street. Such verses, by definition, lack the finish imparted by the revision and editing entailed in written poetry. A number of the elaborations on themes by the *improvvisatore* Sgricci, in Jameson's account of his *accademia*, excite responses that prompt speculation upon the future of the country. The mention of that art, moreover, in a work that cites *Corinne*, implicitly raises the possibility of eliding its spontaneity and impetuosity with the vitality of Nature in the South. The heroine of *Corinne* is herself an *improvvisatrice*: a number of her improvisations play a part in the novel, and she defines the art as one aspect of 'la liberalité de la Nature' ('the liberality of Nature') in Italy; when Sicilian boatmen improvise verses, she remarks, 'on diroit que le soufflé pur du ciel et de la mer agit sur l'imagination des hommes, comme le vent sur les harpes éoliennes, et que la poésie, comme les accords, est l'écho de la nature' ('one would say that the pure breath of the sky and the sea acts upon the imagination of men, like the wind on Aeolian harps, and that poetry, like musical harmonies, is the echo of nature').[39]

Improvvisatori and *improvvisatrici* are usually encountered by travellers in Florence or Rome. Another formalized occasion that embodies a fascination with process is more or less confined to the Eternal City: the visit to a sculpture studio, in which the works are, if not always unfinished, at least not yet definitively launched upon the world, and in which pictorial viewing – in the sense of a spectator confronting a fixed pictorial spectacle – is transmuted into a dynamic, participatory social occasion. The second half of Chapter 4 focuses on visits of this kind.

Many of the themes considered in the passages in this book, and the approaches to travel and the foreign that these passages trace, have persisted – often in transmuted but recognizable forms – up until the present day. Throughout the chapters, recent works are quoted from time to time, in order to draw attention to aspects of writing about travel that are

---

in body, and cheered in mind'. He nonetheless dies soon afterwards, in September 1816 (pp. 6–10).

[38] [Jameson,] *Diary of an Ennuyée*, p. 292; see also p. 146.

[39] De Staël, *Corinne*, vol. 1, pp. 76–7; for Jameson's references to the novel see *Diary of an Ennuyée*, p. 110 (quoted in Chapter 1), p. 206 and p. 209.

already apparent in works of the late eighteenth and early nineteenth centuries, and that continue to re-erupt – often in slightly unexpected ways.

II: *The tropes of travel: how to avoid languor in language*

Hyperbole

In investing Naples with a drama that is derived both from natural tumult and from antique associations, Morgan declares that the language of description should prove equal to such drama: 'to the traveller of the present day nothing is left, but cautiously and briefly to obtrude upon the reader some object of overwhelming importance, whose impression is deep-seated, and whose description, if not new, may at least not be languid.' Travel writings, both of this period and of others, take it for granted that the traveller-narrator must aim to represent the foreign as a domain of dramatic difference; in literature of the Grand Tour, discerning some element of drama is defined as essential to the primary aim of the Tour: the appropriation of the topography as a source of pleasure and benefit. Travellers regularly express contempt for other travellers who, for whatever reason, fail to demonstrate that they have grasped the foreign as a topography of otherness. Byron, in a famous passage of his Alpine journal, contemptuously describes a woman 'fast asleep in the most antinarcotic spot in the world' (in the Swiss Alps), and then cites yet another example of dispiriting unresponsiveness: 'I remember at Chamouni – in the very eyes of Mont Blanc – hearing another woman – English also – exclaim to her party – "did you ever see any thing more *rural*" – as if it was Highgate or Hampstead – or Brompton – or Hayes.'[40]

The trope that most directly affirms the drama of the topography is hyperbole: a movement beyond the bounds of utterances that pay strict regard to truth. In travel writing, this narrative structure of exceeding a limit reproduces and dramatizes the narrative of travel as a movement beyond boundaries. The Englishwoman whom Byron judges inadequate to pronouncing on the Alps fails to formulate an expression that is sufficiently hyperbolic, and lapses instead into bathos. Other travellers, too, pour scorn on those who prove incapable of hyperbole. Hester Piozzi, in Naples, concludes her account of Leandro Bassano's *Raising of Lazarus*, at Capo di Monte, with the exclamation: 'the restored Lazarus too – an apparent corpse, re-awakened suddenly to a thousand sensations at once,

---

[40] *Byron's Letters and Journals*, vol. 5, p. 97. This entry in the poet's 'Alpine Journal', written for his sister Augusta Leigh, is dated 18 September 1816. Byron continues: '– "*Rural*" quotha! – Rocks – pines – torrents – Glaciers – Clouds – and Summits of eternal snow far above them – and "*Rural!*"'

wonder, gratitude, and affectionate delight! – How can one coldly sit to hear the connoisseurs *admire the folds of the drapery?*'[41] Charlotte Eaton, in *Rome in the Nineteenth Century* (1820), comments on Raphael's *La Fornarina*, in the Uffizi, in Florence: 'The eye dwells on it with never-satiated delight, and the unlearned and the connoisseur equally experience its fascination. What cold critic can discover a fault while he contemplates it; and who, after seeing it, can say, that Raphael was no colourist?'[42]

Travellers also define hyperbole as a trope that can be recognized as appropriate only by those who have witnessed the wonders of the objects of description on the spot. Anna Jameson, in Rome, observing a popular festival in the Roman Forum declares:

> All this sounds, while I soberly write it down, very sentimental, and picturesque, and poetical. It was exactly what I saw – what I often see: such is the place, the scenery, the people. Every group is a picture, the commonest object has some interest attached to it, the commonest action is dignified by sentiment, the language around us is music, and the air we breathe is poetry.[43]

Such assertions of the necessity for hyperbole assume that this trope, if adeptly employed, will prove more or less equal to the task of describing alterity. Other commentaries go beyond the view that the traveller must search for language that is more or less adequate to the topography, and suggest instead that no forms of language – and, in some cases, no pictorial image, or no form of representation at all – can possibly match up to the qualities of dramatic difference, strangeness and otherness that the topography supplies. In claiming that a particular scene could never be described or painted, the traveller takes for granted that the qualities that resist representation are also qualities that excite the strongest possible responses. Henry Swinburne, in his *Travels in the Two Sicilies*, deploys an expression of this kind to describe the view that he contemplates from Capri: 'The magnificence of this scene would baffle the skill of the greatest painter; how feeble then must be the idea my description can convey of the prospect enjoyed from the chapel of Santa Maria.'[44] Piozzi, in Mantua, declares: 'What can be seen here, and here alone, are the numerous and incomparable works of Giulio Romano; of which no words that I can use

---

[41] Hester Lynch Piozzi, *Observations and Reflections Made in the Course of a Journey through France, Italy, and Germany*, 2 vols (London: A. Strahan and T. Cadell, 1789), vol. 2, pp. 79–80; the painting is still at Capo di Monte.

[42] Charlotte Eaton, *Rome in the Nineteenth Century; Containing a Complete Account of the Ruins of the Ancient City, the Remains of the Middle Ages, and the Monuments of Modern Times*, 3 vols (Edinburgh and London: Archibald Constable & Co. and Hurst, Robinson, & Co., 1820), vol. 1, p. 8.

[43] [Jameson,] *Diary of an Ennuyée*, p. 183.

[44] Henry Swinburne, *Travels in the Two Sicilies, in the Years 1777, 1778, 1779, and 1780*, 2 vols (London: p. Elmsly, 1783–85), vol. 2, p. 3.

would give my readers any adequate idea. – For such excellence language has no praise, and of such performances taste will admit no criticism.'[45] Thomas Watkins, detailing the different tracts of Mount Etna, observes: 'It is impossible for me to describe the pleasure we experienced in passing through the first of these regions'.[46] Forsyth remarks: 'Tivoli cannot be described; no true portrait of it exists: all views alter and embellish it: they are poetical translations of the matchless original.'[47] Henry Sass concurs in his view of the town:

> Indeed, no language can adequately describe the beauties of this delightful retreat. The amenity of the air, the loveliness of the scenery, and the beautiful odour of vegetation, produced a luxurious repose in the mind, a softness of feeling that inclined one to exclaim, 'Here will I rest, and forget the world.'[48]

In accounts of art, hyperboles of unrepresentability often incorporate a declaration that 'markers', as Dean MacCannell has termed them in *The Tourist* – representations that offer information about a sight, such as casts and copies of antique statues – can never give an adequate idea of the sight in question.[49] Both Eaton and Matthews, describing the *Apollo Belvedere* and the *Venus de' Medici* respectively, make declarations of this kind:

> Description would be the excess of absurdity; even the best copies are vain. No cast, drawing, or design, that I ever beheld, had conveyed to my mind the faintest image of its perfection. From every attempt to imprison it in other models, the subtle essence of beauty escapes. The Divinity disdains to inhabit a meaner form.

> A man may give the exact proportions of the Venus de Medicis, with the projections of the nose and chin; – but all this, which is literally *description*, can never impart a single idea of the grace and dignity diffused over that divine statue, – and if he mention that grace, he describes his own sensations rather than the figure.[50]

In these pronouncements, unrepresentability is equated with a vaguely specified transcendence of the concrete. The quality that resists representation, however, is also, in all such hyperboles, a variety of indeterminacy; a more determinate object of scrutiny, it is assumed, would be easier to describe or paint. Forsyth spells out this assumption when he presents sharply defined singularity as easily described:

---

[45] Piozzi, *Observations and Reflections*, vol. 1, pp. 119–20.
[46] Thomas Watkins, *Travels through Switzerland, Italy, Sicily, the Greek Islands to Constantinople; through Part of Greece, Ragusa, and the Dalmatian Isles; in a Series of Letters to Pennoyre Watkins, Esq., from Thomas Watkins, A.M. F.R.S. in the Years 1787, 1788, 1789*, second edition, 2 vols (London: J. Owen, 1794; first published in 1792), vol. 2, pp. 10–11.
[47] Forsyth, *Remarks on Antiquities, Arts, and Letters*, p. 275.
[48] Henry Sass, *A Journey to Rome and Naples, performed in 1817; giving an Account of the Present State of Society in Italy, and containing Observations on the Fine Arts* (London: Longman, Hurst, Rees, Orme and Brown, 1818), pp. 236–7.
[49] Dean MacCannell, *The Tourist: A New Theory of the Leisure Class* (New York: Schocken Books, 1976), pp. 41–4.
[50] Eaton, *Rome in the Nineteenth Century*, vol. 1, p. 169; Matthews, *Diary of an Invalid*, p. 137.

> I found Venice just what I had imagined it to be from books and prints. A singular thing may be fully delineated. It is the sublime or the beautiful, it is the scenery of Naples, or the Belvedere Apollo that baffles description.[51]

Indeterminacy is often presented in travel writings of this period (for example, in Dupaty's description of the coast near Naples in Chapter 3) as a quality that carries the traveller beyond the bounds of mundane experience; part of the allure of the warm South is the array of aquatic experiences of impercepible movement that it offers. ('The water was so smooth that we imperceptibly glided on', says Henry Sass, during 'a most delightful sail' to Baia.)[52] Travel commentaries often present landscape as the product of fleeting effects, and so of natural processes. Anna Jameson, reflecting on the inadequacy of any painting of the cascade at Terni, defines the elements that even 'a good picture' will fail to convey as indeterminacy and infinitude, a sense of process and of the fleeting, and multisensory effects (another preoccupation of the period, upon which Chapter 5 touches, in considering the relation between aesthetic and gastronomic experience in travel writing): 'The lifeless, silent, unmoving image is there: but where is the thundering roar, the terrible velocity, the glory of refracted light, the eternity of sound, and infinity of motion, in which essentially its effect consists?'[53]

Hyperboles of unrepresentability are invested with yet greater rhetorical boldness when the traveller suggests that particular scenes or objects, however difficult to delineate upon the page or the canvas, are nonetheless indelibly inscribed upon the memory. Piozzi combines unforgettability with indescribability when she witnesses the eruption of Vesuvius:

> ... nor shall I ever forget the scene it presented one day to my astonished eyes, while a thick cloud, charged heavily with electric matter, passing over, met the fiery explosion by mere chance, and went off in such a manner as effectually baffles all verbal description.[54]

James Galiffe, approaching the two craters of Vesuvius, anticipates the indescribable scene before him:

> What we had seen was a splendid fire-work, such as supernatural beings might have prepared for some heavenly celebration; what remained behind was a terrifick revelation of the mysteries of hell; and Dante himself would have blenched at the idea of describing it. Scenes of such tremendous sublimity are only debased and disfigured, by the efforts of poetical description; and simplicity of language affords the only escape from affectation and bombast: but it is not easy to find

---

[51] Forsyth, *Remarks on Antiquities, Arts, and Letters*, p. 361.
[52] Sass, *Journey to Rome and Naples*, p. 213.
[53] [Jameson,] *Diary of an Ennuyée*, p. 131.
[54] Piozzi, *Observations and Reflections*, vol. 2, p. 5; see also [Jameson,] *Diary of an Ennuyée*, p. 226. Evelyn Waugh satirises this trope in a much later travel book, *Labels: A Mediterranean Journal* (Harmondsworth: Penguin, [1930] 1985), p. 139.

plain words for the description of things, the mere remembrance of which entirely overpowers the mind and confounds all our ideas.⁵⁵

Two pages later, standing beside the craters and looking down upon 'the river of lava, which gushed out of the valley formed by the craters and the hill we stood on', the traveller declares: 'never, never, can I forget my sensations at that moment! Never can the awful impression of all these elements of terror be effaced from my mind!'⁵⁶

Further 'excitement of the mind'

Having said that the topography is beyond description, travellers usually go on to describe it – as in the commentary just quoted. Alternatively, they may embark on a description and then observe that words fail them: Jameson, under the falls at Terni, exclaims: 'The whole scene was – but how can I say what it was? I have exhausted my stock of fine words; and must be content with silent recollections, and the sense of admiration and wonder unexprest.'⁵⁷ Hyperboles of indescribability (or general unrepresentability), in other words, function as a form of preterition – the trope in which the speaker says something while claiming that he or she is not in fact saying it. Eaton describes one of the most famous sights of Rome in two sentences in which she wonders how she could possibly do so:

> The art of the painter, or the eloquent strains of the poet, might avail, in some degree, to give you a faint image of the Coliseum – but how can I, in plain prose, hope, by mere description, to represent its lofty majesty and ruined splendour? How convey to your mind the sense of its beautiful proportions, its simplicity, its harmony, and its grandeur; of the regular gradations of Doric, Ionic, and the Corinthian orders, that support its graceful ranges of Grecian arcades; of the rich hues with which Time has overspread its massy walls, and of all that is wholly indescribable in its powerful effect on the eye, the mind, and the imagination?⁵⁸

Preterition, then, invites the reader to feel that the topography, whether through its remarkable or its astoundingly unremarkable characteristics, has finally forced the traveller-narrator to pronounce on objects that stoutly resist any translation into forms of language. Another trope, that of litotes, or saying something by denying its opposite, allows the traveller to remain in a state of permanent hesitation, too daunted to offer any positive opinion, and affirming through this hesitation that he or she is confronting a form of authentic strangeness. Jonathan Lamb,

---

⁵⁵ Galiffe, *Italy and its Inhabitants*, vol. 2, p. 279.
⁵⁶ Galiffe, *Italy and its Inhabitants*, vol. 2, p. 280, p. 281.
⁵⁷ [Jameson,] *Diary of an Ennuyée*, p. 130.
⁵⁸ Eaton, *Rome in the Nineteenth Century*, vol. 1, p. 132.

in *Preserving the Self in the South Seas*, has noted that, like hyperboles of indescribability, this trope locates within the topography the *je ne sais quoi*: the quality that, in seventeenth-century and eighteenth-century speculation on aesthetic matters, excites overwhelming responses, but nonetheless resists precise definition.[59] In the face of strangeness, travellers hint at the overwhelming character of the topography's resistance to classification by retreating from any confidently positive assertions, and taking refuge in negatives. Remarks by Piozzi, in Venice, by John Moore, in Rome, and by Robert Gray, in Naples, all set out to categorize otherness by naming absences:

> For it is sure there are in this town many astonishing privations of all that are used to make other places delightful: and as poor Omai the savage said, when about to return to Otaheite – *No horse there! no ass! no cow, no golden pippins, no dish of tea! – Ah, missey! I go without every thing – I always so content there though.*
> It is really just so one lives at this lovely Venice: one has heard of a horse being exhibited for a show there, and yesterday I watched the poor people paying a penny a piece for the sight of a *stuffed one*.

> Here you have few or none of those fair, fat, glistening, unmeaning faces, so common in the more northern parts of Europe.

> In England, thanks to the existence of religion and a respect for the true happiness of life, the value of fidelity and virtue are still felt; and they who depart from them are compelled to affect their appearance or to retreat from society: – such, alas! Is not the case at Naples.[60]

The refusal to utter, in this last comment, pointedly draws attention to those qualities that are, it seems, too shocking to name in positive terms: it supplies a more pointed variant on the 'hypercritical' form of the hyperbole of indescribability, illustrated by Norman Douglas, describing Roman baths at Gafsa, Tunisia, in a much later travel book, *Fountains in the Sand* (1912): 'it would not be easy to describe, in the language of polite society, those features in which it is most repulsive to Europeans'.[61] Matthews suggests a similarly inexpressible repulsiveness when, like Gray, he names an absence:

---

[59] See Jonathan Lamb, *Preserving the Self in the South Seas, 1680–1840* (Chicago and London: University of Chicago Press, 2001), pp. 236–49.

[60] Piozzi, *Observations and Reflections*, vol. 1, p. 167 (Piozzi cites as her rhetorical precedent 'Omai the savage', the Tahitian brought to England on the second Cook voyage). Moore, *View of Society and Manners*, vol. II, pp. 65–6; Robert Gray, *Letters during the Course of a Tour through Germany, Switzerland and Italy, in the Years MDCCXCI, and MDCCXCXII* (London: F. & C. Rivington, 1794), p. 399.

[61] Norman Douglas, *Fountains in the Sand* (Oxford: Oxford University Press, 1986), p. 13. See also Morgan, *Italy*, vol. 2, p. 166: 'The inn, and hostess of Otricoli, were alike beyond description.' The useful term *hypercriticism*, for negative hyperboles, is used by William Hazlitt in his description of the *Venus de' Medici*, in *Notes of a Journey through France and Italy* (London: Hunt and Clarke, 1826), p. 260.

April 5th. Left Naples, in a fit of spleen and disgust at the continued inclemency of the weather, and slept at Capua; where we found none of those seducing luxuries, which enervated the soldiers of Hannibal.[62]

Within the rhetoric of destabilization, litotes supplies a means of naming experiences that cannot be named directly simply because they are too intense. John Bell, at Suza, the town on the Alps that marks the crossing into Italy, uses the trope at the point where his excitement in crossing boundaries is reaching a climax of intensity:

In passing vast boundaries, seemingly planted by nature as barriers between nations, the mind is powerfully awakened to expectation. Every object in a new country, whether in the scenery, or in the customs and manners of the people, excites fresh animation in the traveller. The eye wanders abroad, eager in search of novelty; and the excitement of the mind gives additional charms to the surrounding objects, and new zeal to the spirit of inquiry. *We did not therefore enter Suza without experiencing such emotion;* – we were treading, for the first time, on Italian ground, and were prepared to behold every object with feelings of curiosity and interest.[63]

This last passage demonstrates the usefulness of litotes in supporting hyperbole: whereas preterition registers a will to go on describing and assimilating the objects of commentary, in the face of their power to baffle description, litotes actually traces out the bafflement in its own retreat from too rash and straightforward a form of words. Bell's very hesitation to admit directly to 'such emotion', moreover, distracts the reader from the mild recklessness of the hyperboles – '*every* object' (not just many or most) becomes a source of 'fresh animation' and of 'feelings of curiosity and interest'.

Pierre Fontanier, in his treatise *Les figures du discours* (1821), emphasizes that some element of recklessness is essential to hyperbole, but also notes that this element is never too wildly out of control. While hyperbole increases or diminishes objects of description 'avec excès' ('with excess'), its aim is 'non de tromper, mais d'amener à la vérité même, et de fixer, par ce qu'elle dit d'incroyable, ce qu'il faut réellement croire' ('not to deceive, but to lead to truth itself, and to establish, by means of the unbelievable things that it says, that which we should really believe'). Fontanier then makes another point, highly relevant to late eighteenth-century and early nineteenth-century reflections on what sort of language is best suited to convey 'the excitement of the mind' (to adopt Bell's term). Hyperbole's

---

[62] Matthews, *Diary of an Invalid*, p. 227.
[63] John Bell, *Observations on Italy. By the late John Bell, Fellow of the Royal College of Surgeons, Edinburgh*, &c (Edinburgh and London: William Blackwood and T. Cadell, 1825), pp. 39–40; emphasis added.

excessiveness is reined in not only by its aim of leading to truth, but also by its good faith:

> L'*Hyperbole*, pour être une beauté d'expression et pour plaire, doit porter le caractère de la bonne foi et de la franchise, et ne paraître, de la part de celui qui parle, que le langage même de la persuasion. Ce n'est pas tout, il faut que celui qui écoute puisse partager jusqu'à un certain point l'illusion, et ait besoin peut-être d'un peu de réflexion pour n'être pas dupe, c'est-à-dire, pour réduire les mots à leur juste valeur.[64]
>
> Hyperbole, to possess a beauty of expression and to please, must bear the character of good faith and sincerity, and must seem, on the part of the speaker, like the language of persuasion itself. And this is not all: the person who constitutes the audience for this figure must share the illusion, up to a point, and must need to reflect a little in order not to be taken in – that is to say, in order to reduce the words to their true value.

This passage provides a means of understanding a fault that travellers, at least from the late eighteenth century onwards, repeatedly discover in the hyperboles of other travellers. When traveller-narrators note the danger of affectation, as Galiffe does when he observes that 'simplicity of language affords the only escape from affectation and bombast', they are usually referring to the risk that hyperboles will fail to produce a convincing effect of sincerity – in other words, to supply the 'bonne foi' and 'franchise' that are needed in order to draw the reader into the illusion.[65] W.H. Auden, in his *Letters from Iceland* (1937), touches gently on the failure of excessive enthusiasm to sound convincing:

> Staying here is a Scotch girl, an English lecturer at one of our provincial universities, and a great Icelandophil. She thinks them like the Greeks. Terribly enthusiastic, rushing at life like a terrier. I wonder if she really enjoys herself as much as she protests. I can imagine her in a siege saying at dinner, 'What? Fried rats? Goody. How awfully exciting.' But she is intelligent and extremely good-hearted.[66]

Failures in sincerity, it is argued (or, more often, simply assumed), generate inflated, hackneyed and redundant forms of language. Elizabeth Bowen, in *A Time in Rome* (1960), summarizes the arguments of acquaintances who attempt to dissuade her from making a book of her experience of the Eternal City: 'Language seldom fails quietly; it fails noisily.' The dissuaders have some evidence to muster in support of their view: 'Attempts to write about Rome made writers rhetorical, platitudinous, abstract, ornate, theoretical, polysyllabic, pompous, furious.'[67]

Criticisms of Eustace often focus upon a noisy failure of this kind. John

---

[64] Pierre Fontanier, *Les figures du discours* (Paris: Flammarion, 1977), p. 123, pp. 123–4.
[65] Galiffe, *Italy and its Inhabitants*, vol. 2, p. 279.
[66] W.H. Auden and Louis MacNeice, *Letters from Iceland* (London: Faber and Faber, 1985; first published in 1937), p. 142.
[67] Elizabeth Bowen, *A Time in Rome* (London: Longmans, 1960), p. 50.

Cam Hobhouse, in a footnote to the passage in Canto IV of Byron's *Childe Harold's Pilgrimage* concerned with the Sabine Hills, vents his 'extreme disappointment' in Eustace's *Tour*, with its penchant for hackneyed rhetorical 'decorations':

> Indeed the *Classical Tour* has every characteristic of a mere compilation of former notices, strung out by those decorations which are so easily supplied by a systematic adoption of all the common places of praise, applied to every thing, and therefore signifying nothing.
> The style which one person thinks cloggy and cumbrous, and unsuitable, may be to the taste of others, and such may experience some salutary excitement in ploughing through the periods of the *Classical Tour*. It must be said, however, that polish and weight are apt to beget an expectation of value. It is amongst the pains of the damned to toil up to a climax with a huge round *stone*.[68]

Jameson, picking up a copy of Eustace's *Tour* at the inn at Terni, claims that his laboriousness has prompted in her a physical gesture of disgust: 'I ... quickly threw down the book with indignation, deeming all his verbiage, the merest nonsense I had ever met with: in fact, it is nonsense to attempt to image in words an individual scene like this.'[69]

Digression

In attempting to elude suspicions of affectation and cumbrousness, travellers make use of another trope: digression. The very name of this figure is, of course, a metaphor that summons up an approach to the practice of travel – an approach that suggests a certain scepticism about a sequential *progression* through sights and wonders. Paradoxically, digression itself allows language to proliferate in an ostensibly unrestrained – and highly capricious – manner. The first-person travel narrative – a genre that begins to split away from the guide book by at least the middle of the eighteenth century – adopts as one of its defining characteristics the assumption that the subject of commentary is free to pronounce on any topic that might spring to mind: history, aesthetics, natural history, demography, epidemiology, to name just a few. Digressions are, in fact, sometimes signalled directly: Galiffe, in his 'Table of Contents' at the start of his second volume, includes in the outline of Chapter 7: 'Grotto of Pausilippo

---

[68] [George Gordon Noel Byron, Baron], *The Complete Poetical Works*, edited by Jerome J. McGann, 7 vols (Oxford: Oxford University Press, 1980–92), vol. 2, p. 262; note to line 1566. Hobhouse contributed a number of footnotes to Canto IV, as well as entire book of more extended annotations: *Historical Illustrations of the Fourth Canto of Childe Harold: containing dissertations on the ruins of Rome, and an essay on Italian literature* (London: John Murray, 1818).
[69] [Jameson,] *Diary of an Ennuyée*, p. 131. See Eustace, *Tour through Italy*, vol. 1, pp. 183–7.

– Digression on the Inaccuracies of "Corinna" and Vindication of Italian Females.'[70]

Corinne is criticized here for 'inaccuracies', as though it were a travel book, constrained by its generic rules to offer the reader information which is useful because it is correct. Digression, however, at this time, often draws attention to the affinity between the two genres in an opposite manner, by registering a fictionalizing impulse within the travel narrative. A tradition of 'sentimental' straying off the point is founded by Laurence Sterne's *Sentimental Journey through France and Italy* (1768). Sterne's fictionalized traveller-narrator, Yorick, resolutely affirms the crucial role of digression, both literal and metaphorical, in the assimilation of the foreign:

> The man who either disdains or fears to walk up a dark entry may be an excellent good man, and fit for a hundred things; but he will not do to make a good sentimental traveller. I count little of the many things I see pass at broad noon day, in large and open streets. – Nature is shy, and hates to act before spectators; but in such an unobserved corner, you sometimes see a single short scene of her's worth all the sentiments of a dozen French plays compounded together – and yet they are *absolutely* fine.[71]

Yorick moves on to a particular dark passage, and to an evening when he walked along it and saw 'two ladies standing arm in arm' within it. The sight of them prompts desires that seem about to take the narrator into novelistic territory; voicing these desires with cautiously conditional formulations, and revealing that his own role in the anecdote that follows will in fact be that of a mere spectator, he hovers on the boundary between the travel narrative and the novel: 'they seem'd to be two upright vestal sisters, unsapp'd by caresses, unbroke in upon by tender salutations: I could have wish'd to have made them happy – their happiness was destin'd, that night, to come from another quarter.'[72]

The traveller-narrator defines his digressiveness as a quality that prompts a cheerful irreverence towards the established itinerary of the Grand Tour, with its sequence of sights and wonders, all demanding a hyperbolic responsiveness. His own responsivenss, he explains to a French count, will be accorded instead to women – more specifically, to 'the *nakedness* of their hearts' – a preoccupation that will supply him with a sequence of sights to rival those sought out by travellers of a less 'sentimental' disposition:

---

[70] Galiffe, *Italy and its Inhabitants*, vol. 2, p. vii, p. 84; see pp. 79–86.
[71] Laurence Sterne, '*A Sentimental Journey*', with '*The Journal to Eliza*' and '*A Political Romance*', edited by Ian Jack (Oxford: Oxford University Press, 1991; first published in 1768), p. 107. On sentiment and sentimentalism in the late eighteenth century, see William M. Reddy, *The Navigation of Feeling: A Framework for the History of Emotions* (Cambridge: Cambridge University Press, 2001).
[72] Sterne, *Sentimental Journey*, pp. 107–8, p. 108.

> It is for this reason, Monsieur le Compte, continued I, that I have not seen the Palais royal – nor the Luxembourg – nor the Façade of the Louvre – nor have attempted to swell the catalogues we have of pictures, statues, and churches – I conceive every fair being as a temple, and would rather enter in, and see the original drawings and loose sketches hung up in it, than the transfiguration of Raphael itself.[73]

Yorick does in fact devote much of his narrative to chronicling the minutiae of social encounters – in large part, flirtatious encounters with women. Satire of the conventional progression through sights and wonders is apparent in such encounters even before his declaration of his programme of sightseeing: glimpsing a woman in the courtyard of his inn at Calais ('– Good God! How a man might lead such a creature as this round the world with him! –'), he reaches ahead to Rome, and to the discourse of antiquarianism allotted to that city:

> I had not yet seen her face – 'twas not material; for the drawing was instantly set about, and long before we had got to the door of the Remise, *Fancy* had finished the whole head, and pleased herself as much with its fitting her goddess, as if she had dived into the TIBER for it.[74]

The narrative ends on the Alps, where Yorick dismisses the conventional hyperboles through which travel books acclaim natural sublimity:

> Let the way-worn traveller vent his complaints upon the sudden turns and dangers of your roads – your rocks – your precipices – the difficulties of getting up – the horrors of getting down – mountains impracticable – and cataracts, which roll down great stones from their summits, and block his road up.[75]

In Yorick's 'sentimental' narrative, however, this last feature, so integral to the narrative of crossing boundaries and witnessing natural features that themselves exceed their limits, turns out to be more than mere rhetorical decoration: there is indeed 'a fragment of this kind' in the road, and Yorick is trapped in an inn, where he becomes embroiled in complex negotiations with an attractive Piedmontese woman who is constrained to share a room with him.[76] The anticipation of crossing the great natural boundary of Europe is displaced onto uncertainties as to whether their carefully negotiated attempt to maintain a boundary between their beds will be entirely successful. (The abrupt suspension of Yorick's tour at the end of the second volume is usually explained by reference to Sterne's death before he could write Volume III; it is, however, entirely in keeping

---

[73] Sterne, *Sentimental Journey*, p. 84.
[74] Sterne, *Sentimental Journey*, p. 17.
[75] Sterne, *Sentimental Journey*, pp. 120–1. For a longer analysis of this episode, see Chloe Chard, 'Crossing Boundaries and Exceeding Limits: Destabilization, Tourism and the Sublime', in *Transports: Travel, Pleasure and Imaginative Geography, 1600–1830*, edited by Chloe Chard and Helen Langdon (New Haven and London: Yale University Press, 1996), pp. 117–49; pp. 117–25.
[76] Sterne, *Sentimental Journey*, p. 121; see pp. 120–5.

with the irreverent disregard of conventional orderings in the existing text.)

Chapter 2 includes a number of narratives in which digressions in the sentimental tradition displace hyperboles, yet protect these hyperboles from suspicions of affectation and pomposity through an ironic movement from the sublime to the ridiculous. Even in more straightforward commentaries, moreover, a divagatory disorderliness is proclaimed by traveller-narrators as proof of their sincerity and spontaneity. Martin Sherlock, in his *Nouvelles Lettres d'un voyageur anglois* (1780), which he himself translates as *New Letters from an English Traveller* (1781), addresses his correspondent, in a letter from northern Italy, in a manner that implies that disorderliness of expression must be prompted not only by sincerity but also by a strength of feeling, unrestrained by 'art':

> Me blâmez-vous, mon cher ami, de ce que je quitte trop souvent mon sujet? J'écris sans art et je vous présente un mélange de mouvemens et d'idées dans le même désordre qu'ils se sont offerts à moi.[77]
>
> Do you blame me, my dear friend, for too often quitting my subject? I write without art, and present you a mixture of emotions and ideas in the same disorder in which they offered themselves to me.

Lewis Engelbach, in *Naples and the Campagna Felice* (1815), is equally concerned to impress upon his correspondent that he is writing 'without art':

> You know my antipathy to systems; you recollect, I dare say, the friendly altercation which took place, a few days before my departure, at Somerset-house, when I was for examining first the most important pictures in preference to beginning the review at the door of every room in the exhibition, as proposed by you. You then indulged *my* eccentric propensity. I now curb it into the regular track chalked out by *your* mandate. All fair! a few side-way flights, however, I fear you will have to put up with.[78]

Topographical digression

Digression might be expected to set itself in consistent opposition to hyperbole; since the structure of hyperbole is transgressive (etymologically a 'throwing beyond', and, in terms of its lexical definition, an over-reaching of the limits of language that aims to be understood liter-

---

[77] Martin Sherlock, *Nouvelles Lettres d'un Voyageur Anglois*, second edition (London and Paris: Esprit and La Veuve Duchesne, 1780), pp. 103–4; *New Letters from an English Traveller* (London: J. Nichols, T. Cadell, P. Elmsly, H. Payne and N. Conant, 1781), p. 100.

[78] [Lewis Engelbach,] *Naples and the Campagna Felice. In a Series of Letters Addressed to a Friend in England, in 1802* (London: R. Ackermann, 1815), p. 67.

ally), digression might seem destined always to throw hyperboles into disarray.

Straying and wandering, however, are not completely incompatible with crossing boundaries and exceeding limits. Travellers combine divagation with hyperbole when they allow their thoughts to lead them away from the topography that they have set themselves the task of describing, and reach out to more remote, strange or exotic regions, as though unable to accept the imaginative bounds imposed upon them by the part of the world in which they find themselves. Such expressions of imaginative restlessness are even found in accounts of regions that are themselves defined as wild and unexplored: Jonathan Carver, in his *Travels through America* (1778), comments on 'the Shining Mountains' (the Rocky Mountains) and the range of which they form a part:

> Probably in future ages, this extraordinary range of mountains may be found to contain more riches in their bowels than those of Indostan and Malabar or that are produced on the Golden Coast of Guinea; nor will I except even the Peruvian Mines.[79]

In Italy, however, digressions of this kind affirm the ambiguity of a topography that is in many ways familiar, but that may offer unexpected moments of strangeness, alterity and novelty. Piozzi discovers, 'at Lomellino's villa, in the Genoese state . . . chesnuts, which would not disgrace the forests of America'.[80] Morgan herself, in her description of Vesuvius, deploys this trope: 'Such fatal but inevitable engines rarely allure the proximity of man: they are found lording the desolation where human interests end, amidst the ice deserts of Kamtschatka, the altitudes of the Andes, the outskirts of the world.'

The impatience of imaginative constraint that is inscribed in such hyperbolic digressions is elided with a more general impatience of convention and accepted pieties by William Beckford, when he dreams of constructing a Chinese pavilion in the dome of St Peter's.[81] Charles Dupaty, in a passage in his *Lettres sur l'Italie* (1788), translated as *Sentimental Letters on Italy* (1789), voices a resistance to established social orderings by reaching out to wild regions that provide a space for imaginative speculation.

---

[79] *Jonathan Carver's Travels through America, 1766–1768; An Eighteenth-Century Explorer's Account of Uncharted America*, edited by Norman Gelb (New York and Chichester: Wiley, 1993), p. 99.

[80] Piozzi, *Observations and Reflections*, vol. 1, p. 63.

[81] William Beckford, *Dreams, Waking Thoughts and Incidents* (1783), in *The Travel Diaries of William Beckford of Fonthill*, edited by Guy Chapman, 2 vols (London: Constable and Houghton and Mifflin, 1928), vol. 1, pp. 1–310; pp. 187–8. For an analysis of this passage, see E.S. Shaffer, '"To remind us of China" – William Beckford, Mental Traveller on the Grand Tour: The Construction of Significance in Landscape', in *Transports*, edited by Chard and Langdon, pp. 207–42.

Dupaty pauses before representations of the death of the rich and that of the poor at the Palazzo Pitti, and begins to muse upon this theme, which propels his imagination to regions in which the social constraints of the Old World might be imagined as absent:

> Je réfléchissois sur la societé, sur ce qu'on appelle la justice, qui n'est plus aujourd'hui, en grande partie, qu'une injustice consacrée: mon imagination avoit passé en revue tous les maux de la civilisation; elle entroit dans les forêts du Canada, pour interroger, sur le bonheur, la vie sauvage.[82]
>
> I was reflecting on society, and on what they call justice, which, for the greatest part, is nothing more in these days, than sanctified injustice; my imagination had passed in review all the evils arising from the state of civilization; it was entering the forests of Canada, to reason upon happiness, and a savage life.

The wild excesses of the topographical imagination are sometimes pursued to a point where hyperbole prompts an ironic awareness of how recklessly any sense of the limits of reality has been jettisoned. Anna Jameson, describing her own visit to St Peter's in Holy Week, deploys a topographical digression (prompted by the travels that Maupertuis made famous through his *Figure de la terre*, published in 1738), in order to introduce a mischievously incongruous conjunction between a wonder central to European civilization, on the one hand, and the remote fringes of Europe, on the other:

> As Maupertuis said after his journey to Lapland – for the universe I would not have missed the sights and scenes of yesterday; but, for the whole universe, I would not undergo such another day of fatigue, anxiety, and feverish excitement.[83]

Naples, in particular, attracts hyperbolic topographical digressions – unsurprisingly so, since part of its attraction is that it is a liminal city, where the established topography of the Grand Tour borders on more exotic and less easily assimilated topographies. Martin Sherlock, in his *Lettres d'un voyageur anglois* (London [Geneva], 1779), which he translates as *Letters from an English Traveller* (1780), observes that Naples is 'aussi sauvage que la Russie' ('as savage as Russia')[84] Louis Simond, in his *Voyage en Italie et en Sicile*, translated as *A Tour in Italy and Sicily*, observes cheerfully:

> L'on pourroit comparer les mœurs des Napolitains à celles d'Otahiti, telles qu'elles étaient du temps de Cook; et ces mœurs sont celles de la nature! Quand leur intérêt immédiat paraît s'y trouver, ils font le mal sans honte et sans remords,

---

[82] Dupaty, *Lettres sur l'Italie*, vol. 1, pp. 185–6; *Sentimental Letters on Italy*, vol. 1, p. 146.
[83] [Jameson,] *Diary of an Ennuyée*, p. 304.
[84] [Martin Sherlock], *Lettres d'un voyageur anglois* (London [Geneva]: privately printed, 1779), p. 96, *Letters from an English Traveller* (London: J. Nichols, T. Cadell and N. Conant, 1780), p. 45.

faute de principes et en quelque sorte innocemment. La même irréflexion fait qu'ils jouissent de la vie au jour la journée, sans penser au lendemain.

> The manners and morals of Neapolitans are those of Otaheite, or of Nature. They do wrong without shame or remorse whenever it suits their immediate purpose, enjoying animal life day by day without the smallest care about the next.[85]

Topographical digression, in these passages, indicates an active excessiveness, in Naples, that imaginatively displaces the boundaries of the not-so-distant foreign. Morgan herself, in this city, uses a topographical digression to affirm another form of excessiveness: the excess of restraint represented by monasticism. At the church of Santa Chiara, she describes the 'long iron grating' in the choir that encloses and conceals the nuns when they attend public services. A reference to 'Turkish seraglios' emphasizes the particular horror of their captivity, branding the imprisonment of women in convents as a custom that takes cruelty beyond the usual degree of Gothic oppression to be found even in southern Italy:

> Here the nuns are permitted (themselves unseen) to take glimpses of that world they have abandoned for ever. Here they behold friends! Parents! Perhaps *one* that was more than either, issuing forth in the nave below (their duty paid) to those scenes of sunny loveliness which they themselves shall never more behold! This latticed gallery, and its purposes, remind the observer of the gilt and skreened galleries of the Turkish seraglios, where nuns of another description are imprisoned by the tyranny and folly of man – Nature's laws equally violated or transgressed by the followers of Mahomet and the professors of Christianity.[86]

The traveller's reach of digressive imagination is especially poignant here; the nuns themselves, as Morgan conjures them up, can travel only in their sad and wistful dreams.

---

[85] Louis Simond, *Voyage en Italie et en Sicile*, 2 vols (Paris: A. Sautelet et compagnie, 1828), vol. 2, p. 142; *A Tour in Italy and Sicily* (London: Longman, Orme, Brown and Green, 1828), p. 431.
[86] Morgan, *Italy*, vol. 2, p. 357, p. 358.

Chapter 1
PLEASURE

I: The foreign and the familiar

SCYTHROP
I should have no pleasure in visiting countries that are past all hope of regeneration. There is great hope of our own; and it seems to me that an Englishman, who, either by his station in society, or by his genius, or (as in your instance, Mr Cypress,) by both, has the power of essentially serving his country in its arduous struggle with its domestic enemies, yet forsakes his country, which is still so rich in hope, to dwell in others which are only fertile in the ruins of memory, does what none of those ancients, whose fragmentary memorials you venerate, would have done in similar circumstances.

MR CYPRESS
Sir, I have quarrelled with my wife; and a man who has quarrelled with his wife is absolved from all duty to his country. I have written an ode to tell the people as much, and they may take it as they list.
           Thomas Love Peacock, *Nightmare Abbey* (1818)

Travellers take for granted that deriving pleasure from the foreign affirms their authority and competence as participants in the Grand Tour. They often mock other travellers for regarding the sights of Italy with a perverse moroseness. The most famous dismissal of those who fail in pleasure is the moment in Sterne's *Sentimental Journey* when Yorick, the fictionalized traveller-narrator, summarizes the travels of 'the learned SMELFUNGUS' – Smollett, in his role as traveller-narrator of *Travels through France and Italy* (1766). 'Smelfungus', Yorick explains, 'set out with the spleen and jaundice, and every object he pass'd by was discoloured or distorted'. Smelfungus has failed to appreciate the great sights of the Grand Tour, such as the Pantheon (' – ' *tis nothing but a huge cock-pit*, said he – I wish you had said nothing worse of the Venus of Medicis, replied I'); he also complains bitterly about his treatment by the locals: 'He had been flea'd alive, and bedeviil'd, and used worse than St. Bartholomew, at every stage he had come at –.'[1] John

---

[1] Laurence Sterne, *'A Sentimental Journey' with 'The Journal to Eliza' and 'A Political Romance'*, edited by Ian Jack (Oxford: Oxford University Press, [1768] 1991).

Armstrong, writing under the pseudonym of Lancelot Temple, in his *Short Ramble through some Parts of France and Italy* (1771), cites other travellers who, like Smelfungus, cavil at the beauties of 'the celebrated VENUS':

> As to Shape and Person, nothing can be more perfect or exquisite, though some Connoisseurs complain that her Ancles are rather too thick. I believe they are mistaken: but there are people who think the only office of a critic is to discover Faults; and they may sometimes succeed in that, who are too dull ever to relish a Beauty.[2]

Anna Jameson offers her own dismissal of those who fail to give themselves up to 'illusions of romance':

> I have met persons who think they display a vast deal of common sense, and very uncommon strength of mind, in rising superior to all prejudices of education and illusions of romance – to whom enthusiasm is only another name for affectation – who, where the cultivated and the contemplative mind finds ample matter to excite feeling and reflection, give themselves airs of fashionable *nonchalance*, or flippant scorn – to whom the crumbling ruin is so much brick and mortar, no more – to whom the tomb of the Horatii and Curatii is a *stack of chimneys*, the Pantheon *an old oven*, and the Fountain of Egeria a *pig stye*. Are such persons aware that in all this, there is an affectation a thousand times more gross and contemptible, than that affectation (too frequent perhaps) which they design to ridicule?[3]

Pleasure, however, is defined in many commentaries as a source of anxiety: when voicing a fascination with various aspects of the foreign, travellers often hastily remind themselves – and the reader – either of the more regrettable features of foreign places or of the merits of their own country or region of origin. On the Borromean Islands, swept away by the delights of the famous gardens, Hester Piozzi is presented with currants and gooseberries by a Dutch family, and at once reflects 'that liberty, security, and opulence alone give the true relish to productions either of art or nature; that freedom can make the currants of Holland and golden pippins of Great Britain sweeter than all the grapes of Italy'. Naples elicits from the same traveller expressions of pleasure from which she hastily dissociates herself:

> Here are the most excellent, the most incomparable fish I ever eat; red mullets, large as our maycril, and of singularly high flavour; besides the calamaro, or inkfish, a dainty worthy of imperial luxury; almond and even apple trees in blossom, to delight those who can be paid for coarse manners and confined notions by the beauties of a brilliant climate.[4]

---

[2] Lancelot Temple, *A Short Ramble through some Parts of France and Italy* (London: T. Cadell, 1771), p. 15.

[3] [Anna Jameson,] *Diary of an Ennuyée*, second edition (London: Henry Colburn, 1826), pp. 207–8.

[4] Hester Lynch Piozzi, *Observations and Reflections Made in the Course of a Journey through France, Italy, and Germany*, 2 vols (London: A. Strahan and T. Cadell, 1789), vol. 2, p. 224, p. 58; see also, for example, vol. 1, pp. 150–1.

Sentimental sights and wonders

A slightly earlier part of the commentary on Naples in Piozzi's *Observations and Reflections*, concluding in a similar reversal, is among the passages below. The traveller-narrator begins by proclaiming equably: 'The truth is, the jolly Neapolitans lead a coarse life, but it is an unoppressed one.' After reaffirming the exceptionally 'unoppressed' character of 'female conduct' in the city by invoking Queen Oberea of Tahiti, notorious for her lasciviousness, Piozzi once again takes up a stance of tolerance: 'It is however observable, and surely very praiseworthy, that if the Italians are not ashamed of their crimes, neither are they ashamed of their contrition.' This leads her into a narrative of enthralled viewing. Such narratives are a recurrent element within the 'sentimental' tradition of travel writing. One feature of this tradition has already been mentioned: a resolute digressiveness, which entails an ironic preoccupation with trivial social exchanges rather than with the great sights and wonders. A second feature is the occasional transmutation of a character with whom the traveller-narrator interacts into a human site of enthralment. Such figures are usually female; some of them, like the figures in eighteenth-century French paintings whom Michael Fried, in *Absorption and Theatricality*, has identified as objects of contemporary critical admiration, are presented as absorbed in their own thoughts and feelings to a degree that draws the traveller into an absorptive identification with them, setting up a structure of *mise-en-abîme*: an element within a visual tableau is repeated in the scene of viewing that frames that tableau.[5]

A site of enthralment in Sterne's *Sentimental Journey* supplies a model for women who intermittently fascinate the traveller in this way in other travel writings. Yorick, at Moulines, on his way to Italy, visits a 'disorder'd maid', Maria, who has already appeared in the novelist's *Tristram Shandy* (1757–58). Yorick discovers Maria 'sitting under a poplar', in an attitude that echoes that of the *Weeping Dacia*, in the famous classical bas-relief, in Rome. (One of Joseph Wright's paintings of her – *Maria, from Sterne*, 1777 – emphasizes the resemblance to the *Dacia* especially strongly.) Like the Dacia, Maria is weeping: 'the tears trickled down her cheeks.'[6]

---

[5] Michael Fried notes the approbatory comments of eighteenth-century French art critics when they assess paintings that absorb the beholder: works, in other words, that seem to remove the beholder from a position of spatial detachment in front of the work of art. One of the sorts of painting that are seen as possessing a praiseworthy ability to draw in the beholder, is, Fried suggests, 'the representation of figures absorbed in quintessentially absorptive states and activities' (*Absorption and Theatricality: Painting and Beholder in the Age of Diderot*, Berkeley and Los Angeles: University of California Press, 1980, p. 107).

[6] Sterne, *Sentimental Journey*, p. 113; see Laurence Sterne, *The Life and Opinions of Tristram Shandy, Gentleman*, edited by Graham Petrie (Harmondsworth: Penguin, 1976), pp. 600–2.

Maria, then, is described as a figure who is first apprehended in distanced, pictorial terms – a figure in a well-known classical pose – and is then experienced through a moment of intense emotional identification. Yorick describes in elaborate detail the stages by which her self-absorption draws him into her sorrows: her tears supply an occasion for a drama of identification in which intensity tips over into irony:

> I sat down close by her; and Maria let me wipe them away as they fell with my handkerchief. – I then steep'd it in my own – and then in hers – and then in mine – and then I wip'd hers again – and as I did it, I felt such undescribable emotions within me, as I am sure could not be accounted for from any combinations of matter and motion.[7]

Maria, like other fictional characters, such as Corinne, generates associations that are seen as attracting travellers to particular places on the topography.[8] Piozzi, in her journal, declares 'Molines is a fine Place; I know not if 'tis the Town Sterne places his Maria near: but I caught myself looking for her, and listening to hear the Pipe as We approached it both Times.'[9]

In her account of Naples, Piozzi describes another such human site of enthralment. She begins by establishing herself in the position of detached pictorial spectator, emphasizing that, as a foreigner, she is struck by many objects of observation that fail to make any impact on the local inhabitants: 'I saw this very morning an odd scene at church, which, though new to me, appeared, perhaps from its frequent repetition, to strike no one but myself.'[10] She then describes 'a lady with a long white dress, and veiled', who prostrates herself in front of the high altar; her tears, as she rises, are, Piozzi declares, 'mingled with sobs of no affected or hypocritical penitence I am sure'. The indifference of the Neapolitans emphasizes, by contrast, the extent to which the traveller herself is fascinated and moved by the penitent: she feels her heart 'quite penetrated by her behaviour'. By invoking Nicholas Rowe's *Jane Shore* and Milton's *Paradise Lost*, she locates

---

[7] Sterne, *Sentimental Journey*, p. 114.

[8] For the 'romantic and charming associations' conferred on Terracina by Corinne, see [Jameson,] *Diary of an Ennuyée*, p. 209.

[9] *The Piozzi Letters: Correspondence of Hester Lynch Piozzi, 1784–1821 (formerly Mrs. Thrale)*, edited by Edward A. Bloom and Lillian D. Bloom, 6 vols (Newark, London and Toronto: University of Delaware Press and Associated University Presses, 1989–96), vol. 1, p. 391. See also W[lliam] Hazlitt, *Notes of a Journey through France and Italy* (London: Hunt and Clarke, 1826), p. 175: 'As we left Moulins, the crimson clouds of evening streaked the west, and I had time to think of Sterne's *Maria*.'

[10] In Milan, too, Piozzi emphasizes that the customs of the Italians are striking to foreigners but not to themselves: she asks a young married woman what the attitude of her confessor is to her compliance with the custom of taking on a *cicisbeo* – a man who escorts her to social occasions, and spends much of his time with her. The reply is: '"Oh, why he *is used to it*" – in the Milanese dialect –*è assuefaà*' (*Observations and Reflections*, vol. 1, p. 101).

this poignant figure in a literary tradition of women repenting of their errors, and so lifts her above the continuum of everyday existence, and defines her as, however fleetingly, one of the sights of the city.

At this point, Piozzi observes sharply: 'Let not this story, however, mislead any one to think that more general decorum or true devotion can be found in churches of the Romish persuasion than in ours'; noting that 'this burst of penitential piety was in itself an indecorous thing', the traveller reminds herself of a string of other lamentable features of Neapolitan society and manners (including a propensity to 'filthiness' – a frequent preoccupation in travel writing, upon which Charlotte Eaton elaborates in one of the passages in the second part of this chapter). In other words, she suddenly defines the pleasure of allowing herself to become enthralled by the penitent as a pleasure to which some sense of the forbidden is attached – and so, of course, invests the experience of enthralment with yet greater allure.

The second passage from *Observations and Reflections*, placed at the conclusion of the narrative, attempts to pin down the reasons why the delights of travel must be treated with suspicion. Piozzi's reflections begin on a rather less disenchanted note, as she muses on the increased sophistication and diminished sense of wonder and strangeness that she herself has acquired from travelling: on an earlier visit to the town of Lille, 'it was the first time I had ever crossed the channel, and I thought every thing a wonder'. A dismissive digression to the familiar ('I now feel as if we were at Canterbury') is followed by some digressions to the remote, in which she engages in flights of the restless topographical imagination – but then brings the indulgence of imaginative pleasures to an abrupt end:

> Was one to go to Egypt, the sight of Naples on the return home would probably afford a like sensation of proximity: and I recollect, one of the gentlemen who had been with Admiral Anson round the world told us, that when he came back as near as our East India settlements, he considered the voyage as finished, and all his toils at an end – so is my little book.

These reflections on the relative nature of alterity revive a theme that Piozzi considers at various earlier points in her book: when uttering hyperboles, she suggests, the traveller runs the risk of sounding too easily impressed, and reaching for expressions that would sound naive to those with greater experience of foreign peoples and places. She registers an awareness of this risk at Mantua, when she remarks dismissively: 'The gentleman who shewed us the Ducal palace, seemed himself much struck with its convenience and splendour; but I had seen Versailles, Turin, and Genoa.' In Padua, on her return journey, she launches into a topographical digression that invests the loss of wonder with the inevitability of the physiological changes in perception induced by climbing and descending mountains:

> Well! I have once more walked over St. Antony's church, and examined the bas reliefs that adorn his shrine; but their effect has ceased. Whoever has spent some time in the Musæum Clementinum is callous to the wonders which sculpture can perform.
>
> Has one not read in Ulloa's travels, of a resting-place on the side of a Cordillera among the Andes, where the ascending traveller is regularly observed to put on additional clothing, while he who comes down the mountain feels so hot that he throws his clothes away? So it is with the shrine of St. Antonio di Padua, and one's passion for the sculpture that adorns it: while Santa Giustina's church retains her power over the mind, a power never missed by simplicity, while great effort has often small effect. But we are hastening to Venice, and shall leave our cares and our coach behind; superfluous as they both are, in a city which admits of neither.[11]

Such declarations of diminished awe are common in travel narratives. In Byron's *Childe Harold's Pilgrimage*, the speaker explains at some length that he would be more admiring of the Apennines were he not a man of wider experience:

> Once more upon the woody Apennine,
> The infant Alps, which – had I not before
> Gazed on their mightier parents, where the pine
> Sits on more shaggy summits, and where roar
> The thundering lauwine – might be worshipp'd more;
> But I have seen the soaring Jungfrau rear
> Her never-trodden snow, and seen the hoar
> Glaciers of bleak Mont Blanc both far and near,
> And in Chimari heard the thunder-hills of fear.[12]

Having noted her own changed perceptions, Piozzi then considers other possible effects of travel. Travellers, if they give themselves up too intemperately to the gratification of living abroad, are, she suggests, prone to fall into one of three snares: they become alienated from the familiar, they lose localized loyalties and responsibilities, or they develop an attitude of moral relativism. (The third snare opens up as a result of gaining 'the love of hurrying perpetually from place to place' – restlessness, here, is explicitly defined as a form of addiction.) The second danger – that of irresponsibility – is named in terms that recall Anna Jameson's declaration

---

[11] Piozzi, *Observations and Reflections*, vol. 1, p. 119, vol. 2, p. 182. While Antonio de Ulloa published several works concerned with the Americas, 'Ulloa's Travels' probably refers to his *Relaction historica del viage a la América meridional, hecho de orden de S. Mag., para medir algunos grados de Meridiano terrestre, . . . con otras varias observaciones astronomicas y phisicas*, 4 vols (Madrid: Antonio Maria, 1748); the English translation of 1758 went through numerous editions. I have been unable to trace the precise reference.

[12] Lord Byron, *Childe Harold's Pilgrimage*, Canto IV, stanza 73 (the declaration of superior experience continues in the next stanza); *The Complete Poetical Works*, edited by Jerome J. McGann, 7 vols (Oxford: Oxford University Press, 1980–92), vol. 2, p. 148.

that 'one leaves Naples as a man parts with an enchanting mistress', and suggests a similar identification with a form of pleasure that is gendered as masculine.[13] In Piozzi's case, however, the foreign as mistress is not dangerously 'enchanting', but shabbily neglected; the risk is not of susceptibility to allurements that must in the end be abandoned, but of a failure to live up to social responsibilities: 'Others there are, who . . . learn to treat the world as a man treats his mistress.'[14]

The third passage below, from Anna Jameson's *Diary of an Ennuyée*, demonstrates the ease with which loyalties to the familiar are displaced once the concept of travel as an adventure of the self opens up a new option: the appeal to overwhelming personal need. Reflecting upon the pleasures of Naples, Jameson refers to the merits of the familiar only to explain that her own state of mind makes it necessary for her to seek out the foreign: '– dear England! I love, like an Englishwoman, its fire-side employments, and home-felt delights . . . but for the languid frame, and the sick heart, give me this pure elastic air "redolent of spring;" this reviving sun shine and all the witchery of these deep blue skies.' In contrast to Piozzi, she pointedly maintains that the response demanded by the warm South is one of guiltless irresponsibility; 'to feel that indefinite sensation of excitement, that *superflu de vie*, quickening every pulse and thrilling through every nerve, is a pleasure peculiar to this climate, where the mere consciousness of existence is happiness enough'.

Similar appeals to personal need are, unsurprisingly, often found in more intimate genres, such as the private journal. In her journal entries for 1823, written after she returned to England following her husband's death, Mary Shelley displays a yet more complete lack of concern as to whether her feeling of greater personal freedom and consolatory pleasure while in Italy entails any element of disloyalty to her own country:

> Why am I not in Italy – Italian sun & airs & flowers & earth & hopes – they are akin to love enjoyment freedom – exquisite delight – if they are not them they are masked unto them – but here all wears the hue of grimmest reality – a reality to make me shriek upon the ear of midnight – but I must not.[15]

Jameson adopts the pretence that her *Diary of an Ennuyée* is in fact a secret journal, to which she turns for 'consolation': 'It has gradually

---

[13] [Jameson,] *Diary of an Ennuyée*, p. 308.
[14] For another account of the dangers of disloyalty to the familiar, see John Moore, *A View of Society and Manners in Italy, with Anecdotes Relating to some Eminent Characters*, second edition, 2 vols (London: W. Strahan and T. Cadell, 1781), vol. 2, p. 502. The strategy of hotly denying the benefits of travel, in a work seemingly devoted to displaying such benefits, is satirized by Sterne in Yorick's 'Preface'; see *A Sentimental Journey*, p. 112.
[15] *The Journals of Mary Shelley, 1814–1844*, edited by Paula R. Feldman and Diana Scott-Kilvert, 2 vols (Oxford: Oxford University Press, 1987), vol. 2, p. 469.

become not only the faithful depository of my recollections, but the confidante of my feelings, and the sole witness of my tears.' She herself, she indicates, intends to destroy this 'record of my weakness'; editorial notes affirm that a sympathetic male reader has subsequently discovered it and prepared it for publication.[16]

The *ennuyée's* tears, she repeatedly hints, stem from unhappiness in love; in detailing her efforts to overcome her sorrows in foreign places, she draws the reader into the emotional drama in which her travels play a part. The book, in other words, adopts a version of the sentimental device of enthralment; rather than recounting her absorption in the sorrows of a figure whom she encounters, the traveller-narrator, immersed in her own sufferings, yet struggling to find distraction and diversion in the experience of travel, attempts to draw the reader into an identification with her feelings. This structure had been employed in an earlier travel book: Mary Wollstonecraft's *Letters Written during a Short Residence in Sweden, Norway, and Denmark* (1796). The most immediate point of reference for Jameson, however, is de Staël's *Corinne*, in which the narrator identifies closely with the tribulations of the half-Italian, half-English heroine, who travels round Italy, first as *cicerone* to her Scottish admirer Oswald, Lord Nelvil, and then alone, attempting to console herself for his desertion. Jameson cites the book several times, buying a copy in Florence, where she describes it as 'a fashionable vade mecum for sentimental travellers in Italy', and recounts its effects upon her:

> When I began to cut the leaves, a kind of terror seized me, and I threw it down, resolved not to open it again. I know myself weak – I feel myself unhappy; and to find my own feelings reflected from the pages of a book, in language too deeply and eloquently true, is not good for me. I want no helps to admiration, nor need I kindle my enthusiasm at the torch of another's mind. I can suffer enough, feel enough, think enough, without this.[17]

The structure through which Jameson beckons the readers into her inner world of suffering is established at the very beginning of her book by an introductory note in which the fictional male editor feels driven to express his fascination with the author: 'As a real picture of natural and feminine feeling, the Editor hopes that it may interest others as much as it had interested him.'[18]

Jameson's own confidences about her life, speaking in the first person, begin at Calais; watching 'the shores of England fade away', she is struck

---

[16] [Jameson,] *Diary of an Ennuyée*, pp. 122–3.
[17] [Jameson,] *Diary of an Ennuyée*, p. 110 (for other references to the novel, see p. 206 and p. 209); see [Germaine] de Staël, *Corinne, ou l'Italie*, edited by Claudine Herrmann, 2 vols (Paris: Éditions des Femmes, 1979), vol. 2, pp. 236–8.
[18] [Jameson,] *Diary of an Ennuyée*, p. 1.

by 'the conviction that I should never behold them more', but nonetheless attempts to maintain some suspense as to whether a return to happiness might still be possible:

> I know not yet whether I ought to rejoice and be thankful for this opportunity of travelling, while my mind is thus torn and upset; or rather regret that I must visit scenes of interest, of splendour, of novelty – scenes over which, years ago, I used to ponder with many a sigh, and many a vain longing; now that I am lost to all the pleasure they could once have excited: for what is all the world to me now? But I will not weakly yield . . . Who knows but this dark cloud may pass away. Continual motion, continual activity, continual novelty, the absolute necessity for self-command may do something for me.[19]

As she progresses through France and Italy, the traveller minutely assesses every place that she visits for its therapeutic or destructive effects on her, and for the insights that it offers into her own condition. Meditating on her own enchantment, in Paris, on viewing 'the Pont des Arts, on a fine moonlight night', she muses: 'it appears to me that those who from feeling too strongly, have learnt to consider too deeply, become less sensible to the works of art, and more alive to nature'. The sublime landscape that surrounds her in Geneva prompts the reflection: 'Now I feel the value of my own enthusiasm: now am I repaid in part for many pains and sorrows and errours it has cost me.' In Venice: 'Pleasure and wonder are tinged with a melancholy interest; and while the imagination is excited, the spirits are depressed.' Travelling southwards, she remarks: 'I will say nothing of Bologna; – for the few days I have spent here have been to me days of acute suffering.' In Santa Croce, in Florence, she experiences some respite: 'All memory, all feeling, all grief, all pain were swallowed up in the sublime tranquillity which was within me and around me.'[20]

Once Jameson sets out for Naples, she almost offers a glimmer of hope: '– my senses and my imagination have been so enchanted, my heart so very heavy – where shall I begin?' On the return journey to Rome, her miseries at first predominate: 'Last night, we reached Mola di Gaëta, which looked even more beautiful than before, in the eyes of all but *one*, whose senses were blinded and dulled by dejection, lassitude, and sickness.' Such lassitude leaves her incapable of experiencing and expressing delight:

> When I felt myself passively led along the shore, placed where the eye might range at freedom over the living and rejoicing landscape, when I heard myself repeating mechanically the exclamations of others, and felt no ray of beauty, no sense of

---

[19] [Jameson,] *Diary of an Ennuyée*, pp. 4–5.
[20] [Jameson,] *Diary of an Ennuyée*, p. 29, p. 32, p. 65, p. 84, p. 114.

pleasure penetrate to my heart, shall I own even to myself the mixture of anguish and terror, with which I shrunk back, conscious of the waste within me?[21]

Having noted her 'conviction that now it was all over', Jameson then experiences a remarkable change of mood:

> From my bed this morning I stepped out upon my balcony just as the sun was rising. I wished to convince myself whether the beauty on which I had lately looked with such admiration and delight, had indeed lost all power to touch my heart. The impression made upon my mind at that instant I can only compare to the rolling away of a palpable and suffocating cloud: every thing on which I looked had the freshness and brightness of novelty: a glory beyond its own was again diffused over the enchanting scene from the stores of my own imagination: the sea breeze which blew against my temples, new strung every nerve; and I left Mola with a heart so lightened and so grateful, that not for hours afterwards, nor till fatigue and hurry had again wearied down my spirits, did that impression of happy thankfulness pass away.[22]

At Autun, however, as Jameson travels back towards England, an editorial note informs the reader that the writer has died 'in her 26th year'.[23]

The *ennuyée's* confidences are carefully delimited: she never offers any details of the love affair that has driven her to such misery. In fictionalizing her experiences, she edits out not only the survival of the non-fictional Anna Jameson but also the job as a governess to an English family that allows her to travel to Italy.

Jameson, in other words, despite her gesture of admitting the reader into the secrets of her diary (and her heart), is as reticent about precise biographical detail as Piozzi – who, in *Observations and Reflections*, never mentions directly that she is travelling to Italy in the wake of the scandal caused by her marriage to the Italian musician Gabriele Piozzi, after the death of her first husband, Henry Thrale.[24] Rather, the confidences that the *ennuyée* offers mark a difference in the attitude of the two traveller-narrators towards the interaction of human passions and sensibilities, on

---

[21] [Jameson,] *Diary of an Ennuyée*, p. 208, p. 265.
[22] [Jameson,] *Diary of an Ennuyée*, p. 265, p. 266.
[23] [Jameson,] *Diary of an Ennuyée*, p. 354.
[24] Hester Piozzi's friend Elizabeth Montagu wrote in a letter, soon after the event: 'Mrs. Thrales marriage has taken such horrible possession of my mind I cannot advert to any other subject. '*The Piozzi Letters*, vol. 1, p. 99; letter dated [25] July 1784. Montagu adds: 'female delicacy, and male wisdom, will be much shocked', and comments: 'when one . . . weeps over the disgrace of a Friend bitter are the sensations'.

The autobiographical references in her travel book are brief and discreet: she refers to her 'demi-naturalization' as an advantage in gaining the opportunity to chat confidentially with Italian women (*Observations and Reflections*, vol. 1, p. 67), and, in Florence, is at pains to emphasize the respectable role that she and her husband occupy in society there; see, for example, vol. 1, p. 328; after noting that she has 'dined at Prince Corsini's table', Piozzi adds: 'I had the honour of entertaining, at my own dinner on the 25th of July, many of the Tuscan, and many of the English nobility; and Nardini kindly played a solo in the evening at a concert we gave in Meghitt's great room' (see also vol. 1, p. 272).

the one hand, and the topography, on the other. When Piozzi mentions odd personal details, such as as 'a distracting tooth-ach' while visiting the Palazzo Barberini, in Rome, she never reflects at any length upon the ways in which her own state of mind might influence her perception of particular places. In Florence, she presents love as well as pain as a mere distraction:

> Readers . . . want no further telling that one traveller was in pain, and one in love when the tour of Italy was made by them; and so they pick out their intelligence accordingly, from various books, written like two letters in the Tatler, giving an account of a rejoicing night; one endeavouring to excite majestic ideas, the other ludicrous ones of the very same thing.[25]

Jameson, in contrast, assumes that passions and pain draw the topography into a drama of dynamic interaction between self and world. Such a drama demands a narrative more overarching than the incidental interludes of sentimental travel writing, and imposes this bolder narrative strategy through the heroine's struggle to fend off the doom that awaits her.[26] (Henry Matthews, when he assesses the effect of Italy on his spirits, and so on his physical health, in his *Diary of an Invalid*, sets up a similar narrative.)

Impatience of limits

In Jameson's account of the effect of Naples upon her troubled spirits, the absence of spatial limitation is noted as one of the features of the prospect that imbues her with 'that indefinite sensation of excitement'. Enjoying 'the enchantment of the earth, air, and skies' from her balcony, the traveller suggests a vast sweep of the natural world; she then refers to 'the atmosphere without a single cloud', and places 'the blue sea' that results from this cloudlessness in implicit contrast to the 'vapoury atmosphere' of the North, and the enclosed domestic space within which the English take refuge from mists and cold. The plot of desire that Jameson maps out is repeated in many different versions in succeeding centuries; to cite a well-known, example, it follows – in a much more restrained manner

---

[25] Piozzi, *Observations and Reflections*, vol. 1, p. 418 (recounting her visit to the Palazzo Barberini); vol. 1, p. 289. Ironically, two of the travel books that most conspicuously advertise their authors' personal preoccupations in the early nineteenth century, focus, respectively, on pain and on love: Henry Matthews's *Diary of an Invalid* and Anna Jameson's *Diary of an Ennuyée*.

[26] Jonah Siegel, in *Haunted Museum: Longing, Travel and the Art-Romance Tradition* (Princeton: Princeton University Press, 2005), notes this aspect of Jameson's *Diary of an Ennuyée* when (pp. 56–7) he situates it within the fictional genre of the 'art romance' ('the kind of story that emerges at the confluence of . . . the nineteenth century's fascination with creative genius and the same period's insatiable appetite for tales of the European South'; p. 5).

– the same movement away from the constraining bounds of domesticity that Freud traces when he notes, in his essay 'A Disturbance of Memory on the Acropolis': 'I had long seen clearly that a great part of the pleasure of travel . . . is rooted . . . in dissatisfaction with home and family', and merges this desire with the experience of crossing the unbounded ocean: 'When first one catches sight of the sea, crosses the ocean and experiences as realities cities and lands which for so long had been distant, unattainable things of desire – one feels oneself like a hero who has performed deeds of improbable greatness.'[27]

Both Jameson and Freud, in these passages, draw on the founding text of the theory of the sublime: Longinus' *Peri Hypsous*. ('On the Sublime'). Longinus is, in this work, concerned mainly with sublimity in poetry and rhetoric, but shifts momentarily to the sublime in nature, and equates the desire for sublimity with an impatience of limits and limitations. As translated by William Smith, in one of many eighteenth-century versions of the text, Longinus declares:

> Nature never designed man to be a grov'ling and ungenerous animal, but brought him into life, and placed him in the world, as in a crouded theatre, not to be an idle spectator, but spurr'd on by an eager thirst of excelling, ardently to contend in the pursuit of glory. For this purpose, she implanted in his soul an invincible love of grandeur, and a constant emulation of whatever seems to approach nearer to divinity than himself. Hence it is, that the whole universe is not sufficient, for the extensive reach and piercing speculation of the human understanding. It passes the bounds of the material world, and launches forth at pleasure into endless space.[28]

The treatise then suggests that this spirit of aspiration leads us to admire natural features that themselves display a proclivity to go beyond bounds. Such features not only draw our imagination beyond the limits of the domestic and familiar, and exceed more mundane objects in size, but, in addition, in at least two cases, actively transgress their own boundaries: he includes in his list the Nile, a river famous for annually overflowing its banks, and Etna, famous for its volcanic eruptions:

> Thus the impulse of nature inclines us to admire, not a little clear transparent rivulet that ministers to our necessities, but the *Nile*, the *Ister*, the *Rhine*, or still much more, the Ocean. We are never surprised at the sight of a small fire that burns clear, and blazes out on our own private hearth, but view with amaze the celestial fires, tho' they are often obscured by vapours and eclipses. Nor do we reckon any thing in nature more wonderful than the boiling furnaces of *Ætna*,

---

[27] Sigmund Freud, 'A Disturbance of Memory on the Acropolis' [1936; first English translation 1941], in *The Pelican Freud Library* (Harmondsworth: Penguin, 1972-), translated under the general editorship of James Strachey, vol. 11, edited by Angela Richards, pp. 443–55; p. 455.

[28] *Dionysius Longinus on the Sublime*, translated by William Smith, fourth edition (London: E. Johnson, 1770), pp. 145–6.

which cast up stones, and sometimes whole rocks, from their labouring abyss, and pour out whole rivers of liquid and unmingled flame. And from hence we may infer, that whatever is useful and necessary to man, lies level to his abilities, and is easily acquired; but whatever exceeds the common size, is always great, and always amazing.[29]

Jameson positions her account of the Bay of Naples just after a long narrative of her ascent of Vesuvius in order to witness the mountain 'spouting fire to a prodigious height'. In moving from visions of 'romantic interest and terrible magnificence' to English 'fire-side enjoyments' and 'hearth rugs', Jameson obliquely invokes Longinus' opposition between sublime natural features such as volcanoes and 'the Ocean', on the one hand, and 'our own private hearth', on the other; in doing so, she endorses the pleasures of escaping bounds and limitations as a source of delight – a delight that, in her case, is not so much ennobling but, rather, a source of emotional refuge.[30]

More equivocations about pleasure

In the next passage, from Henry Sass's *Journey to Rome and Naples* (1818), the traveller tries out a series of different approaches to pleasure. Like Jameson, Sass sees Naples as allowing the traveller to transcend mundane experience: 'The deliciousness of the climate, the fertility of the earth . . . the grandeur of the bay, and the magnificence of the scenery, caused that degree of inspiration which renders us above ourselves.' Like Sydney Morgan in the environs of the same city, he is gratified by 'poetic visions': beyond Posillipo, he notes, is 'poetic ground, with all its pleasing associations'. These expressions of delight, however, are prefaced by a lament about a major constraint on pleasure: the 'moans and pitiful plaints' of the Neapolitan poor prevent the traveller and his party from enjoying their ices. The degraded condition of the Neapolitans is then implicitly defined as yet more lamentable by virtue of their indifference to the great natural amentiy that is available to them: the sea. As in Piozzi's account of the lack of interest that the Neapolitans display towards the penitent, such indifference nonetheless adds piquancy to the pleasures of the traveller, who views the foreign, he feels, with sharper curiosity and more complex sensibilities.

At this juncture, the traveller surveys the landscape, like Jameson, from his balcony, and signals a change of mood: 'The sun was just setting; there was a most glorious sky, scenes of misery vanished from our minds,

[29] *Dionysius Longinus on the Sublime*, pp. 146–7.
[30] [Jameson,] *Diary of an Ennuyée*, p. 228, p. 231.

and we gave ourselves up to the enjoyment of the scene around.' Even a reminder of more mundane existence – 'the rattling of a carriage' – sets off a train of dreamy fabulation.

Hester Lynch Piozzi, *Observations and Reflections Made in the Course of a Journey through France, Italy, and Germany*, 2 vols (London: A. Strahan and T. Cadell, 1789), vol. 2, pp. 26–31

The truth is, the jolly Neapolitans lead a coarse life, but it is an unoppressed one. Never sure was there in any town a greater shew of abundance: no settled market in any given place, I think, but every third shop full of what the French call so properly *ammunition de Bouche*, while whole boars, kids and small calves dangle from a sort of neat scaffolding, all with their skins on, and make a pretty appearance.[31] Poulterers hang up their animals in the feathers too, not lay them on boards plucked, as at London or Venice.

The Strada del Toledo is at least as long as Oxford Road, and straight as Bond-street, very wide too, the houses all of stone, and at least eight stories high. Over the shops live people of fashion I am told, but the persons of particularly high quality have their palaces in other parts of the town; which town at last is not a large one, but full as an egg: and Mr. Clarke, the antiquarian, who resides here always, informed me that the late distresses in Calabria had driven many families to Naples this year, beside single wanderers innumerable; which wonderfully increased the daily throng one sees passing and repassing.[32] To hear the Lazaroni shout and bawl about the streets night and day, one would really fancy one's self in a semi-barbarous nation; and a Milanese officer, who has lived long among them, protested that the manners of the great corresponded in every respect with the idea given of them by the little. His account of female conduct, and that even in the very high ranks, was such as reminded me of Queen Oberea's sincerity, when Sir Joseph Banks joked her about Otoroo.[33] It is however observable, and surely very praiseworthy, that if the Italians are not ashamed of their crimes, neither are they ashamed of their contrition. I saw this very morning an odd scene at church, which, though new to me, appeared, perhaps from its frequent repetition, to strike no one but myself.

---

[31] [Literally 'Ammunition for the mouth'.]

[32] [James Clark (c.1745–1800), painter and antiquary, who lived in Naples more or less continuously from 1771 until his death in 1800.]

[33] [This may be a slightly misremembered account of an anecdote in John Hawkesworth, *An Account of the Voyages Undertaken by Order of his Present Majesty for Making Discoveries in the Southern Hemisphere*, 3 vols (London: W. Strahan and T. Cadell, 1773), vol. 2, p. 107; Banks finds Oberea (now known to scholars as Purea), a Tahitian woman of high social rank, 'in bed with a handsome young fellow about five and twenty, whose name was OBADÉE'; Banks 'retreated in haste and confusion, but was soon made to understand, that such amours gave no occasion to scandal'.]

A lady with a long white dress, and veiled, came in her carriage, which waited for her at the door, with her own arms upon it, and three servants better dressed than is common here, followed and put a lighted taper in her hand. *En cet état*, as the French say, she moved slowly up the church, looking like Jane Shore in the last act, but not so feeble;[34] and being arrived at the steps of the high altar, threw herself quite upon her face before it, remaining prostrate there at least five minutes, in the face of the whole congregation, who, equally to my amazement, neither stared nor sneered, neither laughed nor lamented, but minded their own private devotions – no mass was saying – till the lady rose, kissed the steps, and bathed them with her tears, mingled with sobs of no affected or hypocritical penitence I am sure. Retiring afterwards to her own seat, where she waited with others the commencement of the sacred office, having extinguished her candle, and apparently lighted her heart; I felt mine quite penetrated by her behaviour, and fancied her like our first parent described by Milton in the same manner:

> To confess
> Humbly her faults, and pardon beg; with tears
> Watering the ground, and with her sighs the air
> Frequenting, sent from heart contrite, in sign
> Of sorrow unfeign'd, and humiliation meek.[35]

Let not this story, however, mislead any one to think that more general decorum or true devotion can be found in churches of the Romish persuasion than in ours – quite the reverse. This burst of penitential piety was in itself an indecorous thing; but it is the nature and genius of the people not to mind small matters. Dogs are suffered to run about and dirty the churches all the time divine service is performing; while the crying of babies, and the most indecent methods taken by the women to pacify them, give one still juster offence. There is no treading for spittle and nastiness of one sort or another, in all the churches of Italy, whose inhabitants allow the filthiness of Naples, but endeavour to justify the disorders of other cities; though I do believe nothing ever equalled the Chiesa dei Cavalieri at Pisa, in any Christian land. Santa Giustina at Padua, the Redentore at Venice, St. Peter's at Rome, and some of the least frequented churches at Milan, are exceptions; they are kept very clean, and do not, by the scandalous neglect of those appointed to keep them, disgrace the beauty of their buildings.

---

[34] [Literally 'In this state'. The eponymous heroine of the play (1714), by Nicholas Rowe (1674–1718), one of the parts in which Hester Piozzi's friend Sarah Siddons became famous early in her career; Rowe included *Jane Shore* among his 'She-Tragedies', which place particular emphasis on the suffering and penitence of the heroines.]

[35] [Adapted from *Paradise Lost*, Book 10, lines 1100–4.]

Here has, however, been a dreadful accident which puts such slight considerations out of one's head. A Friar has killed a woman in the church just by the Crocelle inn, for having refused him favours he suspected she had granted to another. No step is taken though towards punishing the murderer, because he is *religioso, è di più cavaliere*.[36] What a miracle that more such outrages are not daily committed in a country where profession of sanctity, and real high birth, are protections from law and justice! Surely nothing but perfect sobriety and great goodness of disposition can be alleged as a reason why worse is not done every day. I said so to a gentleman just now, who assured me the criminal would not escape very severe castigation; and that perhaps the convent would inflict such severities upon that gentleman as would amply supply the want of activity in the exertion of civil power.

Piozzi, *Observations and Reflections*, vol. 2, pp. 385–8

On her return journey, Hester Piozzi finds herself in Lille.

How fine I thought these churches thirteen years ago, comes now thirteen times a-day into my head; they are not fine at all; but it was the first time I had ever crossed the channel, and I thought every thing a wonder, and fancied we were arrived at the world's end almost; so differently do the self-same places appear to the self-same people surrounded by different circumstances! I now feel as if we were at Canterbury. Was one to go to Egypt, the sight of Naples on the return home would probably afford a like sensation of proximity: and I recollect, one of the gentlemen who had been with Admiral Anson round the world told us, that when he came back as near as our East India settlements, he considered the voyage as finished, and all his toils at an end – so is my little book; and (if Italy may be considered, upon Sherlock's principle, as a sort of academy-figure set up for us all to draw from) my design of it may have a chance to go in the portfolio with the rest, after its exhibition-day is over.[37]

With regard to the general effect travelling has upon the human mind, it is different with different people. Brydone has observed, that the magnetic needle loses her habits upon the heights of Ætna, nor ever

---

[36] ['A man of religion and, what is more, a gentleman'.]

[37] [George Anson's circumnavigation of the globe is recounted in *A Voyage round the World in the Years MDCCXL, I, II, III, IV*, compiled by Richard Walter (London: W. Bowyer and J. Nichols, 1776); Martin Sherlock, *Nouvelles Lettres d'un Voyageur Anglois*, second edition (London and Paris: Esprit and La Veuve Duchesne, 1780), pp. 52–3; *New Letters from an English Traveller* (London: J. Nichols, T. Cadell, P, Elmsly, H. Payne and N. Conant, 1781), p. 64 (Piozzi summarizes the comment two pages earlier; *Observations and Reflections*, vol. 2, p. 384); Sir James Edward Smith quotes this passage from 'Mrs. Piozzi's Travels' – and embroiders upon it – on the title page of each of the three volumes of *A Sketch of a Tour on the Continent, in the Years 1786 and 1787* (London: B. and J. White, 1793).]

more regains her partiality for the *north*, till again newly touched by the loadstone:[38] it is so with many men who have lived long from home; they find, like Imogen,

> That there's living out of Britain;[39]

and if they return to it after an absence of several years, bring back with them an alienated mind – this is not well. Others there are, who, being accustomed to live a considerable time in places where they have not the smallest intention to fix for ever, but on the contrary firmly resolve to leave *sometime*, learn to treat the world as a man treats his mistress, whom he likes well enough, but has no design to marry, and of course never provides for – this is not well neither. A third set gain the love of hurrying perpetually from place to place; living familiarly with all, but intimately with none; till confounding their own ideas (still undisclosed) of right and wrong, they learn to think virtue and vice ambulatory, as Browne says;[40] profess that climate and constitution regulate men's actions, till they try to persuade their companions into a belief most welcome to themselves, that the will of God in one place is by no means his will in another; and most resemble in their whirling fancies a boy's top I once saw shewn by a professor who read us a lecture upon opticks; it was painted in regular stripes round like a narrow ribbon, red, blue, green, and yellow; we set it a-spinning by direction of our philosopher, who, whipping it merrily about, obtained as a general effect the total privation of all the four colours, so distinct at the beginning of its *tour*, – *it resembled a dirty white!*

[Anna Jameson,] *Diary of an Ennuyée* (London: Henry Colburn, 1826), pp. 238–40

[February] 26. – The Eruption burst forth again to-day, and is exceedingly grand; though not equal to what it was on Sunday night. The smoke rises from the crater, in dense black masses, and the wind having veered a few points to the southward, it is now driven in the direction of Naples. At the moment I write this, the skies are obscured by rolling vapours, and the sun which is now setting just opposite to Vesuvius, shines, as I have seen him, through a London mist, red, and shorn of his beams. The sea is angry and

---

[38] [Patrick Brydone, *A Tour through Sicily and Malta*, 'A New Edition', 2 vols (London: W. Strahan and T. Cadell, 1775); first published in 1773, vol. 1, pp. 115–16.]

[39] [Adapted from Shakespeare, *Cymbeline*, 3.4.142]

[40] [Sir Thomas Browne, *Christian Morals*, 'published from the Original and Correct Manuscript of the Author' by John Jeffery (London and Cambridge: Cambridge University Press, Knapton and Morphew, 1716), p. 11:'Think not that Morality is ambulatory; that Vices in one age are not Vices in another; or that Virtues, which are under the everlasting Seal of right Reason, may be stamped by Opinion.']

discoloured; the day most oppressively sultry, and the atmosphere thick and sulphureous.

March 4. – We have had delicious weather almost ever since we arrived at Naples, but these last three days have been perfectly heavenly. I never saw or felt any thing like the enchantment of the earth, air, and skies. The mountain has been perfectly still, the atmosphere without a single cloud, the fresh verdure bursting forth all around us, and every breeze visits the senses, as if laden with a renovating spirit of life, and wafted from Elysium. Whoever would truly enjoy nature, should see her in this delicious land: 'Où la plus douce nuit succède au plus beau jour;' for here she seems to keep holiday all the year round.[41] To stand upon my balcony, looking out upon the sunshine, and the glorious bay; the blue sea, and the pure skies – and to feel that indefinite sensation of excitement, that *superflu de vie*, quickening every pulse and thrilling through every nerve, is a pleasure peculiar to this climate, where the mere consciousness of existence is happiness enough. Then evening comes on, lighted by a moon and starry heavens, whose softness, richness, and splendour, are not to be conceived by those who have lived always in the vapoury atmosphere of England – dear England! I love, like an Englishwoman, its fire-side enjoyments, and home-felt delights: an English drawing-room with all its luxurious comforts – carpets and hearth rugs, curtains let down, sofas wheeled round, and a group of family faces round a blazing fire, is a delightful picture; but for the languid frame, and the sick heart, give me this pure elastic air 'redolent of spring;' this reviving sun shine and all the witchery of these deep blue skies. [42]

Henry Sass ('student of the Royal Academy of Arts'), *A Journey to Rome and Naples, performed in 1817; giving an Account of the Present State of Society in Italy, and containing Observations on the Fine Arts* (London: Longman, Hurst, Rees, Orme and Brown, 1818), pp. 174–9.

In various parts of Naples we were assailed by the Vetturini, offering to convey us to Rome, Milan, Paris; and then, perceiving we were Englishmen,

---

[41] [The fourth line of Germaine de Staël's translation of Goethe's 'Song of Mignon' from *Wilhelm Meisters Lehrjahre* (*Wilhelm Meister's Apprenticeship*); in translating these words, de Staël silently quotes Voltaire's *La Henriade*, line 147: 'La plus affreuse nuit succède au plus beau jour.']

[42] [John Dryden, 'Of the Pythagorean Philosophy' (translated from Ovid, *Metamorphoses*, 15), line 110.

Jameson was of Irish birth and ancestry; her maiden name was Murphy. Like many of her contemporaries, she treats national identity as a relatively flexible point of reference for self-definition. In her account of Naples, her view of herself as an Englishwoman is useful in setting up an opposition between domestic enclosure and reviving space and freedom.]

to London. At the coffee-houses every luxury can be commanded: the ices, which are delicious, are served up in various shapes of fruit, and so firm, that the spoon will hardly make an impression on them. But how is it possible to enjoy these, when the doors are beset with crowds of miserable beings, men, women, and children, whose moans and pitiable plaints ring in our ears. To feed on luxuries when surrounded by misery is impossible. Once we endeavoured to distribute a certain sum among about thirty of these wretched creatures; when they became so clamorous and importunate, many who had already received shifting their places, that it was out of our power to make any distinction. Before we had half done, hundreds came running from the surrounding houses; and, attempting to make our way out by another door, we were again assailed, and were only indebted to our speed in running for our escape.

The men of the lower classes wear neither shoes nor stockings, and some are without shirts; the children have merely a short tunic, but the women are in general more clothed. The latter never think of cutting their hair, which is disgustingly profuse, frizzed out on all sides and one head will present all the different shades from the lightest to the darkest brown. The higher classes are very gay in their habiliments; but the Neapolitan women are universally ugly, having somewhat of the Egyptian character, thick lips, heavy eyelids, flat foreheads, and sallow complexions.

Although the Neapolitans have a luxuriant sea before them, and a shore of the softest sand, they never enter on it; and the few that are seen bathing near the King's garden, are generally English. In walking along the streets of an evening, there may be seen, under the porticos of palaces, at the gates of churches, on the steps of houses and terraces, and by the sides of streets, crowds of Lazaroni sunk in slumber, those being their usual places of rest.

On the evening after our return from Vesuvius we took tea in the balcony of our window, which overlooked the sea. The sun was just setting; there was a most glorious sky, scenes of misery vanished from our minds, and we gave ourselves up to the enjoyment of the scene around. The deliciousness of the climate, the fertility of the earth, producing excellent corn in abundance, and quantities of the finest fruits and vegetables, the grandeur of the bay, and the magnificence of the scenery, caused that degree of inspiration which renders us above ourselves; and when night had fallen, what a time for reflection! The balcony of my window commanded the whole bay; and from the bay, the Mediterranean spread itself to the horizon. On the left rose Vesuvius, with its burning top, to the clouds; on the right were the grotto and mountain of Posilipo; and beyond that, poetic ground, with all its pleasing associations. Above, the moon was shining in splendour with its borrowed light, in a pure atmospheric region; and the more distant stars, twinkling with original lustre, gave animation to the scene. Lamps lined the shore; and nothing was heard but the confused murmur of distant sounds from the busy haunts of men, the softness of which was occasionally interrupted by the barking of the watchful dog. The rattling of a carriage announced some one, who, it was possible, might be returning filled with *ennui* from a resort of public amusement – or with mortified vanity from the precincts of a court, – or with an aching heart from domestic calamity – or with the joyfulness of a lover well received by his beloved – or with a breast wounded with the pangs of jealousy – or with a bosom callous to sensibility, from plundering the pocket of – perhaps his friend; or possibly it might be one flying to the arms of a beloved wife – or conveying agreeable news to a sincere friend – or in the buoyancy of expectation of meeting a lovely mistress. It passed swiftly by, and was no longer heard – silence prevailed – music was wafted through the air – some one serenading – or perhaps chanting to the Virgin. It died away – silence again prevailed. Mortality was sunk in sleep, while wakeful angels guard. Address thyself to thy Creator, and retire to thy couch. Who can behold the vast firmament, but must exclaim with the poet, 'That there is a God above, all nature cries aloud through all her works; he must delight in virtue; and that which he delights in must be happy.'[43]

II: Tourism: the management of pleasure

'No postmasters abuse me'

In all the passages surveyed so far in this chapter, the discussions of pleasure and travel are concerned in some way with cultural loyalties. During the late eighteenth and early nineteenth centuries, however, many of the accounts of pleasure in travel writing focus on the problem of how to manage pleasure so as to avoid any risk to the stability or identity of the self; they take up, in other words, the problem mapped out by the touristic approach to travel, which seeks to manage pleasure by keeping danger at bay.

Anna Jameson, in the first of the passages below, forgets her cares for a while, as she describes herself listening to a conversation about Italian politics between two men, and then attempting to set the topic aside, as one too distressing to contemplate. In a version of the trope of preterition, she allows her own views to flow forth in any case, as though too impassioned to brook restraint ('A spirit is silently and gradually working its way beneath the surface of society, which must, ere long, break forth either for good or for evil'). At this point, she not only denies that she will allow herself to become embroiled in the distressing topic of 'politics and dis-

---

[43] Adapted from Joseph Addison, *Cato, a Tragedy* (1713), 5.1.15–18.

cord' but claims that she has also managed to avoid the minor irritations of which other travellers complain: 'no tradesmen cheat me, no hired menials irritate me, no innkeepers fleece me, no postmasters abuse me'.

Jameson indicates, in other words, that she is committed to avoiding any preoccupations that might impair 'that state of calm benevolence towards all around me, which leaves me undisturbed to envy, admire, observe, reflect, remember, with pleasure, if not with profit'. This strategy seems to entail avoiding almost all encounters with the local inhabitants: 'I have no dealings with the lower classes, little intercourse with the higher.' Instead, she turns to 'all the treasures of art and nature'.

In making this declaration, Jameson adopts the touristic approach: she assumes that danger must be kept at bay through a careful management of pleasure. In impressing upon the reader that she is aiming to achieve a sympathetic identification with both Italy and the very Italians with whom she claims to have so few exchanges, she twice invokes Sterne's *Sentimental Journey* – paradoxically, the very travel book that most resolutely abandons art and nature for encounters with human beings. In asserting that she comes to Italy 'not with the impertinent inquisition of a book-maker, nor the gloomy calculations of a politician, *nor the sneering selfism of a Smelfungus*' (emphasis added), she invokes Sterne's famous dismissal of those travellers incapable of pleasure. Earlier in the passage, in her declaration that 'I am not come to spy out the nakedness of the land, but to implore from her healing airs and lucid skies the health and peace I have lost', she silently quotes another section of the *Sentimental Journey*: the same section in which Yorick, seeking a passport from a French count, explains that his interest in the female heart is greater than his concern with the usual sights and wonders:

> Excuse me, Monsieur Le Count, said I – as for the nakedness of your land, if I saw it, I should cast my eyes over it with tears in them – and for that of your women (blushing at the idea he had excited in me) I am so evangelical in this, and have such a fellow-feeling for what ever is *weak* about them, that I would cover it with a garment, if I knew how to throw it on – But I could wish, continued I, to spy the *nakedness* of their hearts, and through the different disguises of customs, climates, and religion, find out what is good in the, to fashion by own by – and therefore am I come.[44]

Process and 'poetic fervour'

In invoking Sterne, then, and proclaiming the value of sentimental sympathy, Jameson raises the possibility that she might in fact feel slightly

---

[44] Sterne, *Sentimental Journey*, p. 84.

equivocal about rejecting animate beings for art and nature. When she moves on to a new object of attention, the sight that she selects is one that accentuates the equivocations implicit in her definition of safely touristic viewing. The sight that she chooses – an *accademia*, or performance by an *improvvisatore*, is a form of art, but also a social occasion – one to which an invitation must be secured ('Lady C** has just sent us tickets'). The art of improvisation, of which Jameson provides a succinct and informative account, often entails moments in which the audience suggests themes or words to the performer (in Jameson's narrative, Sestini rejects one word and accepts another). This element of exchange not only emphasizes the social character of the event, but also draws attention to the most striking feature of improvisation: it is an art of process rather than completion. As such, it supplies a metaphor for the state of incipient transformation of Italy itself, in which Jameson has just discerned a promising but unpredictable ebullition of political energies. She sees in Sestini's improvisation on the death of Alfieri an upsurge of spontaneous 'poetic fervour', which elicits from the audience a display of patriotic ardour; the traveller emphasizes that it is this response, as well as 'the animation of the poet', that moves her to tears.

As in many accounts of improvisation, the performer is presented as drawing on ancient myth: 'The subject proposed was from the story of Ulysses, which afforded him an opportunity of bringing in the whole sonorous nomenclature of the Heathen mythology, – which says Forsyth, enters into the web of every Improvisatore.' The passage that Jameson cites, from Joseph Forsyth's *Remarks on Antiquities, Arts, and Letters* (1813) is, in fact, an account of the famous *improvvisatrice* Fortunata Sulgher Fantastici, in Florence, in which the traveller registers a sense of irony at the incongruity between the theme of 'the sofa' that he proposes – with reference to the first book of William Cowper's *The Task* (1785) – a poem that focuses on rural domesticity – and the high-flown mythological references on which La Fantastici draws:

> So extensive is her reading that she can challenge any theme. One morning, after other classical subjects had been sung, a Venetian count gave her the boundless field of Apollonius Rhodius, in which she displayed a minute acquaintance with all the argonautic fable. Tired at last of demigods, I proposed the sofa for a task, and sketched to her the introduction of Cowper's poem. She set out with his idea, but, being once entangled in the net of mythology, she soon transformed his sofa into a Cytherean couch, and brought Venus, Cupid, and Mars on the scene; for such embroidery enters into the web of every improvvisatore. I found this morning-accademia flatter than the first. Perhaps Poetry, being one of the children of pleasure, may, like her sisters, be most welcome in the evening.[45]

[45] Joseph Forsyth, *Remarks on Antiquities, Arts, and Letters during an Excursion in Italy in the Years 1802 and 1803*, first edition (London: T. Cadell and W. Davies, 1813), pp. 55–6.

Jameson herself, however, refrains from any sense of ludicrous 'embroidery' or artifice, merely noting, with reference to Forsyth, that 'the Heathen Mythology' has its own part to play in the process of improvising; it 'assists the poet both with rhymes and ideas'. Only the 'jingling harpsichord' intrudes upon her absorption – musical accompaniment is, she notes, another source of support to the *improvvisatore*. Sestini's 'still increasing animation', over 'between thirty and forty stanzas', implicitly testifies to his spontaneity and sincerity.

The haunted

The third passage below – the second of two from Charlotte Eaton's *Rome in the Nineteenth Century* (1820) – also allows a bearer of cultural memory to assume a human form, and so to play a part in a commentary that strives to put into effect the strategy of concentrating only on art and nature. The passage begins with an account of the Coliseum by moonlight – a scene that is included in many travel books of this period, and is described in Byron's *Manfred* (1817), as well as in Canto IV of *Childe Harold's Pilgrimage*.[46] As in the similar set piece of visiting the Capitoline Museum at night, and viewing the antique sculptures by torchlight (the same context of display in which Matthews, at the Vatican, complains about fig leaves in the second passage in Chapter 4), the lighting effect supplies the traveller with a framing device, which facilitates the task of editing out any elements in the topography that might prove unsettling, distracting or dangerous.[47] For Piozzi, moonlight allows the Coliseum to aspire to the condition of art:

> We were driving last night to look at the Colisseo by moon-light – there were a few clouds just to break the expanse of azure and shew the gilding. I thought how like a sky of Guercino's it was; other painters remind one of nature, but nature when most lovely makes one think of Guercino, and his works.[48]

For Jameson, the framing device is one that fails to operate as it should: she is distressed, on visiting the monument on a night when it is illuminated by 'a brilliant full moon', both by the behaviour of some members of her own party ('young men too, and classical scholars, who

---

[46] Byron, *Manfred*, lines 3:4:8–46 (the passage is quoted by Matthews, p. 155), *Childe Harold's Pilgrimage*, Canto IV, stanza 144; *The Complete Poetical Works*, edited by Jerome J. McGann, 7 vols (Oxford: Oxford University Press, 1980–92), vol. 4, pp. 97–8, vol. 2, pp. 172–3.
[47] For Dean MacCannell's account of touristic 'framing and elevation', see *The Tourist: A New Theory of the Leisure Class* (New York: Schocken Books, 1976), pp. 44–5.
[48] Piozzi, *Observations and Reflections*, vol. 1, p. 414.

perhaps thought it fine to affect a well-bred *nonchalance*, a fashionable disdain for all romance and enthusiasm'), and by the guard of Austrian soldiers who 'walked close after our heels, smoking, spitting and sputtering German'.[49]

For Eaton, however, the scene is one of gratifying 'solitude and silence': 'Would that I could describe it to you, as it stood in its ruined loneliness amidst the deserted hills of Ancient Rome.' As in many other such descriptions (both of the Coliseum and of other Roman ruins), plants serve as metonyms for an enduring absence of human activity: 'the wild weeds waved as the night breeze passed over them.'[50] The scene is one from which human activities, energies and aspirations have been emptied: 'Nature holds her eternal course; – the works of man perish.'

As Eaton and her party move on to the Roman Forum, 'the silver moonlight' continues to mark the scene as an occasion for moralizing on departed glories: 'how beautifully its pale and mournful ray harmonized with the mouldering arches sunk in earth, like the deeds they commemorate!' The silence is broken, however, by 'a bell from a distant convent':

> At the sound, a figure glided from the shade of the Temple of Concord, passed before us like a shadow, and disappeared among the trees. We were somewhat startled at this apparition, which, according to all the rules of romance, should have served as the prelude to some mysterious adventure; but it only served to warn us to go home to bed; and, as it appeared to us no more, nor even condescended to explain why it had appeared at all, you may conceive it to have been a ghost or a man, a monk or an assassin, as best suits your fancy.

The 'apparition', then, allegorizes the role of Italy as a topography of the haunted, in which cultural memory is always poised to resurge, in unsettling ways. At the same time, it prompts in Eaton a sense of irony. 'It only served to warn us to go home to bed.' (The reader has already been prepared for a moment of bathos through an adaptation of lines from Byron's satirical poem 'The Curse of Minerva'.) The plunge from the sublime to the ridiculous implicit in such an admonition is emphasized by Henry Matthews's account of a similar reminder, in the moonlit Coliseum, welling up unprompted within him:

> A man should go *alone* to enjoy, in full perfection, all the enchantment of this moonlight scene; and if it do not excite in him emotions, that he never felt before,

---

[49] [Jameson,] *Diary of an Ennuyée*, p. 137, p. 138.
[50] Among the most famous accounts of weeds in ruins are Byron's lines on the Fountain of Egeria in Canto IV of *Childe Harold's Pilgrimage* (stanzas 116–20, lines 1036–80; *Complete Poetical Works*, edited by Jerome J. McGann, vol. 2, p. 163) and Shelley's description of the Baths of Caracalla; *The Letters of Percy Bysshe Shelley*, edited by Frederick L. Jones, 2 vols (Oxford: Oxford University Press, 1964), vol. 2, pp. 84–5.

– let him hasten home, – eat his supper, – say his prayers, – and thank Heaven that he has not one single grain of romance or enthusiasm, in his whole composition.[51]

Such a shift from the intense or unsettling to the comic can be seen as one of the strategies that serves the purposes of the touristic approach, in keeping the more destabilizing elements within the topography at bay. The haunted character of Italy offers travellers endless occasions for flirting with danger, yet reminding themselves that unsettling experiences may be based merely on the illusions of an over-active imagination.[52]

Framed intensity, set in contrast to filth

Tourist sights, then, offer an experience of intensity. For Eaton, on the Palatine, the 'flood of light and glory' in which the sun sinks is 'such as no power of language or of painting can pourtray'. At the same time, this intensity must be contained in some way. Containable intensity, in the first of the two passages from *Rome in the Nineteenth Century* below, is defined by opposition to the attributes of a less satisfactory sight. Eaton marshals the oblique acerbity of litotes: 'The beautiful solitude which surrounds the Coliseum, adds a secret charm to the pleasure we feel in surveying it. Not so the Pantheon.' The problem with this latter monument, she suggests, is precisely that the traveller's experience of it lacks any element of framing: the Pantheon is insufficiently separated from the chaotic continuum of everyday life around it – the 'incessant uproar' and 'congregated filth' that beset the monument on all sides.

References to dirt are extremely common in travel writing. Hester Piozzi, noting the dogs that are suffered to ruin and dirty the churches' in Naples, in the first passage in the earlier part of this chapter, moves on to a more wide-ranging survey of the disregard for cleanliness in Italian ecclesiastical settings. One of the most ebullient accounts of the filth of Rome, in Tobias Smollett's *Travels through France and Italy* (1766), begins with a description of the 'nastiness' of modern Rome, raising the expectation that the ancients, who have just been credited with founding the tradition of providing fountains in the city, might be judged more leniently. Far from it: observing nonchalantly, 'I have a great notion that their ancestors were not much more cleanly', Smollett launches into a detailed, satirically inflated catalogue of the multifarious sources of evidence that

---

[51] Henry Matthews, *The Diary of an Invalid. Being the Journal of a Tour in Pursuit of Health in Portugal, Italy, Switzerland and France in the Years 1817, 1818 and 1819*, second edition (London: John Murray, 1820); first published in 1820, p. 155.

[52] An apparent ghost, who turns out not to be so spectral after all, appears in the Coliseum in [Constantine Henry Phipps,] Marquis of Normanby, 'The Sentimental Baronet', in *The English in Italy*, 3 vols (London: Saunders and Otley, 1825), vol. 2, pp. 82–6.

testify to the utter squalor in which the ancient Romans lived ('we must naturally conclude they were strangely crouded together, and that in general they were a very frowzy generation').[53]

Descriptions of dirt emphasize the feat that the traveller has accomplished in selecting objects of observation, separating them from the surrounding confusion, and shifting them into a domain of personal experience – while nonetheless surviving the threat of contamination that filth and disorder evoke.[54] In dramatizing incipient contamination, travellers repeatedly set up a drama in which they confront a world so frighteningly chaotic that it drives them to make a gesture of separation: to affirm their distinct identity in reaction to it. In *Rome in the Nineteenth Century*, Eaton initially attempts to explain the Pantheon and its filthy surroundings by trying to imagine Westminster Abbey moved to Covent Garden Market. She then claims in resounding terms that this task defeats her: 'Nothing resembling such a hole as this could exist in England; nor is it possible that an English imagination can conceive a combination of such disgusting dirt, such filthy odours and foul puddles, as that which fills the vegetable market in the Piazza Della Rotonda at Rome.'

The ancient Romans look back at British savages

Eaton then introduces a dramatic shift of perspective:

> Still, while I gazed upon the beauty of the Pantheon itself, I could not but remember that this noble monument of taste and magnificence was already built in those times when our savage ancestors still roamed through their ancient forests, scarcely raised above the level of the beasts they chaced; their very name unknown to all the world besides, excepting to the Romans, by whom they were considered much the same as the South-Sea islanders are by us.

In imagining the Romans gazing at 'our savage ancestors', the traveller employs a variant of the common device of emphasizing cultural distance by describing foreigners reflecting on the behaviour or culture of those travellers who are attempting to understand them – or commenting on some aspect of the travellers' own culture. Piozzi, for example, describes Italians travelling in England who are dismayed to find that 'an exorbitant expence is incurred by the journey, not well repaid to them by the

---

[53] Tobias Smollett, *Travels through France and Italy*, edited by Frank Felsenstein (Oxford: Oxford University Press, 1981), p. 243; to cite one of many other accounts of dirt, Morgan, visiting the *palazzi* of Rome, is struck by the paradoxes of 'filth and ostentation' and 'superb flights of filth and marble' (*Italy*, vol. 2, p. 215, p. 217).

[54] Susan Stewart, in *On Longing: Narratives of the Miniature, the Gigantic, the Souvenir, the Collection* (Durham and London: Duke University Press, 1993), offers a persuasive account of the role of contamination in tourism, in the course of her analysis of the souvenir (pp. 146–7).

waiters white chitterlins, tambour waistcoats, and independent "*No, Sir*," echoed round a well-furnished inn or tavern.'[55]

Eaton, however, moves back boldly across time, and as she does so she maps out a cultural distance yet more daunting than that which 'an English imagination' confronts in observing the contemporary Italians. The ancient Romans, in her simile, regard our ancestors not as we regard their modern counterparts, but, rather, as we regard the more remote 'South-Sea islanders'. In introducing this rapid series of cultural shifts – from the more muted filth of Covent Garden Market to that of the Piazza della Rotonda, from the ancient Romans to the ancient Britons and then from the contemporary British to the South Sea islanders – Eaton unleashes a meditation on the vertiginous possibilities of strangeness; as though imagining Westminster Abbey in Covent Garden were not odd and incongruous enough, she implies, we are in fact forced to recognize that the world is full of the most stupendous cultural incongruities and reversals.

This device of displacing one cross-cultural encounter onto another, and imagining savagery amid the familiar, is taken up in a more chilling form in one of the classic texts of alterity: Joseph Conrad's *Heart of Darkness* (1902). In anticipation of the horror that Conrad's seafaring narrator discovers in the Congo, the novel begins by summoning up sombre moments in the Thames Estuary: '"And this also," said Marlow suddenly, "has been one of the dark places of the earth."' Reverting to 'very old times, when the Romans first came here', he reflects: 'Imagine the feelings of a commander of a fine – what d'ye call 'em – trireme in the Mediterranean, ordered suddenly to the north.' A series of negatives play their part in banishing all qualities consonant with civilization and comfort:

> Imagine him here – the very end of the world, a sea the colour of lead, a sky the colour of smoke . . . Sandbanks, marshes, forests, savages, – *precious little to eat fit for a civilised man, nothing but Thames water to drink. No Falernian wine here, no going ashore*. Here and there a military camp lost in a wilderness, like a needle in a bundle of hay – cold, fog, tempests, disease, exile, and death, – death skulking in the air, in the water, in the bush. They must have been dying like flies here. Oh yes – he did it. Did it very well, too, no doubt, and without thinking much about it either, except afterwards to brag of what he had gone through in his time, perhaps. They were men enough to face the darkness.[56]

Marlow then imagines another Roman who comes to Britain and encounters 'all that mysterious life of the wilderness that stirs in the forest':

---

[55] Piozzi, *Observations and Reflections*, vol. 2, p. 168.
[56] Joseph Conrad, *'Heart of Darkness' with 'The Congo Diary'*, edited by Robert Hampson (London: Penguin, 2000), p. 18, p. 18, p. 19; emphasis added.

> He has to live in the midst of the incomprehensible, which is also detestable. And it has a fascination too, that goes to work upon him. The fascination of the abomination – you know.[57]

When she reflects upon 'our savage ancestors' roaming through their ancient forests, 'scarcely raised above the level of the beasts they chaced', Eaton suggests that if the dirt of Rome can prompt such visions of abomination within the familiar topography of Britain it must itself be invested with an extraordinarily powerful potential for horror.

She also, perhaps, in these elucubrations, obliquely satirizes the eagerness of travellers to incorporate those features of foreign topography and culture that they regard as culturally superseded in their own countries – above all, dirt – within a *mise-en-scène* of the foreign that gains added piquancy from 'the fascination of the abomination'. Such an eagerness is voiced explicitly in Jameson's account of the topographical specificity of the picturesque:

> Civilization, cleanliness, and comfort, are excellent things, but they are sworn enemies to the picturesque: they have banished it gradually from our towns, and habitations, into remote countries, and little nooks and corners, where we are obliged to hunt after it to find it; but in Italy the picturesque is every where, in every variety of form; it meets us at every turn, in town and in country, at all times and seasons; the commonest object of every-day life here becomes picturesque and assumes from a thousand causes a certain character of poetical interest it cannot have elsewhere.[58]

A similar recognition that dirt and the picturesque may be rather closely entangled with each other is spelt out more ruthlessly, much later in this tradition, by Aldous Huxley, in his essay 'The Pierian Spring':

> A picturesque object may be defined as a thing which has some quality or qualities in excess of the normal. The nature of the excessive quality is almost a matter of indifference. Thus, even an excess of dirtiness is sufficient to render an object picturesque. The ideally picturesque object or scene possesses several excessive qualities in violent contrast one with another – for example, . . . excess of magnificence contrasting with excess of squalor.[59]

This last sentence could hardly describe more precisely Eaton's account of a 'noble monument of taste and magnificence' battling for attention with 'disgusting dirt', 'filthy odours' and 'foul puddles'.

---

[57] Conrad, *Heart of Darkness*, p. 19, p. 20.
[58] [Jameson,] *Diary of an Ennuyée*, p. 332. Malcolm Andrews, in his essay 'Dickens, Turner and the Picturesque' – an unusually subtle exploration of the diversity of concepts that the picturesque encompasses – provides a useful analysis of the role in picturesque aesthetics of objects that resist human control or modernizing improvements. (In *Imagining Italy: Victorian Writers and Travellers*, edited by Catherine Waters, Michael Hollington and John Jordan; Newcastle-upon-Tyne: Cambridge Scholars Publishing, 2010, pp. 177–94).
[59] Aldous Huxley, 'The Pierian Spring', in *Along the Road: Notes and Essays of a Tourist* (London: Chatto and Windus, 1925), pp. 190–201; p. 199.

[Jameson,] *Diary of an Ennuyée*, pp. 292–9

To-day we have remained quietly at home recruiting after the exertions of yesterday. After dinner Colonel –, and Mr. W** began to discuss the politics of Italy, and from abusing the governments, they fell upon the people, and being of very opposite principles and parties, they soon began an argument which ended in a warm dispute, and sent me to take refuge in my own room. How I detest politics and discord! How I hate the discussion of politics in Italy! And above all, the discussion of Italian politics, which offer no point upon which the mind can dwell with pleasure. I have not wandered to Italy, – 'this land of sun-lit skies and fountains clear,' as Barry Cornwall calls it, – only to scrape together materials for a quarto tour, or to sweep up the leavings of the 'fearless' Lady Morgan; or to dwell upon the heart-sickening realities which meet me at every turn; evils, of which I neither understand the cause, nor the cure. And yet say not to Italy

'Caduta è la tua gloria – e tu nol' vedi!'[60]

She does see it, – she does feel it. A spirit is silently and gradually working its way beneath the surface of society, which must, ere long, break forth either for good or for evil. Between a profligate and servile nobility, and a degraded and enslaved populace, a middle class has lately sprung up; the men of letters, the artists, the professors in the sciences, who have obtained property, or distinction at least, in the commotions which have agitated their country, and those who have served at home or abroad in the revolutionary wars. These all seem impelled by one and the same spirit; and make up for their want of numbers by their activity, talents, enthusiasm, and the secret but increasing influence which they exert over the other classes of society. But on subjects like these, however interesting, I have no means of obtaining information at once general and accurate; and I would rather not think, or speak, or write upon 'matters which are too high for me.'[61] Let the modern Italians be what they may, – what I hear them styled six times a day at least, – a dirty, demoralized, degraded, unprincipled race, – centuries behind our thrice blessed, prosperous, and comfort-loving nation in civilization and morals: if I were come among them as a resident, this picture might alarm me; situated as I am, a nameless sort of person, a mere bird of passage, it concerns me not. I am not come to spy out the nakedness of the land, but to implore from her healing airs and lucid skies the health and peace I have lost, and to worship as a pilgrim at the tomb of her departed glories. I have not

---

[60] [Adapted from Barry Cornwall, *Marcian Colonna*, part 1, line 3; Petrarch, 'Canzoniere "Che debb'io far? Che mi consigli, Amore"', line 23: 'Your glory is in ruins, and you don't wish to see it.' The term *fearless* is famously applied to Lady Morgan's *Italy* by Byron, in an appendix to *The Two Foscari* (Byron, *Complete Poetical Works*, vol. 6, p. 222).]

[61] [Adapted from Psalms, 131:1.]

many opportunities of studying the national character; I have no dealings with the lower classes, little intercourse with the higher. No tradesmen cheat me, no hired menials irritate me, no innkeepers fleece me, no postmasters abuse me. I love these rich delicious skies; I love this genial sunshine, which, even in December, sends the spirits dancing through the veins; this pure elastic atmosphere, which not only brings the distant landscape, but almost Heaven itself nearer to the eye; and all the treasures of art and nature which are poured forth around me; and over which my own mind, teeming with images, recollections, and associations, can fling a beauty even beyond their own. I willingly turn from all that excites the spleen and disgust of others; from all that may so easily be despised, derided, and reviled, and abandon my heart to that state of calm benevolence towards all around me, which leaves me undisturbed to envy, admire, observe, reflect, remember, with pleasure, if not with profit, and enables me to look upon the glorious scenes with which I am surrounded, not with the impertinent inquisition of a bookmaker, nor the gloomy calculations of a politician, nor the sneering selfism of a Smelfungus,[62] – but with the eye of the painter, and the feeling of the poet.

Apropos to poets! – Lady C** has just sent us tickets for Sestini's Accademia to-morrow night. So far from the race of Improvisatori being extinct, or living only in the pages of Corinne, or in the memory of the Fantastici, and the Bandinelli, the Giannis and the Corillas of other days, – there is scarcely a small town in Italy, as I am informed, without its Improvisatore; and I know several individuals in the higher classes of society, both here, and at Florence more particularly, who are remarkable for possessing this extraordinary talent, – though, of course, it is only exercised for the gratification of a small circle. Of those who make a public exhibition of their powers, Sgricci and Sestini are among the most celebrated – and of these Sgricci ranks first. I never heard him; but Signor Incoronati who knows him well, described to me his talents and powers as almost supernatural. A wonderful display of his art was the Improvisazione – we have no English word for a talent which in England is unknown, – of a regular tragedy on the Greek model, with the choruses and dialogue complete. The subject proposed was from the story of Ulysses, which afforded him an opportunity of bringing in the whole sonorous nomenclature of the Heathen mythology, – which says Forsyth, enters into the web of every Improvisatore, and assists the poet both with rhymes and ideas.[63] Most of the celebrated Improvisatori have been Florentines: Sgricci is, I believe, a Neapolitan, and his rival Sestini a Roman.

*   *   *   *   *   *

---

[62] [See Sterne, *Sentimental Journey*, pp. 28–9; discussed on p. 59, above.]
[63] [See pp. 60–1 above.]

April 7. – Any public exhibition of talent in the Fine Arts is here called an *Accademia*. Sestini gave his Accademia in an antichamber of the Palazzo –, I forget its name, but it was much like all the other *Palaces* we are accustomed to see here; exhibiting the same strange contrast of ancient taste and magnificence, with present meanness and poverty. We were ushered into a lofty room of noble size and beautiful proportions, with its rich fresco-painted walls and ceiling faded and falling to decay; a common brick floor, and sundry window panes broken, and stuffed with paper. The room was nearly filled by the audience, amongst whom I remarked a great number of English. A table with writing implements, and an old shattered jingling piano occupied one side of the apartment, and a small space was left in front for the poet. Whilst we waited with some impatience for his appearance, several persons present walked up to the table and wrote down various subjects; which on Sestini's coming forward, he read aloud, marking those which were distinguished by the most general applause. This selection formed our evening's entertainment. A lady sat down in her bonnet and shawl to accompany him; and when fatigued, another fair musician readily supplied her place. It is seldom that an Improvisatore attempts to recite without the assistance of music. When Dr. Moore heard Corilla at Florence, she sang to the accompaniment of two violins.* La Fantastici preferred the guitar; and I should have preferred either to our jingling harpsichord.[64] However, a few chords struck at intervals were sufficient to support the voice, and mark the time. Several airs were tried, and considered, before the poet could fix on one suited to his subject, and the measure he intended to employ. In general they were pretty and simple, consisting of very few notes, and more like a chant or recitative, than a regular air: one of the most beautiful I have obtained, and shall bring with me to England.

The moment Sestini had made his choice, he stepped forward, and without further pause or preparation, began with the first subject upon his list, – '*Il primo Navigatore*.'

Gesner's beautiful Idyl of 'The First Navigator,' supplied Sestini with the story, in all its details; but he versified it with surprising facility: and, as far as I could judge, with great spirit and elegance.[65] He added, too, some

---

* Corilla (whose real name was Maddalena Morelli) often accompanied herself on the violin; holding it, not against her shoulder, but resting it in her lap. She was reckoned a fine performer on this instrument; and for her distinguished talents was crowned in the Capitol in 1799. – ED. [Jameson appears to refer to John Moore, whose *View of Society and Manners in Italy* does not, however, include any reference to Corilla.]

[64] [Fortunata Sulgher Fantastici (1755–1825), described by Piozzi as 'successor to the celebrated Corilla' (*Observations and Reflections*, vol. 1, p. 318). See also the account of her talents, some years later, in Forsyth, *Remarks on Antiquities, Arts, and Letters*, pp. 54–6, partially quoted above, pp. 60–1.]

[65] [Salomon Gesner, Swiss poet and painter (1730–88)]

trifling circumstances, and several little traits, the *naïveté* of which afforded considerable amusement. When an accurate rhyme, or apt expression, did not offer itself on the instant it was required, he knit his brows and clenched his fingers with impatience; but I think he never hesitated more than half a second. At the moment the chord was struck the rhyme was ready. In this manner he poured forth between thirty and forty stanzas, with still increasing animation; and wound up his poem with some beautiful images of love, happiness, and innocence. Of his success I could form some idea by the applauses he received from better judges than myself.

After a few minutes repose and a glass of water, he next called on the company to supply him with rhymes for a sonnet. These, as fast as they were suggested by various persons, he wrote down upon a slip of paper. The last rhyme given was '*Ostello,*' – (a common ale-house,) – at which he demurred, and submitting to the company the difficulty of introducing so vulgar a word into an heroic sonnet, respectfully begged that another might be substituted. A lady called out '*Avello,*' the poetical term for a grave, or a sepulchre, which expression bore a happy analogy to the subject proposed. The poet smiled, well pleased; – and stepping forward with the paper in his hand, he immediately, without even a moment's preparation, recited a sonnet on the second subject upon his list, – '*La Morte di Alfieri.*' – I could better judge of the merit of this effusion, because he spoke it unaccompanied by music; and his enunciation was remarkably distinct.[66] The subject was popular, and treated with much feeling and poetic fervour. After lamenting Alfieri as the patriot, as well as the bard, and as the glory of his country, he concluded, by indignantly repelling the supposition that 'the latest sparks of genius and freedom were buried in the tomb of Vittorio Alfieri.' A thunder of applause followed; and cries of 'O bravo Sestini! bravo Sestini!' were echoed from the Italian portion of the audience, long after the first acclamations had subsided. The men rose simultaneously from their seats; and I confess I could hardly keep mine. The animation of the poet, and the enthusiasm of the audience, sent a thrill through every nerve and filled my eyes with tears.

---

[66] [Vittorio Alfieri (1749–1803), dramatist and poet, known not only for his writing but also for his long love affair with the Countess of Albany, who was unhappily married to Prince Charles Edward Stuart, the Young Pretender.]

Charlotte Eaton, *Rome in the Nineteenth Century . . . In a Series of Letters Written during a Residence at Rome, in the Years 1817 and 1818*, 3 vols (Edinburgh and London: Archibald Constable & Co. and Hurst, Robinson, & Co., 1820), vol. 1, pp. 328–30.

THE PANTHEON

Rome presents no greater attraction to the stranger than the Pantheon, now the Rotonda, one of the largest and most beautiful temples of antiquity; the boast of the Romans themselves in the proudest era of their arts, and perhaps the only pagan temple in the world, which, after eighteen centuries have passed away, still preserves its primeval form and its ancient grandeur.

The beautiful solitude which surrounds the Coliseum, adds a secret charm to the pleasure we feel in surveying it. Not so the Pantheon. Its situation, on the contrary, tends as much as possible to dissolve the spell that hangs over it. It is sunk in the dirtiest part of Modern Rome; and the unfortunate spectator, who comes with a mind filled with enthusiasm to gaze upon this monument of the taste and magnificence of antiquity, finds himself surrounded by all that is most revolting to the senses, distracted by incessant uproar, pestered with a crowd of clamorous beggars, and stuck fast in the congregated filth of every description that covers the slippery pavement; so that the time he forces himself to spend in admiring its noble portico, generally proves a penance from which he is glad to be liberated, instead of an enjoyment he wishes to protract.

We escaped none of these nuisances except the mud, by sitting in a open carriage to survey it; the smells and the beggars were equally annoying. You may perhaps form some idea of the situation of the Pantheon at Rome, by imagining what Westminster Abbey would be in Covent-Garden Market: – But I wrong Covent Garden by such a parallel. Nothing resembling such a hole as this could exist in England; nor is it possible that an English imagination can conceive a combination of such disgusting dirt, such filthy odours and foul puddles, as that which fills the vegetable market in the Piazza Della Rotonda at Rome. Still, while I gazed upon the beauty of the Pantheon itself, I could not but remember that this noble monument of taste and magnificence was already built in those times when our savage ancestors still roamed through their ancient forests, scarcely raised above the level of the beasts they chaced; their very name unknown to all the world besides, excepting to the Romans, by whom they were considered much the same as the South-Sea islanders are by us.

The beauty of the Pantheon is as honourable to the ancient Romans as its filth is disgraceful to the moderns. But its present state of dirt and degradation is nothing to that from which it has emerged. There was a time when it was built round with beggarly hovels, when the very columns themselves, the admiration of every age, were walled up; and the portico, thus enclosed, was filled with stalls, booths, and hucksters' shops. Pope Eugenius the Fourth, about the middle of the fifteenth century, turned these 'money changers and dove sellers out of the temple,'[67] and freed the imprisoned columns.

Eaton, *Rome in the Nineteenth Century*, vol. 3, pp. 419–24

SUNSET ON THE PALATINE. – THE COLISEUM AND THE FORUM BY MOONLIGHT

On one of those delicious evenings that close the bright and beautiful days of autumn in this country, I lingered on the Palatine until the sun sunk in a flood of light and glory, such as no power of language or of painting can pourtray. Vainly would imagination try to body forth the beauty of an hour like this, beneath the heavenly sun of Italy. The soft mist that floated over the landscape like a silver veil, softened, without obscuring every object, and gave a shadowy beauty to the grey tombs that covered the wide plain of the Campagna; while the hues that painted the Sabine Hills, the purple lights that, fading, blended into distance, and the last crimson glow that was reflected from the tops of the embattled Apennines, altogether formed a picture that would have awakened admiration in the coldest breast.

I stood on the terrace of the Palace of the Cæsars, – on that ancient hill where the Kings of Rome, the heroes of the Republic, and the imperial tyrants of the world, had successively triumphed and passed away.

The last horizontal beam of the God of Day, darting under the broad shade of the pine-tree, fell on the shattered ruins at my feet. Eighteen centuries had now almost completed their course since first his radiance had illumined the golden walls of this magnificent fabric; a thousand years his light had seen them laid in ruins, and still his setting ray seemed to shine with redoubled splendour on the fallen marbles of that proud Fane, within which he was once adored.*

> 'Slow sinks, more lovely ere his course be run
> O'er *Latium's* desert plains – the setting sun;
> Not as in northern climes, obscurely bright,
> But one unclouded blaze of living light:
> O'er *Rome's* proud seat, o'er *Tiber's* sacred isle,
> The God of Gladness sheds his parting smile;
> O'er his own regions lingering loves to shine,
> Though there his altars are no more divine.'[68]

---

[67] [Matt. 21:12, Mark 11:15]

* The broken Corinthian columns, and capitals of a temple on this hill, are supposed to be the ruins of the famous Temple of Apollo on the Palatine.

[68] [Adapted from Byron, 'The Curse of Minerva', lines 1–4, 7–10; Lord Byron, *The Complete Poetical Works*, edited by Jerome J. McGann, 7 vols (Oxford: Oxford University Press, 1980–

Transitory as beautiful, the deep glow of the western sky gradually faded away; – the shades of evening rapidly closed around, – no twilight here interposed its meditative hour, but the moon arose with a brightness and beauty unknown to our wintry climate, and the evening star lighted her glowing lamp in the west; as beneath their mingled rays, which trembled through the dark shade of the tall cypresses, we slowly passed along the now forsaken triumphal way, towards the Coliseum. Would that I could describe it to you, as it stood in its ruined loneliness amidst the deserted hills of Ancient Rome, surrounded with the remains of overthrown temples, imperial palaces, triumphal arches, and buried thermæ, – mighty even in decay!

The still, pale moonbeam fell on the lines of its projecting columns, range above range, to the lofty attic, in silvery light, leaving the black arches in mysterious darkness.

We passed under the great arch of entrance, crossed the grass-grown area, ascended the long staircases, and traversed the circling corridors. No sound met our ear but the measured tread of our own footsteps, and the whispered murmurs of our own voices. The deep solitude and silence, – the immensity and the ruin of the great fabric that surrounded us, filled our minds with awe; and as we caught the view of the stars appearing and disappearing through the opening arcades – marked the moonbeams illuminating the wide range of these lofty walls, and raised our eyes to the beauty of the calm clear firmament above our head, – we could not but remember, that hundreds of ages past, these eternal lights of heaven had shone on the sloping sides of this vast amphitheatre, when they were crowded with thousands of human beings, impatient for the barbarous sports of the rising day, – where now, only the wild weeds waved as the night breeze passed over them.*

Nature holds her eternal course; – the works of man perish. Earth is strewed over with the mouldering vestiges of his vanity and ambition; and yet, compared with his own little space, how durable are even those mute memorials! How wonderful is the discrepancy between the duration of his works and his own existence. The buildings he raises, the characters he impresses on the page, the colours he spreads on the canvas, the forms he creates in the breathing marble – live; they enjoy a species of immortality on earth, but he passes away like a shadow.

We gazed around us on the gigantic wreck of this mighty fabric; and as

---

92), vol. 1, p. 320. The poem (set not in Rome but in Athens) is dated 1811; it was published in a pirated edition in Philadelphia in 1815, and then in London, after Byron's death, in 1828. Amid the scene that Byron describes, the goddess Minerva appears, and berates the speaker for the destruction and spoliation wrought by his fellow-Briton, Lord Elgin.]

* It was customary for the common people thus to secure places to see the games over night.

we recalled what it had once been; – the long procession of years which had gone by – the silent march of time – the countless generations that had gone down to the dust, rushed forcibly upon our mind. The proud masters of the world were no more; and we, pilgrims from a then despised and barbarous land, were wandering amidst the ruined monuments of their pride and their power, to admire their grandeur, and to mourn over their decay!

We quitted the Coliseum: we passed along the long track of the Via Sacra, amidst ruined temples, and tottering arches; we beheld before us the once-proud Capitol; we stood in the Roman Forum. How well did this hour of stillness, when nature itself seemed hushed, accord with this scene of ancient glory! How softly the silver moonbeams fell on the Corinthian columns, and broken porticos of the temples, whose very gods are forgotten! How distinctly its clear light marked the dark decaying marble of that proud sculpture meant to immortalize the triumphs of heroes; and how beautifully its pale and mournful ray harmonized with the mouldering arches sunk in earth, like the deeds they commemorate! I could almost have fancied that I saw Time seated amidst the ruins he had made, mocking at their vanity, as he worked at their destruction. Our thoughts turned upon those over whom he had no power, – for whom there is no monument, – but whose memory is immortal on earth; and we felt, not without emotion, that we stood on the venerable soil where Camillus and Scipio, and Brutus and Cicero had trod. Whilst our hearts were touched with feelings such as these, a bell from a distant convent on the Cælian Hill, which tolled to call the Friars to their midnight orisons, broke upon the silence of night. At the sound, a figure glided from the shade of the Temple of Concord, passed before us like a shadow, and disappeared among the trees. We were somewhat startled at this apparition, which, according to all the rules of romance, should have served as the prelude to some mysterious adventure; but it only served to warn us to go home to bed; and, as it appeared to us no more, nor even condescended to explain why it had appeared at all, you may conceive it to have been a ghost or a man, a monk or an assassin, as best suits your fancy. Farewell.

Chapter 2

RISING AND SINKING IN SUBLIME PLACES

Had Mr. Raycie ever really frightened Lewis? Why, now he was not even frightened by Mont Blanc!
 He was still gazing with a sense of easy equality at its awful pinnacles when another travelling carriage paused near his own.
  Edith Wharton, 'False Dawn (The 'Forties)', in *Old New York* (1924)

When this pack of girls gets in The Great Open Spaces goodness knows what is going to happen. Sprained ankles is the least I should think.
  W.H. Auden and Louis MacNeice, *Letters from Iceland* (1937)

Bewildered and confounded

The previous chapter, in considering Jameson's description of the Bay of Naples, noted two sources of the sublime: uninterrupted and unbounded extent, inducing a sense of infinitude, and the contemplation of vast natural objects – especially those objects (erupting volcanoes, for example) that exceed their own bounds. In either case, the plot of the sublime includes, potentially, two separate moments: a moment in which the imagination and understanding are unable to assimilate the vastness of nature, and a moment of self-affirmation, in which the viewer identifies with the grandeur of the objects that he or she contemplates. Patrick Brydone, describing Mount Etna, in his *Tour through Sicily and Malta* (1773), places his most dramatic emphasis on the first of these moments: 'The senses, unaccustomed to the sublimity of such a scene, are bewildered and confounded; and it is not till after some time, that they are capable of separating and judging of the objects that compose it.'[1]

The sublime, then, entails an experience of destabilization, which can readily be elided with the destabilizing properties assigned to travel as an adventure of the self. In most versions, it also entails a moment of

---

[1] P[atrick] Brydone, *A Tour through Sicily and Malta. In a Series of Letters to William Beckford, Esq. of Somerly in Suffolk*, 2 vols (London: W. Strahan and T. Cadell, 1775; first published in 1773), vol. 1, p. 204.

relative stability – a summoning up of the faculties that will enable the viewer, suffused with sublime aspiration, to feel 'capable of separating and judging of' the elements of the scene of sublimity.

When stressing the self-affirmatory moment, theorists of the sublime usually invoke the narrative of identification mapped out by Longinus in Section VII of his treatise on the sublime, in analysing effects of sublimity in poetry and rhetoric:

> The mind is naturally elevated by the true *Sublime*, and so sensibly affected with its lively strokes, that it swells in transport and an inward pride, as if what was only heard had been the product of its own invention.[2]

Burke, citing this passage in his *Philosophical Enquiry into the Origin of our Ideas of the Sublime and Beautiful* (1757), incorporates within it a new concept of the sublime 'delight' that we experience 'when we have an idea of pain and danger, without being actually in such circumstances':

> Now whatever either on good or upon bad grounds tends to raise a man in his own opinion, produces a sort of swelling and triumph that is extremely grateful to the human mind; and this swelling is never more perceived, nor operates with more force, than when without danger we are conversant with terrible objects, the mind always claiming to itself some part of the dignity and importance of the things which it contemplates. Hence proceeds what Longinus has observed of that glorying and sense of inward greatness, that always fills the reader of such passages in poets and orators as are sublime; it is what every man must have felt in himself upon such occasions.[3]

Burke's principle that the sublime is produced by distanced terror, however, is often invoked in a manner that registers a sharper awareness of terror than of distancing. Frances Reynolds, in her *Enquiry concerning the Principles of Taste* (1785), implicitly voices doubt as to whether the subject of the sublime – the viewer of a landscape of vast dimensions, for example – can maintain control, having once undergone an experience of danger: 'It is a pinnacle of beatitude, bordering upon horror, deformity, madness! An eminence from whence the mind, that dares to look farther, is lost! It seems to stand, *or rather to waver*, between certainty and uncertainty, between security and destruction.'[4]

Hester Piozzi, looking back on the Alps from Turin, in the first of the passages below, begins her account of sublimity by invoking Burke: 'the

---

[2] *Dionysius Longinus on the Sublime*, translated by William Smith, fourth edition (London, 1770), p. 21.

[3] Edmund Burke, *A Philosophical Enquiry into the Origin of our Ideas of the Sublime and Beautiful*, edited by James Boulton (Oxford: Blackwell, 1987), pp. 50–1.

[4] Frances Reynolds, *Enquiry concerning the Principles of Taste, and the Origin of our Ideas of Beauty* (London: Baker and Galabin, 1785), p. 18; emphasis added.

portion of terror excited either by real or fancied dangers on the way, is just sufficient to mingle with the pleasure, and make one feel the full effect of sublimity.' The chairmen carrying her supply a test case for the Burkean sublime, since they have grown indifferent to the dangers that lead her to cry out 'prenez garde', yet respond to the grandeur of the scenery in a manner that makes it evident that 'the glories of these objects have never faded'.

Sydney Morgan, in the second passage below, is more reckless in dramatizing the destabilizing power of sublimity: 'Here experience teaches the falsity of the trite maxim, that the mind becomes elevated by the contemplation of nature in the midst of her grandest works.' On the contrary: 'The mind in such scenes is not raised. It is stricken back upon its own insignificance.' She enlarges at length on the ways in which such a sense of insignificance is induced, through the astonishing turbulence of scenes 'at once the wreck and the monument of changes, which scoff at human record, and trace in characters that admit no controversy the fallacy of calculations and the vanity of systems'.

Exceeding limits

The first three passages in this chapter are concerned with the Alpine crossing: in other words, the traversal of the great natural boundary between northern and southern Europe. The sublime, in the Alps, thematizes this movement beyond a limit, as well as the more general crossing of geographical and symbolic boundaries constantly entailed in the Grand Tour, and in any journey. Sublimity also (like travel) demands the figure defined as a crossing of rhetorical limits: hyperbole. Morgan, at one point, emphasizes that the Alps, unlike many other sights witnessed by experienced travellers, do not disappoint the improbably high expectations raised by 'the promises of books'. Piozzi brings hyperbole and the traversal of boundaries into close metaphorical entanglement by introducing two bold topographical digressions to introduce and conclude her account of the sublime, as though prompted by her aesthetic transcendence of limits to reach out imaginatively beyond the bounds of regions directly known to her. Speculating on travellers' tales of 'a region of the air so subtle as to extinguish the two powers of taste and smell', she establishes a new range of topographical reference: 'those who have crossed the Cordilleras of the Andes say, that situations have been explored among their points in South America, where those senses have been found to suffer a temporary suspension.' The town of Novalesa prompts a reference to the icy regions known to eighteenth-century readers from Maupertuis' *Figure de la terre* (1738):

> One's quiet is here so disturbed by insects, and polluted by dirt, that one recollects the conduct of the Lapland rein-deer, who seeks the summit of the hill at the hazard of his life, to avoid those gnats which sting him to madness in the valley.

Morgan, too, after her initial analysis of the particular depths of exhaustion to which she sinks in the Alps, reaches out in her imagination to this same topography of the frozen North: 'the murky huts of Lans-le-bourg looked like a Lapland village.' Her hyperboles, however, are mainly derived from elisions between geological turbulence and historical vicissitudes, and from the extremes of oppression and aspiration that have imprinted the human will on the region – above all, through road-building. She laments a burst of 'road-making' in the feudal, pre-Napoleonic past, during which the Corvée has been exacted 'in all its terrible rigour', in order to facilitate 'the passage of a Piedmontese princess, on her way to some royal bridegroom of France'. On Mont Cenis, 'natural obstacles' and 'political change' appear as alternative agents of destruction, thwarting the efforts of road-builders, whose labours leave only 'vestiges of greater projects and bolder facilities than were yet effected'.

The sublime impulse to exceed boundaries that drives these road-builders is, above all, elided with the aspiration that propels Napoleon across the Alps, not simply as head of a victorious French army, but also in his role as the builder of the Simplon Pass: 'All that had been danger, difficulty, and suffering, but twenty years back, was now safe, facile, and enjoyable; secure beyond the chance of accident, sublime beyond the reach of thought.'

Such elisions between Napoleon's ambitions as general and road-builder and the sense of a movement beyond limits experienced in scenes of grandeur are common in travel writings of the period. Henry Matthews, for example, as he gazes in astonishment and awe 'at the monstrous masses, which nature has her heaped one upon another, in every mode of shapeless desolation', remarks: 'it is impossible not to be filled with admiration of the man, who had the boldness to undertake, and the genius to accomplish, a complete triumph over such fearful obstacles.' While Hannibal crossed the Alps, he notes, Napoleon constructed 'this *"royal road;"* by which every puny whipster may do the same': the road stands 'as a lasting record of his contempt of all impediments, physical as well as moral, that stood in the way of the execution of his purpose'.[5]

William Hazlitt, in the third of the passages below, moves directly from his own version of the narrative of the sublime into an account of

---

[5] Henry Matthews, *The Diary of an Invalid. Being the Journal of a Tour in Pursuit of Health in Portugal, Italy, Switzerland and France in the Years 1817, 1818 and 1819*, second edition (London: John Murray, 1820), pp. 308–9.

Napoleon's exploits. He describes the Alps as inducing a sense of inadequacy and of self-affirmation simultaneously:

> Any one, who is much of an egotist, ought not to travel through these districts; his vanity will not find its account in them; it will be chilled, mortified, shrunk up: but they are a noble treat to those who feel themselves raised in their own thoughts and in the scale of being by the immensity of other things, and who can aggrandise and piece out their personal insignificance by the grandeur and eternal forms of nature!

Napoleon, in the next sentence, is differentiated from the rest of humanity by heroically proving equal to sublime nature:

> He alone (the Rob Roy of the scene) seemed a match for the elements, and able to master 'this fortress, built by nature for herself.' Neither impeded nor turned aside by immoveable barriers, he smote the mountains with his iron glaive, and made them malleable.

The very thought of Napoleon then prompts the traveller to register his own modest, momentary resistance to established authority: he pointedly claims to be unimpressed by the information that the King of England has stayed at the same inn as him.

The intoxication of arrival

At the culmination of her narrative of traversal, Morgan presents Napoleon as the successor both to Hannibal and to a sixth-century invader of Italy. She dramatizes the famous moment when the Carthaginian general looks down upon the plains of Lombardy – a moment that affirms the pleasures awaiting the contemporary traveller through the trope of prolepsis, or anticipation. (One of the many other evocations of 'the fierce Carthaginian' gazing down upon Italy is in Canto III of Byron's *Childe Harold*.)[6] This moment is repeated, here, not only in the experience of Napoleon, but in that of 'the Lombard Alboin', whose anticipation of the delights of Italy wittily combines aspirational bellicosity with a taste of the pleasures of the warm South: 'From such a site as this the Lombard Alboin paused amidst his ferocious hosts, to contemplate the paradise of his future conquest, and quaffed from the skull of his enemy his first draught of Italian wine.'

Hazlitt, too, anticipates the pleasures of Italy through a moment of vinous indulgence. With implicit allusion to Sterne's *Sentimental Journey*, he presents the Alps as the site not only of sublimity but also of rustic domesticity. (In 'The Supper' and 'The Grace', the two episodes of *A*

---

[6] Lord Byron, *Childe Harold's Pilgrimage*, Canto III, stanza 110, lines 1022–5; *The Complete Poetical Works*, edited by Jerome J. McGann, 7 vols (Oxford: Oxford University Press, 1980–92), vol. 2, p. 117.

Sentimental Journey at the very beginning of Yorick's attempt to cross the Alps, his horse's loss of its shoes throws him upon the hospitality of a peasant family; he joins them in sitting down to 'lentil-soup', 'a large wheaten loaf', and 'a flaggon of wine', and then watches the dance with which they pay 'thanks to heaven'.)[7] The traveller describes a 'rude tenement' into which he and his fellow-passengers in the Diligence are 'cordially welcomed . . . by a young peasant (a soldier's wife) with a complexion as fresh as the winds, and an expression as pure as the mountain-snows'. As she serves 'three earthen bowls filled with sparkling wine, heated on a stove with sugar', she satisfies the expectation, frequently inscribed in travel writing of this period, that the Italians, like many elements in their surroundings, will rise naturally towards the condition of art: 'The woman stood by, and did the honours of this cheerful repast with a rustic simplicity and a pastoral grace that might have called forth the powers of Hemskirk and Raphael.'[8]

A hyperbole of enduring memory then introduces a note of ironic inflation. The traveller declares: 'I shall not soon forget the rich ruby colour of the wine, as the sun shone upon it through a low glazed window that looked out on the boundless wastes around, nor its grateful spicy smell as we sat around it.'

During the final stage of the crossing, Hazlitt moves from wine as a metonym for anticipated pleasures to a metaphorical intoxication, on approaching the joys of Italy more closely. In doing so, he reiterates Morgan's account of the intoxication of arriving in a land of both sun and strangeness:

> The traveller who ascends from *Lans-le-bourg*, shivering with cold and shuddering with apprehension, descends into the town of Susa, glowing under the rays of summer suns, and not more intoxicated, by their '*soft ethereal warmth*,' than by the pleasurable consciousness which attends the first arrival in a country unknown and unexplored.[9]

Hazlitt once again adds his own ironic twist: 'My arrival at Turin was the first *and only* moment of intoxication I have found in Italy' (emphasis added).

---

[7] Laurence Sterne, *'A Sentimental Journey' with 'The Journal to Eliza' and 'A Political Romance'*, edited by Ian Jack (Oxford: Oxford University Press, 1991), pp. 118–20.

[8] The southern grace of this 'young peasant' is emphasized especially strongly by the implied contrast between her and the less pliable Englishwoman whom Hazlitt earlier describes at Lans-le-Bourg, who has 'died a short time before of pure chagrin and disappointment in this solitary place, after having told her tale of distress to every one, till it fairly wore her out'.

[9] Lady Morgan, *Italy*, 2 vols (London: Henry Colburn, 1821), vol. 1, p. 29, quoting Milton, *Paradise Lost*, Book 2, line 601.

Odd travellers

Hazlitt's traversal is punctuated by other moments of humour: he is entertained by the attempts of various travelling companions to assimilate the foreign and translate it into forms of language. As he walks on from Lans-le-bourg with two Frenchmen, he himself adopts a simile so flatly domestic that it implies a certain reservation about unrelieved hyperboles: 'We noticed some of the features of the scenery; and a lofty hill opposite to us being scooped out into a bed of snow, with two ridges or promontories projecting (something like an arm-chair) on each side.' One of the Frenchman, however, seizes the rhetorical opportunity that this 'arm-chair' offers:

> '*Voilà!*' said the younger and more volatile of our companions, '*c'est un trône, et le nuage est la gloire!*' – A white cloud indeed encircled its misty top. I complimented him on the happiness of his allusion, and said that Madame was pleased with the exactness of the resemblance.

In his ironic indulgence ('Madame was pleased'), Hazlitt implicitly invokes the passage of *A Sentimental Journey* in which Yorick considers 'the French sublime'. The narrative follows a trajectory that is almost the opposite of Hazlitt's – Yorick is struck by a French rhetorical eccentricity that moves resolutely from the mundane to the sublime, whereas Hazlitt's Frenchman seizes upon a mundane feature of the scene of grandeur – the 'arm-chair' – and makes a hapless effort to lift it out of banality. In both travel books, however, the French are presented as disconcerting in their sense of how to match up word and world. In Paris, Yorick's barber deals with the traveller-narrator's expression of anxiety about the buckle of his wig by an unexpected declaration: 'You may immerge it, replied he, into the ocean, and it will stand.' Observing that 'the utmost stretch of an English periwig-maker's ideas could have gone no further than to have "dipped it into a pail of water"', Yorick initially endorses the attractions of the sublime hyperbole that goes beyond such mundane terminology. In doing so, however, he obliquely defines such a version of hyperbole as, at the same time, a form of digression; as he points out in the subsequent paragraph, the pail of water is 'in the next room', and the ocean is not:

> I confess I do hate all cold conceptions, as I do the puny ideas which engender them; and am generally so struck with the great works of nature, that for my own part, if I could help it, I never would make a comparison less than a mountain at least. All that can be said against the French sublime in this instance of it, is this – that the grandeur is *more* in the *word*; and *less* in the *thing*. No doubt the ocean fills the mind with vast ideas; but Paris being so far inland, it was not likely I should run post a hundred miles out of it, to try the experiment.[10]

---

[10] Sterne, *A Sentimental Journey*, pp. 49–50.

In Hazlitt's narrative, unlike Sterne's, irony soon evaporates; the Frenchman is berated for his lack of inventiveness:

> He then turned to the valley, and said, 'C'est un berceau.' This is the height to which the imagination of a Frenchman always soars, and it can soar no higher. Any thing that is not cast in this obvious, common-place mould, that had been used a thousand times before with applause, they think barbarous, and as they phrase it, *originaire*.

These two commentaries, however, have a feature in common: it is the sublime that destabilizes the relation between 'word' and 'thing', whether because the French seize upon it too eagerly (as Yorick believes) or (as Hazlitt affirms) because their imagination cannot rise to its heights.

At once, in Hazlitt's commentary, another traveller, glimpsed earlier in the narrative, also goes comically awry in attempting to get to grips with the topography of strangeness and alterity:

> 'What has become,' said the elder of the Frenchmen, 'of Monsieur l'Espagnol? He does not easily quit his seat; he sits in one corner, never looks out, or if you point to any object, takes no notice of it; and when you come to the end of the stage, says – "What is the name of that place we passed by last?" – takes out his pocket-book, and makes a note of it. "That is droll."' And what made it more so, it turned out that our Spanish friend was a painter, travelling to Rome to study the Fine Arts!

As Hazlitt and the Frenchmen continue along the road, however, 'our cautious Spaniard brushed by us, determined to shew he could descend the mountain, if he would not ascend it on foot'. Sublime scenery, it appears, may in the end galvanize into restlessness even those most indifferent to their surroundings: the Spaniard 'seemed bent on redeeming the sedentary sluggishness of his character by one bold and desperate effort of locomotion'.

Figures such as these, who respond to the foreign in ways that seem absurd, are often deployed, in travel writing, as a means of defining, by opposition, what is required of the traveller who wishes to demonstrate his or her adequacy as a participant in the Grand Tour. They can also, however, be seen as fulfilling another function, suggested by Hazlitt's own lecture 'On Wit and Humour'. Hazlitt, here, describes laughter as arising in situations in which oddity and absurdity distract us from a concern for those afflicted by some disagreeable or distressing circumstance, so that 'the ludicrous prevails over the pathetic, and we receive pleasure in stead of pain from the farce of life which is played before us'.[11] Freud, in his essay 'On Humour', offers a similar account of what happens when we laugh,

---

[11] William Hazlitt, 'On Wit and Humour' [1818], in *Lectures on the English Comic Writers* (Oxford: Oxford University Press, 1943), pp. 1–35; p. 2.

which takes the power of laughter one step further, and sees it as dissipating a sense of distress excited not only by our sympathy for others but by the sense of 'the farce of life' impinging upon our own well-being:

> The ego refuses to be distressed by the provocations of reality, to let itself be compelled to suffer. It insists that it cannot be affected by the traumas of the external world; it shows, in fact, that such traumas are no more than occasions for it to gain pleasure.[12]

Both these analyses provide a model for the rhetorical strategy that traveller-narrators adopt, in passages that describe the risible approaches towards the topography adopted by others; in deploying effects of laughter, they seek to set aside anxieties that trouble all travellers – at least when faced with certain situations or embroiled in certain activities, such as the viewing of landscape or art – and they accomplish this aim by deflecting anxiety and unease onto travellers whose 'oddity', 'absurdity' or 'unaccountableness' of behaviour, to adopt Hazlitt's terms, distract the reader from his or her own unease by providing an apparent explanation for the difficulties that they face.[13] Such figures include travellers who are, from the narrator's point of view, foreigners. Patrick Brydone, in his *Tour through Sicily and Malta* (1773), comments on the 'degree of lassitude' induced by the sirocco in Naples:

> It is not perhaps surprising, that it should produce these effects on a phlegmatic English constitution; but we have just now an instance, that all the mercury of France must sink under the load of this horrid, leaden atmosphere. A smart Parisian marquis came here about ten days ago: he was so full of animal spirits that the people thought him mad. He never remained a moment in the same place; but, at their grave conversations, used to skip from room to room with such amazing elasticity, that the Italians swore he had got springs in his shoes. I met him this morning, walking with the step of a philosopher; a smelling bottle in his hand, and all his vivacity extinguished. I asked what was the matter? 'Ah! mon ami,' said he, 'je m'ennui à la mort; – moi, qui n'ai jamais sçu l'ennui. Mais cet execrable vent m'accable; et deux jours de plus, et je me pend.'[14]

The two Frenchmen and the Spaniard, in Hazlitt's traversal of the Alps, clearly fall into this category of the odd traveller-foreigner – with the added twist that the Spaniard is so utterly lacking in the visual curiosity expected of a traveller – especially one who is 'travelling to Rome to study the Fine Arts' – that even the Frenchmen find him 'droll'.

---

[12] Sigmund Freud, 'On Humour' (1927), in *Art and Literature*, translated under the general editorship of James Strachey, edited by Albert Dickson, The Pelican Freud Library, vol. 11 (Harmondsworth: Penguin, 1985), pp. 425–33; p. 429.
[13] Hazlitt, 'On Wit and Humour', p. 2.
[14] Brydone, *Tour through Sicily and Malta*, vol. 1, pp. 7–8 ('Ah! my friend . . . I am wearied to death; I, who never knew *ennui* before. But this accursed wind is too much for me; two days more, and I shall hang myself.').

What, then, is the source of the unease that stories about odd travellers serve to deflect? The alacrity with which traveller-narrators turn from their own responses to report on those of others suggests an anxiety that the task of observing the topography of the foreign and finding fluent and confident forms of language in which to comment on it may draw the unwary into revealing themselves as inadequate. Hazlitt's Frenchmen and Spaniard exemplify two of the ways in which travellers fail to rise to the demands of viewing and commenting: the Spaniard is disinclined to make any effort to observe his surroundings at all, and the Frenchmen are lacking in the personal spontaneity and powers of imagination that might allow them to find forms of language adequate to the sublime scenery around them.

Amid such scenery, a particular rhetorical pitfall is often perceived: the traveller will fall into trite, conventionalized and insincere forms of utterance – as, Hazlitt maintains, the Frenchmen do. Striving for hyperbolic responsiveness does not necessarily save the traveller from suspicions of insincerity and affectation; on the contrary, it may only add to such suspicions; the first of the hapless Frenchmen outdoes the narrator in hyperbole when he sees the hill with two ridges not as 'something like an arm-chair' but as a throne surrounded by a glory.

The three final passages below all underline the risks of hyperbolic responses to the sublime, and attempt to find ways of keeping such risks at bay.

From the sublime to the ridiculous

In striving to fend off the damning suspicion of affectation, travellers have the option of recognizing and exploiting one of the risks of hyperbole: its tendency to surge out of control, and reach such heights that it cannot help but tip over into bathos. Travel writings of this period often employ a self-protective effect of irony or comedy, which acknowledges the potential for a plunge from the sublime to the ridiculous, and turns it to the traveller-narrator's advantage, reminding the reader that, even when travellers allow themselves to be tempted by the rhetorical force of hyperbole, they may nonetheless retain some of their powers of critical detachment.

Brydone, in his account of ascending Etna (the fourth passage below), recounts the story of Empedocles, throwing himself into the crater 'that he might be looked upon as a god, and that the people might suppose he was taken up to heaven', but punished for his hubris when 'the treacherous mountain threw out his slippers, which were of brass, and announced to the world the fate of the philosopher'. This plot is then ironically repeated, in a less violently destructive form, in the fate that the traveller-narrator himself meets with on the mountain. The grandeur of his surroundings induces a conviction 'that the soul, in approaching the æthereal regions, shakes off its earthly affections, and already acquires something of their celestial purity'. A sprained ankle, however, reduces him once again to the state of 'a poor miserable mortal': 'your poor philosopher was obliged to hop on one leg, with two men supporting him, for several miles over the snow; and our wags here allege, that he left the greatest part of his philosophy behind him, for the use of Empedocles's heirs and successors.' The return to mundane reality is emphasized by a shift to gastronomy: Brydone enjoys 'an excellent dish of tea, the most refreshing and agreeable I ever drank in my life'.

Piozzi, ascending Vesuvius (in the fifth passage below), and anticipating dramatic contrasts of 'snow and flame!', also allows the trivial and the mundane to displace the sublime. She expresses her delight at becoming embroiled in a conversation with the resident hermit, some way up, when he suddenly reveals that he knows her already, from the days when he was her hairdresser in London. Sydney Morgan, describing her own ascent of the same mountain in the subsequent extract, makes similar use of the disarming power of a moment of bathos. She relates how her party reach a spot 'which a few days before had been liquid fire, and from which smoke and a sulphureous vapour were emitted at frequent air-holes', and are startled when, 'by the sudden turn of an angle, we came unexpectedly upon a group of English dandies, of both sexes, of our acquaintance – the ladies with their light garments something the worse for the adventure, and all laughing, flirting, and chattering over a chasm, which exhibited the lava boiling and bubbling up within a few feet below where they stood.' The traveller's choice of words reminds us that they are flirting not only with each other but also with danger. Morgan ironically maintains the language of aesthetic theory in her observation that 'this was a terrible sacrifice of the sublime to the agreeable!' (See Figure 1.)

All three travellers, then, situate themselves in the tradition of Sterne's *Sentimental Journey*. In their vignettes of rising and sinking in sublime places, as in Yorick's exposition of his approach to the Grand Tour, responsiveness is defined as too readily channelled into reverential acclamations of sights and wonders in a formalized itinerary: in digressing, the traveller-narrator claims for his or her responses a more disorderly spontaneity. Odd incidents supply a distraction from piously conventional sightseeing that is equivalent to the distraction that women provide for Yorick when he declares to the French count: 'I conceive every fair being as a temple, and would rather enter in, and see the original drawings and loose sketches hung up in it, than the transfiguration of Raphael itself.'[15]

Hester Lynch Piozzi, *Observations and Reflections Made in the Course of a Journey through France, Italy, and Germany*, 2 vols (London: A. Strahan and T. Cadell, 1789), vol. 1, pp. 36–44.

Piozzi writes this account of the Alps from Turin.

October 17, 1784

We have at length passed the Alps, and are safely arrived at this lovely little city, whence I look back on the majestic boundaries of Italy, with amazement at his courage who first profaned them: surely the immediate sensation conveyed to the mind by the sight of such tremendous appearances must be in every traveller the same, a sensation of fulness never experienced before, a satisfaction that there is something great to be seen on earth – some object capable of contenting even fancy. Who he was who first of all people pervaded these fortifications, raised by nature for the defence of her European Paradise, is not ascertained; but the great Duke of Savoy has wisely left his name engraved on a monument upon the first considerable ascent from Pont Bonvoisin, as being author of a beautiful road cut through the solid stone for a great length of way, and having by this means encouraged others to assist in facilitating a passage so truly desirable, till one of the great wonders now to be observed among the Alps, is the ease with which even a delicate traveller may cross them. In these prospects, colouring is carried to its utmost point of perfection, particularly at the time I found it, variegated with golden touches of autumnal tints; immense cascades mean time bursting from naked mountains on the one side; cultivated fields, rich with vineyards, on the other, and tufted with elegant shrubs that invite one to pluck and carry them away to where they would be treated with much more respect. Little towns sticking in the clefts, where one would imagine it was impossible to clamber; light clouds often sailing under the feet of the high-perched inhabitants, while the sound of a deep and rapid though narrow river, dashing with violence among the insolently impeding rocks at the bottom, and bells in thickly-scattered spires calling the quiet Savoyards to church upon the steep sides of every hill – fill one's mind with such mutable, such various ideas, as no other place can ever possibly afford.

    I had the satisfaction of seeing a chamois at a distance, and spoke with a fellow who had killed five hungry bears that made depredation on his pastures: we looked on him with reverence as a monster-tamer of antiquity, Hercules or Cadmus; he had the skin of a beast wrapt round his middle,

---

[15] Sterne, *Sentimental Journey*, p. 84.

which confirmed the fancy – but our servants, who borrowed from no fictitious records the few ideas that adorned their talk, told us he reminded *them* of *John the Baptist*. I had scarce recovered the shock of this too sublime comparison, when we approached his cottage, and found the felons nailed against the wall, like foxes heads or spread kites in England. Here are many goats, but neither white nor large, like those which browze upon the steeps of Snowdon, or clamber among the cliffs of Plinlimmon.

I chatted with a peasant in the Haute Morienne, concerning the endemial swelling of the throat, which is found in seven out of every ten persons here: he told me what I had always heard, but do not yet believe, that it was produced by drinking the snow water. Certain it is, these places are not wholesome to live in; most of the inhabitants are troubled with weak and sore eyes: and I recollect Sir Richard Jebb telling me, more than seven years ago, that when he passed through Savoy, the various applications made to him, either for the cure or prevention of blindness by numberless unfortunate wretches that crowded round him, hastened his quitting a province where such horrible complaints prevailed.[16] One has heard it related that the goître or gozzo of the throat is reckoned a beauty by those who possess it; but I spoke with many, and all agreed to lament it as a misfortune. That it does really proceed merely from living in a snowy country, would be well confirmed by accounts of a similar sickness being endemial in Canada; but of an American goître I have never yet heard – and Wales, methinks, is snowy enough, and mountainous enough, God knows; yet were such an excrescence to be seen *there*, the people would never have done wondering, and blessing themselves.

The mines of Derbyshire, however, do not very unfrequently exhibit something of the same appearance among those who work in *them*; and as Savoy is impregnated with many minerals, I should be apter to attribute this extension of the gland to their influence over the constitution, than to that of snow water, which can scarcely be efficacious in a degree of power equal to the producing so very violent an effect.

The wolves do certainly come down from these mountains in large troops, just as Thomson describes them:

Burning for blood; boney, and gaunt, and grim. –[17]

But it is now the fashionable philosophy every where to consider this creature as the original of our domestic friend, the dog. It was a long time

---

[16] [Dr Richard Jebb (1729–87), created a baronet in 1778; in 1771 Jebb was sent by George III with Dr Robert Adair to provide medical treatment for the Duke of Gloucester, who had fallen ill in Italy, and in 1777 the two physicians were again summoned to the help of the Duke at Trent, and stayed briefly in Venice.]

[17] [James Thomson, *The Seasons*, 'Winter', line 394.]

before my heart assented to its truth, yet surely their hunting thus in packs confirms it; and the Jackall's willingness to connect with either race, shews one that the species cannot be far removed, and that he makes the shade between the wolf and rough haired shepherd's cur.

Of the longevity of man this district affords us no pleasing examples. The peasants here are apparently unhealthy, and they say – short-lived. We are told by travellers of former days, that there is a region of the air so subtle as to extinguish the two powers of taste and smell; and those who have crossed the Cordilleras of the Andes say, that situations have been explored among their points in South America, where those senses have been found to suffer a temporary suspension.[18] Our *voyageurs aeriens** may now be useful to settle that question among others, and Pambamarca's heights may remain untrodden.

As for Mount Cenis, I never felt myself more hungry, or better enjoyed a good dinner, than I did upon its top: but the trout in the lake there have been over praised; their pale colour allured me but little in the first place, nor is their flavour equal to that of trout found in running water. Going down the Italian side of the Alps is, after all, an astonishing journey; and affords the most magnificent scenery in nature, which varying at every step, gives new impression to the mind each moment of one's passage; while the portion of terror excited either by real or fancied dangers on the way, is just sufficient to mingle with the pleasure, and make one feel the full effect of sublimity.[19] To the chairmen who carry one though, nothing can be new; it is observable that the glories of these objects have never faded – I heard them speak to each other of their beauties, and the change of light since

---

[18] [One of Piozzi's probable sources is Oliver Goldsmith's 'Essay towards a Natural History of the Air', in *An History of the Earth, and Animated Nature*, 8 vols (London: J. Nourse, 1774), vol. 1, p. 335 (a work that she draws upon at other points in her travel narrative): 'Those who are willing to augment the catalogue of the benefits we receive from this element, assert also, that tastes themselves would be insipid, were it not that the air presses their parts upon the nerves of the tongue and palate, so as to produce their grateful effects. Thus, continue they, upon the tops of high mountains, as on the Pike of Teneriff, the most poignant bodies, as pepper, ginger, salt, and spice, have no sensible taste, for want of their particles being thus sent home to the sensory. But, we owe the air sufficient obligations, not to be studious of admitting this among the number: in fact, all substances have their tastes, as well on the tops of mountains, as in the bottom of the valley; and I have been one of many, who have ate a very savoury dinner on the Alps.']

* Our aerostatic travellers. [In Paris, Piozzi witnesses 'aërial travellers' who rise upwards 'in the new-invented flying chariot fastened to an air-balloon' (*Observations and Reflections*, vol. 1, p. 23, p. 22). She translated a sonnet 'Sopra il pallone aerostatico' ('Sonnet on an Air Balloon'), by the Abbate Parini; see B[ertie] Greatheed, R[obert] Merry, W[illiam] Parsons and Mrs. [Hester Lynch] Piozzi, *The Florence Miscellany* (Florence: G. Cam, 1785), pp. 58–9.]

[19] [At Terni, Piozzi again invokes Burke's concept of the sublime: 'one feels a thousand sensations of sublimity unexcited by less accidents, and soon obliterated by real danger.' See *Observations and Reflections*, vol. 2, p. 154.]

Rising and sinking in sublime places 89

they had passed by last time, while a fellow who spoke English as well as a native told us, that having lived in a gentleman's service twenty years between London and Dublin, he at length begged his discharge, chusing to retire and finish his days a peasant upon these mountains, where he first opened his eyes upon scenes that made all other views of nature insipid to his taste.

If impressions of beauty remain, however, those of danger die away by frequent reiteration; the men who carried me seemed amazed that I should feel any emotions of fear. *Qu'est ce donc, madame?** was the coldly-asked question to my repeated injunction of *prenez garde*†: not very apparently unnecessary neither, where the least slip must have been fatal both to them and me.

Novalesa is the town we stopped at, upon entering Piedmont; where the hollow sound of a heavy dashing torrent that has accompanied us hitherto, first grows faint, and the ideas of common life catch hold of one again; as the noise of it is heard from a greater distance, its stream grows wider, and its course more tranquil. For compensation of danger, ease should be administered; but one's quiet is here so disturbed by insects, and polluted by dirt, that one recollects the conduct of the Lapland rein-deer, who seeks the summit of the hill at the hazard of his life, to avoid those gnats which sting him to madness in the valley.[20]

Suza shewed nothing that I took much interest in, except its name; and nobody tells me why it is honoured with that old Asiatick appellation. At the next town, called St. Andrè, or St. Ambroise, I forget which, we got an admirable dinner; and saw our room decorated with a large map of London, which I looked on with sensations different from those ever before excited by the same object, Amsterdam and Constantinople covered the other sides of the wall; and over the door of the chamber itself was written, as our people write the Lamb or the Lion, '*Les trois Villes Heretiques*'‡.

---

* What's the matter, my lady?
† Take care.
[20] [See [Pierre Louis Moreau de] Maupertuis, *La Figure de la terre* (Paris: chez Jean Catuffe, 1738), p. 14; translated as *The Figure of the Earth* (London: T. Cox, 1738), pp. 41–2; Maupertuis, however, describes behaviour exactly opposite to that cited by Piozzi: he mentions that he and his party are 'exposés aux Mouches qui y sont si cruelles, qu'elles forcent les Lappons et leurs Reenes d'abandonner le pays dans cette saison, pur aller vers les côtes de l'Océan' ('exposed to the Flies, which in this Season are so insufferable as to drive the *Laplanders* and their Rein-Deer to seek shelter on the Coasts of the Ocean'). Oliver Goldsmith, in *An History of the Earth*, vol. 3, pp. 156–7, describes the behaviour of reindeer in the same way that Piozzi does, which suggests that he may be her immediate source: one of their remedies against the attacks of the gnats, which 'drive the poor animal almost to distraction' is, he says, 'to ascend to the highest summit of the mountains, where the air is too thin, and the air too cold for the gnats to come'.]
‡ The three Heretical Cities.

Sydney Morgan, *Italy*, 2 vols (London: Henry Colburn, 1821), vol. 1, pp. 18–25

Savoy, with all its wild variety of soil and scene, its vestiges of extinct volcanos, and sunny vales of pastoral beauty, may be considered as the vestibule of the Alps. As their mightier regions are approached, the country gradually loses its character of civilization; the last stunted vine withers upon the heights of Modane, and culture has ceased to clothe the interstices of rocks with its forced products, ere that acclivity is ascended, where in the midst of '*regions dolorous*,' stand the clustered hovels of the village of Lans-le-bourg.[21]

The exhaustion of a long journey is a species of malady; and the peculiar weariness, physical and moral, which hangs on the close of each day's progress, may be said to be the periodical paroxysm of the disease. The truth of this remark is only to be verified in all its intensity by Continental travellers; and it is never perhaps more strongly illustrated than by those, who like the writer of these pages, reaches the foot of the Alps at the close of a wearisome day, and catches through the deepening shadows of a dreary twilight, and the drifting eddies of a snow shower, the first glimpses of those regions, which appear to the morbid perceptions of of exhausted nature –

'An universe of death, which God by curse
Created evil, for evil only good.' – MILTON.[22]

The dark, narrow, plashy lane of Lans-le-bourg is terminated to the left by a spacious building, which rises directly opposite to the ascent of Mount Cenis. This building includes a barrack, and an inn*, built by the French. All else around was one wild waste of snow; and the murky huts of Lans-le-bourg looked like a Lapland village.

The passage of the Alps, from Hannibal to Napoleon, has been always described as awful and terrific; as something worse

'Than fables yet have feign'd, or fear conceived.'[23]

Benvenuto Cellini's journey over them to France, in the sixteenth century; Evelyn's in the seventeenth; and Lady Mary Wortley's, and Horace Walpole's in the eighteenth, are all described in terms which seem to exhaust the details of possible danger. 'I intend to set out to-morrow,' says the brilliant

---

[21] [Adapted from John Milton, *Paradise Lost*, Book 2, line 619.]
[22] [Milton, *Paradise Lost*, Book 2, lines 622–3.]
* This inn is kept by an English family, and, contrary to general custom, afforded greater accommodation, comfort, and civility, than are usually offered by our emigrating countrymen. Good beds and good fare are peculiarly valuable, and valued, in this dreary spot, where the sudden diminution of temperature which necessarily accompanies a rapid ascent, leaves the body more susceptible of disagreeable impressions.
[23] [Milton, *Paradise Lost*, Book 2, line 627.]

ambassadress to the Ottoman Porte, 'and pass those *dreadful* Alps so much talked of. If I come to the bottom, you shall hear of me.' 'We began to ascend Mount Cenis, being carried on little seats of twisted osier fixed upon poles, upon men's shoulders.'[24]

Horace Walpole's description is still more formidable. 'At the foot of Mount Cenis we were obliged to quit our chaise, which was taken to pieces and loaded on mules; and we were carried in low arm-chairs on poles, swathed in beaver bonnets, beaver gloves, beaver stockings, muffs, and bear-skins.' 'The dexterity and nimbleness of the mountaineers is inconceivable; they run down steeps and frozen precipices.' – 'We had twelve men and nine mules to carry us.' – 'On the top of the highest Alps, by the side of a wood of firs, there darted out a young wolf, seized poor dear Tory by the throat; and before we could possibly prevent it, sprung up the side of the rock, and carried him off.'[25]

To this perilous mode of passing the Alps Lalande offers an alternative. '*Cela s'appelle se faire ramasser.*' One of the preliminaries of this speedy mode of travelling might be deemed quite sufficient to render it an experiment of rare occurrence; and the whole is sufficiently uninviting, from the first precipitation down the frozen snows of the mountain, till the half-dead traveller is picked up, or '*ramassé,*' at the base of his rapid descent.*

When, however, the passage of a Piedmontese princess, on her way to some royal bridegroom of France, was expected, the Corvée was exacted in

---

[24] [*Letters of the Right Honourable Lady M—y W—y M—e: Written during her Travels in Europe, Asia and Africa*, 4 vols (London: T. Becket and P. A. de Hondt, 1763-7), vol. 3, p. 95, p. 97. Cellini's narrative of traversing these mountains is found in *Vita di Benvenuto Cellini scritta da lui medesimo*, transcribed and edited by Giuseppe Molini, 2 vols (Florence: 'Tipograifa all'insegna di Dante', 1832), vol. 1, pp. 260-7. See *The Life of Benvenuto Cellini*, translated by John Addington Symonds, second edition, 2 vols (London: John C. Nimmo, 1888), vol. 2, pp. 6-14. For Evelyn's account of crossing the Alps, written in May 1646 and initially published (in the first edition of his *Diary*) in 1818, see *The Diary of John Evelyn*, edited by E.S. de Beer, 6 vols (Oxford: Oxford University Press, 1955), vol. 2, pp. 506-19.]

[25] [*The Yale Edition of Horace Walpole's Correspondence*, edited by W.S. Lewis, 40 vols (London and New Haven: Yale University Press, 1937-83), vol. 13, p. 189 (with slight alterations); the letter by Walpole from which Morgan takes these excerpts is dated 11 November 1739, N.S., and, according to this edition, was first published in *The Works of Horatio Walpole, Earl of Orford*, 5 vols (London: G.G. and J. Robinson and J. Edwards, 1798).]

* 'This is only practised on the Savoy side, the Piedmontese mountains not being adapted to the process. For the operation, the traveller is seated on a traineau; and a guide is placed before him, (with iron spikes in his shoes, to stop the machine when it goes too fast,) who throws himself back on the traveller, to prevent the effect of the shock from pitching him out. Thus arranged, the whole are projected down the frozen snow on the side of the mountain, and a quarter of an hour brings them to the foot of Mount Cenis.' – Lalande. [See [Joseph Jérôme le Français de Lalande,] *Voyage d'un Français en Italie, fait dans les années 1765 et 1766*, 8 vols (Venice and Paris: chez Desaint, 1769), vol. 1, p. 23. In observing 'cela s'appelle *se faire ramasser*' (literally: 'it is known as *being gathered up*'), Lalande refers to an extremely swift descent in a sledge.]

all its terrible rigour; and the whole vassalage of Piedmont and Savoy were put into requisition to clear a path for the traineau of the royal bride.* But all under royalty passed, or perished, as it might be.

Impressed with all this perilous imagery, which the last book of travels, looked into over night, had revived in the memory, it was a dreary thing to rise with the dawn, the following morning, and from the window of *Lans-le-bourg* Inn, to behold that *'frozen continent, deep snow and ice, where armies whole have sunk.'*[26] Immediately opposite the door, a black track in the snow was pointed out, as the old line of road over which the shuddering traveller was borne in osier baskets, on the shoulders of those porters of the Novalese, and of Lans-le-bourg, who were of necessity reduced to the state of beasts of burden; and who frequently were obliged to fortify themselves against the severity of the elements they encountered, by means which sometimes endangered, and sometimes lost the lives of the persons committed to their care. † Beaver swathings! reeling porters! frozen precipices! young wolves! and dislocated carriages on mules' backs, were predominating ideas, when, descending to the inn-yard to begin our journey, we found our carriage undisturbed, four post-horses, and two smart postilions, whose impatient 'Allons, Monsieur, allons, Madame,' recalled the technical jargon of the first stage from Paris. Their '*vif, vif,*' put the horses into motion; and we ascended in a trot that broad, smooth, magnificent road, which, carried over the mightiest acclivities of the mightiest regions, exceeds the military highways of antiquity, and shames the paved roads of modern France, whose price was the degradation of a nation.‡ The road, indeed, when we passed it, was covered with snow; but the fences on either side marked its breadth; and the facility of its winding ascent, proved the boldness, ingenuity, and perfection of its design. At certain distances arose the safe asylums (maisons de refuge) against the *tormenta*, or the avalanche: and the Cantonieri presented themselves with their pick-axes and shovels, giving courage where aid was not wanted. A post-house, or a barrack, disputed the site with the *bears* and *wolves*; and the rapidity of the whole passage rendered beaver swathings, or any other extraordinary precautions against cold, unnecessary. All that had

---

* This was the case in 1775, on the marriage of the present King of France and his brother the Count d'Artois, to the two princesses of Savoy.

[26] [Adapted from Milton, *Paradise Lost*, Book 2, lines 587, 591, 594.]

† 'On the very highest precipice of Mount Cenis, the devil of discord, in the similitude of sour wine, had got amongst our Alpine savages, and set them a-fighting with Gray and me in the chairs: they rushed him by me on a crag, where there was scarce room for a cloven foot.' – Walpole's Correspondence. [*The Yale Edition of Horace Walpole's Correspondence*, edited by W.S. Lewis, 40 vols (London and New Haven: Yale University Press, 1937–83), vol. 13, pp. 188-9, dated 11 November 1739; see note 25 above. (Morgan omits a comma after Gray, which confuses the sense.)]

‡ The Corvée. [In other words, forced labour.]

been danger, difficulty, and suffering, but twenty years back, was now safe, facile, and enjoyable; secure beyond the chance of accident, sublime beyond the reach of thought. Legitimate princes! divine-righted sovereigns! houses of France! Austria and Savoy! *'which of you have done this?'* There is not one among you, descendants of a Clovis, a Barbarossa, or an Amadeus, but may in safe conscience shake his innocent head, and answer, *'Thou canst not say 'twas I did it!'* – Neither does the world accuse you.

Whoever has wandered far and seen much, has learned to distrust the promises of books; and (in respect of the most splendid efforts of human labour) must have often felt how far the unworn expectation starts beyond its possible accomplishment. But *nature* never disappoints. Neither the memory nor the imagination of authorship can go beyond the fact she dictates, or the image she presents. If general feelings can be measured by individual impressions, Italy, with all her treasures of art, and associations of history, has nothing to exhibit, that strikes the traveller like the Alps which meet his view on his ascent to the summit of Mount Cenis, or of the Semplon. That is a moment in which the imagination feels the real poverty of its resources, the narrow limits of its range. An aspect of the material world then presents itself, which genius, even in its highest exaltation, must leave to original creation, as unimitated and inimitable. The sensation it produces is too strong for pleasure, too intense for enjoyment. There, where all is so new, novelty loses its charm; where all is so safe, conscious security is no proof against *'horrible imaginings;'* and those splendid evidences of the science and industry of man, which rise at every step, recede before the terrible possibilities with which they mingle, and which may render the utmost precaution of talent and philanthropy unavailable.[27] It is in vain that the barrier rises and the arch springs; that the gulf is platformed and the precipice skreened – still the eye closes and the breath is suspended, while danger, painted in the unmastered savagery of remote scenes, creates an ideal and proximate peril. Here experience teaches the falsity of the trite maxim, that the mind becomes elevated by the contemplation of nature in the midst of her grandest works, and engenders thoughts *'that wander through eternity.'*[28] The mind in such scenes is not raised. It is stricken back upon its own insignificance. Masses like these sublime deformities, starting out of the ordinary proportions of nature, in their contemplation reduce man to what he is – an atom. In such regions nothing is in conformity with him, all is at variance with his end and being, all is commemorative of those elementary convulsions, which sweep away whatever lives and breathes, in the general wreck of inanimate matter. Engines and agents of the destructive elements that rage around them,

---

[27] [Shakespeare, *Macbeth*, 1.3.138.]
[28] [Milton, *Paradise Lost*, Book 2, line 148.]

these are regions fitted only to raise the storm and to launch the avalanche, to cherish the whirlwind, and attract the bolt; until some convulsive throe within their mystic womb, awakens fiercer contentions: then they heave and shift, and burst and burn, again to subside, cool down, and settle into awful stillness and permanent desolation; at once the wreck and the monument of changes, which scoff at human record, and trace in characters that admit no controversy the fallacy of calculations and the vanity of systems. Well may the countless races of successive ages have left the mysteries of the Alps unexplored, their snows untracked: but immortal glory be the meed of them, the brave, bold spirits, whose unaccommodated natures, in these regions, where 'cold performs the effect of fire,'[29] braved dangers in countless forms, to oppose the invading enemies of their country's struggling rights; who climbing where the eagle had not soared, nor the chamois dared to spring, raised the shout of national independence amidst echoes which had never reverberated, save to the howl of the wolf, or the thunder of the avalanche.* Gratitude as eternal as the snows of Mont Blanc to them or him, who grappled with obstacles coeval with creation, levelled the pinnacle and blew up the rock, pierced the granite and spanned the torrent, disputing with nature in all her potency her right to separate man from man, and made straight in the desert an highway for progressive civilization!

Than such great works as this, one only greater remained – to facilitate the communion of knowledge, and spread the means of civil liberty from pole to pole by their sole omnipotent agent, A FREE PRESS. He who did much, did not this – he who levelled mountains and turned aside torrents, and did more than a thousand ages of feudal patrons could effect, of all his possible performances left this *'greater still behind;'* and by that one false calculation, made on the model of examples he derided and of men he had crushed, he fell himself; and now remains *'unrespited, unpitied, unreprieved,'* the victim of the system he revived and of the policy he cherished.[30]

The art of road-making ranks high in the means of civilization; and its utility, better felt than understood in the dark ages, was sufficiently appreciated to

---

[29] [Milton, *Paradise Lost*, Book 2, line 595.]

* 'Les pièces d'artillerie et les caissons sont portés à bras: les grenadiers arrivés au sommet du mont, jettèrent en l'air leurs bonnets ornés de plumets rouges. Un cri de joie s'élève de l'armée, Les Alpes sont franchies.' – Campagne d'Italie, 1796. ['The artillery and the caissons were carried in the arms of the grenadiers, who, once they arrived at the summit of the mountain, threw their bonnets, trimmed with red plumes, in the air. A cry of joy rose up from the army: "We have crossed the Alps"'.] The probable source for this quotation is [François René Jean, Baron] de Pommereul, *Campagne du Général Buonaparte en Italie, pendant les années IVe et Ve de la République Français, par un officier général* (Paris: 'chez Plassan, chez Bernard', 1797), but I have been unable to find the precise reference.

[30] ['This greater still behind' seems to invoke Shakespeare, *Macbeth*, 1.3.117: 'The greatest is behind.' Milton, *Paradise Lost*, Book 2, line 185.]

render it an object of monopoly to the Church.* To build a bridge, or clear a forest, were deeds of salvation for the next world, as for this; and royal and noble sinners very literally paved their way to heaven, and reached the gates of paradise by causeways made on earth. St. Benedict laid the basis of his own canonization with the first stone of the famous bridge of Avignon; which, says Pope Nicholas the Fifth, was raised by the inspiration of the Holy Ghost. The *Frères Pontifs* by dint of brick and mortar built up a reputation which rendered their order the most opulent as well as the most revered of their day; and the 'viceregents of God on earth'[31] could find no higher title to indicate their power than that, borrowed from Roman priests and emperors, of Pontifex Maximus, or chief bridge-builder.† But if there is one, by whom this significant epithet is merited more than by all others, it is he who made roads, cleared forests, and built bridges, from the Alps to the Pontine marshes.

We found the plain, which terminates the ascent of Mount Cenis, covered with snow. Its lake, so famous for excellent trout, was a sheet of ice. The windows of the post-house, the inn, the convent, and the barrack, (the colony of this frozen region) were defended by closed shutters. A friar and a few discontented-looking soldiers were loitering about. An old woman offered some scentless lilies for sale, which she called 'fiori di Cenisa,' and some little children sat on the steps of the convent up to their knees in snow. The atmosphere was rarified, and the sky one deep, dark tint of unvaried blue. Even with all that had been done to provide against danger and ensure accommodation, desolation reigned unabated through the scene.

---

* Some remains of the Cantonieri, or *Utricularii*‡, established in Gaul under the Romans, were discoverable in the early part of the middle ages in Provence, where they plied in bands on the banks of rivers and marshes. But this living machinery was not always to be trusted; for in undertaking to forward the traveller to another shore, they sometimes sent him to another world.

---

‡ So called from their rafts used in crossing rivers, which were floated on inflated skins.

31 [Summary of Genesis 1: 28. Milton, in *Paradise Lost*, refers to Christ as God's 'viceregent': see, for example, Book 5, line 609. Morgan extends the scope of this title to the popes as part of her argument for the prestige attached to the title of 'Pontifex Maximus', and, therefore, the importance assigned to bridge-builiding.]

† 'Pontifices ego à ponte arbitror; nam ab iis sublicius est factus primum, ut restitutus sæpe, cum ideo sacra et uls et cis Tyberim non mediocri ritu fiant.' – Varro de Ling. Latina, l.iv. [Varro, *De Lingua Latina*, 5.83. 'For my part I think that the name [pontifices] comes from *pons* 'bridge'; for by them Bridge-on-Piles was made in the first place, and it was likewise repeatedly repaired by them, since in that connexion rites are performed on both sides of the Tiber with no small ceremony.' [Marcus Terentius] Varro, *On the Latin Language*, with an English translation by Roland G. Kent, 2 vols (Cambridge, Massachusetts: Harvard University Press [1951]), vol. 1, p. 81.]

It is probable, however, that, in the rude ages of early Roman history, the priests, imported with the religion from more civilized countries, were alone capable of turning an arch. The Gothic architects of the 11th century, who raised our most beautiful cathedrals, were in a manner like priests. If this conjecture be just the term *pontifex* arose from a general, and not a particular fact.

The first step of the descent was not calculated to lessen unpleasant sensations. The winding precipitous road hung suspended for fathoms down, terrace below terrace: an arch flung across a gulf, which, when reached, was carelessly trotted across, seemed as it was viewed from on high, scarce passable by the chamois' foot. Here and there blown-up rocks lay scattered in black masses, unfinished excavations yawned, and vestiges of greater projects and bolder facilities than were yet effected, evinced some daring intention suddenly cut short by natural obstacles, or by political change. Torrents of melted snow swelled the stream of the Cenisella; an undulating region of mountains spread round on every side, like the waves of northern seas suddenly frozen in the moment of their stormy fermentation; until gradually the tintless surface of the soil exhibited spots of black earth, a patch of vegetation, a clump of underwood, a tree putting forth its nipped buds, an hut, a sheepfold, a vine. Winter blasts softened into vernal gales, and the doubling of a bold projecting promontory, revealed the sunny plains of Italy:

> 'To all delight of human sense exposed,
> Nature's whole wealth; nay, more – an heaven on earth.'[32]

From such a site as this, it is said, Hannibal halted his Carthaginians, and pointed to the recompense of all their arduous undertakings. From such a site as this the Lombard Alboin paused amidst his ferocious hosts, to contemplate the paradise of his future conquest, and quaffed from the skull of his enemy his first draught of Italian wine.* From such a site as this Napoleon Bonaparte, at the head of an ill-appointed, long-suffering, and neglected army, pointed to the plains of Lombardy, and promised victory. His soldiers accepted the pledge†, rushed like an Alpine torrent over crags and precipices, and won that Italy, in two brief and splendid campaigns, which had through ages resisted the forces, and witnessed the disasters, of millions of Frenchmen, led on by kings, and organized by experienced generals.‡

---

[32] [Milton, *Paradise Lost*, Book 4, condensed from lines 206–8.]

* 'Secondo i costume di quei tempi, in un gran convito dei Longobardi, beveva nel cranio de Cunemondo legato in oro.' – Pignotti, vol. ii. [The reference is presumably to one of the 'favole' or 'novelle' of Lorenzo Pignotti (1739–1812), which went through numerous editions in the late eighteenth an dearly nineteenth centuries. 'According to the customs of those times, at a great feast of the Lombards, he drank from the skull of Cunemonde, bound with gold.']

† Bonaparte, before his departure for this campaign, traced a slight sketch of his intended operations at a private house. In this plan Millissimo is marked, in the confidence of success, as being the first site of the defeat of the enemy. 'Je chasserois,' he says, 'les Autrichiens des gorges du Tyrol;' and he finishes the sketch with these words: 'C'est aux portes de la Vienne que je vous donnerai la paix.' Speaking afterwards of his treaty of Millissimo, he said, 'C'étoit la plus forte sensation de ma vie.' ['I should chase . . . the Austrians from the gorges of the Tyrol'; 'It is at the gates of Vienna that I shall give you peace'; 'It was the strongest sensation I ever felt.']

‡ Under Charles VIII., Louis XII., and Francis I.; and in more recent times, under Louis XIII., XIV., and XV.

William Hazlitt, *Notes of a Journey through France and Italy* (London: Hunt and Clarke, 1826), pp. 198–210

On the previous evening, the travellers have descended into Chambéry, and arrived in Savoy.

We set out early the next morning, and it was the most trying part of our whole journey. The wind cut like a scythe through the valleys, and a cold, icy feeling struck from the sides of the snowy precipices that surrounded us, so that we seemed enclosed in a huge well of mountains. We got to St. Jean de Maurienne to breakfast about noon, where the only point agreed upon appeared to be to have nothing ready to receive us. This was the most tedious day of all; nor did we meet with any thing to repay us for our uncomfortable setting out. We travelled through a scene of desolation, were chilled in sunless valleys or dazzled by sunny mountain-tops, passed frozen streams or gloomy cavities, that might be transformed into the scene of some Gothic wizard's spell, or reminded one of some German novel. Let no one imagine that the crossing the Alps is the work of a moment, or done by a single heroic effort – that they are a huge but detached chain of hills, or like the dotted line we find in the map. They are a sea or an entire kingdom of mountains. It took us three days to traverse them in this, which is the most practicable direction, and travelling at a good round pace. We passed on as far as eye could see, and still we appeared to have made little way. Still we were in the shadow of the same enormous mass of rock and snow, by the side of the same creeping stream. Lofty mountains reared themselves in front of us – horrid abysses were scooped out under our feet. Sometimes the road wound along the side of a steep hill, overlooking some village-spire or hamlet, and as we ascended it, it only gave us a view of remoter scenes, 'where Alps o'er Alps arise,' tossing about their billowy tops, and tumbling their unwieldy shapes in all directions – a world of wonders![33] – Any one, who is much of an egotist, ought not to travel through these districts; his vanity will not find its account in them; it will be chilled, mortified, shrunk up: but they are a noble treat to those who feel themselves raised in their own thoughts and in the scale of being by the immensity of other things, and who can aggrandise and piece out their personal insignificance by the grandeur and eternal forms of nature! It gives one a vast idea of Buonaparte to think of him in these situations. He alone (the Rob Roy of the scene) seemed a match for the elements, and able to master 'this fortress, built by nature for herself.'[34] Neither impeded

---

[33] [Alexander Pope, *Essay on Criticism*, part 2, line 32.]
[34] [The fame of Rob Roy, a Scottish outlaw and folk hero, was augmented by the publication of Sir Walter Scott's novel *Rob Roy* in 1817; Shakespeare, *Richard II*, 2.1.44.]

nor turned aside by immoveable barriers, he smote the mountains with his iron glaive, and made them malleable; but roads through them; transported armies over their ridgy steeps; and the rocks 'nodded to him, and did him courtesies!'[35]

We arrived at St. Michelle at night-fall (after passing through beds of ice and the infernal regions of cold), where we met with a truly hospitable reception, with wood-floors in the English fashion, and where they told us the King of England had stopped. This made no sort of difference to me.

We breakfasted the next day (being Sunday) at Lans-le-Bourg, where I observed my friend the Spaniard busy with his tables, taking down the name of the place. The landlady was a little, round, fat, good-humoured, black-eyed Italian or Savoyard, *saying* a number of good things to all her guests, but sparing of them otherwise. We were now at the foot of Mount Cenis, and after breakfast we set off on foot before the Diligence, which was to follow us in half an hour. We passed a melancholy-looking inn at the end of the town, professing to be kept by an Englishwoman; but there appeared to be nobody about the house, English, French, or Italian. The mistress of it (a young woman who had married an Italian) had, in fact, died a short time before of pure chagrin and disappointment in this solitary place, after having told her tale of distress to every one, till it fairly wore her out. We had leisure to look back to the town as we proceeded, and which, with its church, stone-cottages, and slated roofs, shrunk into a miniature-model of itself as we continued to advance farther and higher above it. Some straggling cottages, some vineyards planted at a great height, and another compact and well-built village, that seemed to defy the extremity of the seasons, were seen in the direction of the valley that we were pursuing. Else all around were shapeless, sightless piles of hills covered with snow, with crags or pine-trees or a foot-path peeping out, and in the appearance of which no alteration whatever was made by our advancing or receding. We gained on the mountain by a broad, winding road that continually doubles, and looks down upon the point from whence you started half an hour before. Some snow had fallen in the morning, but it was now fine, though cloudy. We found two of our fellow-travellers following our example, and they soon after overtook us. They were both French. We noticed some of the features of the scenery; and a lofty hill opposite to us being scooped out into a bed of snow, with two ridges or promontories projecting (something like an arm-chair) on each side. '*Voilà!*' said the younger and more volatile of our companions, '*c'est un trône, et le nuage est la gloire!*' – A white cloud indeed

---

[35] [Adapted from Shakespeare, *A Midsummer Night's Dream*, 3.1.174: 'Nod to him, elves, and do him courtesies.']

encircled its misty top.³⁶ I complimented him on the happiness of his allusion, and said that Madame was pleased with the exactness of the resemblance. He then turned to the valley, and said, '*C'est un berceau.*'³⁷ This is the height to which the imagination of a Frenchman always soars, and it can soar no highter. Any thing that is not cast in this obvious, common-place mould, that had been used a thousand times before with applause, they think barbarous, and as they phrase it, *originaire*. No farther notice was taken of the scenery, any more than if we had been walking on the Boulevards at Paris, and my young Frenchman talked of other things, laughed, sung, and smoked a cigar with a gaiety and lightness of heart that I envied. 'What has become,' said the elder of the Frenchmen, 'of Monsieur l'Espagnol? He does not easily quit his seat; he sits in one corner, never looks out, or if you point to any object, takes no notice of it; and when you come to the end of the stage, says – "What is the name of that place we passed by last?" – takes out his pocket-book, and makes a note of it. "That is droll."' And what made it more so, it turned out that our Spanish friend was a painter, travelling to Rome to study the Fine Arts! All the way as we ascended, there were red posts placed at the side of the road, ten or twelve feet in height, to point out the direction of the road in case of a heavy fall of snow, and with notches cut to shew the depth of the drifts. There were also scattered stone-hovels, erected as stations for the *Gens d'armes*, who were sometimes left here for several days together after a severe snow-storm, without being approached by a single human being. One of these stood near the top of the mountain, and as we were tired of the walk (which had occupied two hours) and of the uniformity of the view, we agreed to wait here for the Diligence to overtake us. We were cordially welcomed in by a young peasant (a soldier's wife) with a complexion as fresh as the winds, and an expression as pure as the mountain-snows. The floor of this rude tenement consisted of the solid rock; and a three-legged table stood on it, on which were placed three earthen bowls filled with sparkling wine, heated on a stove with sugar. The woman stood by, and did the honours of this cheerful repast with a rustic simplicity and a pastoral grace that might have called forth the powers of Hemskirk and Raphael. I shall not soon forget the rich ruby colour of the wine, as the sun shone upon it through a low glazed window that looked out on the boundless wastes around, nor its grateful spicy smell as we sat around it. I was complaining of the trick that had been played by the waiter at Lyons in the taking of our places, when I was told by the young Frenchman, that, in case I returned to Lyons, I ought to go to the Hotel de l'Europe, or to the Hotel du Nord, 'in which latter case he should have the honour

---

36 ['*Voilà!* It is a throne, and the cloud is the halo.']
37 ['It is a cradle.']

of serving me.'[38] I thanked him for his information, and we set out to finish the ascent of Mount Cenis, which we did in another half hour's march. The *traiteur* of the Hotel du Nord and I had got into a brisk theatrical discussion on the comparative merits of Kean and Talma, he asserting that there was something in French acting which an English understanding could not appreciate; and I insisting loudly on bursts of passion as the *forte* of Talma, which was a language common to human nature; that in his *Œdipus*, for instance, it was not a Frenchman or an Englishman he had to represent – '*Mais c'est un homme, c'est Œdipe*' – when our cautious Spaniard brushed by us, determined to shew he could descend the mountain, if he would not ascend it on foot.[39] His figure was characteristic enough, his motions smart and lively, and his dress composed of all the colours of the rainbow. He strutted on before us in the snow, like a flamingo or some tropical bird of variegated plumage; his dark purple cloak fluttered in the air, his Montero cap, set a little to one side, was of fawn colour; his waistcoat a bright scarlet, his coat a reddish brown, his trowsers a pea-green, and his boots a perfect yellow. He saluted us with a national politeness as he passed, and seemed bent on redeeming the sedentary sluggishness of his character by one bold and desperate effort of locomotion.

The coach shortly after overtook us. We descended a long and steep declivity, with the highest point of Mount Cenis on our left, and a lake to the right, like a landing-place for geese. Between the two was a low, white monastery, and the barrier where we had our passports inspected, and then went forward with only two stout horses and one rider. The snow on this side of the mountain was nearly gone. I supposed myself for some time nearly on level ground, till we came in view of several black chasms or steep ravines in the side of the mountain facing us, with water oozing from it, and saw through some *galleries*, that is, massy stone-pillars knit together by thick rails of strong timber, guarding the road-side, a perpendicular precipice below, and other galleries beyond, diminished in a fairy perspective, and descending 'with cautious haste and giddy cunning,'[40] and with innumerable windings and re-duplications to an interminable depth and distance from the height where we were. The men and horses with carts, that were labouring up the path in the hollow below, shewed like crows or flies. The road we had to pass was often immediately under that we were passing, and cut from the side of what was all but a precipice out of the solid rock by the broad, firm master-hand that traced and executed this mighty work. The share that art has in the scene is as appalling as the scene itself – the

---

[38] [For the story of the 'trick' at Lyons, see Hazlitt, *Notes of a Journey*, pp. 185–7.]

[39] [The actors Edmund Kean (1789–1833) and François-Joseph Talma (1763–1826); 'But it is a man, it is Oedipus.']

[40] [An Ironic play on Milton, 'L'Allegro', line 141: 'With wanton heed and giddy cunning.']

strong security against danger as sublime as the danger itself. Near the turning of one of the first galleries is a beautiful waterfall, which at this time was frozen into a sheet of green pendant ice – a magical transformation. Long after we continued to descend, now faster and now slower, and came at length to a small village at the bottom of a sweeping line of road, where the houses seemed like dove-cotes with the mountain's back reared like a wall behind them, and which I thought the termination of our journey. But here the wonder and the greatness began: for, advancing through a grove of slender trees to another point of the road, we caught a new view of the lofty mountain to our left. It stood in front of us, with its head in the skies, covered with snow, and its bare sides stretching far away into a valley that yawned at its feet, and over which we seemed suspended in mid air. The height, the magnitude, the immoveableness of the objects, the wild contrast, the deep tones, the dance and play of the landscape from the change of our direction and the interposition of other striking objects, the continued recurrence of the same huge masses, like giants following us with unseen strides, stunned the sense like a blow, and yet gave the imagination strength to contend with a force that mocked it. Here immeasurable columns of reddish granite shelved from the mountain's sides; here they were covered and stained with furze and other shrubs; here a chalky cliff shewed a fir-grove climbing its tall sides, and that itself looked at a distance like a huge, branching pine-tree; beyond was a dark, projecting knoll, or hilly promontory, that threatened to bound the perspective – but, on drawing nearer to it, the cloudy vapour that shrouded it (as it were) retired, and opened another vista beyond, that, in its own unfathomed depth, and in the gradual obscurity of twilight, resembled the uncertain gloom of the background of some fine picture. At the bottom of this valley crept a sluggish stream, and a monastery or low castle stood upon its banks. The effect was altogether grander than I had any conception of. It was not the idea of height or elevation that was obtruded upon the mind and staggered it, but we seemed to be descending into the bowels of the earth – its foundations seemed to be laid bare to the centre; and abyss after abyss, a vast, shadowy, interminable space, opened to receive us. We saw the building up and frame-work of the world – its limbs, its ponderous masses, and mighty proportions, raised stage upon stage, and we might be said to have passed into a unknown sphere, and beyond mortal limits. As we rode down our winding, circuitous path, our baggage, (which had been taken off) moved on before us; a grey horse that had got loose from the stable followed it, and as we whirled round the different turnings in this rapid, mechanical flight, at the same rate and the same distance from each other, there seemed something like witchcraft in the scene and in our progress through it. The moon had risen, and threw its gleams across the fading twilight; the snowy tops of the mountains were blended with the clouds and stars; their sides were shrouded in mysterious gloom, and it was not till we entered Susa, with its fine old drawbridge and castellated walls, that we found ourselves on *terra firma*, or breathed common air again. At the inn at Susa, we first perceived the difference of Italian manners; and the next day arrived at Turin, after passing over thirty miles of the straightest, flattest, and dullest road in the world. Here we stopped two days to recruit our strength and look about us.

CHAPTER XV

My arrival at Turin was the first and only moment of intoxication I have found in Italy. It is a city of palaces. After a change of dress (which, at the end of a long journey, is a great luxury) I walked out, and traversing several clean, spacious streets, came to a promenade outside the town, from which I saw the chain of Alps we had left behind us, rising like a range of marble pillars in the evening sky. Monte Viso and Mount Cenis resembles two pointed cones of ice, shooting up above the rest. I could distinguish the broad and rapid Po, winding along at the other extremity of the walk, through vineyards and meadow grounds. The trees had on that deep sad foliage, which takes a mellower tinge from being prolonged into the midst of winter, and which I had only seen in pictures. A Monk was walking in a solitary grove at a little distance from the common path. The air was soft and balmy, and I felt transported to another climate – another earth – another sky. The winter was suddenly changed to spring. It was as if I had to begin my life anew. Several young Italian women were walking on the terrace, in English dresses, and with graceful downcast looks, in which you might fancy that you read the soul of the Decameron.[41] It was a fine, serious grace, equally remote from French levity and English sullenness, but it was the last I saw of it.

P[atrick] Brydone, *A Tour through Sicily and Malta. In a Series of Letters to William Beckford, Esq. of Somerly in Suffolk*, 2 vols (London: W. Strahan and T. Cadell, 1775; first published in 1773), vol. 1, pp. 210–19

We now had time to examine a fourth region of this wonderful mountain, very different, indeed, from the others, and productive of very different sensations; but which has, undoubtedly, given being to all the rest; I mean the region of fire.

The present crater of this immense volcano is a circle of about three

---

[41] [Giovanni Boccaccio, *Decameron*, written 1350–53.]

miles and a half in circumference. It goes shelving down on each side, and forms a regular hollow like a vast amphitheatre. From many places of this space, issue volumes of sulphureous smoke, which being much heavier than the circumambient air, instead of rising in it, as smoke generally does, immediately on its getting out of the crater, rolls down the side of the mountain like a torrent, till coming to that part of the atmosphere of the same specific gravity with itself, it shoots off horizontally, and forms a large track in the air, according to the direction of the wind; which, happily for us, carried it exactly to the side opposite to that where we were placed. The crater is so hot, that it is very dangerous, if not impossible, to go down into it; besides, the smoke is very incommodious, and, in many places, the surface is so soft, there have been instances of people sinking down in it, and paying for their temerity with their lives. Near the center of the crater is the great mouth of the volcano. That tremendous gulph so celebrated in all ages, looked upon as the terror and scourge both of this and another life; and equally useful to ancient poets, or to modern divines, when the Muse, or when the Spirit inspires. We beheld it with awe and with horror, and were not surprised that it had been considered as the place of the damned. When we reflect on the immensity of its depth, the vast cells and caverns whence so many lavas have issued; the force of its internal fire, to raise up those lavas to so vast a height, to support it as it were in the air, and even force it over the very summit of the crater, with all the dreadful accompaniments; the boiling of the matter, the shaking of the mountain, the explosions of flaming rocks, &c. we must allow, that the most enthusiastic imagination, in the midst of all its terrors, hardly ever formed an idea of hell more dreadful.

It was with a mixture both of pleasure and pain, that we quitted this awful scene. But the wind had risen very high, and clouds began to gather round the mountain: In a short time they formed like another heaven below us, and we were in hopes of seeing a thunder-storm under our feet: A scene that is not uncommon in these exalted regions, and which I have already seen on the top of the high Alps: But the clouds were soon dispelled again by the force of the wind, and we were disappointed in our expectations.

I had often been told of the great effect produced by discharging a gun on the top of high mountains. I tried it here, when we were a good deal surprised to find, that instead of increasing the sound, it was almost reduced to nothing. The report was not equal to that of a pocket-pistol: We compared it to the stroke of a stick on a door; and surely it is consistent with reason, that the thinner the air is, the less its impression must be on the ear; for in a vacuum there can be no noise, or no impression can be made; and the nearer the approach to a vacuum, the impression must always be the smaller. Where those great effects have been produced, it must have been amongst a number of mountains, where the sound is reverberated from one to the other.

When we arrived at the foot of the cone, we observed some rocks of an incredible size, that have been discharged from the crater. The largest that has been observed from Vesuvius, is a round one of about twelve feet diameter. These are much greater; indeed almost in proportion of the mountains to each other.

On our arrival at the Torre del Filosofo, we could not help admiring, that the ruins of this structure have remained uncovered for so many ages, so near the top of Ætna, when thousands of places at a great distance from it, have been repeatedly buried by its lavas, in a much shorter time. A proof that few eruptions have risen so high in the mountain.

Empedocles was a native of Agrigentum, and is supposed to have died 400 years before the Christian æra. Perhaps his vanity more than his philosophy led him to this elevated situation; nay, it is said to have carried him still much farther: – That he might be looked upon as a god, and that the people might suppose he was taken up to heaven, he is recorded to have thrown himself headlong into the great gulph of mount Ætna, never supposing that his death could be discovered to mankind; but the treacherous mountain threw out his slippers, which were of brass, and announced to the world the fate of the philosopher, who, by his death, as well as life, wanted only to impose upon mankind, and make them believe that he was greater than they.

However, if there is such a thing as philosophy on earth, this surely ought to be its seat. The prospect is little inferior to that from the summit; and the mind enjoys a degree of serenity here, that even few philosophers, I believe, could ever boast of on that tremendous point. – All Nature lies expanded below your feet, in her gayest and most luxuriant dress, and you still behold united under one point of view, all the seasons of the year, and all the climates of the earth. The meditations are ever elevated in proportion to the grandeur and sublimity of the objects that surround us; and here, where you have all Nature to arouse your admiration, what mind can remain inactive?

It has likewise been observed, and from experience I can say with truth; that on the tops of the highest mountains, where the air is so pure and refined; and where there is not that immense weight of gross vapours pressing upon the body; the mind acts with greater freedom, and all the functions both of soul and body are performed in a superior manner. It would appear, that in proportion as we are raised above the habitations of men, all low and vulgar sentiments are left behind; and that the soul, in approaching the æthereal regions, shakes off its earthly affections, and already acquires something of their celestial purity. – Here, where you stand under a serene sky, and behold, with equal serenity, the tempest and storm forming below your feet; the lightning, darting from cloud to cloud, and the thunder rolling round the mountain, and threatening with destruction the poor wretches below; the mind considers the little storms of the human passions as equally below her notice. – Surely the situation alone, is enough to inspire philosophy, and Empedocles had good reason for chusing it.

But, alas! How vain are all our reasonings! In the very midst of these meditations, my philosophy was at once overset, and in a moment I found myself relapsed into a poor miserable mortal; was obliged to own, that pain was the greatest of evils; and would have given the world to have been once more arrived at those humble habitations, which, but a moment before, I had looked down upon with such contempt. – In running over the ice, my leg folded under me, and I received so violent a sprain, that in a few minutes it swelled to a great degree, and I found myself unable to put my foot to the ground. Every muscle and fibre was at that time chilled and froze by the extreme cold, the thermometer continuing still below the point of congelation. It was this circumstance, I suppose, that made the pain so violent; for I lay a considerable time on the ice in great agony: However, in these exalted regions, it was impossible to have a horse, or a carriage of any kind; and your poor philosopher was obliged to hop on one leg, with two men supporting him, for several miles over the snow; and our wags here allege, that he left the greatest part of his philosophy behind him, for the use of Empedocles's heirs and successors.

I was happy to get to my mule, but when I once more found myself on our bed of leaves in the Spelonca del Capriole, I thought I was in Paradise: So true it is, that a removal of pain is the greatest of pleasures. The agony I suffered, had thrown me into a profuse sweat and a fever; however, in an instant I fell asleep, and in an hour and a half, awaked in perfect health. We had an excellent dish of tea, the most refreshing and agreeable I ever drank in my life.

Piozzi, *Observations and Reflections*, vol. 2, pp. 61–4

To-morrow we mount the Volcano, whose present peaceful disposition has tempted us to inspect it more nearly. Though it appears little less than presumption thus to profane with eyes of examination the favourite alembic of nature, while the great work of projection is carrying on; guarded as all its secret caverns are too with every contradiction; snow and flame! solid bodies heated into liquefaction, and rolling gently down one of its sides; while fluids congeal and harden into ice on the other; nothing can exceed the curiosity of its appearance, now the lava is less rapid, and stiffens as it flows;

stiffens too in ridges very surprisingly, and gains an odd aspect, not unlike the pasteboard waves representing sea at a theatre, but black, because this year's eruption has been mingled with coal. The connoisseurs here know the different degrees, dates, and shades of lava to a perfection that amazes one; and Sir William Hamilton's courage, learning, and perfect skill in these matters, is more people's theme here than the Volcano itself. Bartolomeo, the Cyclop of Vesuvius as he is called, studies its effects and operations too with much attention and philosophical exactness, relating the adventures he has had with our minister on the mountain to every Englishman that goes up, with great success. The way one climbs is by tying a broad sash with long ends round this Bartolomeo, letting him walk before one, and holding it fast. As far as the Hermitage there is no great difficulty, and to that place some chuse to ride an ass, but I thought walking safer; and there you are sure of welcome and refreshment from the poor good old man, who sets up a little cross wherever the fire has stopt near his cell; shews you the place with a sort of polite solemnity that impresses, spreads his scanty provisions before you kindly, and tells the past and present state of the eruption accurately, inviting you to partake of

> His rushy couch, his frugal fare,
> His blessing and repose.
>
> GOLDSMITH.[42]

This Hermit is a Frenchman. *J'ai dansé dans mon lit tans de fois**, said he: the expression was not sublime when speaking of an earthquake, to be sure; I looked among his books, however, and found Bruyere. 'Would not the Duc de Rochefoucault have done better?' said I. 'Did I never see you before, Madam?' said he; 'yes, sure I have, and dressed you too, when I was a hair-dresser in London, and lived with Mons. Martinant, and I dressed pretty Miss Wynne too in the same street. *Vit'elle encore? Vit'elle encore*†? Ah I am old now,' continued he; 'I remember when black pins first came up.' This was charming, and in such an unexpected way, I could hardly prevail upon myself ever to leave the spot; but Mrs. Greatheed having been quite to the crater's edge with her only son, a baby of four years old; shame rather than inclination urged me forward; I asked the little boy what he had seen; I saw the chimney, replied he, and it was on fire, but I liked the elephant better.

That the situation of the crater changed in this last eruption is of little consequence; it will change and change again I suppose. The wonder is, that nobody gets killed by venturing so near, while red-hot stones are flying

---

[42] [Adapted from Oliver Goldsmith, 'The Hermit', lines 19–20.]
* I have danced in my bed so often this year.
† Is she yet alive? Is she yet alive?

about them so. The Bishop of Derry did very near get his arm broke; and the Italians are always recounting the exploits of these rash Britons who look into the crater, and carry their wives and children up to the top; while we are, with equal justice, amazed at the courageous Neapolitans, who build little snug villages and dwell with as much confidence at the foot of Vesuvius, as our people do in Paddington or Hornsey.[43]

Morgan, *Italy*, vol. 2, pp. 343–4

As soon becomes obvious, Sydney Morgan is describing an episode in her visit to Naples.

During the whole of our stay in that capital, the mountain, though it never raged with that fury which adds alarm to admiration, was sufficiently active to excite an incessant interest. The ascent commences at Portici, where carriages are abandoned, and mules hired. The road is steep, but picturesque; and affords frequent views of the town and bay of Naples, of the greatest loveliness. As the elevation increases, the road is more frequently intersected by lava, the products of old eruptions, which pass, like dark and turbid torrents, through the vineyards. In one place we found a small space of a few square feet, between two streams of lava, an oasis in the desert, where the vegetation was not destroyed. On passing the hermitage, (where prayers and provisions, Litanies and Lacryma Christi, are prepared for adventurous travellers by two Franciscan monks, who constantly inhabit it,) an extensive plain, black and wavy with old lava, leads at once to the external base of the crater. Here the mules are left, and the journey is continued on foot. The guide takes the bridle of his mules, and, winding it round his body, gives one end to the traveller, and almost drags him up a nearly perpendicular acclivity, partly formed of lava and partly of loose sand: this ascent, which requires an hour and a half to accomplish, is descended, on returning, in a few minutes. On arriving at the summit, the great crater was visible at a short distance, throwing up, at intervals, showers of stones, with a tremendous noise, which kept us at a respectful distance; and we turned to the right, towards the side of the hill, to seek a lateral opening, at that time discharging a constant torrent of lava. To accomplish this object, we passed over an

---

[43] [Sir William Hamilton, in *Observations on Mount Vesuvius, Mount Etna, and Other Volcanos: in a Series of Letters, Addressed to the Royal Society* (London: T. Cadell, 1772), p. 8, recounts the incident during the Bishop of Derry's visit as one that happened in March 1766. Frederick Augustus Hervey (1730–1803), Bishop of Derry (1768) and later Earl of Bristol (1779), was one of the best known travellers and collectors of the time; he spent eighteen years in Italy, in the course of five visits, and is commemorated throughout much of Europe by numerous Hotel Bristols.]

1. Henry Tresham, *The Ascent of Vesuvius* (1785–90), watercolour over graphite, 44.8 x 69.5 cm. Yale Center for British Art, Paul Mellon Collection (B1977.14.6296)

extensive surface, which resembled a sea suddenly congealed in the midst of its wildest agitation; and was covered with huge masses of scoriæ, often sufficiently warm to be unpleasant. On reaching the desired spot, (which a few days before had been liquid fire, and from which smoke and a sulphureous vapour were emitted at frequent air-holes,) by the sudden turn of an angle, we came unexpectedly upon a group of English dandies, of both sexes, of our acquaintance – the ladies with their light garments something the worse for the adventure, and all laughing, flirting, and chattering over a chasm, which exhibited the lava boiling and bubbling up within a few feet below where they stood. This was very pleasant, but it was very provoking! To have travelled so far! – to have endured all the exhaustion of inordinate fatigue, and other annoyances equally out of the sphere of daily habits of ease, in the vain hope of snatching at a new and a strong sensation (the great spell of existence) – of meeting Nature, all solitary and sublime, in the awful process of one of her profoundest mysteries! – and then, to be put off with a *rechauffée* of the St. Carlos party of the preceding evening, and the sight of faces seen for nothing in the Paris circles during the preceding winter; – this was a terrible sacrifice of the sublime to the agreeable! – for, after all, it was no ungracious sight to behold so many laughing lovely English faces;

and to see their fair owners led by a laudable curiosity and an energy of character that belongs alone to British women, seemingly superior to fatigue, reckless alike of the sun that sullied their bloom, and the lava that burnt their *chaussure*, and excoriated their feet. Still the intention of the visit was frustrated; it was in vain the mind returned to its sublime and terrific object. There was no awe mingled with its contemplation! It was vain to gaze on the thin and trembling crust which vaulted the crater, and separated the spectator from an abyss of flame! There was no recoil of the imagination: inquiries, compliments, and recognitions, mingled with the deep subterranean murmurs of the volcano; parties were made, for distant days, on the brink of the engine of instant destruction; and the surprise most audibly evinced, was that of a rencontre so strange! Each knew the other's face was

– 'Neither new nor rare –
But wonder'd how the devil it got there!'[44]

---

[44] [Adapted from Alexander Pope, 'Epistle to Dr Arbuthnot', lines 171–2.]

Chapter 3
DANGER AND DESTABILIZATION

> I remember saying something like 'I feel a bit lightheaded; maybe you should drive...' And suddenly there was a terrible roar all around us and the sky was full of what looked like huge bats, all swooping and screeching and diving around the car, which was going about a hundred miles an hour with the top down.
>
> Hunter S. Thompson, *Fear and Loathing in Las Vegas: A Savage Journey to the Heart of the American Dream* (1971)

> 'Bridle Road to...' When I see this notice in England it has the same effect on me as Mescalin does on Mr Aldous Huxley. Here there are no such notices but you can see the bridle roads leading over the plains and the sierras in every direction and to an addict the sight is intoxicating. Every one has his weaknesses: some people run after women, others after Dukes; I run after priests and along *carrils* which, with their alluringly sinuous ways, are gravely tempting me to throw all my family duties to the wind and to go on riding along them for ever.
>
> Penelope Chetwode, *Two Middle-aged Ladies in Andalusia* (1963)

I: Indolent delicious reverie

Charles Dupaty concludes his *Lettres sur l'Italie* (1788), translated by Giovanni Povoleri as *Sentimental Letters on Italy* (1789), with a walk beside the Bay of Naples (the second passage below), during which he muses upon a landscape 'where breathed voluptuousness and pleasure'. Evoking the unbridled hedonism of the ancients in such a place, he reflects:

> Even I find this place, though so much changed by volcanos and time..., – yes, I find it still dangerous: methinks the air has retained something of its ancient corruption, as yet unpurified; the heart begins to feel the forcible influence of it.

Dupaty concludes by suggesting ironically that he needs to tear himself away from such a spot: 'Let us quit this dangerous shore, and re-embark for Naples.'

'Ancient corruption', in other words, anticipates danger and incipient destabilization in the present. Such danger is conceived in two ways in this commentary: ancient 'voluptuousness' is equated both with active dissipation ('Propertius suspected the fidelity of his Cynthia, the moment she reached that fatal, bewitching spot') and with a form of dreamy abandonment: 'these delightful shores, so fatal to modesty, and so favourable to love, where the zephyrs, the sea, the air – all contributed to relax the mind, and the heart, from the severe yoke of thought.'

At moments such as this, Dupaty vaunts the pleasures of enervation – the same experience that Anna Jameson analyses, in the extract from her *Diary of an Ennuyée* below, when she turns her attention from the extraordinary animation of popular life in Naples to a more pressing preoccupation: her own state of mind. She describes an experience of partial relief from the burden of bounded selfhood while overlooking the sea in Naples: 'a kind of pensive dreamy rapture, which if not quite pleasure, had at least a power to banish pain'. Hours pass 'insensibly', while the quotation from Wordsworth's 'Peter Bell' places the scene in the category of those on which humans have 'gazed [themselves] away'. Enervation borders on utter inanition: 'All my activity of mind, all my faculties of thought and feeling, and suffering, seemed lost and swallowed up in an indolent delicious reverie, a sort of vague and languid enjoyment.'

Softness and vivacity

An implicit point of reference in discussions of feeling 'vague and languid' in a warm climate, from the middle of the eighteenth century onwards, is Montesquieu's *De l'esprit des lois* (1748). In his chapter explaining 'combien les hommes sont différents dans les divers climats' ('Of the difference of Men in different Climates', as Thomas Nugent's translation of 1750 puts it), Montesquieu claims that cold air has a bracing effect on bodily fibres, and warm air a relaxing effect. As a result, changes in climate correspond to different degrees of receptiveness to sensory gratification: 'Dans les pays froids, on aura peu de sensibilité pour les plaisirs; elle sera plus grande dans les pays tempérés; dans les pays chauds, elle sera extrême' ('In cold climates, they have very little sensibility for pleasures; in temperate climates they have more; in warm countries their sensibility is exquisite'). A warm climate, moreover, induces a more intense abandonment to the passions: 'Approchez des pays du midi, vous croirez vous éloigner de la morale même; des passions plus vives multiplieront les crimes' ('If we draw near the south, we fancy ourselves removed from all morality; the strongest passions multiply all manner of crimes'). At the same time, a yet greater degree of heat induces not passion but utter indolence:

> La chaleur du climat peut être si excessive, que le corps y sera absolument sans force. Pour lors, l'abattement passera à l'esprit même; aucune curiosité, aucune noble entreprise, aucun sentiment généreux; les inclinations y seront toutes passives; la paresse y sera le bonheur.

> The heat of the climate may be so excessive as to deprive the body of all vigor and strength. Then the faintness is communicated to the mind; there is no curiosity, no noble enterprize, no generous sentiment; the inclinations are all passive; indolence constitutes the greatest happiness.¹

De Staël, in *Corinne*, brings together languor and passion in her reference to 'la mollesse et la vivacité du midi' ('the effeminate softness and the liveliness of the South').² Jameson, just before her account of her own 'indolent delicious reverie', produces a similarly paradoxical formulation: 'I never saw such eyes before, as I saw to-day, half languor and half fire, in the head of a ruffian Lazzarone, and a ragged Calabrian beggar girl.'

Pleasure and indolence in antiquity

Travellers, however, are concerned not only with the effects of a warm climate on the natives but with the power of the warm South to transform the behaviour of foreigners. The literature and history of antiquity provide them with convenient examples of such figures – whether the Romans who are summoned to the imagination by Dupaty, transmuted into voluptuaries as they absent themselves from the high seriousness of Rome, or the more generalized victims of an alluring climate invoked by Henry Swinburne, in the passage from his *Travels in the Two Sicilies* below. Swinburne considers the myth of the Sirens, whom Homer introduces into the *Odyssey* as sea-songstresses, living on an island near Scylla and Charybdis, who lure mariners to their doom.³ Speculating upon possible historical points of reference for these mythical figures, the traveller turns from a vision of 'some female sovereign', using her 'piratical subjects' to intercept mariners, to the perception that 'it is more natural to vest the power of the Sirens in the arts and corruptions of peace'. He then shifts historical time into personal time – a task that travel writing of this period constantly sets itself – by an evocation of foreigners ineluctably lured to the spot:

---

¹ [Charles Louis de Secondat, Baron de] Montesquieu, *De l'esprit des lois*, edited by Victor Goldschmidt, 2 vols (Paris: Flammarion, 1979), vol. 1, p. 375, p. 375, p. 375, p. 376; *The Spirit of Laws*, translated by Thomas Nugent, 2 vols (London: J. Nourse and P. Vaillant, 1750), vol. 1, p. 319, p. 320, p. 320.

² Madame de Staël [Anne Louise Germaine de Staël-Holstein], *Corinne, ou l'Italie*, edited by Claudine Herrmann, 2 vols (Paris; Éditions des Femmes, 1979), vol. 1, p. 97; de Staël includes this paradoxical formulation in a part of the novel that is set in Rome; the symbolic boundaries of the South are often flexible. William Beckford, in his account of Naples, prises the two terms of the paradox apart; see William Beckford, *Dreams, Waking Thoughts and Incidents* (1783), in *The Travel Diaries of William Beckford of Fonthill*, edited by Guy Chapman, 2 vols (London: Constable and Houghton and Mifflin, 1928), vol. 1, pp. 1–310; pp. 253–4.

³ *Odyssey*, 12.39.

> The sweet retreats that abound in the Surrentine peninsula; the enchanting prospects; the plenty of all the necessaries, and even luxuries of life, and the soft temperature of the climate could not fail of attracting strangers: there they must insensibly have acquired a relish for pleasure and indolence that enervated both their bodies and minds, and rendered every other country odious to them ...

The term *insensibly*, here, summons up an indeterminacy of perception: pleasure banishes any power to make the distinctions on which a sober judgement might be based. Dupaty, too, associates the seductive power of the South with an erasure of distinctions, induced by sensory indeterminacy. While the traveller begins the letter with a description of the sunrise 'separating the heavens from the waves', he nonetheless paints his mental picture of the antics of the ancients 'at the hour the sun rapidly descends from the heavens into the sea': in other words, he explains, 'at that hour, which is the most inviting of all the evening hours, to soft endearments, and to dalliance'. The link between a visual blurring of distinctions and a loss of moral certainty is spelt out explicitly: 'the thoughts are incessantly rendered more flexible by that vague and light shade, spreading a sable veil over the last glimpses of day.' Such flexibility of thought is enhanced by an effect of aural indeterminacy, towards which the sea makes its contribution; the sentence just quoted continues:

> ... but above all by the silence, which every moment diffuses itself on this coast, and from the bosom of which rises by degrees the affecting concert of the evening, composed of the melancholy sound of oars dashing the foaming waves, of the distant bleating of flocks, scattered over the mountains; of the hollow murmurs of the sea, expiring on the rocks; of the rustling of the leaves, where the zephyrs never rest; of all those insensible sounds, in short, which, extended far off in the heavens, on the water, and on the earth, form at this instant an uncertain whisper – a kind of melodious breathing of reposing nature!

In the evocation of ancient 'pleasure and voluptuousness', different sounds, some of them individually indistinct, produce a general effect of indeterminacy by merging with each other: 'amidst the voluptuous accents of voices and effeminate instruments, intermixed with the murmurs of gentle zephyrs, and the sweet notes of the feathered songsters, were dying away the sounds of warlike trumpets.'

The role of aquatic elements in erasing distinction is emphasized especially strongly early in the passage: at the amphitheatre of Misena, the waves of 'the foaming sea' have manifested their power to erase visual boundaries; for the past eight hundred years, they have attempted to blur the boundary between sea and land, by constantly lapping at the walls that prevent them from entering the structure.

Such effects of 'insensible gradation' are linked by Edmund Burke to the beautiful, the category that he sets in opposition to the sublime. His account of the beautiful, in fact, deploys a concept of 'relaxation' that, though formulated without any explicit reference to Montesquieu's analysis of the relaxing effects of a warm climate, obliquely invokes the elision between such a climate and indolent voluptuousness established in *De l'esprit des lois*. In his *Philosophical Enquiry into the Origin of our Ideas of the Sublime and Beautiful*, entitled 'The physical cause of LOVE', Burke describes both the physical reactions ('The head reclines something on one side; the eyelids are more closed than usual') and the 'inward sense of melting and languor' induced by 'such objects as excite love and complacency'. He observes:

> From this description it is almost impossible not to conclude, that beauty acts by relaxing the solids of the whole system. There are all the appearances of such a relaxation; and a relaxation somewhat below the natural tone seems to me to be the cause of all positive pleasure. Who is a stranger to that manner of expression so common in all times and in all countries, of being softened, relaxed, enervated, dissolved, melted away by pleasure.[4]

The experience of being 'melted away by pleasure', however, as charted in travel writings, might equally well be defined as a southern, aquatic version of the sublime. The sea and sky, in Dupaty's description and in others of this region, exhibit not only indeterminacy but also infinitude, which Burke cites as a source of sublimity.[5] This southern sublime is less concerned with crossing boundaries than with the loss of a sense of bounded self, amid a natural world that promotes a sense of erasure of boundaries: in other words, with the kind of experience that Freud classifies by reference to the 'Nirvana principle', or tendency towards the suppression of all internal tensions, and corresponding extinction of a sense of individual being.[6] Allusions to the air, as well as to the waves, promote the sense of boundaries dissolving: as Forsyth declares, silently quoting *Macbeth*, this is 'a climate where heaven's breath smells sweet and wooingly'.[7]

Such a dissolution of boundaries is perceived as a more gentle experience than the wild urge to transgress boundaries and exceed limits. For

---

[4] Edmund Burke, *A Philosophical Enquiry into the Origin of our Ideas of the Sublime and Beautiful*, edited by James Boulton (Oxford: Blackwell, 1987), p. 149, pp. 149–50.

[5] Longinus, moreover, in a passage cited in Chapter 2, names 'ocean' as the culminatory natural feature that our aspiring mind leads us to admire; see *Dionysius Longinus on the Sublime*, translated by William Smith, fourth edition (London, 1770), p. 146. On infinitude, see Burke, *Philosophical Enquiry*, pp. 73–4, p. 77.

[6] Sigmund Freud, 'Beyond the Pleasure Principle', in *The Pelican Freud Library*, (Harmondsworth: Penguin, 1972–), translated under the general editorship of James Strachey, vol. 11, edited by Angela Richards, pp. 269–338, p. 329; Freud takes this term from Barbara Low's *Psycho-Analysis; A Brief Account of the Freudian Theory* (London: George Allen and Unwin Ltd, 1920), p. 73.

[7] Joseph Forsyth, *Remarks on Antiquities, Arts, and Letters during an Excursion in Italy in the Years 1802 and 1803*, first edition (London: T. Cadell and W. Davies, 1813), p. 299, adapted from Shakespeare, *Macbeth*, 1.6.5–6.

Swinburne and Dupaty, it is nonetheless identified as dangerous. For Jameson, it is a permissible and harmless pleasure, endorsed not only by her own intense need for relief from emotional suffering but also by her view of her 'vague and languid enjoyment' as 'the true *"dolce far niente"* of this enchanting climate'. The *dolce far niente*, in early nineteenth-century travel writings (literally, the 'sweet doing nothing'), is a form of gratification that is innocent because it offers a relief from care and responsibility that is only temporary; in accordance with the needs of tourism, it allows the traveller to flirt with destabilization, while nonetheless avoiding any truly unsettling loss of agency.[8] Jameson's ironic allusion to her arm, stiff from leaning upon her elbow in her long 'pensive dreamy rapture', delicately indicates the absence of any more serious consequences.

Henry Swinburne, *Travels in the Two Sicilies, in the Years 1777, 1778, 1779, and 1780*, 2 vols (London: P. Elmsly, 1783–85), vol. 2, pp. 162–5

The traveller recounts a journey by sea, sailing past Cape Conca.

When the passage of Capri began to open upon us, we steered S.W. to the Galli, supposed to be the Syrenusæ, or islands once inhabited by the Sirens, which Ulysses passed with so much caution and hazard. Great revolutions have been occasioned in their shape, size, and number, by the effects of subterranean fire; and some learned persons go so far as to assert that these rocks have risen from the bottom of the sea since Homer sang his rhapsodies; consequently, that those monsters dwelt upon some other spot, probably Sicily or Capri. The tradition of Sirens residing hereabouts is very ancient, and universally admitted; but what they really were, divested of their fabulous and poetical disguise, is not easy to discover. It is remarkable, that all the islands at the points of land, which advance into the seas of Italy, were supposed to be the place of residence, or burial of a Goddess or Siren; from which opinion we may argue, that on those promontories some female sovereign once dwelt in times of which no records are existing. As the ancient Germans and Greeks were wont to pay obedience to persons of the weaker sex, it is not absurd to suppose that the old inhabitants of Italy, perhaps sprung from the same stock, were also accustomed to entrust the sceptre in the hands of a woman; the post she chose for her residence was, no doubt, strongly fortified, and well situated for her piratical subjects to dart out upon, and intercept all vessels that navigated those seas in ages when it was impossible to sail at any considerable distance from land. Thus they may have rendered themselves formidable to mankind by violence and

---

[8] See Chapter 5, pp. 230–1.

martial exploits; but it is more natural to vest the power of the Sirens in the arts and corruptions of peace, and more consonant to the idea generally entertained of them. The sweet retreats that abound in the Surrentine peninsula; the enchanting prospects; the plenty of all the necessaries, and even luxuries of life, and the soft temperature of the climate could not fail of attracting strangers: there they must insensibly have acquired a relish for pleasure and indolence that enervated both their bodies and minds, and rendered every other country odious to them. Perhaps, in very remote ages, when Italy was possessed by nations, whose very names are now unknown, there was a period of wealth, elegance, refinement and learning succeeded by ages of barbarism that have effaced all remembrance of it: the subjects of the Sirens may then have excelled in arts and sciences. Their interest and policy might make them superlatively ingenious and industrious in enticing foreigners to their abodes, and equally expert in tainting their rude minds with vice and effeminacy. We have almost certain authority that learning flourished in this part of Europe before the Trojan war, but it was probably in the hands of the priests; the ancient rites practised on the banks of the Avernan lake corroborate this opinion; superstition thus called in to the assistance of vice must have been irresistible, and made it dangerous indeed for an adventurer to land at any port on this coast.

These islands are five in number; on the largest is a watch tower, and the next has a deserted hermitage. We went ashore on the principal one in a cove formed by a crack in the great mass of rocks; a crowd of fishermen were come in to dine and dry their nets.

[Charles Marguerite Jean Baptiste Mercier Dupaty,] ***Sentimental Letters on Italy*, translated by J. [i.e. Giovanni] Povoleri, 2 vols (London: printed for the translator by J. Crowder, and sold by J. Bew, 1789), vol. 2, pp. 206–12. In the French original, *Lettres sur l'Italie, en 1785*, 2 vols (Rome and Paris: de Senne, 1788), the passage is in vol. 2, pp. 301–9, and the number of the letter is 115.**

LETTER CX.
AND THE LAST.

NAPLES

I embarked yesterday before dawn, and went to visit, with the sun, the beautiful islands scattered in the gulph of Naples.

I saw the sun emerging from the sea, and separating the heavens from the waves – the heavens seemed majestically rising, and the waves widely extending their domain. One would have thought that Phœbus had been reposing during the night in the midst of them. I saw him darting his rays on the top of Posilipo, running over the promontory of Miseno, sparkling upon the curling waves that surround the islands of Procida, Ischia and Nisida; then I perceived him towards the horizontal boundary, where the sky rests on the sea, glancing his soft genial rays over Baja and Pozzoli, and the gulph which separates them, over Monte Novo, formed in one night by the eruption of a volcano; and Monte Barbaro, where once ripened the Falernian grape; over the elysian fields, the solemn remains of Cuma, and the ruins of seven cities, which flourished, in happier times, on these delightful shores.

Stay thy course for a moment, bright god of day! – let me run over all these enchanting spots, which nature seems to have created on purpose to relieve and recreate the Romans after the conquest of the world; or to make them forget it, in these delightful retreats!

Here I am, with the foaming sea, on the second portico of the amphitheatre of Misena. After viewing it attentively, I ascend hastily the upper one; thence I contemplate the steps the waves have been making, these eight hundred years, to enter this amphitheatre. How many ages has nature then to herself for completing her revolutions! – I descend at last, and wander, with dry feet, over that astonishing pool called *Piscina Ammirabile*; that immense reservoir, supported at intervals by so many enormous pillars, which present, by their elevation, their mass, their number, their indestructible cement, their majestic vaults, and their ruins, a striking resemblance of the foundations of the Roman empire. I passed before three rows of tombs raised one above another, and half opened to the light by the powerful hand of time.

The bodies of the inhabitants of Misena were deposited on the borders of these waves, separated by a canal from the rest of the sea, which, deprived of all motion, becomes there black, hideous and fœtid; it actually flows no more, it lives no longer, and is a perfect *dead* sea. Behold the elysian fields! – how silent! – how tranquil! – how cool! – how delightful it is to pass a pensive evening under these thick shades, and in these solitary paths! – But see the infernal regions not far off!

Wonderful contrast! How faithfully does Tibullus express it in his beautiful lines, which these awful mansions recall to the mind![9] – Peruse them again, and be struck with horror at the description he gives. After quitting the elysian fields, I went to see the remains of the temples of Venus Genitrix, Diana, and Mercury; the ruins of Nero's baths, and numberless country seats; of stoves, where health was restored, and of baths, where breathed voluptuousness and pleasure; but above all, these delightful shores, so fatal to modesty, and so favourable to love, where the zephyrs, the sea, the air – all contributed to relax

---

[9] [In the original, French edition (*Lettres sur l'Italie*, vol. 2, pp. 304–5), Dupaty inserts here his own translation of lines by Tibullus.]

the mind, and the heart, from the severe yoke of thought;[10] where, amidst the voluptuous accents of voices and effeminate instruments, intermixed with the murmurs of gentle zephyrs, and the sweet notes of the feathered songsters, were dying away the sounds of warlike trumpets, celebrating every where the victories of Rome, and soliciting new ones; where, in short, while generals, consuls, and emperors were singing, dancing and sighing, all the nations were wiping their tears, and breathing for a moment, in peace.

Yes, in the midst of these ruins, even in the condition these shores are in at present, I can easily conceive, that when these temples were entire, when the festivals and mysteries of Venus were celebrating in them, and sacrifices were offered to Mercury; when these various mineral waters, these stoves, these baths, these resorts of voluptuousness, health and strength, were incessantly frequented; when all the theatres were filled with the most distinguished Romans, and the most renowned beauties of Italy; when this gulph was covered with purple sails, flowing streamers, and masts curiously decked with flowers, continually conveying backward and forward frolicksome and brilliant youths, on a sea bestrewed with roses; when, in short, at the hour the sun rapidly descends from the heavens into the sea – at that hour, which is the most inviting of all the evening hours, to soft endearments, and to dalliance; for all then here abandoned themselves to voluptuousness and pleasure, agreeably to the charms of the evening and the place – yes, I can conceive, that then Cicero might be reproached for having a country-house at Baja; that Seneca, when travelling, was afraid of sleeping there more than one night; and that Propertius suspected the fidelity of his Cynthia, the moment she reached that fatal, bewitching spot.

Even I find this place, though so much changed by volcanos and time, though desart, and covered with hanging and falling ruins, every instant disappearing under the waves, – yes, I find it still dangerous: methinks the air has retained something of its ancient corruption, as yet unpurified; the heart begins to feel the forcible influence of it – in this aspect, and in this situation, the thoughts are incessantly rendered more flexible by that vague and light shade, spreading a sable veil over the last glimpses of day, in the heavens, on the sea, and on the summits of the hills and the trees; but above all by the silence, which every moment diffuses itself on this coast, and from the bosom of which rises by degrees the affecting concert of the evening, composed of the melancholy sound of oars dashing the foaming waves, of the distant bleating of flocks, scattered over the mountains; of the hollow murmurs of the sea, expiring on the rocks; of the rustling of the leaves, where the zephyrs never rest; of all those insensible sounds, in short, which,

---

[10] [See Shakespeare, *Hamlet*, 3.1.84–5: 'And thus the native hue of resolution | Is sicklied o'er with the pale cast of thought.']

extended far off in the heavens, on the water, and on the earth, form at this instant an uncertain whisper – a kind of melodious breathing of reposing nature! – Let us quit this dangerous shore, and re-embark for Naples. – After to-morrow we shall return thither.

[Anna Jameson,] *Diary of an Ennuyée*, second edition (London: Henry Colburn, 1826); first published in 1826, pp. 260–2.

Jameson describes a day in March.

8th. – Forsyth might well say that Naples has no parallel on earth.[11] Viewed from the sea it appears like an amphitheatre of palaces, temple and castles, raised one above another, by the wand of a necromancer: viewed within, Naples gives me the idea of a vast Bartholomew fair. No street in London is ever so crowded as I have seen the streets of Naples.

It is a crowd which has no pause or cessation: early in the morning, late at night, it is ever the same. The whole population seems poured into the streets and squares; all business and amusement is carried on in the open air: all these minute details of domestic life, which, in England, are confined within the sacred precincts of *home*, are here displayed to public view. Here people buy and sell, and work, wash, wring, brew, bake, fry, dress, eat, drink, and sleep, &c. &c. all in the open streets. We see every hour, such comical, indescribable, appalling sights; such strange figures, such wild physiognomies, picturesque dresses, attitudes and groups – and eyes – no! I never saw such eyes before, as I saw to-day, half languor and half fire, in the head of a ruffian Lazzarone, and a ragged Calabrian beggar girl. They would have *embrasé* half London or Paris.

I know not whether it be incipient illness, or the enervating effects of this soft climate, but I feel unusually weak, and the least exertion or excitement is not only disagreeable but painful. While the rest were at Capo di Monte, I stood upon my balcony looking out upon the lovely scene before me, with a kind of pensive dreamy rapture, which if not quite pleasure, had at least a power to banish pain: and thus hours passed away insensibly –

> 'As if the moving time had been
> A thing as stedfast as the scene,
> On which we gazed ourselves away.'*

All my activity of mind, all my faculties of thought and feeling, and suffering, seemed lost and swallowed up in an indolent delicious reverie,

---

[11] [Forsyth, *Remarks on Antiquities, Arts, and Letters*, p. 293: 'Naples, in its interior, has no parallel on earth.']

* Wordsworth. ['Peter Bell. A Tale', lines 268–70, slightly altered; William Wordsworth, *Poetical Works*, edited by Thomas Hutchinson and revised by Ernest de Selincourt (Oxford: Oxford University Press, 1981), p. 190.]

a sort of vague and languid enjoyment, the true '*dolce far niente*' of this enchanting climate. I stood so long leaning on my elbow without moving, that my arm has been stiff all day in consequence.

II: Disease, debilitation and delusions of revival

Malarial topographies

Disease, infection and contagion are named in accounts of Italy (as in writings on many other topographies of the foreign) as perils that lurk even – or especially – amid scenes of the greatest allure: Sir William Gell, in his *Pompeiana* (1824), concludes a survey of Campania with the warning:

> This delightful region, the 'pompa maggior della natura,' says Micali, was ever considered, for its soft climate and fertile soil, the compendium of all the prerogatives of Italy. Its wines, its roses, its vases, were equally celebrated; though its diseases should not be forgotten in ancient or modern times.[12]

The disease most often mentioned in writings of this period – malaria – is located in three main regions: the Roman Campagna, Rome itself and the Pontine Marshes, between Rome and Naples. All these areas prompt reflections upon the theme of a lurking peril amid beauty and pleasure. Morgan, in Rome, in her account of the Villa Albani, begins with scenes of delight: 'Its gardens, studded with temples, command a view, terminated by a waving line of acclivities, whose very names are poetry.' She concludes by commenting darkly upon a less obvious presence in these gardens: 'In summer even the custode vacates his hovel, and the Villa Albani is left in the undisputed possession of that terrible scourge of Roman policy and Roman crimes – the Mal-aria; the causes and effects all morally connected, and the strictest poetical justice every where visible.'[13] In the passage from Morgan's *Italy* below, such ironies assume yet more sinister dimensions: the travellers are accosted by 'a lovely creature, that looked on the verge of girlhood and the tomb', who, unknowingly invoking the allure of cultural memory, 'touched my arm playfully with a myrtle branch, and begged with the smile of a young Sibyl to accompany us'.

Malaria, in fact, often becomes entangled, literally and metaphorically,

---

[12] 'Nature at her most splendid.' Sir William Gell and John P. Gandy, *Pompeiana. The Topography, Edifices, and Ornaments of Pompeii*, new edition, 2 vols (London: Rodwell and Martin, 1824), vol. 1, pp. xxiii–xxiv.

[13] Lady Morgan, *Italy*, 2 vols (London: Henry Colburn, 1821), vol. 2, p. 225. For another account of malarial danger in the midst of imaginative pleasure on the road from Rome to Naples, see Henry Sass, *A Journey to Rome and Naples, performed in 1817; giving an Account of the Present State of Society in Italy, and containing Observations on the Fine Arts* (London: Longman, Hurst, Rees, Orme and Brown, 1818), pp. 137–8.

with speculation about pleasure and danger. In *Corinne*, Lord Nelvil, a Scotsman on the Grand Tour, embarking on a romantic relationship with the eponymous heroine, visits the Campagna with her, and suggests that danger not only erupts insidiously amid the charms of the Italian climate, but actually imparts an added allure to such delights (just as, it is implied, his relationship with Corinne gains added piquancy from the dangers that hover over it): 'J'aime . . . ce danger mystérieux, invisible, ce danger sous la forme des impressions les plus douces' ('I love . . . this mysterious, invisible danger; this danger concealed in the form of the softest impressions').[14] John MacCulloch, formulating a sternly admonitory account of the dangers of malarial 'misery and death' in his treatise *On Malaria* (1827), acknowledges the fascination of the pleasures that ensnare travellers to malarial regions by the very effect of irony through which he attempts to dismiss such delights: 'he who, in the language of the poets, wooes the balmy zephyr of the evening, finds death in its blandishments.'[15] The rhetorical usefulness of disease in general, and malaria in particular, in indicating the pleasurable but destructive destabilization that may befall the traveller to Italy, is recognized in a malarial metaphor in William Hazlitt's essay on 'English Students at Rome'. Hazlitt comments on the visitor to this city: 'if ever he wishes to do anything, he should fly from it *as he would from the plague*.' He continues:

> There is *a species of malaria* hanging over it, which infects both the mind and the body. It has been the seat of too much activity and luxury formerly, not to have produced a corresponding torpor and stagnation (both in the physical and moral world) as the natural consequence at present . . . You have no stimulus to exertion, for you have but to open your eyes and see, in order to live in a continued round of delight and admiration.[16]

A change of air

Accounts of malaria merely constitute one element in a more general debate about the reviving and debilitating effects of travel. Sir Thomas Morgan, in an appendix to the first volume of his wife's travel book ('On the state of medicine in Italy, with brief notices of some of the universities and hospitals'), prefaces his account of the 'poison' of malaria by noting other dangers:

---

[14] De Staël, *Corinne*, vol. 1, pp. 132–3.
[15] John MacCulloch, *On Malaria: an Essay on the Production and Propagation of this Poison, and on the Nature and Localities of the Places by which it is Produced* (London: Longman, Rees, Orme, Brown and Green, 1827), p. 381.
[16] William Hazlitt, *Criticisms on Art: and Sketches of the Picture Galleries of England*, edited by W[illiam] Carew Hazlitt, 2 vols (London: 1843–44), vol. 2, pp. 203–4; emphasis added.

> Upon the slightest suspicion of pulmonary disease, it is our custom in England to hurry the patient off to Italy; and the public papers abound with that bitter sarcasm on the practice, 'died in Italy, where he went for the recovery of his health.' From the experience which a rather extensive journey has afforded me, I should think no climate less adapted to an invalid. The extremes of heat in summer are insufferable, and must necessarily prove debilitating to oppressed and feeble constitutions. In winter the cold in some places, and especially at Florence, is intense ... During the early months of spring, the cold at Naples was of the same dry and piercing quality as that which attends our March winds, and the contrast between the sunny and shady side of the street was formidable.[17]

In the Marquis of Normanby's short story 'Change of Air', reproduced in full below, 'the malaria' is mentioned only glancingly, as yet one more danger amid the vagaries of the Italian climate: 'At Pisa and Lucca the very stones perspire the winter through with the terrible Siroc. Rome hath its Malaria: and of all climates under the sun, the most variable perhaps is Naples.' The story is concerned with the same readiness 'to hurry the patient off to Italy' that troubles Sir Thomas Morgan; it recounts the travels of a young Englishman, Augustus Bouverie, who has been sent abroad, on the advice of a physician, in order to recover from the enfeebling effects of 'over-exertion in his last studies at Oxford'. The narrator comments darkly on 'the practice of ordering patients to the South for "change of air"': 'If the victim be of the young, the drooping plant is borne from the fresh and pure air of our isle to the hot-house of the South, there to revive for an interval in appearance, from flushed and fevered blood, and then to sink more rapidly under the influence of the most varying temperatures, extreme in all its variations.'

As in other interventions in this debate, diverse effects of travel and of particular topographies are considered. The narrator of 'Change of Air' declares, at one point: 'The mind and body are closely linked together certainly, and in most cases the disorder of one occasions the derangement of the other.' He then examines the contrary point of view, and is led to conclude that 'as the bodily powers sink in utter languor and prostration, the spirit still retains not only its wonted vigour, but seems to exert itself with more than usual power, to shine with unearthly splendour, and to anticipate, as it were, by the loftiness of its views and conceptions, the pure state of being which it then approaches'. (This provides him with an explanation for the inordinate excitement of the young traveller Augustus Bouverie on finding himself in the vicinity of Rome: 'his sole wonder was, how he could have tarried so long in that dull Lombardy and trifling

---

[17] Morgan, *Italy*, vol. 1, pp. 311–48: p. 346, p. 345.

Tuscany, instead of having hurried by a bird's path at once to the scenes, where all associations of past greatness centred.')

One of the main aspects of travel that is classified as harmful in 'Change of Air' is solitude – the very experience that leads Germaine de Staël to describe travel as 'un triste plaisir', and that prompts Henry Matthews, at Terni, to observe resignedly but mournfully:

> – So I jog on, contented at least, if not happy, to be alone; – though not perhaps, without often feeling the truth of Marmontel's observation:
> 'Il est triste de voir une belle campagne, sans pouvoir dire à quelqu'un, Voilà une belle campagne!'[18]

Lord Normanby quotes the same reflection by Marmontel at the point where he observes that many other young men 'would have joined the pleasures of companionship to those of travel, and have thus provided an antidote against the oppressive feelings of solitude and sadness, that come so unexpectedly over the solitary wanderer in foreign realms'. While he endorses Bouverie's disdain for company 'in enjoying nature's noble scenes', he soon returns to the alarming consequences of solitary travel:

> For the purposes of restoring health and relieving languor, I need not say, that the delights and amusements, which instead of being equal and continuous, are of excitement, and consequently are succeeded by a state of depression proportionate to the degree of elation, must be far more pernicious than beneficial. It is this which renders a companion in society so necessary abroad, as a soother in those intervals, when the spirits flag.

Reminders of the 'desolation' of solitary travel – and the corresponding miseries of being thrown into uncongenial society – recur throughout the narrative, until Augustus, 'tended by the careless hands of strangers', dies in Rome, 'the victim, I am conscious, of an idle counsel, in consequence of southern air, and of the oppressive gloom that attends unbroken solitude'.

Amid the various stages of his decline, Bouverie experiences some moments of revival. (An implicit argument, in this narrative, is that the effects of travel upon health are so diverse that it is hardly surprising that medics and travellers have trouble assessing them in a

---

[18] De Staël, *Corinne*, vol. 1, p. 25. Matthews, *Diary of an Invalid*, p. 250: 'It is sad to see a scene of beauty, without being able to say to someone, "There is a scene of beauty."' The remark, quoted in translation in the Marquis of Normanby's 'Change of Air' (see below, p. 128), seems to be adapted from Jean-François Marmontel's reflection: 'Un Auteur a dit que ce n'est pas tout que d'être dans une belle campagne, si l'on n'a quelqu'un à qui l'on puisse dire: la belle campagne!'; Marmontel, 'Alcibiade, ou le Moi' in *Contes Moraux*, 'nouvelle édition, corrigée et augmentée', 3 vols (Paris: chez Merlin, 1770), vol. 1, pp. 11. I am grateful to Jean-Clément Martin and David A. Powell for their help in tracing this quotation.

level-headed manner.) The first is the initial susceptibity to 'very strong momentary excitements', experienced after crossing the Channel. The second occurs just after his inauspicious arrival in Rome, which he marks by fainting – 'the strongest tribute that perhaps ever pilgrim paid to the overpowering grandeur of Roman greatness': 'A night's repose, however, obviated the immediate bad effects of his journey: and the ardour with which he rose to commence his researches, and gratify his long-nourished curiosity, led him to flatter himself that his health was restored.'

Henry Matthews, in his account of a few days in February, charts a sequence of such moments of revival. While sunshine, in Rome, fails to distract him from the 'constant irritation' of declining health, the works of art in the Palazzo Borghese have some beneficial effect – in particular, the painting by Domenichino that he terms 'his *Chace of Diana*' (see Figure 2). A visit to the studio of Maximilien Laboureur revives him further, by supplying, in the form of a sculpture, an allegory of Hope, which, as he phrases it, speaks 'affectingly' to him.

On the road to Naples, moreover, the salutary effects of motion become apparent. While Matthews is, like other travellers, struck by the pathos of the 'animated spectres' in the malarial terrain, and strongly aware of the danger of banditti, he twice notes the excellence of the road, and comments on the gratifying 'richness and luxuriance' of the landscape.

Lady Morgan [Sydney Morgan, née Owenson], *Italy*, 2 vols (London: Henry Colburn, 1821), vol. 2, pp. 325–7

The inn of Terracina lies down on the coast, a new and spacious building; and on either side the road lie scattered a few small white-washed houses. The ascent to the old town is sufficiently arduous for weary travellers, but we could not neglect a spot where Horace met Mæcenas after his hard day's journey towards Brundisium. If this was the Anxur of Horace! if the ancient town resembled that which now presents itself (and to judge by Pompeii, we may suppose it did) what dens the cities of antiquity must have been! The steep dark streets were narrow passages; in the centre of which the miserable population appeared to live in common. Some were supping, others working; but most lounging on the pavement, which, though filthy, was strewed with myrtles, in honour of some festa*. As we proceeded with difficulty, and suffocated with stench,

---

* Mr. Eustace says, 'this town Terracina *seems* to have been rising rapidly into consideration by its increasing commerce, till the late invasion of the French checked its growth, and threw it back into insignificance!!! With respect to the truth of this observation, it is

to the convent of St Francis (now a college), a lovely creature, that looked on the verge of girlhood and of the tomb, sprang from a group of rickety imps – her eyes of fire, her white teeth, and her dark complexion deeply tinted with the hues of the mal-aria, formed a frightful contrast. She touched my arm playfully with a myrtle branch, and begged with the smile of a young Sibyl to accompany us, being, she said, a good '*cicerone per gli antiquità;*' but alas! we had already our *cicerone*, a poor lame distorted creature, hobbling with difficulty, and telling us, 'the *mal-aria* (in his own words) *had done his business.*'[19]

On reaching the convent (which crowns a fertile acclivity above this ancient town), and entering its cloistered court, perfumed with the fruit and blossoms of a gigantic orange-tree, the first thing that met my eye was an inscription of

'Le donne non entranno qui;'[20]

and I was staring back at the prohibition, when a troop of the young students*, in their clerical habits, passed under the cloister, two by two – all courteously bowing; while the monk who accompanied them, after a few words of conversation, politely observed, that, 'when ladies came so far to see their convent, the general prohibition lost its force.' We found it clean and simple: a supper of vegetables was preparing in the kitchen for the boys. Over each little dormitory was written 'viva Gesu, viva Maria.'

The antiquities of Terracina are rather sites than ruins; and the close atmosphere drove us away before we could examine some broken columns, said to be the remains of the Temple of Apollo, where the Cathedral now stands.

---

only necessary to quote, that he adds, "few places seem better calculated for bathing and public resort than Terracina." – Terracina, infected by the *mal-aria*, and infested by *banditti*; approached and left in all seasons under a military escort, not always then safe!! In summer the direst necessity only induces the natives to pass the road; to sleep on it is death; and the difficulty of overcoming an unnatural drowsiness is well described in Corinna, who trembles for the life of Oswald, regardless of her own.' [See John Chetwode Eustace, *A Tour through Italy, Exhibiting a View of its Scenery, its Antiquities, and its Monuments; Particularly as they are Objects of Classical Interest and Elucidation*, 2 vols (London: J. Mawman, 1813), vol. 1, p. 470 and de Staël, *Corinne*, vol. 2, p. 8; it is in fact Oswald who hastens anxiously to reawaken Corinne, every time that she closes her eyes.]

[19] ['Guide to the antiquities.']
[20] ['Women may not enter here.']
* We were much affected by reading in the public papers lately, that this seminary had been attacked by the banditti, and several of the youth carried to the mountain. We have since heard, that those who were not instantly ransomed were put to death. These poor boys were from all parts of the Roman and Neapolitan States – some of them not above ten or twelve years old. The elevation of the college preserved them from the mal-aria; and their health, appearance, and manners, seemed sedulously attended to.

[Constantine Henry Phipps,] Marquis of Normanby, *The English in Italy*, 3 vols (London: Saunders and Otley, 1825), vol. 2, pp. 112–35

The short story forms part of a collection of similar sketches, in many of which travellers fall into traps or allow themselves to be lured into dangerous entanglements with Italy and the Italians.

CHANGE OF AIR.

The French have a most cruel fashion of disposing, not only of their dead but their dying. They have establishments called *Maisons de Santé*, so named for a similar reason as *lucus a non lucendo*;[21] to which *Houses of Health*, those whose life is despaired of, are, unless they be amongst kind and immediate relatives, handed over. It is like an anticipated burial; and the attempt to deceive patients thus abandoned, concerning the ominous place to which they are removed, is impossible. They are told the change is for better air, for variety, for several promising reasons; but the mansion and its inmates always belie the cheat. In vain the apartments are filled with flowers, and saturated with perfumes, the atmosphere of death that reigns there is rendered but more perceptible to the acute senses of the invalid by these means. The features too, the demeanour of the master and domestics of the fatal abode, inured to behold the last stage of life in so many victims, fail not to strike the nervous attention of the patient, who thus may be said to suffer burial twice, once at the hands of man's unkindness, before the last obsequies are to be gone through from necessity.

Having myself been once a witness of this delicate dread of death, evinced by the host of a young Englishman in Paris, I have entertained ever since an horror of the pretext, under which they got rid of the trouble of watching and soothing his last moments. This was 'change of air;' such was the delusive remedy held out to him, as they caused him to be removed away from their roof and anxieties, to one of these Houses of Health, which might be termed more properly Houses of Death.

In our own country we have no custom of similar, at least of equal barbarity; still there is one, which I cannot but regard with the same feeling. This is the practice of ordering patients to the South for 'change of air.' Many of the physicians who issue this mandate must entertain a very erroneous idea of what the South is. No doubt they imagine it the land of eternal zephyrs, of never varying summer, sunshine, and fragrant vegetation.

---

[21] ['A (dark) grove (*lucus*) by virtue of not being light (*lucendo*)': in other words, named after the quality that represents its exact opposite. A mock-etymology originally formulated by the fourth-century grammarian Maurus Servius Honoratus, in his commentaries on Virgil.]

I fear few of them take into account the Bise or the Siroc, or that the 'land of the South, the clime of the sun,' is the most variable of all climes, and that perhaps in which most precaution is necessary, even on the part of the strong and healthy.[22]

No event is to me more melancholy than one of those warrants, at once of death and exile passed upon the member of a happy family. If it be one of the heads of the family, the whole frame and system of domestic life is disjointed, and away the wanderers are driven forth in discomfort, that they may return mourners with tripled expense, and with the unpleasant reflection of having been compelled to abandon, in a foreign soil, the remains of one that was dear to them. If the victim be of the young, the drooping plant is borne from the fresh and pure air of our isle to the hot-house of the South, there to revive for an interval in appearance, from flushed and fevered blood, and then to sink more rapidly under the influence of the most varying temperatures, extreme in all its variations. With respect to the South of France, Avignon, Montpelier, Hyeres, and neighbouring situations, Petrarch's word may still be taken, '*Ibi cum vento male vivitur, sine vento pessime.*' – 'There with wind life is bad enough, without wind wretched.'[23] Throughout all the South of Italy, even to Florence, the extremes of heat and cold, in summer and winter, rival those of the United States. At Pisa and Lucca the very stones perspire the winter through with the terrible Siroc. Rome hath its Malaria: and of all climates under the sun, the most variable perhaps is Naples. The duration of the cold or northern wind there is generally three days, seldom more, three, six, or nine days being the limits of its continuance. Whilst it blows, the Orkneys are not more frozen than are the beautiful shores of Naples, and even the burning Vesuvius is compelled to bear snow and ice upon its smoking and sulphuric sides. Beneath its influence you see the Neapolitan population briskly moving about enwrapped in their furred *ferraioli*; and in an hour afterward, perhaps, the wind will have changed, the Siroc blowing, and you behold the same people stripped, bent, and feebly crawling under the enervating effects of a wind that actually thaws the marrow in one's bones.

An acquaintance with one victim especially of this medical edict, has led me to bestow a few pages upon it, as hastening in many instances the catastrophe, which it professed to ward off. Over-exertion in his last studies

[22] [Adapted from Byron, *The Bride of Abydos: A Turkish Tale* (1813); see lines 16–17 ("Tis the clime of the East; 'tis the land of the Sun – Can he smile on such deeds as his children have done?'); [George Gordon Noël Gordon,] Lord Byron, *The Complete Poetical Works*, edited by Jerome J. McGann, 7 vols (Oxford: Oxford University Press, 1980–92), vol. 3, p. 103. Lord Normanby quotes the lines just before this in another of the narratives in this collection, 'L'Amoroso'; see vol. 1, pp. 133–4.]
[23] [The quotation is from Francesco Petrarch's *Rerum Senilium Libri*, or *Letters of Old Age*, Book 7.]

at Oxford had enfeebled the health of young Bouverie to an alarming degree. He languished even in the leisure of his paternal home. It was a languor, however, proceeding from a too continued tension of the mental powers, that a continuance of leisure and amusement would have obviated in a little time. But this time is a physician, whose aid, in some cases the only effectual one, anxious parents can seldom bring themselves to await. The expense of calling in an eminent practitioner is looked on as a sacrifice of duty, and in this case was accordingly complied with. The experienced physician saw plainly that drugs were not the remedies fit for removing mere languor; but to order nothing, or to say nothing, after being called in, would be awkward. He mentioned casually in consequence, that a 'change of air' would be recommendable. – 'The continent?' 'Yes, the more variety the better.' And this brief dialogue was considered sufficient ground for dispatching Augustus Bouverie with still unrallied health to the continent. Travelling was but a little physical exertion, and variety, with the 'change of air,' would far counterbalance it, and restore Augustus to his wonted health.

With many youths, no doubt, the simple nostrum would have been effectual; they would have joined the pleasures of companionship to those of travel, and have thus provided an antidote against the oppressive feelings of solitude and sadness, that come so unexpectedly over the solitary wanderer in foreign realms. Augustus himself was delighted with the recipe and the project, and fancied for himself worlds of amusement. But he was naturally reserved and lonely, and thought the very opposite of the French sentimentalist, who esteemed it a sad enjoyment, 'to look on a beautiful scene without having a friend near, to whom he might observe, this is beautiful.'[24] The sentiment, by the bye, is thoroughly French; for my part, I should esteem any friend *de trop* in enjoying nature's noble scenes, and Augustus was of the same opinion, and he resolved to proceed upon his journey with as many letters of introduction to foreigners as would be necessary for his instruction and convenience; but determined to avoid, as much as possible, all connection with his countrymen.

Young Bouverie, in forming this resolution, over-rated considerably the sources of pleasure, which foreign scenes prove to the traveller; or rather he considered falsely such enjoyment to be like a fresh ray of sunshine evenly spread over the whole of one's thoughts and time. On the contrary, he experienced the delights of foreign travels to consist in very strong momentary excitements, awakened at intervals, and at first perhaps of some duration, but gradually and in a little time of a very passing kind. The twenty-four hours subsequent to his landing upon a foreign soil, the two hours of his first morning ramble in Paris – these were moments that indeed

---

[24] [See note 18 above.]

might be reckoned among the choice ones of existence, nay might for enjoyment be classed amongst those hallowed by affection and friendship, – among

> 'The greenest spots
> On Memory's waste.'[25]

But for the purposes of restoring health and relieving languor, I need not say, that the delights and amusements, which instead of being equal and continuous, are of excitement, and consequently are succeeded by a state of depression proportionate to the degree of elation, must be far more pernicious than beneficial. It is this which renders a companion in society so necessary abroad, as a soother in those intervals, when the spirits flag, and cease to be uplifted by the novel scenes in which the fancy has been revelling for some time past to satiety. Augustus Bouverie however had reckoned himself independent for amusement or companionship, or any aid more than his own thoughts, which, with the food of a new world almost before them, he could scarcely look forward to, as even to feel palled, or languid, or melancholy.

Those who have known what it is to find one's self alone in a foreign land, for the first time, surrounded with unfamiliar faces, the ears saluted by sounds harsh and unintelligible, and every object suggesting the present isolation from sympathy or kindness – those who have experienced the fearful weight of despondency, which then presses upon the mind so lately excited to the enjoyment of these same, and now oppressive objects; they can tell how unwisely August reasoned upon the inexhaustibility of his sources of self-amusement, how grievously he was disappointed by the first visitations of languor and ennui abroad. It was unexpected, discredited, and therefore doubly felt; and to shake it off ten times more impossible, than it would have been to dissipate the cloud of English spleen, which the youth had fled from at home.

If this natural feeling of uneasiness in a foreign land be increased to the foreigner in England by the consciousness of an indispensable extravagance of expence, the same feeling is heightened more to the Englishman abroad by the want of the customary comfort of his own dear isle. The walls, the floors, the furniture, are so uncouth, naked, cold, and comfortless; the windows are prison-like, and the mansion itself has the aspect of a jail, with its lodgers, its numbered rooms, and its common stairs. And oh! what desolation is to be compared to that felt by a stranger upon a fine summer or autumnal evening, treading the promenades of a gay city, thronged with faces, of which he knows not one, and resounding with gaiety of which

[25] [Adapted from Thomas Moore, 'Love's Young Dream', lines 25–6.]

he cannot partake – the bustle forbidding him the enjoyment of reverie or pensive thought, whilst the heart is all too young, too aspirant after those joys in view, to allow it to moralize in cold indifference upon the scene. Augustus thought, that continuing his journey south would bring a remedy to these lonely feelings; at least, thought he, Italian solitude will be real solitude in the midst of scenes that cannot but excite and ennoble lonely thought; and to wait here for introductions to arrive, would be useless; the ice would be scarcely broken, when I should be obliged to continue my journey.

He proceeded southward. But for all the promised good effects of change of air, the fatigue of travel counterbalanced them, and Augustus felt his accessions of languor more frequent and deep. No doubt they were increased considerably by exile from the society of the family circle, from the genial friendly faces, in whose presence he had felt cheered and at ease. Now as he journeyed on, his solitude was often though not agreeably interrupted by formal visits, which he was obliged to pay in order to deliver a letter of introduction to some personage famed for literary or scientific acquirements. This sage perhaps conversed theatrically with the young Englishman, much such matter as he had found in their volumes, too close attention to which had worked him his present harm. In return, for which condescension he had his tribute of flattery to pay, followed by the usual superlatives of esteem on the part of the illustrious foreigner. An invitation to resume the *talk* at another opportunity accompanied this, and Augustus departed from the interview, nothing delighted, except with the being able to pass judgment on the personal appearance of the sage of whom he had heard so much.

To pay his passing court to the petty literary potentates became at length as irksome to Augustus, as attendance on the actual courts of the petty reigning potentates of the land would have been to him, had he been a courtier. In both cases there were the same parade and pretensions, rancour, poverty, real prejudice, and affected liberality; the same habit of cringing elsewhere, and being worshipped at home; the same want of power, disguised under a profusion of all the regalia of importance.

Amidst these and other *videnda* of Switzerland and Lombardy were the attentions of the poor Augustus divided, whilst his health was by no means improved under the effects of the Lombard autumnal sun, although the year was somewhat advanced. In the immense plains of the north of the peninsula too, fever and ague were known to lurk. Venice, with its dock-savouring canals, its swarms of musquitos, denial of exercise and crowded lanes, was no tempting abode for the convalescent; and moreover there, above all other places, that peculiar feeling of solitude that drove young Bouverie from Paris, reigns especially. The almost oriental seclusion of the fair, the churlishly closed gondola, the absence of all gentility from even the streets, render the queen of the Adriatic more lonely than Palmyra to the foreigner, who does not intend a stay long enough to permit any attempt to introduce himself into its society.

Hence the delicate youth betook himself to the capital of Tuscany; and here indeed society was every way accessible – Italian and English mingled or apart, high life, low life, middling life, any might be tried, for either experiment or amusement sake. His countrymen too, still on the move, wherever he had not yet encountered them south of Paris, had here drawn up their reins to rest, and even of his fellow Oxonians there were sufficient to have formed a club. But Augustus, much as he admired Englishmen in their proper sphere, that is, at home, failed not to perceive how metamorphosed, spoiled, affected, they all, to a man, became abroad: their characters seemed stretched on the wheel of extravagance, were strained, and disjointed; not one remained the natural islander, the Briton; and flesh fishified is not more unpalatable than your Englishmen, babbling the virtuoso, or aping the gusto, which the Italians have for licentiousness. At Oxford Augustus was not much given to society, his choice of companions was select; but he found many, who had been tolerable on the banks of the Isis, altogether intolerable puppies transported to those of the Arno. His state of health too, did not allow of a flow of spirits able to keep pace with that of his countrymen, excited by foreign scenes and sunshine; and even when elevated to a cheerful mood, his mind sunk at once into gloom, as soon as it came in contact with the still more buoyant feelings of his fellows.

Augustus too was a youth who could not rest contented with the second place even in the scale of mirth and wit; and he shrunk even to his late dreaded solitude, as a refuge from the more tormenting society of his young compatriots. In this determination Florence no longer suited him as a residence; it was too gay, wore too much an air of *fête*, and the sound of his mother tongue was by far too predominant in the streets. The English papers, journals, and publications, procured by the assiduity of Vieusseux, and allowed by the liberality of the ducal government, turned all general conversation more upon England and English affairs, than at all harmonized with the Italian sky and scene, or with the mind that gave itself up with devotion to the contemplation and enjoyment of these.[26] Tilburies too rolled on the smooth pavement of Florence, and the graceful forms of dandies glided in its quays and places. British grooms and valets thronged its hotel doors, and their drunken cockneyisms were heard vociferated in the streets at an hour when every Florentine was in the arms of sleep, and when the restless Augustus walked forth to contemplate the delicious spectacle of

---

[26] [The Gabinetto Vieusseux, founded in 1819, supplied copies of well-known European periodicals.]

an Italian moon-light night, he hoped, in the undisturbed solemnity of the hour.

All these inconveniences, joined with an irrepressible wish to tread the soil of the Eternal City, drove Augustus still further south; and languor, sickness and ennui were all instantly forgotten as soon as the carriage that bore him from Florence was in motion, and ascending the Appenines towards Rome

Poor Augustus! in that journey I happened to be his companion, and never shall I forget the almost unearthly elevation that his spirits rose to with the consciousness of whither he was journeying. In a mind like his, the very enthusiasm of excitement was pernicious to his feeble health, and the restless desire and anxiety awakened by the approach to Rome in this journey was the original cause of the slow fever that afterwards preyed upon Augustus Bouverie, till it consumed him.

The mind and body are closely linked together certainly, and in most cases the disorder of one occasions the derangement of the other. Still that philosophy is sublime and not irrational, which argues the contrary, and founds itself on their disunion; and however the former remark may hold true where actual pain is felt, the arguments of the latter are exemplified in the decay of the body gradually and without pain, by the withdrawing or pining away of the vital principle. It is then, that as the bodily powers sink in utter languor and prostration, the spirit still retains not only its wonted vigour, but seems to exert itself with more than usual power, to shine with unearthly splendour, and to anticipate, as it were, by the loftiness of its views and conceptions, the pure state of being which it then approaches.

It was not the wanness of the cheek of Augustus that struck me with forebodings of his fate, but some of those eccentric flights of fancy, seldom indulged in by those who have a strong hold of life. For his own art, he seemed to lose sight altogether of his precarious state of health: one idea alone occupied his mind; and his sole wonder was, how he could have tarried so long in that dull Lombardy and trifling Tuscany, instead of having hurried by a bird's path at once to the scenes, where all associations of past greatness centred. His day was one long, though interrupted, monologue of raving; from which he sunk, at intervals, to a dreary lethargy, and started thence again each moment to some anticipation of the immortal city, or some recollection of its story. The road by which we travelled was one well calculated to feed the dreamy mood. Spoleto, Narni, and the Thrasymene lay upon our path, and from Hannibal to Octavian, an hundred names of heroic interest were recalled by the scenes through which we passed.

Enthusiasm of this kind lays a firmer hold on the weak frame than on the strong. The robust have their attention and interest so much excited by different external objects, that they shake off the yoke, which one predominant train of feeling would impose upon them. Long abstinence from food, even inanition, and consequent weakness, proves in this way often the strongest of all excitements to the imagination, and even to the spirits; and for a similar reason Augustus was absorbed, inspired almost, by the present exclusive object of his thoughts. He went foodless, sleepless, for both which states he might have found, indeed, an excuse in the beds and fare of Italian hotels. But such were not the causes of his abstinence. He was in consequence worn out completely, ere he did reach Rome; and I shall never forget the fixed, vacant, and scarcely waking, though unwinkling stare, with which he regarded the white houses and steeples of the city, as we descended to it from the hillocks of the Campagna. Before poor Augustus reached the hotel where he was to stop, he paid the strongest tribute that perhaps ever pilgrim paid to the overpowering grandeur of Roman greatness. He had felt ill on approaching the gate; he supported himself during the continuance of the motion; but no sooner had the carriage rolled under the portal, and stopped for the inspection of the officers of police and customs stationed there, than the youth fainted utterly.

A night's repose, however, obviated the immediate bad effects of his journey: and the ardour with which he rose to commence his researches, and gratify his long-nourished curiosity, led him to flatter himself that his health was restored. Augustus wrote home in high spirits a letter to that effect; and his parents congratulated themselves on the superior restorative effect of 'change of air.'

Their son, in the meantime, shunning all society, which he deemed almost sacrilege in such a scene, given up to solitary rambles, was imbibing in long draughts the southern air of Rome, that sovereign remedy that had been prescribed for his debility. His days were spent amidst the hills and desert places of the ancient city – he roamed over the ruined Palatine, through the lanes and by-roads that transect the Cœlian hill, and he more than once utterly lost his way amidst the rural solitude of the once popular Aventine. The sturdy peasant of the Church's realm seldom survives a season of labour in these spots; that the young and weak Englishman felt the little strength he had left undermined by it, is not to be wondered at. In the morn, perhaps, the youth set forth with ardour on his wanderings, but languor and sadness did not fail to accompany him home. Friendly society was that which seemed to restore him to himself most effectually; but when the gloom had begun to prey upon him, he seemed to prefer indulging it, and, like the bird fixed by the witching eye of the snake, he steadily contemplated the spirit of melancholy, until he fell a victim to its voracity.

Augustus still pined; and at Rome as in London, the same forlorn hope, in the shape of a remedy, was held out – 'change of air.' He allowed himself to be borne to Naples. But scenery had lost all charms for his sunken eye. The Sirocco was here far more powerful than at Rome, and blew more incessantly; and the pestiferous blast came even from the sea, whither the sick youth would have looked for pure and refreshing air. The unequalled variability of this boasted climate he found more insufferable, more of harm, and oppressive to him, than any he had as yet visited; and the youth, at his earnest request, was again borne back to Rome. The air of the South was then declared ineffectual, unfit for his case; and a return to England was recommended; but time or strength were not allowed for this new experiment. Augustus Bouverie, alone and exiled from his family, sunk gradually through all the melancholy stages of his disease, tended by the careless hands of strangers, and at last expired, the victim, I am conscious, of an idle counsel, in consequence of southern air, and of the oppressive gloom that attends unbroken solitude.

Henry Matthews, *The Diary of an Invalid. Being the Journal of a Tour in Pursuit of Health in Portugal, Italy, Switzerland and France in the Years 1817, 1818 and 1819*, second edition (London: John Murray, [1820] 1820), pp. 164–70. The synopsis of Chapter VI, after the heading, has been omitted.

This narrative begins in Rome.

February 5th. My health grew worse and worse! Constant irritation. – Day without rest, – night without sleep; at least, sleep without repose, and rest without recreation.

If life, with health and wealth, and all 'appliances and means to boot,'[27] be nothing but vanity and vexation of spirit; what is it, alas! when deprived of all these embellishments?

February 6th. Beautiful day. – The sun shines upon every thing but me. – My spirits are as dark as November; – but *levius fit patientia*![28] Went to the Borghese Palace, to see and admire again Dominichino's *Sibyl*.[29] – His *Chace of Diana* too is a superb picture. – Raphael's *Deposition from the Cross* has too much of his first manner in the execution; – though it is a noble work in conception and design.[30] Here is a fine collection of Titians; – but, with all

---

[27] Shakespeare, *King Henry IV*, 3.1.29.
[28] ['Patience makes lighter'; Horace, *Odes*, 1.24.]
[29] [See Matthews, *Diary of an Invalid*, p. 158, for his earlier account of 'the charming sibyl of Domenichino'.]
[30] [With reference to Vasari's life of the painter, Raphael's 'manner' is usually seen as improving in 'strength' after he comes to Rome, is influenced by Michelangelo, and paints his *Isaiah*. See Giorgio Vasari, 'Vita di Raffaello da Urbino, pittore et archittetto', in *Le Vite de' piu eccelenti pittori scultori e archittettori, nelle redazioni del 1550 e 1568*, edited by Rosanna Bettarini and Paola Barocchi, 6 vols (Florence, Sansoni, 1966–99), vol. 4, pp. 155–214; pp. 175–6; ' Raphael of Urbino, Painter and Architect', in *The Lives of the Painters, Sculptors, and Architects*, translated by A.B. Hinds, 4 vols (London and New York: Dent and Dutton, 1950), vol. 2, pp. 221–49; p. 231.]

2. After Domenichino, *Diana and her Nymphs*, engraved by Giovanni Franco Venturini. 47.4 x 36.1 cm. Victoria and Albert Museum, V&A Images/Victoria and Albert Museum, London (Museum No: 21136). The painting depicted here is now in the Villa Borghese, Rome

their glowing beauties, I doubt, whether the Venetian painters ever give us more than the *bodies*, – either of women, or of men.[31]

February 7th and 8th. Very unwell; – but Democritus was a wiser man than Heraclitus. Those are the wisest, and the happiest, who can pass through life as a play; who, – without making a farce of it, and turning every thing into ridicule, – or running into the opposite extreme of tragedy, – consider the whole period, from the cradle to the coffin, as a well-bred comedy; – and maintain a cheerful smile to the very last scene. For, what is happiness, but a Will-o-the-whisp, a delusion; – a terra incognita, – in pursuit of which thousands are tempted out of the harbour of tranquillity, to be tossed about, the sport of the winds of passion, and the waves of disappointment, to be

---

[31] [The Venetian school was especially known for alluring use of colour. Sir Joshua Reynolds, for example, refers to 'the *Venetian* and *Flemish* schools, which owe much of their fame to colouring'; *Discourses on Art*, edited by Robert R. Wark (New Haven and London: Yale University Press, 1975), p. 34.]

wrecked perhaps at last on the roads of despair; – unless they be provided with the sheet-anchor of religion, – the only anchor that will hold in all weathers. This is a very stupid allegory, but it was preached to me this morning, by a beautiful piece of sculpture, in the *studio* of Maximilian Laboureur. A female figure of Hope has laid aside her anchor, and is feeding a monstrous chimæra. The care and solicitude of Hope, in tending this frightful creature, are most happily expressed; and, if all stones spoke as affectingly as this, Shakspeare's phrase of *Sermons in stones* would be more intelligible than it is.[32]

CHAPTER VI.

February 9th. When the mind is full of fret and fever, the best remedy is to put the body in motion, which, by establishing an equilibrium between the two, may perhaps restore something like tranquillity to the whole system. It was with this hope that I left Rome, before day-break, on my way to Naples, – as fast as four wheels and sixteen legs would carry me; – and there is nothing like the rattling of wheels, to scare away blue devils. The road is excellent; and the posting, however defective it may be in the appearance and appointments of the horses, is in point of celerity, equal to that on the best regulated road in England.

The Pontine Marshes, of which one has heard such dreadful accounts, appeared to me to differ but little from many parts of Cambridgeshire; though the livid aspect of the miserable inhabitants of this region is a shocking proof of its unwholesomeness. – The short, but pathetic reply, made to an inquiring traveller, is well known. – 'How do you manage to live here?' said he, to a group of these animated spectres – 'We die!' – The excellent road which runs through these marshes for twenty-five miles, in a direct line, as straight as an arrow, was the work of the late Pope Pius VI., for which he will receive the thanks of every traveller; but this, like most of his other undertakings, exposed him to the satire of his contemporaries, and it became a proverb, when talking of sums expended in extravagance, to say, '– sono andate alle paludi Pontine.'[33]

Early in the evening, we reached Terracina, – the ancient *Anxur* of the Romans. Its situation is strikingly beautiful, at the foot of the Apennines, and on the shore of the Mediterranean; and it is backed, as Horace has accurately described, '*saxis late candentibus.*'[34] We were induced to halt here, by the representations that were made to us of the dangers of travelling after dark. It seems, we are now in the strong hold of the robbers, where they commit the most barefaced outrages.

[32] [Shakespeare, *As You Like It*, 2.1.17.]
[33] ['They have gone to the Pontine Marshes.']
[34] [Horace, *Satires*, 1.5.26: 'by white rocks that dazzle far and wide'.]

The man, who had no money in his pocket, might formerly dismiss all fear of robbers; – but in these days, an empty purse is no longer a security. These modern desperadoes carry men away even from their homes, for the sake of the ransom, which they think they may extort for their liberation. We are told that two men were lately kidnapped from this neighbourhood, and taken up into the mountains. The friends of the one sent up nearly the sum that was demanded; – the other had no friends to redeem him. The robbers settled the affair, in the true spirit of that cold-blooded savage disposition, that has leisure to be sportive in its cruelty. They sent the first man back without his ears; detaining these, as a set-off against the deficiency in the ransom; – and the other poor fellow was returned in *eight pieces!* – So much for the Italian government. An edict has been lately issued against ransoms, as operating to encourage kidnapping. This may be an excellent law for the public; but it would require the patriotism of Regulus, in an individual falling into the hands of these marauders, to consider the public interest, in preference to his own.[35]

February 10th. Soon after quitting Terracina, we entered the Neapolitan territory, where the road begins to wind among the Apennines; and, for many miles, it is one continued pass through a wild and rugged country. It seems intended by nature for the region of robbers. The government of Naples has adopted the most vigorous measures for the protection of travellers. Small parties of soldiers are encamped, at half a mile's distance from each other, during the whole line of road, from Terracina to Capua. But, *quis custodiet ipsos custodes*?[36] – it is said that the soldiers themselves, after dark, lay aside their military dress, and act as banditti. The richness and luxuriance of the country, between Terracina and Naples, are very striking. Hedges of laurestinus, olives, and vineyards; – orange and lemon groves, covered with fruit; – myrtle, fig, and palm trees, give a new and softer character to the landscape.

The orange-tree adds richness to the prospect, but its form is too *clumpy*, – too round and regular – to be picturesque.

III: Banditti

After 1815, when travel to Italy resumes, in the wake of the final defeat of Napoleon, traveller-narrators constantly touch upon the banditti who prey on travellers between Rome and Naples. Travellers sometimes

---

[35] [Marcus Attilius Regulus, Roman consul, was defeated and captured by the Carthaginians, under the Spartan Xantippus, in Spring 255, and sent to Rome, in order to negotiate peace terms (or, in another version of the tale, to arrange an exchange of prisoners), which he urged he Senate to decline. He kept his word to return if these negotiations were unsuccessful, and was, at least according to legend, put to a cruel death.]

[36] ['Who will guard the guards themselves?'; Juvenal, *Satires*, 6.347–8.]

identify malaria as an element within the social and agricultural conditions that produce brigandage (as Maria Graham does in the second passage below, from her *Three Months Passed in the Mountains East of Rome*); very often, they deploy these wild, lawless figures as metaphors for less readily identifiable dangers. (The fascination with danger in travel writing of this period is perhaps indicated by the fact that, at the very time when the journey onwards to Naples is defined as most dangerous, increasing numbers of travel books proclaim that the traveller has made such a journey.) For Hazlitt, in Rome, the banditti first appear as figments of the disordered English imagination, with only a tenuous basis in reality. Frequent reports of 'murder and robberies' in the papers, he observes, do not lead the English to question the 'goodness, honesty, and industry' of their own countrymen. Nonetheless, 'one similar fact occurring once a year abroad fills us with astonishment, and makes us ready to *dub* the Italians (without any further inquiry) a nation of assassins and banditti'. Ignorance, he argues, fuels unbridled exaggeration:

> If a single Italian commit a murder or a robbery, we immediately form an abstraction of this individual case, and because we are ignorant of the real character of the people or state of manners in a million of instances, take upon us, like true Englishmen, to fill up the blank, which is left at the mercy of our horror-struck imaginations, with bugbears and monsters of every description.[37]

Hazlitt confesses that he himself is not exempt from the influence of these accounts of horror:

> I am at present kept from proceeding forward to Naples by *imaginary* bands of brigands that infest the road the whole way. The fact is, that a gang of banditti, who had committed a number of atrocities and who had their haunts in the mountains near Sonino, were taken up about three years ago, to the amount of two-and-thirty: four of them were executed at Rome, and their wives still get their living in this city by sitting as models to artists, on account of the handsomeness of their features and the richness of their dresses.[38]

Some pages later, at the start of the passage below, Hazlitt returns to the themes of banditti and danger. He and his party, it seems, set out for L'Ariccia, on the road to Naples, but decide not to stay there as planned. He lists a series of presages of danger: 'the deep sandy roads', the sentinels posted along these roads, 'the dreary marshes' and 'the story of Hippolytus painted on the walls of the inn'. The traveller then proclaims his 'strong desire' to cross one further boundary on his Tour:

---

[37] William Hazlitt, *Notes of a Journey through France and Italy* (London: Hunt and Clarke, 1826), p. 310, p. 310, pp. 311–12.
[38] Hazlitt, *Notes of a Journey*, p. 313.

> L'Ariccia, besides being, after Cortona, the oldest place in Italy, is also one step towards Naples, which I had a strong desire to see – its brimming shores, its sky which glows like one entire sun, Vesuvius, the mouth of Hell, and Sorrentum, like the Islands of the Blest.

At this point, the traveller embarks on a more extended account of the considerations that prevent him from crossing the territory that separates Rome and Naples: among them, the very accounts of robbers that he has already dismissed – and continues to dismiss – as exaggerated. Hazlitt stops short of any scrutiny of the concealed desires, impulses and fears that might lurk behind his rationalization of his decision – a refinement of the approach to travel as an adventure of the self that is most famously exemplified by a twentieth-century travel narrative: Freud's 'Disturbance of Memory on the Acropolis'. (In this 'open letter' the traveller-narrator and his brother, on holiday at Trieste, are advised by an acquaintance to travel on to Athens. They spend the hours before they can buy their tickets in a state of gloom, foreseeing 'nothing but obstacles and difficulties'; once the Lloyd offices open, however, they go and book their passages 'as though it were a matter of course'. Freud's later experience of 'derealization' on the Acropolis offers clues to the reasons for this strange behaviour.)[39] Nonetheless, through his declaration that he could resolve the question of proceeding from Rome to Naples only by an apparently arbitrary decision, the traveller at least half-acknowledges that an inner struggle is taking place, and is causing him a certain degree of discomfiture as he cedes to fears rather than desires. A sense of confusion and shiftiness is generated not only by his receptiveness to fears that he has already dismissed as exaggerated, but also by the sequence of completely diverse justifications that he offers for drawing back before a boundary that so many others have crossed.

After a measured assessment of 'the real amount of the danger', then, Hazlitt starts off on a different tack, invoking a friend who sees capture by banditti as an alluring element in the experience of travel as adventurous and destabilizing:

> A friend of mine said that he thought it *the only romantic thing going*, this of being carried off by the banditti; that life was become too tame and insipid without such accidents, and that it would not be amiss to put one's-self in the way of such an adventure.

---

[39] Sigmund Freud, 'A Disturbance of Memory on the Acropolis' (1936; first English translation 1941), in *On Metapsychology: the Theory of Psychoanalysis*, vol. 2 of *The Penguin Freud Library*, translated under the general editorship of James Strachey, edited by Angela Edwards (Harmondsworth: Penguin, 1985), pp. 443–56; p. 450. Freud's allusions to his failure to visit Rome for some years tell another story of inner obstacles to travel overcome: see for example, *The Interpretation of Dreams*, vol. 4 of *The Penguin Freud Library*, translated by James Strachey, edited by James Strachey and Alan Tyson, revised by Angela Richards, The Penguin Freud Library (Harmondsworth: Penguin, 1997), p. 282.

The term *romantic*, here, would seem to denote, in part, an adventure that might play a part in the narrative of a romance. One of the plots of romance on which tales of banditti draw is that of the Gothic novel, in which, in most instances, the topography and culture of southern, feudal, Roman Catholic Europe unleash diverse perils upon those who travel through it. In Ann Radcliffe's *Sicilian Romance* (1790), the Duke de Luovo, a feudal oppressor pursuing two fugitives through the 'wild and savage country' of Sicily in gathering darkness, sees a light among some rocks, and conjectures that 'it might possibly proceed from a party of the banditti with which these mountains were said to be infested'. He is drawn towards a cavern, in which 'the sound of many voices in high carousal' gives way to a drinking song.[40] (Both Hazlitt, in his story of a captured French artist, – and Maria Graham, in her anecdote about Pope Sixtus V in the second passage below, take up this element in the character of literary banditti, and emphasize the brigands' impatience of restraint by accounts of their immoderate drinking.)

The Duke de Luovo also registers an awareness of the feature of these wild, lawless figures that forms the basis for Hazlitt's implicit debate with his romantically inclined friend: the equivocation of banditti between the role of dangerous and violent ruffians, on the one hand, and, on the other, figures so heavily mediated by art and literature, and therefore so readily perceived as characters of romance, that, as Hazlitt explains in the text below, the 'wives or mistresses' of captured bandits (his uncertainty as to their marital status again emphasizing disregard of order and convention) can earn a living as artists' models. Radcliffe's Sicilian duke finds himself in a state of uncertainty as to whether he is encountering ruffians or merely free spirits: 'He would not have hesitated to pronounce this a party of banditti, had not the delicacy of expression preserved in the song appeared unattainable by men of their class.' As he attempts to decipher the clues on offer, he lurches towards the 'romantic' point of view: 'The countenances of the men exhibited a strange mixture of fierceness and sociality; and the duke could almost have imagined he beheld in these robbers a band of the early Romans before knowledge had civilized, or luxury had softened them.'[41]

Thinking that one of the fugitives whom he is pursing is with them, the Duke de Luovo impulsively draws his sword, and then at once turns to flee, but is discovered 'when the light of the fire glittering upon the bright

---

[40] Ann Radcliffe, *A Sicilian Romance*, edited by Alison Milbank (Oxford: Oxford University Press, 1993), p. 84, p. 85.
[41] Radcliffe, *A Sicilian Romance*, p. 85.

blade of his weapon, caught the eye of one of the banditti'. Two of the banditti seize him, and bring him before their chief:

> What were the emotions of the duke, when he discovered in the person of the principal robber his own son! who, to escape the galling severity of his father, had fled from his castle some years before, and had not been heard of since.
> He had placed himself at the head of a party of banditti, and, pleased with the liberty which till then he had never tasted, and with the power which his new situation afforded him, be became so much attached to this wild and lawless mode of life, that he determined never to quit it till death should dissolve those ties which now made his rank only oppressive.[42]

The Duke is in fact allowed to continue on his way, though he does so 'with thoughts agitated in fierce and agonizing conflict' at 'the discovery of his son in a situation so wretchedly disgraceful'.[43] The account of the son's motives nonetheless emphasizes as strongly as possible the lure of the 'romantic' aspect of banditti: while appearing as dangerous and violent captors, they at the same time allegorize the impulse to cross boundaries and exceed limits that, it is assumed, plays a part in the motivation even of the most sedate traveller on the Grand Tour. Danger in the outside world, in other words, literalizes the forces of destabilization within the self. As Hazlitt satirically observes, in commenting on his friend's fascination with capture, the romance plot promises an escape from dull familiarity and stability: 'Assuredly, one is not likely to go to sleep in such circumstances: one person who was detained in this manner, and threatened every hour with being dispatched, went mad in consequence.'

Much of the description in the narrative of encountering banditti in *A Sicilian Romance* obliquely invokes the work of Salvator Rosa, a painter whose frequent depictions of banditti in wild landscapes provides a starting-point for diverse forms of biographical fiction and speculation about his entanglement with such figures. William Beckford, in his *Biographical Memoirs of Extraordinary Painters*, includes artists who evoke Rosa in two of his satirical narratives, 'Andrew Guelph and Og of Basan, Disciples of Aldrovandus Magnus' and 'Blunderbussiana'; in the second, the artist is the son of a bandit chief, and benefits in his art from the abundance of bodies to dissect with which his father's chosen profession supplies him.[44] Radcliffe includes in her narrative of discovering the banditti several references to gleams of light against the darkness – a feature regularly associated with Rosa's work: 'they perceived a light break from among the rocks at some distance', 'it . . . cast a bright reflection upon

---

[42] Radcliffe, *A Sicilian Romance*, p. 85, p. 86, pp. 86–7.
[43] Radcliffe, *A Sicilian Romance*, p. 88.
[44] William Beckford, *Biographical Memoirs of Extraordinary Painters* (London: William Clarke, 1824; first published in 1780), pp. 25–88 and pp. 97–111; see pp. 102–5.

the overhanging rocks and shrubs', 'he beheld, by the light of the fire, a party of banditti', 'the light of the fire glittering upon the bright blade of his weapon, caught the eye of one of the banditti.'[45] Sydney Morgan, in her *Life and Times of Salvator Rosa* (1824), notes this feature of Rosa's work when she describes the paintings inspired, in her account, by his youthful journey into 'the trackless solitudes of Nature' – a journey in which exceeding topographical limits allegorizes his impatience of the constraints of parental authority: his parents oppose his choice of profession. In some works from this period, Morgan observes, the viewer discerns 'a dark and desolate plain, dimly lighted by the livid flashes of a turbulent and stormy sky'. Brigands soon make an appearance:

> The event which most singularly marked the fearless enterprises of Salvator in the Abruzzi, was his captivity by the banditti, who alone inhabited them, and his temporary (and it is said voluntary) association with those fearful men. That he did for some time live among the picturesque outlaws, whose portraits he has multiplied without end, there is no doubt; and though few of his biographers allude to the event, and those few but vaguely, yet tradition authenticates a fact, to which some of his finest pictures afford a circumstantial evidence.[46]

Hazlitt's friend, then, has plenty of mediatory art and literature on which to draw when viewing capture by the banditti as 'the only romantic thing going'. The traveller-narrator himself invokes the 'livid flashes' of Salvator Rosa when he mentions the glare of the assassin's knife (albeit in conjunction with sunlight rather than darkness). He counters the impulse to romanticize banditti by ironic understatement: 'A French Artist was laid hold of by a gang of the outlaws, as he was sketching in the neighbourhood of their haunts, about a year ago; he did not think their mode of life at all agreeable.'

Hazlitt, in other words, endorses his own decision by satirizing those who are attracted by the 'romantic' side of capture – clearly not the only alternative to giving up on the road to Naples altogether. After a digression to Lucien Bonaparte, he sets up another opposition through which to justify not visiting Naples, defining his own disinclination to taking risks in contrast to an absurdly dauntless 'national propensity to contend with difficulty and to resist obstacles':

> A young Englishman returned the other day to Italy with a horse that he had brought with him for more than two thousand miles on the other side of Grand Cairo; and poor Bowdich gave up the ghost in a second attempt to penetrate to the source of the Niger, the encouragement to persevere being in proportion to the impossibility of success!

---

[45] Radcliffe, *A Sicilian Romance*, p. 84, p. 84, p. 85, p. 85, p. 86.
[46] Lady [Sydney] Morgan, *The Life and Times of Salvador Rosa*, 2 vols (London: Henry Colburn, 1824), vol. 1, pp. 108–9.

At this juncture, Hazlitt tries to persuade the reader of the positive charms of caution: declaring that 'the height of my ambition in this line would be to track the ancient route up the valley of the Simplon, leaving the modern road', he touches on the reassuringly mundane pleasures of gastronomy, as the culmination to the more modest adventure of 'clambering up the ledges of rocks, and over broken bridges, at the risk of a sprained ankle or a broken limb, to return to a late, but excellent dinner at the post-house at Brigg!'

One page later (just after the passage reproduced here), the traveller concludes his discussion of banditti by a summary that seems to dismiss such caution as unnecessary: 'In short, any one I believe can pass with proper precaution from Rome to Naples and back again, with tolerable, if not with absolute security.'[47] His sequence of vacillations and near-contradictions invest the road to Naples with a sinister drama – a power to throw any sense of self-possession into disarray – that would be absent from a more confident and consistent account of its dangers.

Dodging real and 'romantic' banditti

Maria Graham, in the second commentary on banditti below, presents herself as tempted by the 'romantic' aspects of her theme, at the same time as she attempts to remain within the sphere of 'authentic fact':

> The notices of the banditti might have been more full and more romantic, but the writer scrupulously rejected all accounts of them, upon the truth of which she could not rely, thinking it better to give one authentic fact, than twenty doubtful, though more interesting, tales.[48]

Graham, however, uses the term *romantic* in a rather different way from Hazlitt: she evokes, here, merely the wild fabrication characteristic of local gossip. In her next few sentences, she suggests that the categories supplied by folkloric and literary tradition need not in fact mislead us, but can be used to make sense of information acquired through precise, on-the-spot observation:

> The banditti or forusciti of Italy are what the forest outlaws of England were in the days of Robin Hood. They are not of the poorest or vilest of the inhabitants. They generally possess a little field and a house, whither they retire at certain seasons, and only take the field when the hopes of plunder allure them, or the fear of a stronger arm drives them to the woods and rocks.[49]

---

[47] Hazlitt, *Notes of a Journey*, p. 325.
[48] Maria Graham, *Three Months Passed in the Mountains East of Rome, during the Year 1819* (London: Longman, Hurst, Rees, Orme and Brown; Edinburgh: A. Constable & Co., 1820), p. v.
[49] Graham, *Three Months*, p. v.

Graham draws on literary texts, in combination with works of scholarship, throughout her narrative, and uses the former as well as the latter to affirm her views on the society that produces brigandage. In the passage below, an epigraph from Gray's 'Alliance of Education and Government' designates the 'mountain cliffs' as 'the rough abode of want and liberty' – a theme that she explores further in the course of the chapter that follows.

The traveller combines commentary on society and manners with a narrative of adventure and danger. Both these elements are introduced at the beginning of her initial chapter:

> To avoid the great heat of Rome during the summer of 1819, the writer of the following pages, and two other persons, determined to go to some of the neighbouring villages to spend a few weeks. Accident determined in favour of Poli, between Tivoli and Palestrina: and as circumstances occurred whilst we were there which we believed might give some insight into the manners of a class of inhabitants not often brought into contact with foreigners, and therefore little known in England, – namely, the farmers and peasants, – a sort of journal was kept of every thing material that occurred. During the last days of our stay at Poli, however, the interest we had taken in the people around us was superseded by one to which a considerable degree of danger was joined.[50]

A company of banditti, she reveals, have stationed themselves at 'the rock of Guadagnola, two hours' walk from Poli', and have been making excursions 'to our very gates'.[51]

In the chapters that follow, Maria Graham, her husband and a friend, together with 'our servant, a Caffre, from the Mozambique channel', travel from Rome to Poli, find themselves trapped there by the proximity of the brigands, but eventually escape to Tivoli and then back to Rome.[52] The passage below begins at the end of Chapter 5, as they return to Poli after a brief visit to Palestrina. A reference to the banditti acquires added premonitory force from the ostensibly casual manner in which they are introduced, in a mere subordinate clause: 'as we were ignorant that at that very moment a troop of banditti, which the government has not power to suppress, was within a short distance of our road, our little journey was one of uninterrupted enjoyment.'

For much of the next chapter, the effect of suspense produced by this elliptical introduction of the brigands is maintained: prolonged reflections on the social habits of mountain-dwellers delays any further information about the specific inhabitants of the region threatening the travellers. These reflections, we are eventually told, are prompted by 'a

---

[50] Graham, *Three Months*, pp. 1–2.
[51] Graham, *Three Months*, p. 3.
[52] Graham, *Three Months*, p. 180.

shocking scene': 'something that we took for a heap of linen for bleaching' turns out to be, instead, 'a young man just murdered'. The murder, though not directly attributable to the banditti, indicates the state of the country that allows them to flourish. Danger now impinges more closely: Graham's party are threatened by the mother of one of the murderers when they refuse to employ him as a servant and so 'screen him from punishment'.

As the chapter concludes, 'a gang of gypsies' appears. The gypsies provide occasions for further literary mediation of the topography (references to Autolycus in *The Winter's Tale*), but also for a new warning of danger: both the travellers and the local inhabitants regard them as forerunners of the banditti. The lurking menace of these figures is briskly noted through an invocation of vices too unpalatable to specify: 'Their character is not at all more respectable here than in other countries.'

Reports of the approach of brigands are mentioned at this point, but it is only at the beginning of chapter 7 that Graham positively affirms that their arrival on the scene is imminent: 'The morning after, at day-break, the gypsies had all disappeared, and we learned with certainty that the banditti were at Guadagnola' (see Figures 3 and 4).[53]

Both locals and gypsies supply occasions for bold cross-cultural comparisons. After quoting Gibbon's 'observation, that the pastoral manners, which have been "adorned with the fairest attributes of peace and innocence, are much better adapted to the fierce and cruel habits of a military life"', Graham notes that this remark, 'though it concerns the wandering Tartars, is equally applicable to the shepherds of the Appenines, between whom and the wandering tribes of northern Asia there are some points of resemblance'. 'A regular annual migration from the mountain to the plain' befits the shepherd for 'the wandering life and desultory habits of the outlaw', and, while Switzerland is an exception to this rule, 'the Spanish mountaineers, in the Guerilla war, displayed a spirit too like the banditti of the Appenines, and it is scarcely "sixty years since," the Caterans of the Highlands of Scotland might have emulated the brigands of Sonnino'. The gypsies prompt a similarly wide range of reference:

> One of them said, her mother was born at Alexandria, in Egypt, and was the head of the tribe in Italy. We talked with them some time, and found that their own dialect was the same with that of the gypsies of England and Spain, and the Bohemians of France and Germany, which Richardson and Schlegel have long since recognised to be that of the Nats of Hindostan.

---

[53] Maria Graham, *Three Months*, p. 151.

The gypsy children, however, 'looked so like a scene at Hampstead, or Blackheath, that we felt almost good-will towards what reminded us so much of home'. The sudden deflection to the familiar, after the traveller's speculations have drawn her to diverse and far-flung topographies, impresses upon the reader the paradoxical role of Italy, as a country in which strangeness and familiarity are combined and intermingled.

'Pose'

In the next chapter of her book, Graham offers a description, gleaned at second hand, of the mode of dress and general appearance of the brigands; she also includes an illustration of these savage figures, and of local peasants searching for them (Figures 3 and 4).[54] Hazlitt, too, emphasizes the visual impact of banditti, in mentioning the work that the 'wives or mistresses' of captured brigands find as artists' models, and noting the costume and demeanour of those captives who are employed as forced labourers on the streets of Rome.

In their role as colourful folkloric figures (literally so: the convicts wear 'striped yellow and brown dresses'), banditti join an array of stock figures who, in early nineteenth-century travel writings (and for the rest of the century) summon up these 'streets of Rome', as well as those of Naples and other cities, and supply a spectacle of 'il popolo': the *lazzarone* (in Naples), the *improvvisatore* (the female *improvvisatrice*, anglicized as *improvisatrice*, is usually seen as operating only in the higher echelons of society, however humble her origins), the *pifferare* (or piper), the *trasteverino* and *trasteverina* (for the inhabitants of Trastevere, the *rione*, or quarter, of Rome that lies across the Tiber from the main part of the city) and the *contadino* and *contadina* (respectively, male and female peasants).[55]

By assimilating banditti into this cast of picturesque characters, travellers frequently persuade themselves that even the brutal murderers who threaten them on the very roads crucial to their journey to the warm South can be converted into a source of diversion and delectation.[56] Matthews describes captured banditti not only as a part of the local

---

[54] Maria Graham, *Three Months*, pp. 154–6.

[55] Eustace, in his *Tour through Italy*, vol. 2, p. 43, supplies an etymology for the term *lazzaroni*, so frequently used for the beggars of Naples: 'Its derivation is a subject of conjecture; the most probable seems to be that adopted at Naples itself, which supposes it to originate from the Spanish word *lacero*, derived from *lacerus*, signifying tattered, torn or ragged, pronounced by the Spaniards as by us, *lassero*, and converted by the Neapolitans into *lazzero*, *lazzaroni*.'

[56] On French paintings of imprisoned banditti, among other representatives of 'il popolo', see Stephen Bann, 'Le peuple romain', in *Maestà di Roma: d'Ingres à Degas; les artistes français à Rome*, exhibition catalogue (Rome, Electa, 2003), pp. 244.

scenery but also as figures who, through the absurd paradox of their strategy of survival, comically displace the unease of encountering the more dangerous elements of southern Europe. In Rome, he introduces some sociable (and characteristically bibulous) banditti who are not only on display as tourist attractions, safely framed and bounded by the limits of their prison, but who also demonstrate a spirit of commercial enterprise that fits incongruously with their lawless profession:

> *April* 28. Visited again and again the relics of 'Almighty Rome.' At this delightful season you are tempted to pass the whole night in wandering among the ruins, which make a more solemn impression, than when lighted up by the 'garish eye' of day. I have never encountered any obstruction in these midnight rambles, nor seen any robbers, except the other evening, in the castle of St. Angelo. I had ascended to the roof to enjoy the view, when I observed a party drinking wine on the leads, who very courteously invited me to partake of their good cheer. I found that these fellows were the leaders of a gang of robbers, for whose apprehension a large reward had been offered. As the robbing trade was becoming slack, they hit upon the ingenious expedient of surrendering themselves, in order to obtain it; and it is not a little extraordinary that the Government should have consented to these terms, so that these fellows will, after a confinement of a year in the castle of St. Angelo, be let loose again upon society. In the mean time, they seem to live pleasantly enough; the English go and talk to them about the particulars of their robberies, and I am told that one of our countrywomen has made them a handsome present. This is a strange mode of putting down robbers, but, if it were not to see strange things, who would be at the pains of travelling – for, after all, I believe Madame de Stael is right, when she calls it a '*triste plaisir*'.[57]

When Henry James considers the fascination with such figures in *Italian Hours*, his choice of words registers an awareness that one of the preconditions for converting 'il popolo' into local colour is the longer-established strategy of defining Italy as a country where everything aspires to the condition of art: 'if we think, nothing is more easy to understand than an honest ire on the part of the young Italy of to-day at being looked at by all the world as a kind of *soluble pigment*'. Adopting the term *pose* for this effect, he implies that the terminology of 'il popolo' plays a part in producing it:

> Young Italy, preoccupied with its economical and political future, must be heartily tired of being admired for its eyelashes and its pose. In one of Thackeray's novels occurs a mention of a young artist who sent to the Royal Academy a picture representing 'A Contadino dancing with a Trasteverina at the door of a Locanda, to the music of a Pifferaro.' It is in this attitude and with these conventional accessories that the world has hitherto seen fit to represent young Italy, and one doesn't wonder that if the youth has any spirit he should at last begin

---

[57] Matthews, *Diary of an Invalid*, pp. 242–3.

to resent our insufferable aesthetic patronage . . . I see a new Italy in the future which in many important respects will equal, if not surpass, the most enterprising sections of our native land. Perhaps by that time Chicago and San Francisco will have acquired a pose, and their sons and daughters will dance at the doors of *locande*.[58]

William Hazlitt, *Notes of a Journey through France and Italy* (London: Hunt and Clarke, 1826), pp. 319–24

We had some thoughts of taking a lodging at L'Ariccia, at the Caffé del Piazza, for a month, but the deep sandy roads, the centinels posted every half-mile on this, which is the route for Naples (which shewed that it was not very safe to leave them), the loose, straggling woods sloping down to the dreary marshes, and the story of Hippolitus painted on the walls of the inn (who, it seems, was 'native to the manner here'), deterred us.[59] L'Ariccia, besides being, after Cortona, the oldest place in Italy, is also one step towards Naples, which I had a strong desire to see – its brimming shores, its sky which glows like one entire sun, Vesuvius, the mouth of Hell, and Sorrentum, like the Islands of the Blest – yet here again the reports of robbers, exaggerated alike by foreigners and natives, who wish to keep you where you are, the accounts of hogs without hair, and children without clothes to their backs, the vermin (animal as well as human), the gilded hams and legs of mutton that Forsyth speaks of, gave me a distaste to the journey, and I turned back to put an end to the question.[60] I am fond of the sun, though I do not like to see him and the assassin's knife glaring over my head together. As to the real amount of the danger of travelling this road, as far as I can learn, it is this – there is at present a possibility but no probability of your being robbed or kidnapped, if you go in the daytime and by the common method of a Vetturino, stopping two nights on the road. If you go alone, and with a determination to set time, place, and circumstances at defiance, like a personified representation of John Bull, maintaining the character of your countrymen for sturdiness and

---

[58] Henry James, *Italian Hours*, edited by John Auchard (University Park, Pennsylvania: Pennsylvania State University Press, [1909] 1992), p. 103.

[59] [Shakespeare, *Hamlet*, 1.4.16. In Greek mythology and in Euripides' *Hippolytos*, the son of Theseus is destroyed as a result of the adulterous passion that his stepmother Phaedra expresses towards him; Hippolytus himself rejects her advances. The story, it would seem, reminds Hazlitt of the dangers of crossing boundaries and transgressing limits.]

[60] [See Forsyth, *Remarks on Antiquities, Arts, and Letters*, p. 298; in Naples, the traveller remarks: 'Carving is tormented, and gold-leaf laid on wherever it can find room. A rage for gilding runs through the nation. It disfigures walls, furniture, carriages. Even the hackney calash must have its coat of gold, the collar-maker gilds his harness, the apothecary gilds his pills, the butcher sticks gold-leaf on his mutton.'

In the second edition (London: John Murray, 1816), the traveller employs the expression: 'the collar-maker gilds his hames' (p.272); in the context of gilded legs of mutton, this is presumably the source for Hazlitt's 'gilded hams'.]

independence of spirit, you stand a very good chance of being shot through the head: the same thing might happen to you, if you refused your money to an English footpad; but if you give it freely, like a gentleman, and do not stand too nicely upon a punctilio, they let you pass like one. If you have no money about you, you must up into the mountain, and wait till you can get it. For myself, my remittances have not been very regular even in walled towns; how I should fare in this respect upon the forked mountain, I cannot tell, and certainly I have no wish to try. A friend of mine said that he thought it *the only romantic thing going*, this of being carried off by the banditti; that life was become too tame and insipid without such accidents, and that it would not be amiss to put one's-self in the way of such an adventure, like putting in for the grand prize in the lottery. Assuredly, one is not likely to go to sleep in such circumstances: one person who was detained in this manner, and threatened every hour with being dispatched, went mad in consequence. A French Artist was laid hold of by a gang of the outlaws, as he was sketching in the neighbourhood of their haunts, about a year ago; he did not think their mode of life at all agreeable. As he had no money, they employed him in making sketches of their heads, with which they were exceedingly delighted. Their vanity kept him continually on the alert when they had a moment's leisure; and, besides, he was fatigued almost to death, for they made long marches of from forty to fifty miles a day, and scarcely ever rested more than one night in the same place. They travelled through bye-roads (in constant apprehension of the military) in parties of five or six, and met at some common rendezvous at night-fall. He was in no danger from them in the day-time; but at night they sat up drinking and carousing, and when they were in this state of excitement, he was in considerable jeopardy from their violence or sportive freaks: they amused themselves with presenting their loaded pieces at his breast, or threatened to dispatch him if he did not promise to procure ransom. At last he effected his escape in one of their drunken bouts. Their seizure of the Austrian officer last year was singular enough: they crept for above a mile on their hands and knees, from the foot of the mountain which was their place of retreat, and carried off their prize in the same manner, so as to escape the notice of the sentinels who were stationed at short distances on the road side. Some years since a plan was laid to carry off Lucien Bonaparte from his villa at Frascati, about eleven miles from Rome, on the Albano side, where the same range of Apennines begins: he was walking in his garden and saw them approaching through some trees, for his glance is quick and furtive; he retired into the house, his valet came out to meet them, who passed himself off for his master, they were delighted with their sham-prize, and glad to take 4,000 crowns to release him. Since then Lucien Buonaparte has lived in Rome. I remember once meeting this celebrated character in the streets of Paris, walking arm in arm with Maria Cosway, with whom I had drunk tea the evening before.[61] He was dressed in a light drab-coloured great-coat, and was then a spirited, dashing-looking young man. I believe I am the only person in England who ever read his CHARLEMAGNE. It is as clever a poem as can be written by a man who is not a poet. It came out in two volumes quarto, and several individuals were applied to by the publishers to translate it; among others Sir Walter Scott, who gave for answer, 'that as to Mister Bonaparte's poem, he should have nothing to do with it.' Such was the petty spite of this understrapper of greatness and of titles, himself since titled, the scale of whose intellect can be equalled by nothing but the pitifulness and rancour of his prejudices! The last account I have heard of the exploits of Neapolitan banditti is, that they have seized upon two out of three Englishmen, who had determined upon passing through Calabria on their way to Sicily, and were proceeding beyond Pæstum for this purpose. They were told by the Commandant there, that this was running into the lion's mouth, that there were no patrols to protect them farther, and that they were sure to be intercepted; but an Englishman's will is his law – they went forward – and succeeded in getting themselves into *the only remaining romantic situation*. I have not heard whether they have yet got out of it. The national propensity to contend with difficulty and to resist obstacles is curious, perhaps praiseworthy. A young Englishman returned the other day to Italy with a horse that he had brought with him for more than two thousand miles on the other side of Grand Cairo; and poor Bowdich gave up the ghost in a second attempt to penetrate to the source of the Niger, the encouragement to persevere being in proportion to the impossibility of success! I am myself somewhat effeminate, and would rather 'the primrose path of dalliance tread;'[62] or the height of my ambition in this line would be to track the ancient route up the valley of the Simplon, leaving the modern road (much as I admire the work and the workmen), and clambering up the ledges of rocks, and over broken bridges, at the risk of a sprained ankle or a broken limb, to return to a late, but excellent dinner at the post-house at Brigg!

What increases the alarm of robbers in the South of Italy, is the reviving of old stories, like the multiplication of echoes, and shifting their dates indefinitely, so as to excite the fears of the listener, or answer the purposes of the speaker. About three years ago, a desperate gang of ruffians infested the passes of the Abruzzi, and committed a number of atrocities; but this gang, to the amount of about thirty, were seized and broken up, their ringleaders beheaded in the Square di Popolo at Rome, and their wives or mistresses now live there by sitting for their pictures to English artists. The remainder

---

[61] [Maria Cosway (1760–1838), well-known artist, known also for her romantic entanglements with the Corsican general Pasquale Paoli (an associate of Lucien's brother Napoleon) and (in Paris) with Thomas Jefferson, future president of the United States.]

[62] [Shakespeare, *Hamlet*, 1.3.50–1.]

figure as convicts in striped yellow and brown dresses in the streets of Rome, and very civilly pull off their hats to strangers as they pass.

Maria Graham, *Three Months Passed in the Mountains East of Rome, during the Year 1819* (London: Longman, Hurst, Rees, Orme and Brown; Edinburgh: A. Constable & Co., 1820), pp. 135–50. The long synopsis of Chapter VI that follows the epigraph has been omitted.

Every beauty that a wild country, adorned by the light of a fine setting sun and an Italian sky, can present, we enjoyed in our walk homewards. The mountain rivulets, wild woods, and steep rocks, here and there interrupted by a corn-field or a threshing-floor, and enlivened by flocks of goats, or herds of oxen going to their nightly shelter, were finely contrasted with the long, low line of the Campagna, which now and then appeared through an opening between the hills; and, as we were ignorant that at that very moment a troop of banditti, which the government has not power to suppress, was within a short distance of our road, our little journey was one of uninterrupted enjoyment.

3. 'Peasants in Search of Banditti', in Maria Graham, *Three Months Passed in the Mountains East of Rome, during the Year 1819* (London: Longman, Hurst, Rees, Orme and Brown; Edinburgh: A. Constable & Co., 1820), facing page 170. Drawn by 'C.L.E.' and engraved by I. Clark. 10.7 x 16.5 cm

4. 'Station of the Brigands near Guadagnola', in Maria Graham, *Three Months Passed in the Mountains East of Rome*, facing page 153. Drawn by 'C.L.E.' and engraved by I. Clark. 10.6 x 16.6 cm

CHAP. VI.

The manners speak the idiom of their soil,
An iron race the mountain cliffs maintain,
Foes to the gentler genius of the plain.
And while their rocky ramparts round they see,
The rough abode of want and liberty,
Insult the plenty of the vales below.

GRAY'S Fragment[63]

A day or two after our visit to Palestrina, we walked to the top of a little hill, which had struck us on our way from that place, as a fine point whence we might command the view of the surrounding country. We found it was the direct road to Capranica, which supplies all the neighbouring district with shepherds. From this height, nearly the same objects were seen as from the surrounding hills, and to attempt to describe them, would be to repeat the same words. But, in the natural combinations of objects, the slightest change may often give a life and variety to the picture, which language

---

[63] [Adapted from lines of Thomas Gray's 'The Alliance of Education and Government. A Fragment', Essay 1, lines 87-9, 96-7, 99.]

cannot reach, and to be equalled only by the passing clouds which vary its lights and shadows.

 Here, while resting on the grass, and looking down upon Rome, which was partly obscured by the clouds of smoke rising in different parts of the Campagna, from the chaff burned near the work-people's huts, partly to diminish the effects of the bad air, and partly to destroy the locusts, we naturally thought of the history of the eternal city, and of its heroes. The spot we were on fixed our attention on the middle ages. Here, perhaps on this very rock, was the mule with the jar of oil seized by robbers, which gave Rienzi occasion to exercise his wholesome severity on a nobleman of Rome: the Ursini Lord of Capranica was 'condemned to restore the damage, and to discharge a fine of four hundred florins for his negligence in guarding the high ways.'* The short government of the Tribune freed the country from robbers: travelling became secure; and plenty flowed from all quarters towards Rome, the merchant incurring no risk of the loss of his goods by the way. Unhappily Rienzi grew giddy with power and success. He owed his fall to himself, and one of its first consequences was, the re-assembling of the banditti, and the consequent insecurity of the country.†
This rock was nearly the boundary of the rival houses of the Ursini and Colonna, and witnessed many of their feudal strifes.‡ The Conti, also, whose adopted arms, the bear chained to the column§, refers to the victory they gained in behalf of the Colonna over their rivals, bore no inconsiderable part in these irregular but sanguinary quarrels; and the castle of Poli, in those times, was the chief fastness of their vassals. The hills all around are

---

* Gibbon, chap. lxx. [*Gibbon's Decline and Fall of the Roman Empire*, introduced by Christopher Dawson, 6 vols (London and New York: Dent and Dutton, 1954), vol. 6, pp. 512–63. Much of this chapter is concerned with the career of Nicholas Rienzi Gabrini (1313–54), a popular leader who briefly governed Rome as 'tribune' in the mid-fourteenth century.] See also the curious life of Cola di Rienzi, by a contemporary, written in the low Roman dialect of the time, which is a curious contrast to the language of Petrarch, the friend of the Tribune. When Petrarch went from Avignon, to visit Robert, king of Naples, he stopped at Capranica, where he spent some weeks, and in one of his letters speaks of the beauty of the surrounding country. [The last part of this sentence, after 'some weeks', is an addition inserted in the second edition: see Maria Graham, *Three Months Passed in the Mountains East of Rome, during the Year 1819* (London: Longman, Hurst, Rees, Orme and Brown; Edinburgh: A. Constable & Co., 1821), p. 138.]

† There is a curious burlesque poem, the Maggio Romanesco, that throws some light on the state and character of the Roman populace, in the time of Rienzi. [*Il Maggio Romanesco*, by Giovanni Camillo Peresio (1628–96), was published in 1688.]

‡ Cecconi's History of Palestrina. [Leonardo Cecconi, *Storia di Palestrina, città del prisco Lazio* (Ascoli: 'Per Nicco a Ricci Stampator pubblico', 1756).]

§ See Flaminio Vacca, §105, for the Arms of Conti Cesarini. [This footnote is added in the second edition; see Flaminio Vacca, 'Memorie di varie antichità trovate in diverse luoghi della città di Roma scritte da Flaminio Vacca nell'Anno 1594', in Antonio Nibby, *Roma Antica di Famiano Nardini, riscontrata, ed accresciuta delle ultime scoperte, con note ed osservazioni critico antiquarie* (Rome: 'Nella Stamperia de Roma', [1665] 1818–20), vol. 4, pp. 1–50 (paginated as separate text), p. 41.]

scooped into caves now used for the cattle, but the songs and traditions of the inhabitants, as well as those of the low Romans, assign them to the robbers, from time immemorial.

One of these tales is told of Sixtus V., who went in disguise, like an old man, with an ass laden with wine, into the woods. The robbers, of course, seized him, and caused him to turn the spit in the cave while they examined the wine. Sixtus muttered to himself that he saw them do that with pleasure. 'What say you?' said they. 'Only that I shall eat with pleasure when the roast is done.' 'So you may, but we shall drink all the wine ourselves.' 'Alas, gentlemen, wine is not made for a poor man like me, who only carry it about for others, and who will, perhaps, be put in prison for my misfortune in losing this, which is precious.' So saying, he returned to his office at the fire. At length the meat was done, the supper eaten, and the wine drank, to the great delight of Sixtus, who had mixed opium in it; and, as soon as he saw the band fairly asleep, he whistled, his soldiers came up, and they were every one taken.

From the time of Rienzi, the vigorous government of Sixtus V. is the only one during which the banditti were kept under. After him, all laws and regulations and threats have proved ineffectual, and their depredations have continued, excepting during the short period that the French military government kept them in awe.

We had heard from some peasants bringing their corn to be ground at the mills near Poli, that the robberies lately committed on the road between Rome and Naples, had determined government to rase the town of Sonnino, which had opened its gates to the banditti, and had, in fact, long been their head-quarters, to the ground. Indeed, the first report was, that the town had actually been battered down, and all the inhabitants put to death in the night. The peasants, who gave this evidently exaggerated account, were of opinion that the men must certainly have been absent from the town, or they would never have suffered it to be so surprised; and, in that case, they foretold the most dreadful consequences to whoever should fall into their hands, by way of reprisal for the murder of their wives and children. At any rate, whether Sonnino were destroyed or not, where the brigands, who would certainly leave the town as soon as they heard of the severe proclamation issued against them, would go to, was a matter of serious and anxious conjecture.

Two years ago, on a similar occasion, the noted De Cesaris, who was shot last spring near Terracina, led his followers up to these hills, and for nearly two months they subsisted on the spoil of the neighbouring townships. On such expeditions the banditti are always aided by the shepherds and goat-herds, a race of men apt for their purposes, as their half-savage life, while it gives them enough intercourse with the towns to procure food and intelligence, detaches them so much from all social bonds as to render them indifferent to the crimes of others.

The observation, that the pastoral manners, which have been 'adorned with the fairest attributes of peace and innocence, are much better adapted to the fierce and cruel habits of a military life*,' is confirmed by the manners of the shepherds of these mountains. Where the townships have land enough to employ the inhabitants in agriculture and gardening, as at Poli, the inhabitants are kind and gentle; and when an outrage is committed, the first exclamation always is, he who has done the evil must be an idle fellow, who had not patience to wait while his bread was growing. But Capranica, and some other mountain towns, which have little or no arable land annexed to them, while they supply their neighbours with shepherds, also furnish their annual quota to the ranks of the banditti. The observation of Gibbon, quoted above, though it concerns the wandering Tartars, is equally applicable to the shepherds of the Appenines, between whom and the wandering tribes of northern Asia there are some points of resemblance.

The unhealthiness of that great portion of Italy extending between the mountains and the sea, from the banks of the Arno to Terracina, renders it scarcely habitable during the summer months, and has forced the proprietors to adopt a system of management by which the lands in general only come into tillage every sixth or seventh year in rotation.† Therefore nearly five-sixths appear barren during the summer, but in winter they are covered with flocks of sheep and goats, and herds of oxen and horses, which come down from the mountains, as soon as the influence of the bad air abates, to fatten on the luxuriant winter herbage of the low lands, particularly the Campagna of Rome. The mountain shepherds of course accompany‡ them. Thus by a regular annual migration from the mountain to the plain, the ties to home, which form the most powerful securities for the virtue of the peasant, are loosened, and he becomes fitted for the wandering life and desultory habits of the outlaw. The same causes have worked the same effects in all countries, except, perhaps, in Switzerland,

---

* Gibbon, chap. xxvi of the Decline and Fall. [Vol. 3, p. 3.]
† See Chateauvieux's Letters. [Frédéric Lullin de Chateauvieux, *Lettres écrites d'Italie en 1812 et 13*, 2 vols (Paris and Geneva: chez J.J. Paschoud, 1816), vol. 1, p. 19, pp. 215–16 (although neither of these commentaries gives the precise details of rotation that Graham mentions).]
‡ The following four lines, which are the first stanza of a popular ballad, refer to the departure from the mountain for the plain, by the sea-side, called Maremma, from Leghorn to Terracina. 'Quando Francesco Antonio fece partenza,./ Diss' alla Moglie sua abbia patienza / E quando ti viene occasione / Mandammi in Maremma sto pellicione.' ['When Francesco Antonio left, he said to his wife, "Be patient, and when you have an opportunity, send this fur mantle to me in the Maremma."']

where natural and political circumstances have counterbalanced them. But the Spanish mountaineers, in the Guerilla war, displayed a spirit too like the banditti of the Appenines, and it is scarcely 'sixty years since,' the Caterans of the Highlands of Scotland might have emulated the brigands of Sonnino.[64]

The open trial for crimes, the rigid execution of the laws, and the politic measure of opening roads and erecting bridges throughout the Highlands, have freed Great Britain from the disgrace of harbouring such ruffians. But here, the trial is secret, the judgment uncertain, and the roads generally in such a state of decay, that the culprit may almost defy the pursuit of justice.

We were led to make these reflections by a shocking scene which took place at Poli, on one of the last days of July. We were going out to walk about an hour after day-break, when we heard a voice rather louder and more lamentable than the usual slow morning song of the labourers; we looked towards the quarter whence it came, and perceived some women sitting on the ground, occupied about something that we took for a heap of linen for bleaching, but, on approaching, we distinctly heard the words, 'Oh my good brother,' and discovered a young man just murdered. A single stroke of the dagger had penetrated his heart; he had fallen on the spot, and his relations were weeping round the corpse. The father sat silent, the image of despair: the sisters lamented aloud; and the brothers were in pursuit of the murderers, whom they had seized once, but who were liberated by the women, who were going out to harvest-work, and passed at the moment; and, as there is no legal authority in Poli competent to seize a criminal, without first having recourse to Palestrina, it was feared that if they escaped from the brothers of their victim, they would be safe from all further pursuit. The poor lad who was killed bore an excellent character. He, with one of his brothers, was keeping watch the night before in their master's casale, when the murderers, two very young men, came to steal peas, as they said, to feed their pigeons. The deceased looked from the window, and told them not to touch what did not belong to them, or they might get a *'box on the ear.'* 'A box on the ear to us,' replied the enraged thieves; 'you shall pay for this,' and departed. The next morning, knowing that the young men must go from the casale[65] to the town, about five hundred yards off, for bread, before they could set about their day's work, the villains way-laid them just under the convent wall of San Stefano, and there, seizing the principal object of their revenge, one held him, while the other murdered him in cold blood.

Poli, since the time of the French government, when it formed a regular

---

[64] [Sir Walter Scott's novel about the Jacobite rebellion of 1745–46, published in 1814, was titled *Waverley: or, 'Tis Sixty Years Since*.]

[65] [*Casale*: a small house in the country designed for simple rustic living.]

municipality, with a mayor, &c. has had no efficient magistrates, though the population exceeds twelve hundred souls. There was no one to secure the murderers, and the body must remain where it was, till permission was obtained from Palestrina to send to Tivoli for the proper officer to enquire into the fact, and to pronounce what is equivalent to our coroner's verdict. It was one of the hottest days in summer, the thermometer being at 96: the murder took place at four in the morning. About noon, a violent thunderstorm, with rain and hail, came on: still the body lay across the only road into the town, until about five o'clock in the afternoon, when it was found that the persons who had escaped, had committed wilful murder on the body of the deceased, which was then taken up for interment.

On many following days, when we walked out, we saw the brothers or the friends of the young man, hurrying with bludgeons towards this valley, or that rock, on certain intelligence that the murderers were still lingering about, and that their relations supplied them with food every night. This we afterwards found to be true. They were stout, active young men; one of them could read and write, and his mother applied to us to take him as our servant a few days after the murder, hoping thereby to screen him from punishment. We very unguardedly told her, that so far from assisting in any such plan, we should rather give him up to the magistrate, to receive his due reward. Upon which, she bade us look to ourselves: but her threats were pronounced in anger, and we disregarded them. Her son and his companion wandered about the woods for many weeks. One was recognised in Rome some time afterwards, and imprisoned. He had already contracted a low fever, by sleeping in unhealthy places, and died in gaol. The other was afterwards taken up, and remains in prison, where he will probably stay till some public example is required. He will then be executed in the Piazza del Popolo, in Rome, or be dismissed unpunished, with such additional bad dispositions, as long imprisonment among others, still more wicked, never fails to produce.

As the reports of the approach of the brigands from the southward grew every day stronger, we could not help thinking that a gang of gypsies, which made its appearance rather suddenly one afternoon from Siciliano, was connected with them. The men belonging to the gang seemed to be pedlars; they carried baskets of such wares as Shakspeare's Autolichus has made poetical, and which suit the costume of the young women here. 'Ribbons of all the colours i' th' rainbow, points more than all the lawyers in Bohemia can learnedly handle, though they come to him by the gross; inkles, caddices, cambricks, lawn,' and ballads too in plenty; nor was the song of recommendation wanting.[66] The women, as usual, were fortune-

---

[66] [Shakespeare, *The Winter's Tale*, 4.4.206–9.]

tellers. We had the curiosity to listen to them; and there were the usual promises of good fortunes, great husbands, beautiful wives, and indulgent confessors. One of them said, her mother was born at Alexandria, in Egypt, and was the head of the tribe in Italy. We talked with them some time, and found that their own dialect was the same with that of the gypsies of England and Spain, and the Bohemians of France and Germany, which Richardson and Schlegel have long since recognised to be that of the Nats of Hindostan.[67] Their character is not at all more respectable here than in other countries; and though there was no evidence of their connection with the brigands, they were looked upon as their fore-runners. They professed to be travelling towards Palestrina, to be ready for the feast of Saint Agapet, when they hoped to sell their wares, and exercise their trade of tinkers. Their little camp by the road-side, their asses grazing round, the pigs tethered to the doors of the huts, the little ragged children begging amidst their play, and all having the true gypsey face and expression, looked so like a scene at Hampstead, or Blackheath, that we felt almost good-will towards what reminded us so much of home.

---

[67] [Graham would seem to be invoking John Richardson, *A Dissertation on the Languages, Literature, and Manners of Eastern Nations. Originally Prefixed to a Dictionary Persian, Arabic, and English* (Oxford: Clarendon Press, 1777) and Friedrich von Schlegel, *Über die Sprache und Weisheit der Indier* (Heidelberg: Mohr und Zimmer, 1808).]

Chapter 4

ART, UNEASE AND LIFE

> Upon my asking how he had been taught the art of a connoscento so very suddenly, he assured me that nothing was more easy. The whole secret consisted in a strict adherence to two rules: the one always to observe, that the picture might have been better if the painter had taken more pains; and the other, to praise the works of Pietro Perugino.
>
> Oliver Goldsmith, The Vicar of Wakefield (1766)

> During this conversation, a lady, of about 17 or 18, was occupied at another table in executing an academical drawing. On admiring her proficiency, Donna Nicoletta was introduced as the daughter of the owner of the house. She was employed on a copy of the Farnesian Hercules, the original of which I have since seen in the *Regii Studii*; and the young artist had faithfully copied rude antiquity in all its parts.
>
> Lewis Engelbach, Naples and the Campagna Felice (1815)

Viewing works of art and finding words in which to comment upon them is as central to the Grand Tour as reflecting on antiquity and on landscape; like ancient ruins and scenes of sublimity, works of art present travellers with the task of shifting objects of elevated attention into a domain of intimate, personal experience. In choosing commentaries that give some idea of the range of arguments, debates, concepts and rhetorical ploys that are used to translate art in Italy into forms of language, many different strategies of selection suggest themselves. It would be possible to chart some of the rules of criticism that are formulated either as explicit principles or as unspoken assumptions, for example, or to examine some of the more dramatic and extravagant aspects of the rhetoric of responsiveness (as exemplified by those commentaries in which the traveller claims to have experienced intense and involuntary physical reactions – whether horrified or pleasurable – to a work of art).[1]

---

[1] See, for example, [Anna Jameson,] *Diary of an Ennuyée* (London: Henry Colburn, 1826), p, 254; describing the church of San Severo, in Naples, Jameson comments: 'The Dead Christ covered with a veil, by Corradini . . . is most painful to look upon; and affected me so strongly, that I was obliged to leave the church, and go into the air.'

The strategy of selection that is adopted here, however, is to take two highly specific contexts – a narrative and a *mise-en-scène* of viewing and commenting – as starting-points for an exploration of recurrent themes. In the narrative, the process of finding a language of criticism is apparently thrown off course by a spectator who is in some way odd, unusual or aberrant – for example, a woman, open to the suspicion of specialized female preoccupations that might distract her from pronouncing as a 'man of taste'. The *mise-en-scène* of encountering art is supplied by sculpture studios in Rome, in which the relation between the spectator and the works of art is less fixed and sharply delimited than it would be in a gallery.

Writings that pursue these themes share a series of preoccupations that makes them especially useful in exploring commentary on art at this time: the relation between art and life, the suspicion – or desire – that these two domains might not be as distinct as the orthodoxies of art criticism maintain, and the view of encounters with art as occasions that might unleash feelings of an unpredictable, diverse and powerful kind.

I: Odd spectators

Anxieties about art

Commentaries on art, more than accounts of any other domains of objects, emphasize how daunting the works of art to be seen in Italy are for the traveller. One strategy of hyperbolic response is to claim that the impact of a particular collection is so great that any assimilation or comprehension of the works on view is initially impossible. Anna Jameson, in Florence, at the Uffizi, describes pleasure as only succeeding to generalized sensory breakdown on a second visit:

> Nov. 10. – We visited the gallery for the first time yesterday morning; and I came away with my eyes and imagination so dazzled with excellence, and so distracted with variety, that I retained no distinct recollection of any particular object except the Venus; which of course was the first and great attraction. This morning was much more delightful: my powers of discrimination returned, and my power of enjoyment was not diminished. New perceptions of beauty and excellence seemed to open upon my mind; and faculties long dormant, were roused to pleasurable activity.[2]

James Galiffe, at the Vatican, maps out the same plot: a version of the sublime, in which the spectator is at first overwhelmed, and then rises to the astonishing and elevated character of the scene that he or she is attempting to assimilate:

---

[2] [Jameson,] *Diary of an Ennuyée*, p. 89.

> My heart beat when I entered the gallery which leads to the *Hall of the Belvedere*. A thousand associations filled my mind, and exalted my fancy. I felt as if I had left all the earthly parts of my being; and as if my soul moved on, alone, towards that sanctuary of the fine arts. I might have met my own brother without knowing him. Nor was I conscious of the least sensation till after I had gone round the Hall, seen every thing it contains, – and yet seen nothing of which I could retain a distinct impression. It was only when I began my second circuit that I recovered the free exercise of my faculties, and that I could really observe and enjoy these prodigies of human art.³

Travellers, unsurprisingly, register anxieties about the demands and risks of attempting to translate such daunting objects of commentary into adequate forms of language. Hester Piozzi emphasizes that, in pronouncing on art, the pressure to appear responsive is especially strong, and the risk of appearing affected is correspondingly great:

> When a conceited Englishman starts back in pretended rapture from a Raphael he has perhaps little taste for, it is difficult to persuade these sincerer people that his transports are possibly put on, only to deceive some of his countrymen who stand by, and who, if he took no notice of so fine a picture, would laugh, and say he had been throwing his time away, without making even the common and necessary improvements expected from every gentleman who travels through Italy.⁴

It has already been argued, in Chapter 2, that certain categories of 'odd' traveller, like some digressive incidents, are assigned a useful role in dissipating the unease of attempting to assimilate the topography, and to find appropriate ways of responding to it. If particular characters who make their appearance as participants in the Grand Tour are sufficiently eccentric in their actions or words (or, alternatively, if particular situations are especially unusual and unpredictable), this oddity supplies the precondition demanded by Hazlitt for an effect of humour: 'the ludicrous prevails over the pathetic, and we receive pleasure instead of pain from the farce of life which is played before us'.⁵ In commentary on art, travellers often refer mockingly to other travellers who speak from the specialized viewpoint of connoisseurs, motivated by vanity and

---

³ James Aug. Galiffe, *Italy and its Inhabitants: An Account of a Tour in that Country in 1816 and 1817*, 2 vols (London: John Murray, 1820), vol. 1, pp. 240–1.

⁴ Hester Lynch Piozzi, *Observations and Reflections Made in the Course of a Journey through France, Italy, and Germany*, 2 vols (London: A. Strahan and T. Cadell, 1789). vol. 2, p. 214.

⁵ William Hazlitt, 'On Wit and Humour', in *Lectures on the English Comic Writers* (Oxford: Oxford University Press, 1943; first published in 1818), pp. 1–35; p. 2. The use of an unpredictable situation to produce an effect of humour is found, for example, in John Galt's account of Benjamin West's visit to the Belvedere Courtyard with Cardinal Albani and a party of Italians, who are initially horrified when the American artist exclaims: 'My God, how like it is to a young Mohawk warrior!'; *The Life and Studies of Benjamin West, Esq.*, 2 vols (London: T. Cadell and W. Davies, 1816-20), vol. 1, pp. 104–7, p. 105.

pretentiousness. John Moore, in his *View of Society and Manners in Italy* (1781), implicitly defines a connoisseur as someone 'violently bent upon being a man of very refined taste', who upholds his claim to discernment by drawing on the abundance of books 'which will put you in possession of all the terms of technical applause, or censure, and furnish you with suitable expressions for the whole climax of sensibility'. He then recounts a long story about a spectator of this kind, who pronounces rapturously on a copy of Raphael's *St John the Baptist*, under the impression that it is the original.[6] In the face of such a disaster, the daunting business of commenting on art is viewed for a moment as an occasion not for anxiety but for hilarity.

Another stock figure to whom peculiar and risible habits are often attributed has already appeared, in the form of Hazlitt's French and Spanish travelling companions, in Chapter 2: the traveller-foreigner (or, at times, the traveller-compatriot), whose national peculiarities allow the narrator to displace on to her or him an uneasy sense of the difficulties of appropriating the foreign as a source of pleasure and benefit. Such figures are often introduced into accounts of viewing art. De Sade, describing Bernini's statue of *Santa Bibbiana*, pounces gleefully on remarks uttered by 'un de ces mauvais plaisants de la plus saints de religions, de ces cœurs endurcis pour qui le sang d'une jeune et belle martyre n'est plus intéressant qu'une verre de punch: an Anglais, en un mot' ('one of those reprehensible scoffers at the most holy of religions, of those hardened hearts for whom the blood of a young and beautiful martyr is no more interesting than a glass of punch: an Englishman, in a word'). (He notes that the saint is represented with the branch of a palm tree as a reward for her constancy, but that the Englishman takes this palm to be one of the instruments of her torture, and comments that it was excessively harsh to make her collect up the rods with which she was beaten.)[7]

In Martin Sherlock's *Letters from an English Traveller*, an account of a visit to St Peter's (the first of the passages below) provides an occasion for the unease of commentary on art to be displaced onto three varieties of national oddity: 'I went thither with a Pole, a Frenchman, and an Englishman: the Englishman looked for beauties; the Frenchman for faults; the Pole looked for nothing.'

---

[6] John Moore, *A View of Society and Manners in Italy, with Anecdotes Relating to some Eminent Characters*, second edition, 2 vols (London: W. Strahan and T. Cadell, 1781), vol. 1, p. 63, pp. 63–8. See also, for example, [William Parsons,] 'The Man of Taste, An Epigram', in *A Poetical Tour, in the Years 1784, 1785, and 1786. By a Member of the Arcadian Society at Rome* (London: 'printed at the Logographic Press, for J. Robson, and W. Clarke', 1787), p. 33.

[7] [Donatien Alphonse François] de Sade, *Voyage d'Italie*, in *Bibliothèque Sade*, edited by Maurice Lever, 7 vols (Paris: Fayard, 1993–95), vol. 6, part 1, p. 93.

The last of these travellers, though introduced with more than a tinge of mockery, nonetheless reflects on the topography in a way that obliquely encourages the reader to pause and ponder. The Pole's comment that 'the church was much longer than he imagined' ostensibly provides a comic vision of a traveller utterly at a loss, sinking into a helplessness from which the Frenchman and the Englishman are trying energetically to extract themselves. This comment, however, also intervenes in a long-running debate about whether or not the building is of such perfect proportions that it takes the visitor a while to comprehend its size. The arguments involved in this debate are usually set forth in an elaborate manner: Byron, for example, silently drawing on Montesquieu's 'Essai sur le goût', spends five stanzas of *Childe Harold's Pilgrimage* explaining how we gradually come to grasp the grandeur of the building.[8] The Pole's innocent bemusement is set in ironic contrast to such self-consciously complex structures of argument; the narrator nonetheless uses him, under cover of his apparent naïveté, to allegorize an aspect of travel that is not confined to those completely daunted by sights and wonders: an awareness that encounters with other worlds may have dimensions and implications beyond those that we at first perceive.

A number of accounts of viewing art in Italy by British and French travellers, over the late eighteenth and early nineteenth centuries, introduce figures who are defined as odd on the grounds that they are female. The precise relation between the female spectator and the effect of laughter varies widely: in some such commentaries, a woman may supply an element of wit that sharply enlivens the pleasures of viewing, while in others the traveller may seem to mock a female spectator's responses in tones of doltish jocularity. By examining a few commentaries of this kind in some detail, it is possible to begin to identify in what ways traveller-narrators, when they set in motion a plot in which a woman participates in viewing works of art and discussing them, change or extend their options for translating paintings and sculptures into forms of language.

---

[8] Lord Byron, *Childe Harold's Pilgrimage*, Canto IV, stanzas 155-19; *The Complete Poetical Works*, edited by Jerome J. McGann, 7 vols (Oxford: Oxford University Press, 1980-92), vol. 2, pp. 176–7. See Montesquieu [Charles Louis de Secondat, Baron de], 'Essai sur le goût, dans les choses de la nature et de l'art. Fragment imparfait trouvé parmi les papiers de feu M. le Président de Montesquieu', in Alexander Gerard, *Essai sur le goût, augmenté de trois dissertations sur le même sujet, par Messieurs de Voltaire, d'Alembert et de Montesquieu*, translated by 'M.E***' [M.-A. Eidous] (Paris: chez Delalain, and Dijon, chez la Veuve Coignard and Louis Frantin, 1766), pp. 265–306; p. 298.

Women of innocent perspicacity

Henry Matthews, in the second passage below, from his *Diary of an Invalid* (1820), concludes his account of the sculptures in the Vatican (see Figure 5 for one of the most famous of these works, the *Apollo Belvedere*) by expressing his surprise 'at the squeamishness which has induced the ruling powers at Florence and Rome, to deface the works of antiquity by the addition of a tin fig-leaf, which is fastened by a wire to all the male statues'. He remarks, high-mindedly: 'Nothing can be more ridiculously prudish. That imagination must be depraved past all hope, that can find any prurient gratification in the cold chaste nakedness of an ancient marble.' A female spectator, however, supplies just the slightest hint that some element of 'prurient gratification' might in fact play a part in the pleasures of the antique: 'I was complaining loudly of this barbarous addition, when an Italian lady of the party assented to my criticism, and whispered in my ear, – that I must come again in the *Autumn*.'

By following through the logic of the choice of a leaf of a deciduous tree as the prudish addition to the statues, the 'Italian lady' wittily draws attention to the pointlessness of the Vatican's prudishness – a pointlessness noted more acerbically by the narrator when he observes that 'It is the fig-leaf alone that suggests any idea of indecency'.

More specifically, the woman makes a joke: deploying the techniques of condensation and indirect representation that Freud identifies as two recurrent elements in jokes, she sets up a paradoxical elision between, on the one hand, the biblical fall that forces Adam and Eve to use fig leaves to cover their nakedness and, on the other, the fall of leaves that promises a revelation of the nakedness of the statues.[9]

At the same time, the joke accomplishes the task that Freud views as characteristic of the category of jokes that he terms 'tendentious': it evades the forms of censorship that cultural convention imposes. Such restraints are, in fact, implicitly acknowledged when Matthews specifies that the joke is one that the woman 'whispered in my ear': her oblique mode of utterance, it is assumed, makes it possible to voice a curiosity about the genitalia of classical statues that might perhaps be too down-to-earth to express directly. Such an assumption about the uses of obliquity

---

[9] See the chapter on 'The Technique of Jokes' in Sigmund Freud, *Jokes and Their Relation to the Unconscious*, translated and edited by James Strachey and revised by Angela Richards, *The Pelican Freud Library*, vol. 6 (Harmondsworth: Penguin, 1976), pp. 47–131. The *Oxford English Dictionary* notes that although the term *fall*, for *autumn*, is 'in England now rare in literary use', phrases that incorporate it are fairly common; the *Dictionary* quotes a British instance of the phrase 'spring and fall' from 1826.

5. 'The APOLLO BELVEDERE', plate XI in Joseph Spence, *Polymetis: or, an Enquiry concerning the Agreement between the Works of the Roman Poets, and the Remains of the Antient Artists*, second edition (London: R. and J. Dodsley, 1755), engraved by L.P. Boitard. 31.7 x 18.4 cm. Research Library, The Getty Research Institute, Los Angeles (85-B5725). The sculpture itself is still in the Belvedere Courtyard at the Vatican Museums

is spelt out in more general terms by Freud in his analysis of the category of jokes that he terms 'smut'.

> When we laugh at a refined obscene joke, we are laughing at the same thing that makes a peasant laugh at a coarse piece of smut. In both cases the pleasure springs from the same source. We, however, could never bring ourselves to laugh at the coarse smut; we should feel ashamed or it would seem to us disgusting. We can only laugh when a joke has come to our help, [10]

In making this joke, the woman briskly abandons any pretence that she is aiming to rise to the elevated nature of the ideal. The effect of irony, in other words, follows the model mapped out by Peter Conrad, in *Shandyism*, when he summarizes the aesthetics of Jean Paul Richter: 'In the sublime the senses and imagination despair of responding adequately to the grand phenomenon with which they are confronted; in irony they abandon the attempt and instead lovingly contemplate their own weakness.'[11] The narrator, happily acknowledging the attractions of this latter approach, identifies with the woman in her relinquishment of the ideal, and appropriates her effect of irony as his own.

This effect of irony is, however, combined with gentle mockery of the very ease with which the woman shifts the conversation about art into the domain of sexuality. Alongside the knowingness that she displays in whispering, and so signalling a move towards illicit confidences, she also speaks with an amusing naïveté – or endearing innocence – simply by virtue of her utter unawareness of any need for caution: an Englishwoman, it is assumed, could be expected to display rather greater hesitation in acknowledging the fascinations of the sculpted male body.

The usefulness of female spectators, in drawing attention to erotic qualities in works of art with an air of unembarrassed assurance, and so eliding an awareness of such qualities with a freedom from affectation, is demonstrated by a more elaborate invocation of the thoughts of an Italian woman about sculpted figures. Stendhal, describing Canova's *Three Graces* (see Figures 6 and 7) in *Promenades dans Rome* (1830), also deploys a woman, in this case with a slightly different effect of irony, in order to draw attention to an element of eroticism within the classical ideal. He quotes a description of the group that, he claims, is his own translation of a letter that he has stolen from a young and beautiful Italian woman (whom he implicitly presents as the writer rather than the

---

[10] Sigmund Freud, *Jokes and Their Relation to the Unconscious*, p. 145. On psychoanalysis, gender and wit, see Joel Fineman, '"The Pas de Calais": Freud, the Transference and the Sense of Woman's Humor', in *On Puns: The Foundation of Letters*, edited by Jonathan Culler (Oxford: Blackwell, 1988), pp. 100–14, and Sarah Kofman, *Pourquoi rit-on? Freud et le mot d'esprit* (Paris: Galilée, 1986), pp. 177–85.

[11] Peter Conrad, *Shandyism: The Character of Romantic Irony* (Oxford: Blackwell, 1978), p. 23.

6. Antonio Canova, *The Three Graces*, front view, engraved by Domenico Marchetti, in *Recueil de statues, groupes, bustes, mausolées, colosses et monumens de tout genre, exécutés par Canova, dessinés et gravés sous les yeux de l'auteur* (Rome: Canova, [1816]). 49.4 x 34.0 cm. Research Library, The Getty Research Institute, Los Angeles (91-F0). The sculpture is shared between the Victoria and Albert Museum, London, and the National Gallery of Scotland, Edinburgh

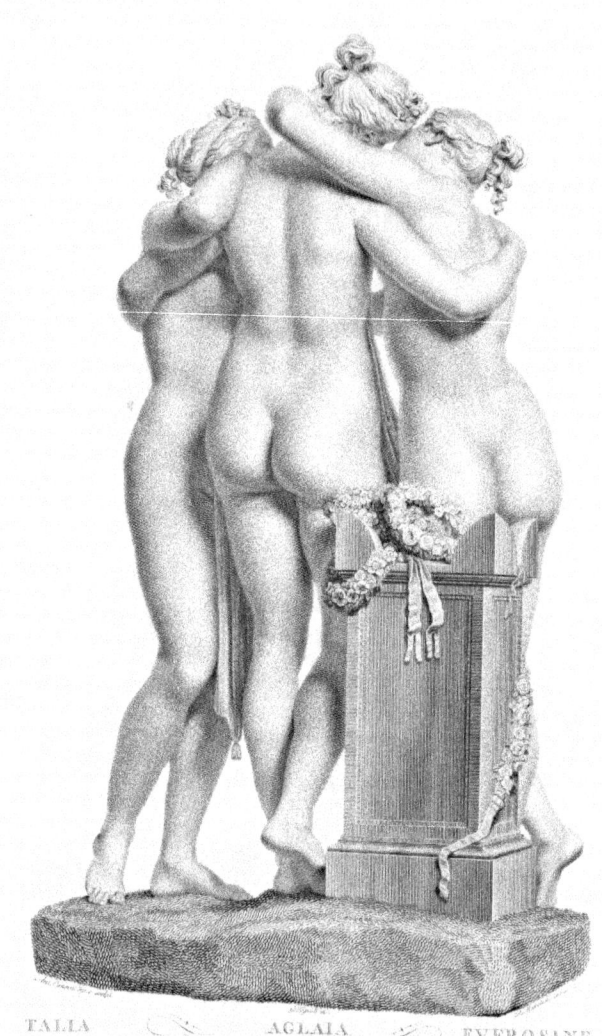

7. Antonio Canova, *The Three Graces*, back view, engraved by Domenico Marchetti, in *Recueil de statues, groupes, bustes, mausolées, colosses et monumens de tout genre*. 49.4 x 34.0 cm. Research Library, The Getty Research Institute, Los Angeles (91-F0)

recipient of this piece of criticism). Once again, therefore, an element of surreptitiousness plays a part in the effect of humour: in introducing a narrative in which a commentary on art is obtained by underhand means, the traveller-narrator obliquely promises that the utterances that follow will transgress culturally imposed forms of censorship, and registers a certain triumph in smuggling such utterances past the usual forms of control. (Through his claim that he is translating the letter from the Italian, he delicately accentuates his own role in offering access to this domain of the veiled and hidden.) The private, confidential nature of the commentary is indicated by the fact that it is addressed to the woman's 'Carissima Sorella' ('Dearest sister'). It is emphasized, too, by the woman's summary of the work itself:

> Les trois sœurs, légèrement enlacées dans les bras l'une de l'autre, sont représentées dans un de ces moments de joie et d'amitié vive et folle que l'on trouve, *loin des regards des hommes*, chez les jeunes filles d'ailleurs les plus retenues. Le sculpteur est indiscret de les avoir ainsi representées; mais c'est la faute de l'art, et non pas celle de ces jolies sœurs. La plus jeune des Grâces demand à sa sœur aînée un baiser que celle-ci lui refuse, et que la seconde essaye de lui faire obtenir.[12]

> The three sisters, lightly entwined in each others' arms, are represented in one of those moments of joy and lively, mad friendship that one sees, *far from the scrutiny of men*, among young girls who are otherwise the most reserved. The sculptor is indiscreet to have depicted them in this way, but this is the fault of art, and not that of these charming sisters. The youngest of the Graces asks her older sister for a kiss that the sister refuses, and that the second sister tries to obtain for her.

In this commentary, however, in contrast to Matthews's account of visiting the Belvedere courtyard, the woman's most salient characteristic is not self-awareness but naïveté. The strategic rhetorical role that Stendhal assigns to the gender of the spectator is emphasized by his decision to appropriate the words of a male travel writer and allot them to her: the passage is in fact adapted from a *Tableau de Rome* by Guinan-Laoureins, published in Brussels in 1816.[13] The traveller-narrator happily assigns it to a figure who proves more useful in gently moving the commentary from the aesthetic to the erotic. Her naïveté – as explicitly noted by him, and exemplified in the letter by her complete lack of self-consciousness – allows the narrator to present the work as a scene sufficiently charged erotically to be startling to find on public view, without defining this way of approaching it as in any way contentious; the element of eroticism,

---

[12] Stendhal [Henri-Marie Beyle], *Promenades dans Rome*, in *Voyages en Italie*, edited by V. del Litto, Bibliothèque de la Pléiade (Paris: Gallimard, 1973), pp. 593–1291; p. 708, p. 708, emphasis added.
[13] See J.B. Guinan-Laoureins [Jean Baptiste Reinolds], *Tableau de Rome vers la fin de 1814* (Brussels: Imprimerie de Weissenbruch, 1816), pp. 224–6.

the traveller suggests, is something that even the most uncomplicated of spectators must perceive. The extended, carefully calibrated assessment of the woman's impassivity covertly promises the reader that this very quality will, by force of contrast, lend added piquancy to the account of erotic exchange that follows:

> Voici la traduction d'une lettre que j'ai volée à Mme Lampugnani, cette femme si naïve, si fière, si belle et si jeune! Cette froideur étonnante qui augmente le charme de sa figure n'est pas celle qui montre l'impossibilité des passions, mais leur absence. Rien ne semble digne de donner de l'émotion. En voyant tant de beauté et tant d'impassibilité pour tout ce qui est commun, l'être le plus calme ne peut se défendre d'un moment de rêverie.[14]

> Here is the translation of a letter that I have stolen from Mme Lampugnani, a woman so naïve, so proud, so beautiful and so young. The astonishing chilliness that increases the charm of her face is not an attribute that suggests the impossibility of the passions, but, rather, one that marks their absence. Nothing seems worthy of exciting emotion. In seeing so much beauty and so much impassivity towards everything that is usual, the calmest of beings can hardly refrain from a moment of reflection.

At the same time, the naïveté of the Italian female critic is, as in Matthews's commentary, combined with an element of knowingness; even the most impassive of Latin women, it is implied, takes it for granted that the classical ideal is not really so far removed from the domain of tender yet impassioned sexuality. Once the portrait of the letter-writer has given way to the letter itself, Madame Lampugnani proceeds to outline the physical contact between the three figures in minute detail, observing that the youngest of the graces is asking her older sister for a kiss, which she refuses, 'tandis que de sa main gauche elle presse doucement la taille de la plus jeune et tempère ainsi la rigueur du refus qu'elle lui fait éprouver' ('while with her left hand she gently presses the waist of the youngest, and so tempers the rigour of refusal that she makes her suffer').[15]

Concluding her account of the sculpture, the letter-writer resorts to language that allows the traveller-narrator to reaffirm the overwhelming innocence and naïveté of the female critic: 'L'intérêt de ce petit drame, *la plus jeune obtiendra-t-elle un baiser?* est suffisant pour animer la scène, mais point assez vif pour faire oublier les formes' ('The interest of this little drama, *will the youngest sister receive a kiss?*, is sufficient to animate

---

[14] Stendhal, *Promenades dans Rome*, p. 708. After the comment on Mme Lampugnani's lack of emotion, Stendhal emphasizes his point by a footnote: 'Ce caractère est souvent joué en Angleterre, par exemple; mais il ne produit d'effet qu'autant qu'on le croit sincère' ('This character is often assumed in England, for example, but it produces a striking effect only when one is convinced of its sincerity').

[15] Stendhal, *Promenades dans Rome*, p. 709.

Art, unease and life 171

the scene, but not sufficient to make one forget the forms').¹⁶ The purpose that the young Italian attributes to the sculptor is the very rhetorical aim that Stendhal pursues here: in his drama of stealing a letter and discovering a woman's secret thoughts, he appropriates the animation of the 'petit drame' that she has detected in the work, without dismissing the sculpture's participation in the ideal. The same rhetorical ploy can be identified in all the commentaries in the first part of this chapter – and many in the second part: travel books repeatedly introduce a 'petit drame' of viewing and commenting in which the formal qualities of the works in question, far from being banished, are made to intervene dynamically in animated scenes of critical activity.

Physicality and prudery

In a third, earlier commentary that introduces a woman into a scene of viewing art (included in the passages below), the traveller-narrator presents his female spectator-critic more harshly and mockingly than either Matthews or Stendhal depict their rhetorically useful women, but nonetheless endorses some of her perceptions. John Moore, commenting on the *Farnese Hercules* (see Figure 8) in his *View of Society and Manners in Italy* (1781), notes that the sculpture 'has been long admired as an exquisite model of masculine strength; yet, admirable as it is, it does not please all the world'. The reflections that follow lead him to introduce a woman whose identity is not explicitly defined, but who appears to be, like him, a traveller from northern Europe. In contrast to the Italian women quoted by Matthews and Stendhal, she is presented as distinctly prudish in her reaction to the sculpture's physicality. The traveller-narrator would seem specifically to invoke Anne, Lady Miller, who, in her *Letters from Italy* (1777), comments on the work: 'It may be very beautiful, and the most perfect model of a man in the world; but I am insensible enough to its charms to own, that if all mankind were so proportioned, I should think them very disagreeable and odious.'¹⁷ Moore's summary of his female companion's remarks takes up the term *odious*, as well as a concern with masculine 'charms', and with the agreeable and disagreeable, and presents these features of Miller's commentary as characteristics of a generalized category of female critical responsiveness: 'I am told that the women in

---

16 Stendhal, *Promenades dans Rome*, pp. 709–10.
17 [Anne, Lady Miller,] *Letters from Italy*, 3 vols (London: Edward and Charles Dilly, 1776), vol. 3, p. 86. For further discussion of this passage, see my essay 'Effeminacy, Pleasure and the Classical Body', in *Femininity and Masculinity in Eighteenth-Century Art and Culture*, edited by Gill Perry and Michael Rossington (Manchester and New York: Manchester University Press, 1994), pp. 142–61; pp. 142–5.

8. 'The FARNESE HERCULES', plate XVI in Joseph Spence, *Polymetis: or, an Enquiry concerning the Agreement between the Works of the Roman Poets, and the Remains of the Antient Artists*, second edition (London: R. and J. Dodsley, 1755), engraved by L.P. Boitard. 32.4 x 18.4 cm. Research Library, The Getty Research Institute, Los Angeles (85-B5725). The sculpture is now in the Museo Archeologico Nazionale, Naples

particular find something unsatisfactory, and even odious, in this figure; which, however majestic, is deficient in the charms most agreeable to them.'

A specific woman is then introduced, whose physical expression of aversion (she turns away from the statue 'in disgust'), is greeted by the traveller-narrator with studied fausse naïveté: 'I could not imagine what had shocked her.' He elicits from her an explanation in which the sexuality implicit in the 'brawny' body is displaced onto a fantastic, Gothic narrative, inspired by 'the old romances':

> She told me, *after recollection*, that she could not bear the stern severity of his countenance, his large brawny limbs, and the club with which he was armed; which gave him more the appearance of one of those giants that, according to the old romances, carried away virgins and shut them up in gloomy castles, than the gallant Hercules, the lover of Omphale.

On the one hand, then, the traveller-narrator mocks the woman's squeamish reaction to the robust physicality of the sculpted body. On the other hand, he employs her in order to voice, directly or obliquely, a number of perceptions that he himself implicitly endorses: her recognition of a troubling element of sexuality in the sculpture, her awareness that 'large brawny limbs' are at odds with a classical ideal within which smoothness and continuity of contour occupy a central role, her sense that such beefiness is in contrast to the usual expectations of the male body in everyday social life and, finally, her conviction that the sculpture is, as a result of its accentuated musculature, disquieting rather than pleasurable to look at. At the same time, the woman's preoccupation with 'the old romances' allows Moore to define his own preoccupation with narrative, voiced in the comments that follow, as more closely linked to the question of the visual impact of sculpture than hers. Implicitly invoking Winckelmann's account of the sculpture in his *Geschichte der Kunst des Alterthums* (*History of the Art of Antiquity*; 1764 [1763]), he goes on to explain that 'the Farnese Hercules is faulty both in his form and attitude: the former is too unwieldy for active exertion, and the latter exhibits vigour *exhausted*'.[18]

---

[18] To cite one of the translations in which the *Geschichte* became well known in France and England, see Johann Joachim Winckelmann, *Histoire de l'art chez les anciens*, translated by Hendrik Jansen, 2 vols (Paris: 'chez l'auteur: Barrois L'Aîné', 1790 – an X/1803), vol. 1, pp. 382–3; Winckelmann in fact associates the muscular body with the same kinds of mythical and literary narratives as those invoked by Moore's female companion; he observes that it is 'l'indication des nerfs et des muscles' ('the display of nerve and muscle'), as in the statue in the Palazzo Farnese, that distinguishes 'un Hercule destiné à combattre les monstres et les brigands, et éloigné encore du terme de ses travaux' ('a Hercules destined to fight monsters and brigands, and still far from reaching the end of his labours'), from representations of Hercules as an immortal, his limbs purified of their mortal grossnesss.

Uninhibited female responsiveness

In the fourth commentary below, in Lewis Engelbach's *Naples and the Campagna Felice* (1815), a female spectator is presented in a more overtly patronizing manner than any of the female art critics in the commentaries considered so far. In the reckless unselfconsciousness with which she throws herself into the risky complexities of speculation on aesthetic matters, she initially resembles two characters from well-known anecdotes about viewing landscape: the Englishwoman (already mentioned in the Introduction) whom Byron mocks in the Alps, exclaiming 'in the very eyes of Mont Blanc . . . "did you ever see any thing more *rural*"', and a figure who distresses Coleridge with a similarly unreflective comment: 'the writer . . . was gazing on a cataract of great height, breadth, and impetuosity, . . . and on his observing, that it was, in the strictest sense of the word, a sublime object, a lady present assented with warmth to the remark, adding – "Yes! and it is not only sublime, but beautiful and absolutely pretty."'[19] (In a twentieth-century version of this same plot, Dorothy Parker describes a traveller who is standing alone at the brink of the Grand Canyon when a woman joins him, 'radiating native friendliness', and we are told that 'woman's world-old need of speech seized her, and seemed as if it would rack her very tweeds apart': '"Well!" she said. "It certainly *is* attractive."')[20]

The woman in Engelbach's commentary, however, is not only unselfconscious in her assumption that she must surely be equal to the hyperboles demanded of her – in the manner of the women just cited; in contrast to these women, who aspire to voice a form of aesthetic responsiveness (however shaky its theoretical basis), she defines her own specific area of expertise not as the domain of the aesthetic but as that of sexuality. In this respect, she resembles the Italian women quoted by

---

On anxieties about the prominent muscles of the Hercules and the more general eighteenth-century concern with continuity of contour, see Chloe Chard, 'Nakedness and Tourism: Classical Sculpture and the Imaginative Geography of the Grand Tour', *Oxford Art Journal*, 18:1 (1995), pp. 14–28, pp. 17–20.

[19] *Byron's Letters and Journals*, edited by Leslie A. Marchand, 13 vols (London: John Murray, 1973-94), vol. 5, p. 97; S[amuel] T[aylor] Coleridge, 'On the Principles of Genial Criticism concerning the Fine Arts, More Especially those of Statuary and Painting, Deduced from the Laws and Motions which Guide the True Artist in the Production of his Works', in *Biographia Literaria, with his Aesthetical Essays*, edited by J. Shawcross, 2 vols (Oxford: Clarendon Press, 1907), vol. 2, pp. 219-43; pp, 224-5.

For an account of some of the questions raised by Coleridge's anecdote, see Ian Balfour, 'Torso: (The) Sublime Sex, Beautiful Bodies, and the Matter of the Text', *Eighteenth-Century Studies*, 39:3 (2006), pp. 323–36: in particular, pp. 324–5.

[20] 'The Artist's Reward', in *The Collected Dorothy Parker*, with an introduction by Brendan Gill (London: Penguin, 2001), pp. 582-8; p. 582.

9. Thomas Rowlandson, 'Don Luigi meets Donna Anna in the Museum', Plate VII, Lewis Engelbach, *Naples and the Campagna Felice* (London: R. Ackermann, 1815). 12.6 x 20.3 cm. Research Library, The Getty Research Institute, Los Angeles (2566-911)

Matthews and Stendhal; she is, in fact, yet more assured than either of these women in insisting upon the amorous nature of a particular work of art. The traveller, in the midst of a long description of paintings of the muses in the museum at Portici, remarks that his attention is greatly distracted by the 'clamorous vociferations' of 'a Neapolitan gentleman, who happened to be viewing the collection with, as I suppose, his lady (for she did not seem to care a pin for him), and two French officers, in gold and buckram' (see Figure 9). The woman, Donna Anna, offers her own interpretations of the narrative content of a series of paintings. By introducing her as an utterly artless, ignorant spectator, yet allowing her ebullient earthiness to displace his own more exalted commentary on ancient art, the traveller-narrator manages, at several points in his story of his visit to Portici, to establish his more carefully honed powers of judgement and response, while at the same time investing the work in question with drama and vitality, as the object of spirited debate, attracting full-blooded instinctual reaction as well as composed reflection. When Donna Anna wants to know what a particular painting represents, he first of all offers a summary to his correspondent (his travel narrative is in epistolary form),

176   *Tristes Plaisirs*

10. Detail from 'Ancient Greek Paintings, from Herculaneum', Plate VI: II, Lewis Engelbach, *Naples and the Campagna Felice*. 7.3 x 6.2 cms. Research Library, The Getty Research Institute, Los Angeles (2566-911)

describing in relatively idealized terms the scene of 'a beautiful young Bacchante' approached by 'an amorous young Faun', who manages 'to – imprint a *faunish* kiss on her blushing cheeks; not, mind! without as fair a portion of the lady's resistance as is demanded by female decorum' (see

Figure 10). A hyperbole of indescribability affirms his admiration for the work:

> Now that is all, believe me; but to describe the beauties of the design, the masterly colouring, the contrast between the delicate snowy carnation of the female, and the dark, yet not copper-coloured skin of the sylvan spark; the expression of lustful desire in the face of the latter (which is not unlike the goat's in the livery-stable opposite our friend B's), and that of blushing surprise in the Bacchante's countenance, it would be fruitless to attempt.

His summary for the woman's benefit is more brisk and down-to-earth: 'I believe, madam, it is a Faun stealing a kiss from a female Bacchante.' She, however, sees his interpretation of the nymph's behaviour as a great deal too polite and anodyne:

> '*Stealing?* Ha! ha! ha!' (Here the penetrating Donna Anna expressed her astonishment at my simplicity, by an immoderate burst of laughter.) 'Pray do tell me, good sir, what is her right hand doing during this pretended robbery?'
> 'What else, but pushing off the head of the impudent intruder?'
> 'Oh! better still! so this hand which she has placed most lovingly over the Faun's head is meant to push him *away*? Nay, now do speak the truth, sir, and tell us if you would care to be pushed *off* in the same manner by a sweetheart of your's?'

Donna Anna then expresses robust scepticism as to the possibility of misinterpreting such a language of gesture; a reference to cross-cultural difference allows her to cast an ironic light on the true motives of the Englishwomen who seem to have led him to pay such deference to female modesty: 'But, who knows, perhaps it is the fashion in your country for ladies to ward off the attacks of gentlemen in this way. There's no knowing, every country has its peculiar customs.'

Since the work is illustrated in the book, the reader has the opportunity to gauge the level of the Bacchante's resistance, and appreciate that the woman might have some justification for her view. While the traveller-narrator overtly presents himself as rising to an appreciation of ideal beauty, moreover – in contrast to Donna Anna, who enthusiastically plunges into the minutiae of everyday flirtatiousness – he covertly encourages an awareness of the very element of roguish sexuality that the female spectator sees as strikingly evident in the painted drama: even in his own account, the 'young Bacchante' (a designation that in itself hardly prompts the reader to expect any great restraint) offers only 'as fair a portion of . . . resistance as is demanded by female decorum'. Through his analogy between the faun's 'expression of lustful desire' and that of the goat 'in the livery-stable opposite our friend B's', he also proclaims his eagerness to establish as firmly as possible that he too has a grasp of the more down-to-earth elements in art.

Laughter and the 'oddity' of female commentary

Women, it has already been suggested, are among the categories of traveller-spectator whose oddities deflect unease. What precise forms of oddity, then, do they supply? The three Italian women are, in one sense, defined as odd precisely on the grounds that they themselves feel no such unease: not only do they express themselves with untroubled fluency but they are, in the eyes of each of the narrators, all too happily at ease when they recognize the element of sexuality within the works in question. Their oddity, in other words, from the point of view of the northern European narrators, lies in their complete lack of awkwardness. Engelbach, viewing another painting, encountered just before the faun and bacchante, which appears to incorporate an amorous element in its narrative content ('three figures, a Centaur in the middle, still grasping a handsome female before him, but seized by the hair from behind by a tall young man carrying a drawn sword'), describes Donna Anna examining it 'with more than female attention'. In turning his attention to the painting of the faun and bacchante, he is more specific in setting this 'more than female attention' in contrast to the 'affected indifference' to be expected from women from cooler climes: 'Not that the bare subject could be termed strictly indecent, but in the design, nay, even in the colouring, there was a degree of amatory warmth which a British female would have disdained noticing through any other medium than her fansticks.' The utter lack of inhibition displayed by his Italian acquaintance is then emphasized yet more strongly: 'Donna Anna's refined taste, however, rose superior to the usual delicacy of her sex, she courageously met the foe face to face; and, *sans cérémonie*, required to be informed of the import of the representation.'[21]

In Matthews's commentary, the woman acknowledges the transgressiveness of her remark by the manner in which she delivers it – whispering in the traveller's ear; this awareness of rules and limits, however, does nothing to dent her self-possession. In Stendhal's commentary, the woman is described as, like Donna Anna, serenely unconscious of such rules; it is the traveller himself who, in claiming to have stolen a letter from one sister to another, implies that he is offering access to a private world of transgressive thoughts. The Italian women, in other words, supply a commentary that is defined as utterly free from insincerity, and suffused with unaffected responsiveness. Travel writings, moreover, draw on a tradition of writing about art in which a 'natural', uninhibited responsiveness can easily be attributed to female spectators: Vasari, in his life of Frà

---

[21] Engelbach, *Naples and the Campagna Felice*, p. 184, p. 184.

Bartolommeo, tells a story about the painter's reaction to taunts that he has no skill in painting the nude: he paints a St Sebastian, which hangs in the church of the monastery to which he is attached, but is removed to the chapter house once the friars begin to report that women are admitting in the confessional that it has aroused lascivious feelings in them.[22] In introducing spectators who are both Italian and female, the various traveller-narrators register an uneasy awareness that art is not concerned only with the ideal, and deflect this awareness onto figures who are 'odd' because they take the virtue of unaffected spontaneity to an extreme.

Moore, on the other hand, presents the Englishwoman in the Palazzo Farnese as exhibiting an oddity that is almost of the opposite kind: while she instinctively recognizes the physicality of the sculpture, she is devoid of the astuteness and frankness in matters of sexuality that characterize the Italian women in the other commentaries, and is therefore reluctant to explore the physical, sexualized nature of her discomfort; instead, she displaces her intuitions onto the plots of romances. When the narrator observes that 'she told me, *after recollection*, that she could not bear the stern severity of his countenance', the moment of 'recollection' supplies a moment in which she might have spoken directly, but fails to do so.

The narrator, of course, is equally disinclined to acknowledge the physicality of the 'brawny' male body directly: the woman supplies him with an oblique, ironic means of doing so, and of shifting onto her, as an 'odd' spectator, all the rhetorically risky naïveté of treating a sculpted body as though it were a real one. Moore uses the opinion of women, as represented by his squeamish Englishwoman, in order to introduce the theme of sexuality with amused detachment and then loftily dismiss it, proclaiming by contrast his own concern with the ideal.

Digression and disruption

In examining this piece of rhetorical legerdemain, it is possible to see a similarity between Moore's use of his female spectator and Engelbach's use of Donna Anna: a strategy which, in each of the two commentaries, supplies a precondition for the effect of somewhat heavy-handed jocularity that both texts produce, in contrast to the more playful wit of

---

[22] Giorgio Vasari, 'Vita di Frà Bartolomeo di S. Marco, pittor fiorentino', in *Le vite de' più eccellenti pittori scultori e architettori*, edited by Rosanna Bettarini and Paola Barocchi, 6 vols (Florence: Sansoni, 1966-99), vol. 4, pp. 91–103; p. 97; for a translation, see Vasari, 'Frà Bartolomeo of S. Marco, Painter of Florence', in *The Lives of the Painters, Sculptors and Architects*, edited by William Gaunt and translated by A.B. Hinds, 4 vols (London and New York: Dent and Dutton, 1963), vol. 2, pp. 191–9; p. 196 I am indebted to Maria Loh for drawing my attention to this anecdote.

Matthews and Stendhal. Moore, in using the woman to draw attention to the brawniness of the *Hercules*, endorses her judgement that the form of the body is 'unwieldy', but goes on to emphasize that he himself is concerned with the sculpted body of the classical ideal, rather than with raw physicality. It is she who takes on the responsibility for digressing: for moving, that is, from the elevated domain of art to the trivial domain of everyday social life, in which men are expected to appear at least moderately attractive in the eyes of women, and are censured if, like the *Hercules*, they are 'deficient in the charms most agreeable to them'.

Donna Anna, too, is a woman who digresses to the trivia of social exchange – who is fascinated by the question of whether a female figure in an antique painting is repulsing a faun or welcoming his embraces. By using a woman to introduce this question, the traveller, in the two commentaries, ensures that he is able to offer his readers the pleasure of digressive speculation on the narrative possibilities of ancient painting without committing himself to a variety of art criticism that verges on gossip. In both these two commentaries, in other words, the narrator disavows his own impulse towards digressiveness, and displaces onto a woman the disorderliness that such an impulse embodies. Ross Chambers has suggested, in *Loiterature*, that 'what makes digression a pleasurable experience is the relaxation of the vigilance, the abandonment of discipline that becomes associated . . . with the way the body impinges on (or distracts from) the activities of the mind, the unconscious on those of consciousness, and with the way desire interferes in matters that are supposed to have nothing to do with libido'.[23] Whereas Matthews and Stendhal, as already noted, covertly recognize the seductiveness of the digression that the woman sets in motion, Moore and Engelbach both sternly distance themselves from any such disruptive impulse.

Matthews and Stendhal, then, both indicate that they are happy to be distracted by the new possibilities for commenting on sculptures that the women open up, Stendhal, as already noted, prefaces the letter that he has supposedly stolen from Mme Lampugnani by a character-sketch, in which he implies that the reader's curiosity can only be increased by his emphasis on her 'froideur étonnante'; his claim to have gone to the trouble of stealing the letter emphasizes that it is likely to offer critical pronouncements of a gratifyingly unpredictable kind. Matthews produces his Italian

---

[23] Ross Chambers, *Loiterature* (Lincoln, Nebraska, and London: University of Nebraska Press, 1999), p. 12.

woman, with her digressive proclivity for exploring the metaphorical dimension of the fig leaf, as a welcome force of disruption.

All four traveller-narrators, in other words, use women as figures who prompt digressions of various kinds – from the ideal to the erotic, and from art to life. The reader might wonder, however, why they bother to deploy a female spectator in order to do this. Travellers, male and female, can digress from art to sexuality, or from art to trivial gossip, without losing authority; they may in fact gain in authority through the insouciance with which they establish that they are equally undaunted by both domains. Charles de Brosses comments on Bernini's *Ecstasy of St Teresa*: 'Si c'est ici l'amour divin, je le connois, on en voit icy-bas maintes copies d'aprez nature' ('If this is divine love, I know it well; there are plenty of copies after nature to be seen here on earth').[24] Byron, having described the great sights of Rome as 'quite inconceivable', nonetheless manages to slide with apparent effortlessness into the jaunty informality of gossip: 'The Apollo Belvidere is the image of Lady Adelaide Forbes – I think I never saw such a likeness' (see Figure 5).[25] Stendhal, commenting on Raphael's *Virgin with Donor*, at the Vatican, sets up an irreverent analogy between art criticism and the brokering of erotic affinities: noting that he would extend to paintings the principle that 'une femme appartient réellement à l'homme qui l'aime le mieux' ('a woman really belongs to the man who loves her best'), he observes, with reference to this painting: 'À Paris, nous en étions si peu amoureux, que nous parlions de notre amour d'une façon presque officielle, comme un mari' ('At Paris, we were so little in love with this one, that we spoke of our love in an almost official manner, as a husband would').[26]

Hester Piozzi, at the Palazzo Borghese, in Rome, launches into an ostensibly conventional catalogue of famous works of art, but concludes her paragraph with a whimsically bathetic, irreverent, digressive comparison:

> Among the pictures here, the entombing our blessed Saviour by Rafaelle is most praised: it is supposed indeed wholly inestimable, and I believe it is so, while Venus, blinding Cupid's eyes, by Titian, engraved by Strange, is possibly one of the pleasantest pictures in Rome. The Christ disputing with the Doctors is inimitable, one of the wonderful works of Leonardo da Vinci: but here is Domenichino's

---

[24] Charles de Brosses, *Lettres familières*, edited by Giuseppina Cafasso and Letizia Norci Cagiano de Azevedo, Mémoires et documents sur Rome et l'Italie Méridionale, Nouvelle Série, 4, 3 vols, continuous pagination (Naples: Centre Jean Bérard, 1991), vol. 2, p. 703.

[25] *Byron's Letters and Journals*, vol. 5, p. 227.

[26] *Promenades dans Rome*, p. 632. The painting in question would appear to be the *Madonna di Foligno*, now in the Vatican; Stendhal refers to his acquaintance with the work in Paris after it was taken there in the wake of Napoleon's Italian campaign.

Diana among her nymphs, very laboured, and very learned. Why did it put me in mind of Hogarth's strolling actresses dressing in a barn?[27]

Piozzi, here, compares Domenichino's representation of the bathing goddess of chastity and her nymphs (see Figure 2), imbued with ideal grace, to Hogarth's portrayal of coarsely comical strolling actresses – women whose profession (and conspicuously lowly place within that profession) hardly suggests dazzlingly chaste and poised demeanour.[28] Through her deceptively casual and dismissive remark, she covertly acknowledges that a certain erotic charge might – paradoxically – be discerned within this 'laboured' and 'learned' painting.

None of these travellers introduces an odd female spectator, and Piozzi does not at this juncture claim any striking oddity for herself as a woman (beyond a faint implication that she might be readier to see through 'very learned' depictions of frolicking females than a man). Traveller-narrators, it would seem from such commentaries, lose nothing by digressing on their own account, and have no need of a female spectator to take the responsibility for digressiveness. Women are nevertheless regularly deployed as figures who lend added *brio* to divagation: who, in other words, promise an extra charge of disorderliness, which will set digression on its course in an especially wild and unpredictable manner.

In writing of this period, women are implicitly recognized as capable of speaking with some or all of the forms of authority required in order to comment on art. They are seen, for example, as easily claiming the authority of the eye-witness, who enjoys the advantage of having inspected paintings and sculptures on the spot, and the authority conferred by an ability to respond emotionally to works of art. The third form of authority that is assigned a crucial role in art criticism is that derived from an ability to speak as a 'man of taste', who, as a result of extensive exposure to the great works of painting and sculpture, can view works of art detachedly, without becoming embroiled in the 'mechanick' of the art, or in distracting details that might monopolize the attention of spectators with a too specialized interest in either the content or the execution of the works concerned.[29] Female spectators, are, on the one

---

[27] Piozzi, *Observations and Reflections*, vol. 1, p. 432.

[28] Melesina Chevenix St George Trench, emphasizing the astonishing vulgarity of Emma Hamilton and her mother, both of whom she encounters in Dresden, quotes the observation of a friend that 'they were exactly like Hogarth's actresses dressing in the barn'; (*Journal Kept during a Visit to Germany in 1799, 1800*, edited by the Dean of Westminster (London: Savil and Edwards, printers, 1861), p. 83. I am grateful to Katharine Kittredge for drawing my attention to this comment.

[29] For a discussion of how works of art may be viewed with detachment, see Daniel Webb, *An Inquiry into the Beauties of Painting; and into the Merits of the most Celebrated Painters, Ancient and Modern* (London: R. and J. Dodsley, 1760), vi–ix, p. 10. Naomi Schor, in *Reading*

hand, assumed, in many or most commentaries, to be perfectly capable of speaking from this position of detachment. On the other hand, traveller-narrators imply, they may also turn out to have odd preoccupations of their own. Rhetorically, the importance of this uncertainty is that it promises the reader a disruption of the established conventions of art criticism, and so invests the commentary with an element of anticipation and excitement.

Laughter, of course, carries its own charge of disorderliness, as Mary Douglas has suggested, in her essay 'The Social Control of Cognition: Some Factors in Joke Perception'. In attempting to find a common element in the theories of laughter formulated by Bergson and Freud, Douglas emphasizes the wild and disruptive elements in jokes, laughing and humour:

> Something is saved in psychic effort, something which might have been repressed has been allowed to appear, a new improbable form of life has been glimpsed. For Bergson it is lifeless encrustation which is attacked in the joke, for Freud the joke lies in the release from control . . . For both the essence of the joke is that something formal is attacked by something informal, something organised and controlled, by something vital, energetic, an upsurge of life for Bergson, of libido for Freud. The common denominator underlying both approaches is the joke seen as an attack on control.[30]

A commentary that deploys intervention by a woman as a means of producing an effect of laughter, then, is doubly disorderly. In colluding with humorous disorder, women are sometimes presented as silly, trivializing critics. At the same time, however, they are ineluctably invested with critical proclivities and powers: to quote Ross Chambers again: 'once one has digressed, the position from which one departed becomes available to a more dispassionate or ironic analysis: it must have been in some sense inadequate or one would not have moved away from it.'[31]

In throwing pieties into disarray, female spectators do not merely set up a conflict between a discourse of orthodoxy and one of aberrancy: they also open up new possibilities, by suggesting that such conflicts might be central to art criticism itself, and that commenting on art might be a more flexible and intriguingly labile enterprise than many critics would

---

in Detail: Aesthetics and the Feminine (New York and London: Methuen, 1987), argues that women are, in the eighteenth century, consigned to a category of spectators who become enmired in trivial detail; she then charts a series of changes through which a sublime transcendence of detail comes to be identified with the feminine.

[30] Mary Douglas, 'The Social Control of Cognition: Some Factors in Joke Perception', *Man: The Journal of the Royal Anthropological Institute*, new series, V (1968), pp. 361–76; p. 364.

[31] Chambers, *Loiterature*, p. 15.

appear to assume.³² Moore, the earliest of the travellers quoted here in this context, tries to set up a sharp distinction between authoritative and naïve departures from orthodoxy when he declares: 'Without such powerful support as that of the fair sex, I should not have exposed myself to the resentment of connoisseurs.' In all three of the later travel books – and especially in the commentaries by Matthews and Stendhal – the narrators are more ready to see disorder as a precondition for new and alluringly unpredictable orderings of language, taste and knowledge.

Martin Sherlock, *Letters from an English Traveller*, translated by the author (London: J. Nichols, T. Cadell and N. Conant, 1780), pp. 60–1. In the original French edition, *Lettres d'un voyageur anglois* (London [Geneva]: privately printed, 1779), the passage is on pp. 127–8.

As the traveller begins this commentary, he is in Rome, reflecting on the comparative merits of Shakespeare and Dante.

The best pieces of Shakespeare have some faults; but each of his good ones seems to me to resemble the church of St. Peter: this temple, the most wonderful in the world, has a thousand faults, a thousand bad things in sculpture, painting, &c. but I pity the man who thinks of looking for them: when a fault presents itself, let him take a step farther, a sublime beauty expects him.

These ideas struck me this morning while I was walking in that church: I went thither with a Pole, a Frenchman, and an Englishman: the Englishman looked for beauties; the Frenchman for faults; the Pole looked for nothing. When we were at the end of the church, 'Behold,' says the Frenchman, 'that *Charity* of Bernini, how bad it is! the air of her head is affected, her flesh is without bone, and she makes frightful faces.' 'These remarks appear to me just enough,' replies the Englishman, 'but, look on the other side of the altar, you will see one of the finest pieces of modern sculpture, the *Justice* of Guilielmo della Porta.' 'You are in the right,' says the Frenchman (without looking at it), 'but that child at the foot of *Charity* disgusts me more than its mother.' While the Englishman continued to praise *Justice*, and the Frenchman to criticize *Charity*, the Pole was observing the door at which

---

³² A useful point of comparison with the rather different role allotted to women in another, earlier genre is provided by Paula Findlen in 'Becoming a Scientist: Gender and Knowledge in Enlightenment Italy', *Science in Context*, 16 (2003), pp. 59–88. Findlen examines dialogues such as Francesco Algarotti's *Dialoghi sopra l'ottica neutoniana* (1737), in which a man is at pains to show his urbanity and charm in instructing a woman in the complexities of natural philosophy, thereby assuring the reader that these complexities will be explored in an agreeable and accessible manner.

he entered, and said to me, that 'the church was much longer than he imagined.'

In passing under the dome, the boldness of Michael Angelo reminded me of the imagination of Shakespeare; and the successive impressions made on me by Justice, Charity, and St. Michael the Archangel of Guido, the St. Jerome of Dominichino, and the Transfiguration of Raphael, were similar to those which I have often felt in reading Othello, &c.[33] The Frenchman has often too much delicacy in his taste; he is too easily chagrined, and he suffers more pain from a fault than he tastes pleasure from ten beauties.

Henry Matthews, *The Diary of an Invalid. Being the Journal of a Tour in Pursuit of Health in Portugal, Italy, Switzerland and France in the Years 1817, 1818 and 1819*, second edition (London: John Murray, 1820) [1820] pp. 132–3.

Went in the evening with a large party, amongst whom was Thorwaldson, to see the Vatican by torchlight. This is absolutely necessary, if you wish to appreciate justly the merit of the statues. Many of them were found in baths, where light was not admitted. They were created therefore for torch-light as their proper element; and the variety of light and shade, which is thus produced, heightens the effect prodigiously. There is something of the same kind of difference between the statues by day and by torchlight, as between a rehearsal in the morning, and the lighted theatre in the evening.

I have endeavoured in vain to admire the Apollo as much as I did the Venus; – and yet, if it were the perfection of the male figure, one ought to admire it more: for sculptors agree, that the male figure is the most beautiful subject for their art. But, perhaps it is impossible to divest oneself entirely of all sexual associations; – and this may be the secret charm of the Venus. – The ladies, I believe, prefer the Apollo. – By the way, I am surprised at the squeamishness which has induced the ruling powers at Florence and Rome, to deface the works of antiquity by the addition of a tin fig-leaf, which is fastened by a wire to all the male statues. One would imagine the Society for the Suppression of Vice had an affiliated establishment in Italy. Nothing can be more ridiculously prudish. That imagination must be depraved past all hope, that can find any prurient gratification in the cold chaste nakedness of an ancient marble. It is the fig-leaf alone that suggests any idea of indecency, and the effect of it is to spoil the statue. I was complaining loudly of this barbarous addition, when an Italian lady of the party assented to my criticism, and whispered in my ear, – that I must come

---

[33] [The three paintings mentioned were reproduced in St Peter's in the form of mosaics, which can still be seen there.]

again in the *Autumn*. This taste has however become so fixed, that Canova now cuts a fig-leaf out of the original block, and it thus becomes an integral part of the statue.

John Moore, *A View of Society and Manners in Italy, with Anecdotes Relating to some Eminent Characters*, second edition, 2 vols (London: W. Strahan and T. Cadell, 1781), vol. 2, pp. 9–12.

Moore, in Rome, refers to 'the ill-directed zeal of the early Christians' – which 'obliged the wretched heathens to hide the statues of their gods and of their ancestors in the bowels of the earth'.

Of those which have been dug up, I shall mention only a few, beginning with the Farnesian Hercules, which has been long admired as an exquisite model of masculine strength; yet, admirable as it is, it does not please all the world. I am told that the women in particular find something unsatisfactory, and even odious, in this figure; which, however majestic, is deficient in the charms most agreeable to them, and which might have been expected in the son of Jupiter and the beauteous Alcmena. A lady whom I accompanied to the Farnese palace, turned away from it in disgust. I could not imagine what had shocked her. She told me, *after recollection*, that she could not bear the stern severity of his countenance, his large brawny limbs, and the club with which he was armed; which gave him more the appearance of one of those giants that, according to the old romances, carried away virgins and shut them up in gloomy castles, than the gallant Hercules, the lover of Omphale. Finally, the lady declared, she was convinced this statue could not be a just representation of Hercules; for it was not in the nature of things, that a man so formed could ever have been a reliever of distressed damsels.

Without such powerful support as that of the fair sex, I should not have exposed myself to the resentment of connoisseurs, by any expression which they might construe an attack upon this favourite statue; but, with their support, I will venture to assert, that the Farnese Hercules is faulty both in his form and attitude: the former is too unwieldy for active exertion, and the latter exhibits vigour *exhausted*. A resting attitude is surely not the most proper in which the all-conquering god of strength could be represented. Rest implies fatigue, and fatigue strength exhausted. A reposing Hercules is almost a contradiction. Invincible activity, and inexhaustible strength, are his characteristics. The ancient artist has erred, not only in giving him an attitude which supposes his strength wants recruiting, but in the nature of the strength itself, the character of which should not be passive, but active.

[Lewis Engelbach,] *Naples and the Campagna Felice. In a Series of Letters Addressed to a Friend in England, in 1802* (London: R. Ackermann, 1815), pp. 184–8.

The traveller, in the museum at Portici, has fallen into conversation with an Italian woman, Donna Anna, and her husband, Don Ignazio.

After a cursory glance over several paintings of minor importance, we arrived before one which, notwithstanding its superlative excellence, one might have supposed a lady would have passed by, with, at least, affected indifference*. Not that the bare subject could be termed strictly indecent, but in the design, nay, even in the colouring, there was a degree of amatory warmth which a British female would have disdained noticing through any other medium than her fansticks. Donna Anna's refined taste, however, rose superior to the usual delicacy of her sex, she courageously met the foe face to face; and, *sans cérémonie*, required to be informed of the import of the representation. – But you, my dear T. shall know it first, however ungallant it may be to leave the lady's curiosity in suspense for a moment.

A beautiful young Bacchante, with her thyrsus and crotalum, was resting from her revels in a sequestered spot on a piece of rock, unconscious of the approach of an amorous young Faun. In an instant he flings away his crook and seven-tubed pipes, and seizes from behind upon the unsuspecting damsel; with one hand he draws her head backwards, the other assists in the operation, and thus he has free play to —— imprint a *faunish* kiss on her blushing cheeks; not, mind! without as fair a portion of the lady's resistance as is demanded by female decorum. Now that is all, believe me; but to describe the beauties of the design, the masterly colouring, the contrast between the delicate snowy carnation of the female, and the dark, yet not copper-coloured skin of the sylvan spark; the expression of lustful desire in the face of the latter (which is not unlike the goat's in the livery-stable opposite our friend B's), and that of blushing surprise in the Bacchante's countenance, it would be fruitless to attempt.

'I believe, madam, it is a Faun stealing a kiss from a female Bacchante.'

'*Stealing?* Ha! ha! ha!' (Here the penetrating Donna Anna expressed her astonishment at my simplicity, by an immoderate burst of laughter.) 'Pray do tell me, good sir, what is her right hand doing during this pretended robbery?'

'What else, but pushing off the head of the impudent intruder?'

'Oh! better still! so this hand which she has placed most lovingly *over* the Faun's head is meant to push him *away*? Nay, now do speak the truth, sir, and tell us if you would care to be pushed *off* in the same manner by a sweetheart of your's? But, who knows, perhaps it is the fashion in your

---

* See plate 7 [Figure 10].

country for ladies to ward off the attacks of gentlemen in this way. There's no knowing, every country has its peculiar customs. – However, wait! my good husband shall decide the point; he is a connoisseur, I assure you.'

Don Ignazio felt greatly flattered at being called upon (by his partner for life too), *tantas componere lites*.[34] After, therefore (*avec réspect*), profusely salivating the bright floor over his left shoulder, *sélon la coutume du pays*, and extricating his right hand from its fashionable resting place in the nankeen hose, in order the better to point at the object of his comment, he declared that, without being usually an abettor of his wife's opinions (for which I gave him full credit), the position of the damsel's hand was such, that it must either move or stand still; if it moved, it must inevitably draw the Faun's head *to* her, and if it did not, it must leave his head in its original place.[35]

'Bravo! bravo!' exclaimed the captian. 'Bravo!' resounded the echo of the subaltern. – '*Benissimo!*' added the lively signora, 'see what it is to have a husband of good parts, that has as much wit in his little finger as — in all his brain.' The latter part of this compliment, it must be said to her credit, was delivered *con sordini*.[36]

'You interrupted me,' continued Don Ignazio, 'before I had done. There is another thing to be observed. This lady has thrown away her thyrsus and crotalum; for no other reason, I suspect, than to enjoy the frolic at her ease; she would otherwise have kept them for her defence. A crotalum appears to me an excellent weapon of defence, which she might have used as a little shield, and with the massy pine-apple-head of the thyrsus she might, if she had chosen, have given the Faun a knock or two on the head, which would, no doubt, have cooled his courage wonderfully.'

This additional observation of Don Ignazio I thought not amiss. It put me in mind of the young woman's pocket handkerchief at one of our assizes.

We were on the point of taking our leave of the Faun, when our female antiquarian was called back by a new object of her curiosity. This sylvan deity had, like every one of his brethren, a pretty little tail, briskly cocked up in a truly caprine attitude, to correspond with the state of mind of its owner; but such was the delicacy of the chaste artist, that this faunian appendix was rather indicated than distinctly pourtrayed, and, as the

---

[34] [Virgil, *Eclogues*, 3.108-9: 'to settle such great disputes'.]
[35] ['With respect'; 'according to the custom of the country'.]
[36] [For *in sordino*: 'under her breath'. In the next speech, *thyrsus*: a rod carried by Dionysus (Bacchus) and his followers, draped with vines and ivy (although these are not discernible in the illustration reproduced in Figure 10) and capped by the 'massy pine-apple-head' that Don Ignazio describes in the next sentence (In the illustration, this looks more like a tuft of plant growth, but it is more clearly visible in the original painting). *Crotalum*: a variety of castanet used in ancient religious dances. Both these objects are visible at the front of the painting, below the bacchante's right foot.]

Faun's position was nearly fronting, five ninths, at most, were visible to the spectator. Yet, for all that, even such a trifle did not escape the argus eye of Donna Anna, which I suspect of microscopic construction in matters of such classic import. Instantly, therefore, five or six very intricate questions were addressed to your humble servant, with all the volubility of the most eager inquisitiveness; to answer which, in a competent and satisfactory manner, nothing short of a dissertation *de Faunorum et Satyrorum caudiculis, earumque forma, usu ac origine*, would have fulfilled the lady's expectations of my antiquarian abilities.[37] For such an undertaking, however, this was neither the time nor place. Under a promise, therefore, to treat this topic at large when I should again have the honour of being in her society (for I had already politely declined her pot-luck invitation for to-day) I began by merely giving a cursory explanation of the matter, when Don Ignazio, whether from a suggestion of his stomach, or an innate aversion to the subject under discussion, looked at his watch, exclaiming, 'It is half past seventeen; we shall be too late for dinner.' – This opportune admonition instantly adjourned the question. Madame as well as the officers thought they had seen enough, and were for returning to town immediately. They very kindly offered me a seat in their carriage, which I thankfully accepted, as I had come to Portici on foot in the morning, with the idea of spending the best part of the day in the museum, taking my chance of finding a dinner at my old landlord's with the night-cap in Resina, and returning at my ease in the cool of the evening. Although it was still early in the day, I confess to you, the company I had been in, and what I had seen and heard among them, diminished, in some measure, the classic zeal with which I had begun my survey of these valuable treasures, and with which I wished to investigate the whole. I consequently determined to return on another early day, and see the remainder at my leisure. Indeed, I think the present day's task is not quite so contemptible (in quantity I mean), allowing for the interruptions I had to encounter.

II: Sculpture studios: socializing with works of art

In the commentaries considered in the first section of this chapter, it is a spectator who draws a work of art into the domain of everyday life, prompts an awareness of erotic undercurrents, and so throws established categories into confusion. A number of accounts of art in travel writing, on the other hand, deploy a particular setting – that of the sculpture studio, in Rome – in order to produce a similar confusion of categories

---

[37] ['On the little tails of Fauns and Satyrs, their form, use and origin.']

11. H.D.C. Martens, *Pope Leo XII Visits Thorvaldsen's Studios near the Piazza Barberini, Rome, on St Luke's Day, October 18th, 1826* (1830). 100 x 138 cm. Thorvaldsens Museum, Copenhagen

(and sometimes, as happens in the first of the passages below, from Matthews's *Diary of an Invalid*, to prompt an especially dynamic relation between the spectator and the work). Narratives of visiting sculpture studios, which might seem merely to affirm the established rules and conventions of sightseeing, can nonetheless disrupt these conventions with surprising force.

Many early nineteenth-century travel writings include accounts of visits to such studios: in particular, those of Canova and Thorvaldsen (see Figure 11).[38] Stendhal, in *Promenades dans Rome* (1830), not only includes both these studios in the fourth day of his 'Manière de voir Rome en dix jours' ('How to see Rome in ten days'), but also, in one of his *Suppléments* to this work, notes how much to tip the workman who conducts visitors

[38] On Canova's studio and mode of working (and, indirectly, travellers' attempts to understand his practice), see Hugh Honour, 'Canova's Studio Practice – I: The Early Years', *The Burlington Magazine*, 114:828 (1972), pp. 146–59, and 'Canova's Studio Practice – II: 1792–1822', *The Burlington Magazine*, 114:829 (1972), pp. 214–29.

around Thorvaldsen's seven or eight ateliers. (The amount specified is 2 paoli.)[39]

Such accounts prompt at least two questions. First, what are the preconditions for this relatively sudden fascination with the studio visit? – preconditions, that is, to be traced within the rhetoric of travel literature, rather than within some traditional structure of explanation, which, imagined in its simplest form, would see traveller-critics as merely responding to developments in the art and culture around them (the gathering of a number of well-known sculptors in Rome).

The second question is simply: what rhetorical purpose does an narrative of a studio visit fulfil – when compared, for example, to an account of viewing works of art in a Roman palazzo?

Behind the scenes

One obvious aim achieved by describing a visit to a studio is that it gives the traveller-narrator an excuse for name-dropping: engaging in a form of 'behind-the-scenes' tourism, and boasting of access to privileged circles.[40] Sydney, Lady Morgan, in the third of the passages below, is eager to impress upon the reader that she has seen Canova ('the master-genius himself') wielding his 'immortal chisel' in person – and cites the very garments that he wears when doing so ('his nankeen jacket and yellow slippers'), as though his engagement with the antique ideal might be expected to raise him, like most of his sculptures, above such mundane conventions as the need to wear clothes.

Charlotte Eaton, in the second passage below, from *Rome in the Nineteenth Century* (1820), smuggles in a similar boast of personal intimacy with a 'master-genius' under the guise of mitigating her censure of one of Canova's most famous works. Introducing 'the groupe of the Graces, the beauty of which is the object of universal admiration here' (see Figures 6 and 7), she pointedly proclaims her own personal spontaneity of response by setting her own views in opposition to the orthodoxy that she has conjured up:

> Beautiful as it is, I own it struck me as being rather *manieré*, especially in the attitude and face of the central figure, which is chargeable with somewhat of affectation, – somewhat of studied Opera-house airs, and put-on sweetness of countenance.

---

[39] Stendhal [Henri Beyle], *Promenades dans Rome*, p. 1184, p. 1268 (Supplément IX).
[40] See Dean MacCannell, *The Tourist: A New Theory of the Leisure Class* (New York: Schocken Books, 1976), pp. 91–107, for an analysis of the role of front and back regions in touristic experience.

Eaton, however, suddenly modifies her censure, and, with an air of resolving the question, remarks conclusively that she herself has been present at its creation:

> But I criticize with reluctance a work, which, whatever may be its faults, has rarely been equalled in modern art, and the progress of which I have long watched with unspeakable interest and delight. It is only a few days since I saw the finishing strokes given to it by the hand of Canova.

The studio visit, in these two commentaries, elicits hyperboles sufficiently intense to designate sculpture studios as places that demand a response of wonder and enthralment. Lady Morgan reaches for a hyperbole of incomparability: 'there was, in our estimation, *nothing in Rome more worthy to be seen* than Canova himself at work, habited in his nankeen jacket and yellow slippers' (emphasis added). Eaton's opportunity to witness the production of the *Three Graces* prompts a hyperbole of indescribability: she feels 'unspeakable interest and delight'.

Travellers endorse their acclamations of sculpture studios as sites of wonder by emphasizing that, in making their way into them, they have acquired an ability to reveal secrets – to unveil the mysteries of the craft. Morgan introduces her visits to Thorvaldsen and Canova by noting 'the rubbish, ruins, and fragments' amongst which their places of work lie concealed. Even within Canova's studio itself, she traces a progress through further bathetic distraction to the object of her quest: 'At the extremity of this suite is the cabinet of the master-genius himself, far from the din and bustle of less inspired workmen.' Eaton beckons the reader into a domain of privileged technical knowledge:

> Perhaps you may have no very clear idea of the progress of a sculptor in his work; at least, I find that many of my countrymen, whom I have introduced to Canova's studio, had previously supposed that his custom was to fall upon a block of marble, and chisel away till he made it into a statue.

An awareness of art as process, far from detracting from the alluring aloofness of the antique ideal, is seen as prompting a more intense awareness of genius: by imagining the sculptor at grips with the work, the traveller defines that work as the product of a dramatic confrontation between heightened imagination and sternly elemental material reality. Matthews, in the first passage below, observes: 'It is curious to see the progress of a statue, from the rough block of marble, to the last *ad unguem* finish; which is all that is done by the master hand.' Eaton, embarking upon a detailed technical account of Canova's mode of working, counteracts her potentially bathetic reference to the humble clay model from which the plaster cast is made, in order to provide a basis for the finished work in marble, by noting the 'visionary' spirit in which this work is conceived – a spirit that propels her beyond the prosaic ordinariness of the English language: 'He forms his model in clay, and this is entirely the work of his own hands; but before he begins, the statue is perfectly *ideato*, – the visionary figure is before him.'

Anna Jameson promises recondite details of the working of sculptural inspiration when describing a visit to the studio of John Gibson, conducted by the artist himself (the sculptor, she confides 'was Canova's favourite pupil', and 'has quite the air of a genius'). She begins her account of 'his exquisite group of Psyche borne away by the Zephyrs' by following the same strategy deployed by Eaton to describe Canova's *Three Graces*: that of invoking an orthodoxy and then proclaiming her own responsiveness by disagreeing with it: 'Psyche was criticised by two or three of our party; but I thought her faultless.' An anecdote of preceptorial intervention by the 'master-genius' then supplies a culminatory hyperbole:

> Mr W** told me that in the original design, the left foot of one of the Zephyrs rested upon the ground; and that Canova coming in by chance while Gibson was working on the model, lifted it up, and this simple and masterly alteration has imparted the most exquisite lightness to the attitude.[41]

Gossiping about art

Visitors to studios, however, constantly oscillate between hyperbole and ironic digression. Stendhal, describing Canova's studio, recognizes the digressive force of the anecdote, and its ability to draw the traveller away from the ideal (and from hyperbolic responsiveness) into divagatory trivia; he asks, ironically, 'veut-on de petites anecdotes d'atelier?' ('would the reader like some little studio anecdotes?'), and then imparts the confidential snippet that the second version of the sculptor's famous *Magdalene* was sculpted from the piece of marble taken from between the legs of the statue of Napoleon.[42]

Offering the reader pieces of inconsequential gossip of this kind allows travellers to voice an oblique criticism of the elevated forms of language so often allotted to art in general, and to the classical ideal in particular. If elevated responsiveness were more satisfying and pleasurable as a mode of approaching neo-classical sculpture, it is implied, the impulse to find ways of eluding its limitations would not be felt so forcefully. This impulse is charted, in some commentaries, by voicing, obliquely, a desire that art should somehow 'join in' – should become embroiled in the messiness and triviality of everyday life. Traveller-critics of the period register enormous fascination with figures who equivocate between art

---

[41] [Jameson,] *Diary of an Ennuyée*, p. 278.
[42] Stendhal, *Promenades dans Rome*, p. 1083.

12. Antonio Canova, *Venere Vincitrice*, front view, engraved by Domenico Marchetti, in *Recueil de statues, groupes, bustes, mausolées, colosses et monumens de tout genre*. 39.5 x 55.3 cm. Research Library, The Getty Research Institute, Los Angeles (91-F0). The sculpture is in the Villa Borghese, Rome

and life, and so endorse an easy movement between the two, in the manner of Emma Hamilton, who imitates the poses of classical sculpture in her famous 'attitudes', while displaying ebullient unrestraint in everyday life, and Paolina Borghese, sculpted by Canova as Venus, and defined as scandalous both in posing for this sculpture and in her amorous excesses (see Figures 12 and 13).[43] In the case of the Princess Borghese, it

[43] For the perception of Emma Hamilton as a work of art, see, for example, Horace Walpole's comment, in a letter, on her marriage to her lover, the British Envoy at Naples, under whose auspices the 'attitudes' are staged: 'Sir William Hamilton has actually married his gallery of statues'; *The Yale Edition of Horace Walpole's Correspondence*, edited by W.S. Lewis, 40 vols (London: Yale University Press, 1937–83), vol. 11, p. 249. For accounts of her unrestraint, see, for example, [Charlotte-Louise-Éléonore-Adélaïde] de Boigne, *Mémoires de la Comtesse de Boigne*, edited by Charles Nicollaud, 4 vols (Paris: Plon-Nourrit, 1907), vol. 1, pp. 113–15, *Life and Letters of Sir Gilbert Elliot, First Earl of Minto, from 1751 to 1806*, edited by the Countess of Minto, 3 vols (London: Longmans, Green, 1874), vol. 2, pp. 364–6, *Souvenirs de Madame Vigée-Lebrun*, 2 vols (Paris: Charpentier, 1891; first published 1835–37), vol. 1, pp. 193–9.

Relevant comments on Paolina Borghese include, in addition to those cited below, [Jameson,] *Diary of an Ennuyée*, p. 273.

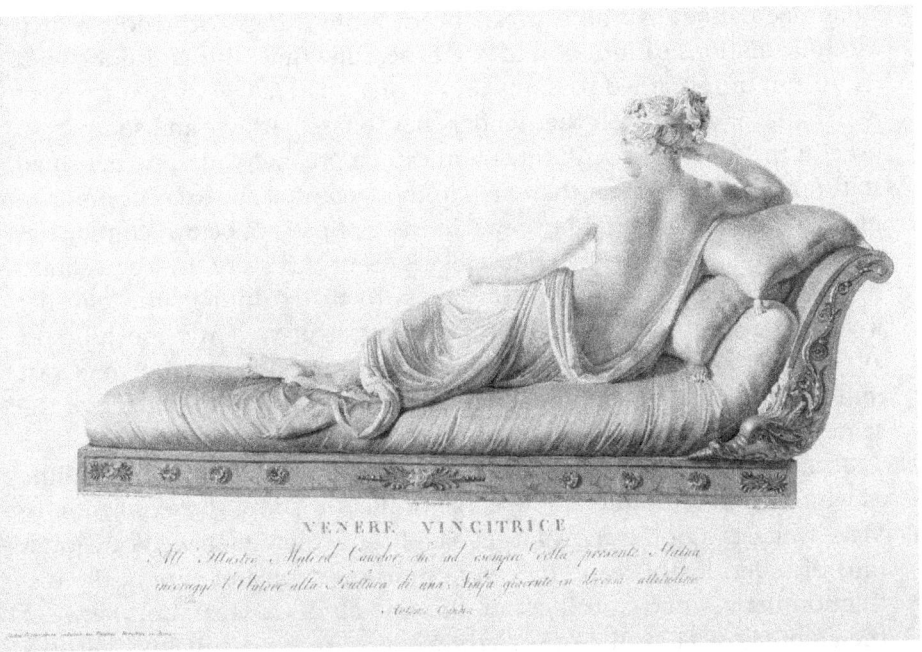

13. Antonio Canova, *Venere Vincitrice*, back view, drawn by Luigi Durantini and engraved by Angelo Bertini, in *Recueil de statues, groupes, bustes, mausolées, colosses et monumens de tout genre*. © The British Library Board (Tab.488.c.). 39.1 x 54.6 cm

is primarily her role as the model for Canova's *Venere Vincitrice* that allows her to be defined both as a sculpted figure and as a woman of flesh and blood. Eaton recounts a well-known anecdote about the Prince Borghese – Paolina's husband – locking the *Venus* away in a room where no-one can view it ('not even Canova himself'); such a narrative invests the sculpture with an eroticized danger beyond that even of the notorious principessa herself – the traveller observes pointedly that the prince makes no attempt to impose any analogous limitations on his wife.[44]

As a woman who, on the one hand, serves as a model for a work that aspires to the classical ideal and, on the other, is known for her everyday dissipations, the principessa invites the ironic or humorous response that

The role assigned to the two women in travel writing is explored in my *Pleasure and Guilt on the Grand Tour: Travel Writing and Imaginative Geography, 1600-1830* (Manchester and New York: Manchester University Press, 1999), pp. 147–53 and p. 168.

[44] Eaton, *Rome in the Nineteenth Century*, vol. 3, p. 47. For other references to the princess as sitter for the sculpture, see Galiffe, *Italy and its Inhabitants*, vol. I, pp. 254–5, and Thomas Love Peacock, *Crotchet Castle*, published in 1831 (*Nightmare Abbey, Crotchet Castle*, edited by Raymond Wright (Harmondsworth: Penguin, 1969)), p. 189.

Coleridge defines as 'the comparison of finite things with those which our imaginations cannot bound'.[45] At the same time, this anecdote, with its hint of unrestrained passions on Paolina's part, suggests that the very penchant for dissipation that renders her so fascinating – and so ready to pose in the nude for a sculpture – indicates a proclivity, despite her small stature, to become 'larger than life', in the sense that she exceeds limits in her everyday behaviour. Matthews, in the first passage below, emphasizes this same quality when he relates a version of this story (in his account, it is Paolina herself who controls access to the sculpture); the traveller invokes her brother Napoleon in order to set up a gently mock-heroic analogy between her impatience of convention and the emperor's vast military and political ambitions: 'her genius seems also to partake of the same character and to scorn the restrictions of ordinary rules.'

Both these commentaries use effects of humour to affirm, in Paolina as woman and sculpture, an 'upsurge of life' (to adopt the expression of Mary Douglas, quoted above), capable of throwing established categories into disorder: in this case, by calling into question not simply the distinction between art and life, but also any absolute separation between the aloof classical ideal and the erotic charge that may attach itself to a neo-classical sculpture (in this case, in part, by virtue of the vitality and transgressiveness of the model). The commentaries cited in the first part of the present chapter, it has been suggested, trace out this same plot of an upsurge of life through a glimpse of erotic undercurrents in works of art. They do so primarily by reference to the spectators and the exchanges between them, but the works themselves, too, are always seen as intervening in the dynamics of viewing: the comments of spectators, however eccentric, are prompted by some element within the paintings and sculptures that is acknowledged by the traveller-narrator. Accounts of sculpture studios have a particularly extended potential cast list: they can, in theory, introduce the artist, the models, the sculptures and the spectators – all interacting in a space that is on the borderline between the public and the private. These multiple participants in the drama of viewing may, it is implied, produce some unpredictable exchanges.

Matthews, in his account of Canova's studio, sets up a drama in which the sculptor, one of his works, a female spectator and the traveller-narrator and his party all play a part. Provocative qualities within the work – in this case, the result of the sculptor's liveliness of 'expression', transgressing the bounds of taste (see Figures 14 and 15) – attract the attention of an

---

[45] See Coleridge's lecture 'Wit and Humour', as summarized by contemporaries in *Coleridge's Miscellaneous Criticism*, edited by Thomas Middleton Raysor (London: Constable, 1936), pp. 111–30, p. 113. (The editor, in a footnote, points out that this sentence is a paraphrase of a passage in Jean Paul Richter's *Vorschule der Ästhetik*, section 32.)

Italian woman, who demonstrates her enthusiasm in a robustly physical manner, which goes far beyond the discreet whisperings of the woman whom the same traveller encounters in the Belvedere Courtyard, and draws Matthews and his companions into the drama of viewing by looking round to them 'for confirmation of her opinion'.

Paradoxically, unrestraint in expression is heightened, in the traveller's assessment, by the failure in invention that prompts Canova to borrow too copiously and conspicuously from the ancients. The model that the sculptor has imitated, here, is the *Hermaphrodite* (see Figure 16), a work that by its very nature directs attention to the parts of the body indicative of gender; the ease with which such a figure can be invested with impropriety is indicated by Charles Dupaty's arch comment on one of the versions of the sculpture: he proclaims, at the Uffizi: 'N'entrez jamais dans le cabinet de l'hermaphrodite, si vous ne voulez pas rougir de plaisir et de honte tout-à-la-fois' ('Never enter the cabinet of the *hermaphrodite*, if you do not wish to blush for pleasure and shame at the same instant').[46] In assessing Canova's sculpture, the traveller-narrator equivocates between pleasure and censure:

> *Chloris* awakened, is an exquisite performance; – but it is plain that Canova's mind was full of the Hermaphrodite, when he modelled it. The introduction of the Cupid is well imagined, as a sort of excuse for the attitude. It is impossible to look at this recumbent nymph, without admiring the delicate finishing of the sculptor, but one cannot applaud the taste of the design. The expression of the whole is scarcely within the bounds of decency; – for, it is the expression, and not the nudity of a statue, 'the disposition, and not the exposition of the limbs,' upon which this depends.

At this point, Matthews introduces his female spectator-critic: an Italian woman who, like her compatriot at the Belvedere Courtyard, possesses the mixture of innocence and knowingness required in order to affirm the erotic qualities of the work more ebulliently than the traveller himself has done. Perceiving the same 'gratification of voluptuousness' that so preoccupies Matthews, she moves with perfect serenity between art and sexuality, and calmly indicates that 'delicate finishing' may be combined with more indelicate elements:

> While we were admiring the exquisite finishing of Canova's chisel, a young Italian lady with a party joined us, who was thrown into an ecstasy of admiration by the charms of Chloris's figure; and she patted the jutting beauties with delight, exclaiming, – while she looked round to us for confirmation of her opinion, – *Bella cosa! Bella cosa! O che bella cosa!*

---

46 [Charles Dupaty,] *Letttres sur l'Italie, en 1785*, 2 vols ('Rome et se trouve à Paris': de Senne, 1788), vol. 1, p. 154, *Sentimental Letters on Italy*, translated by J. Povoleri, 2 vols (London: J. Crowder and J. Bew, 1789), vol. 1, p. 121.

The traveller, then, turns his irony not only against the woman's spiritedly tactile approach to art, but also against the critical decorum that she abandons, and half acknowledges the attractions of her more unaffected responsiveness. Her air of natural spontaneity, in recognizing enthusiastically that very 'expression' that so arouses Matthews's 'squeamishness', ineluctably suggests that the work itself must possess a corresponding naturalness and vitality, even in the face of the traveller's criticisms of Canova's work as too strongly tied to the unnatural affectations of fashion. ('There is a finical fashionable air about his female figures', he remarks, at the beginning of this passage; just after the encounter with the *Chloris*, he qualifies his praise of the *Cupid and Psyche* by the dismissive observation that 'Psyche's hair looks as if it had been dressed by a French friseur'.)

For Matthews, in other words, the material resemblance that sculptures bear to human beings could consign them to a domain of insipidity in which they fail to rise to the condition of art; the woman's recognition of the erotic allure of the sculpture, however, suggests to him that this very resemblance gives sculpture an advantage over painting in allowing the viewer to comment on art with a sense of affectionate intimacy. Sydney Morgan establishes a similarly nonchalant elision between sculptures and animate beings when, in a footnote, she comments on Sommariva: 'I believe he has succeeded in carrying off Canova's favourite *"nymph,"* who had more competitors, when we were at Rome, for her possession, than any living beauty in Europe.'[47]

Through her intervention in the drama of viewing, the woman allows the narrator to enjoy the comic potential of the effect that Georges Bataille, in his essay 'L'expérience intérieure', terms a *dénivellation* – a drop in level. Bataille analyses the pleasure of comic irreverence as a pleasure that goes beyond mere malicious delight at the discomfiture of purveyors of pomposity:

> Si je tire la chaise . . . à la suffisance d'un sérieux personnage succède soudain la révélation d'une insuffisance dernière (on tire la chaise à des êtres fallacieux). Je suis heureux, quoi qu'il en soit, de l'échec éprouvé. Et je perds mon sérieux moi-même, en riant. Comme si c'était un soulagement d'échapper au souci de ma suffisance.[48]

> If I pull the chair out from under someone . . . the sufficiency of a serious character is suddenly succeeded by the revelation of an insufficiency (we pull chairs out from under fallacious beings). I feel happy, in any case, with the sense of a setback

---

[47] Morgan, *Italy*, vol. 2, p. 228n.
[48] Georges Bataille, 'L'expérience intérieure', in *Œuvres complètes*, edited by Michel Foucault, 12 vols (Paris: Gallimard, 1970–88), vol. 5, pp. 7–181, p. 106 (the ellipsis is part of the original text).

that is felt. And I lose my seriousness myself, in laughing. As though it were a relief to escape the anxiety of my sufficiency.

Matthews, then, as in his commentary on the fig leaves in the Belvedere Courtyard, introduces an Italian woman who pulls the chair out from under a fallacious seriousness – that of the discourse of art criticism, with its claim to provide an outlet for the most exalted of responses; in finding himself drawn into her view of art, he experiences the delight of escaping his own seriousness and 'suffisance'. When she ignores the incongruity between the exalted domain of antique art and the more down-to-earth domain of sexuality, and elides the two, the woman opens up the possibility of a cheerful frivolity and irresponsibility; the seriousness that she sweeps aside is initially shared by the traveller – she pulls the chair out from under him as well as from under an implicit critical orthodoxy – but he is sufficiently entranced to enjoy his fall: or, rather, to see the possibilities of flirting with the reader as the woman flirts with him – by inviting the reader, that is, to sample the same delights of easy intimacy, in the presence of great art, that he himself is relishing.

Mingling with art in a serious city

What, then, is the 'suffisance' that it is so pleasurable to escape? – what is it to which the traveller, in this commentary, has been trying to prove himself equal? One answer would be that he has been attempting to find a language that meets the demands of the elevated domain of art – and of the celebrated works of art that assume a place within the sights and wonders of Italy. He has, in particular, been preoccupied with managing his encounter with the high seriousness of Rome – the city in which travellers seek out sculpture studios, as one of its topographically specific attractions.

The sense that the Eternal City places unusual demands on the traveller has already been considered in the Introduction, with reference to John Chetwode Eustace's *Tour through Italy* (1813), in which the traveller observes: 'The *severe majesty* that seems to preside as the genius of the place, proscribes frivolity, and inspires loftiness of thought and gravity of deportment'.[49] The 'loftiness of thought' induced by the city is affirmed with great force and concision later in the nineteenth century by Lord Warburton, in Henry James's *Portrait of a Lady* (1881), when he remarks to

---

[49] John Chetwode Eustace, *A Tour through Italy, Exhibiting a View of its Scenery, its Antiquities, and its Monuments, Particularly as they are Objects of Classical Interest and Elucidation*, 3 vols (London: J. Mawman, 1813–19), vol. 2, p. 67.

Isabel Archer: 'Ah, when I said that I was passing through I didn't mean that one would treat Rome as if it were Clapham Junction.'[50]

Matthews, in order to demonstrate that he has somehow preserved his composure amid the daunting task of translating Rome into forms of language, neatly transforms the viewing of works of art into a social experience: he introduces female spectators who lure the traveller away from high seriousness into a domain of laughter and flirtation, and who do so by taking it for granted that they can establish an easy intimacy and complicity with the sculptures themselves.

Even in a commentary in which a sculpture draws the viewers into a *mise-en-scène* of intense romantic passion, the studio visit emphasizes that reverential wonder is not the only way in which to approach works of art. Germaine de Staël, in *Corinne*, constructs a variant on the narrative in which a woman draws the attention of a man towards the *frisson* to be derived from confusing sculptures with human beings: the heroine, at Canova's studio with her Scottish lover Oswald, Lord Nelvil, responds to a work in a way that draws attention not to herself but to Oswald, and prompts him delicately to touch on their feelings for each other, in tones of sufficient melancholy to hint – very obliquely – at the doomed nature of their passion:

> Il y avoit chez Canova une admirable statue destinée pour un tombeau: elle représentait le Génie de la douleur, appuyé sur un lion, emblème de la force. Corinne, en contemplant ce Génie, crut y trouver quelque ressemblance avec Oswald, et l'artiste lui-même en fut aussi frappé. Lord Nelvil se détourna pour ne point attirer ce genre d'attention; mais il dit à voix basse à son amie: – Corinne, j'étois condamnée à cette éternelle douleur quand je vous ai rencontrée; mais vous avez changé ma vie.[51]

> There was at Canova's studio an admirable statue destined for a tomb: it represented the Spirit of Sorrow, leaning upon a lion, symbol of strength. Corinne, contemplating this Spirit, thought that she discerned in it some resemblance to Oswald, and the artist himself was also struck by this. Lord Nelvil turned aside in order not to attract this sort of attention; but he said to his friend in a low voice: – Corinne, I was condemned to this eternal sorrow at the time when we met; but you have changed my life.

The presence of the artist, here, and his intervention in the discussion, prompt an especially strong awareness of the studio visit as a social space, in which interaction with art becomes entangled with interaction with human beings.

---

[50] Henry James, *The Portrait of a Lady* (Penguin: Harmondsworth, 1971; first published in 1881), p. 292.

[51] Madame de Staël, *Corinne, ou l'Italie*, edited by Claudine Herrmann, 2 vols (Paris, Éditions des femmes, 1979), vol. 1, p. 208.

Artists make spectacles of themselves

Another precondition for the preoccupation with visits to artists' studios, over this period, is the more general fascination that late eighteenth-century and early nineteenth-century travel writings register with travellers who establish a presence within the topography of the foreign and transmute into sights and wonders for other travellers to visit and view. Such travellers include several already mentioned, the Englishwoman Emma Hamilton, in Naples (spectacular by virtue of her 'Attitudes' and her stupendous vulgarity in her social existence), the Corsican Paolina Borghese, in Rome (a sight in her own right, as a visible object of gossip and scandal, and as the model for Canova's *Venere vincitrice*), and the fictional Corinne, who initially seems straightforwardly Italian, but turns out to be half-English, and to have returned to Italy after an unhappy adolescence in England, transmuting into spectacle in her role as an *improvvisatrice*. Forsyth includes artists within this category of sights and wonders by listing them among the noteworthy features of Rome, and explaining how they come to assume their role as part of the scenery:

> Canova, Kauffman, Benvenuti, Denys, Thorwaldeir, all the principal artists of Rome are foreign to it. They came hither to form or to perfect their style. Here they meet congenial society, they catch inspirations from the sights of great works, they contract a dependence on such helps, and at last they can do nothing well out of Rome. Poussin ascribed it to the air: I have heard Angelica say that the water of Rome revived her powers, and gave her ideas.[52]

Travel writings dramatize the paradox by which artists alien to Rome can become integral to it by emphasizing the geographical trajectory that has led them from their far-flung origins. Eaton specifies Thorvaldsen's exotic provenance just after hyperbolically affirming his talents, as though to suggest that his origins somehow contribute to her sense of his worth; at the same time, she allows herself to diverge from sober accuracy in order to invest his transmutation into Roman spectacle with greater drama. The artist, she observes in a footnote 'was born at Copenhagen; his father was an Icelander, who settled there'. On the basis of his paternity, therefore, she is able to declare:

> I feel, in this imperfect sketch, I have done little justice to the merit of this truly great genius, who has come from the frozen shores of Iceland to the land of arts, to astonish the natives of her brilliant clime, with works that might have done honour to her earlier days.[53]

---

[52] Joseph Forsyth, *Remarks on Antiquities, Arts, and Letters during an Excursion in Italy in the Years 1802 and 1803* (London: T. Cadell and W. Davies, 1813), pp. 262–3. See also p. 258: 'Rome has always adopted men of genius; but she has given birth to few.'
[53] Eaton, *Rome in the Nineteenth Century*, vol. 3, p. 305n, pp. 305–6.

Sydney Morgan is equally eager to emphasize the extent to which 'Genius' has travelled:

> Rome is indeed, at this moment, the great studio of the world; and this is the aspect in which it is most delightful to consider her. The congress of talent assembled from all nations of the earth, to promote the arts, is well worth all other congresses; and Genius sending forth her sons from the frozen regions of the Baltic, or the sunny vallies of the dew-dripping South, affords a far more gracious aspect of society, than those portentous meetings of sovereigns, in which the interest of a few takes precedence of the welfare of all; and which are no less fatal to the liberties of the nations they represent, than of those whom they assemble to crush.

Travel writings take care to include Canova, as the principal artist-turned-attraction of Rome, within this category; his birth 'at Possagno, a small village in the Venetian territory' (as Eaton puts it), his initial struggle to gain recognition in the Eternal City, and the extent to which English patrons have helped to establish his reputation all supply travellers with a means of emphasizing that in Rome he is, definitively, a foreigner.[54]

Identifying with artists

Since artists are so eagerly defined not only as sights on the Grand Tour but also as travellers, their experience of Rome supplies a starting-point for allegorizing the encounter with that city in a much wider sense – for eliding the motivation of the artist with the motives that drive travellers in general towards the Eternal City. Jameson, in her analysis of the attraction of Rome for sculptors, opens up the possibility of identifying with these figures through a glancing quotation from the fourth canto of Byron's *Childe Harold's Pilgrimage* (1818):

> It is one of the pleasures of Rome to lounge in the Studij of the best sculptors; and it is at Rome only that sculpture seems to flourish as in its native soil. Rome is truly the *city of the soul*, the home of art and artists. With the divine models of the Vatican ever before their eyes, these inspiring skies above their heads and the quarries of marble at a convenient distance – it is here only they can conceive and execute those works which are formed from the beau-ideal.[55]

On the one hand, here, Jameson is concerned with the specific professional requirements of the artist – 'the quarries of marble at a convenient distance'. On the other hand, she quotes from a stanza of *Childe Harold* that evokes the emotional solace that the city has to offer not to one particular profession but to all those in a state of need:

> O Rome! my country! city of the soul!
> The orphans of the heart may turn to thee,

---

[54] Eaton, *Rome in the Nineteenth Century*, vol. 3, p. 294.
[55] [Jameson,] *Diary of an Ennuyée*, pp. 199–200.

> Lone mother of dead empires! and controul
> In their shut breasts their petty misery.[56]

One of the fantasies that Rome holds out for travellers, in other words, is a dream of dissolution of the bounds of 'petty' selfhood amid the vaster 'woes and sufferance' endured by 'the Niobe of nations' – as Byron terms the city in the next stanza. Such a dream, in Byron's version, incorporates not only the incipient sublimity of this loss of bounded self, but also a rather different, self-affirmatory version of the sublime, in which the traveller identifies with the city of wonders in its 'voiceless woe', and feels not merely consoled by the identification, but ennobled by the attempt to prove equal to it – raised above the pettiness of mere individual misery.[57] Jameson draws on this latter version of the sublime in her narrative of artistic inspiration: sculptors rise to the ideal sketched out for them by 'the divine models of the Vatican' and 'these inspiring skies above their heads'. At the same time, however, the words 'city of the soul' supply a point of continuity between the inspired artists and the more obscure sense of exaltation experienced by travellers for whom inspiration is an emotional need rather than a professional obligation.

A precondition for the dream of rising above 'petty misery' is the view of travel as an adventure of the self, in which stability is placed at risk. In visiting artists' studios, travellers confront this activity as a specialized form of viewing art in Rome – an activity that is consistently seen as exceptionally destabilizing, not only in the exhaustion that it induces, as discussed in the Introduction, but also in the emotional demands that it places upon the traveller (Eaton offers an ironically inflated example: the story of a Frenchwoman who falls in love with the *Apollo Belvedere*, and dies of her hopeless passion).[58] Accounts of the experiences of artists themselves, whose profession confers on them an especially urgent need to grapple with the power and authority embodied in the paintings and sculptures of the Eternal City, supply an occasion for summoning up visions of destabilization, which can then be displaced onto non-specialist travellers, upon whom the city imposes, in slightly more gentle terms, the same demand. Forsyth, in his suggestion that foreign artists who settle in Rome are unable to exercise their talents in any other context, is not the only writer to hint at dangers. Hazlitt, in his essay on 'English Students at Rome', observes darkly: 'If necessity is the mother of invention, it must be

---

[56] Byron, *Childe Harold's Pilgrimage*, Canto IV, stanza 78, lines 1-4; *Complete Poetical Works*, vol. 2 p. 150.
[57] Byron, *Childe Harold's Pilgrimage*, Canto IV, stanza 78, line 5, stanza 79, lines 1, 2; *Complete Poetical Works*, vol. 2, p. 150.
[58] Eaton, *Rome in the Nineteenth Century*, vol. 1, pp. 169–70.

stifled in the birth here, where everything is already done and provided to your hand that you could possibly wish for, or think of.'[59]

Traveller-narrators, then, readily identify with artists, as figures who supply models for the ambitions and fears of all travellers. At the same time, however, artists, when viewed in the context of their studios, supply a means of keeping the fear of destabilization at bay. In mingling with works of art in an atmosphere of easy sociability, the traveller finds in this experience not only a reassurance that the task of commenting on art may not be any more daunting than engaging in daily gossip, as suggested earlier, but also a model for mingling equally easily with the other wonders of art by which he or she is surrounded. Studios, in other words, supply a reassurance that viewing art may only be an extension of everyday social life.

At the same time, the very 'behind the scenes' details that travellers cite (Canova's 'nankeen jacket and yellow slippers') reinforce the suggestion that everyday life continues even amid the struggle to prove equal to the overwhelming plenitude and excellence of art in Rome, and that the two might in fact co-exist with each other in an unexpectedly easy and casual manner.

The status of artists as travellers who have transmuted into spectacle, moreover, affirms that travellers may indeed prove equal in one sense to the sights and wonders around them: as part of the spectacle of Rome, artist-travellers have actually been admitted within the ranks of these sights and wonders. They therefore offer hope of being in some way part of the life of a city that is very often defined – as it is by Byron when he claims it as his 'city of the soul' – as one whose identity is shaped as much by the demands of foreigners as by the day-to-day activities of locals.

Sculpture studios supply another reassuring option: since they contain many works that are for sale, and plasters that are to form the basis of commissions, they allow travellers to remind themselves that at least some of the sights of Rome are destined to circulate through other regions of the world; accounts of studio visits often name the destinations of particular works (Eaton, in the second passage below, notes that the most recent version of Canova's 'Venus coming out of the Bath' is 'destined for Lord Lansdowne'). They also mention the acquisitive impulse that sculptures excite – implicitly, in most cases, a desire to transport the works concerned to some other part of the globe. Anna Jameson, visiting Gibson's studio, is surprised that his *Psyche* remains unsold: 'Could I but afford to

---

[59] William Hazlitt, 'English Students at Rome', in *Essays on the Fine Arts*, edited by W. Carew Hazlitt (London: Reeves and Turner, 1873), pp. 321–33; p. 321.

bestow seven hundred pounds on my own gratification, I would have given him the order on the spot.'[60] Sydney Morgan begins her account of studios by dramatizing the seductions of art through an admirably equivocal metaphor of a consumerism that, like travel itself, prompts a desire to go beyond limits: '"Rome," says Evelyn, "is most tempting for a great person or a wanton purse;" a truth particularly felt in visiting the *studii*, or workshops of sculptors and painters, by those who are not *great persons*, and have not a *wanton purse*.'

Matthews, *The Diary of an Invalid*, pp. 124–8

[January] 9th. Went for the third time to Canova's *Studio;* who has, perhaps, attained a reputation beyond his merits. There is much grace in his works, but the effect is too often spoiled by an affected prettiness, or a theatrical display. There is a finical fashionable air about his female figures; and his men are all attitudinarians. He is too fond of borrowing from the ancients. This is to be lamented, for it does not seem to be necessary for him to borrow; and, his best works perhaps are those in which he has borrowed least; as the *Hercules and Lychas, Dœdalus and Icarus,* which he finished at 18, the *Cupid and Psyche,* and the *Venus and Adonis.*

But you can too often trace every limb and feature, to its corresponding prototype in the antique. This is pitiful. It is no excuse to say that all the beautiful attitudes have been forestalled, and that repetition is necessary. There certainly is nothing new under the sun; but, invention is displayed in a new *arrangement* of the same materials; and the human figure may be varied, in its attitudes and contours, *ad infinitum.*

Chloris awakened, is an exquisite performance; – but it is plain that Canova's mind was full of the Hermaphrodite, when he modelled it. The introduction of the Cupid is well imagined, as a sort of excuse for the attitude. It is impossible to look at this recumbent nymph, without admiring the delicate finishing of the sculptor, but one cannot applaud the taste of the design. The expression of the whole is scarcely within the bounds of decency; – for, it is the expression, and not the nudity of a statue, 'the disposition, and not the exposition of the limbs,' upon which this depends; and it is a prostitution of sculpture to make it subservient to the gratification of voluptuousness.

This criticism may however perhaps savour of squeamishness; – for, while we were admiring the exquisite finishing of Canova's chisel, a young Italian lady with a party joined us, who was thrown into an ecstasy of admiration by the charms of Chloris's figure; and she patted the jutting beauties with

---

[60] [Jameson,] *Diary of an Ennuyée,* p. 279.

14. Antonio Canova, *Naiad* (also known, more specifically, as *Chloris*), front view, drawn by G. Tognoli and engraved by Angelo Bertini, in *Recueil de statues, groupes, bustes, mausolées, colosses et monumens de tout genre*. © The British Library Board (Tab.488.c.). 41.6 x 54.2 cm. The sculpture is in the Royal Collection at Buckingham Palace, London

delight, exclaiming, – while she looked round to us for confirmation of her opinion, – *Bella cosa! Bella cosa! O che bella cosa!*

It is curious to see the progress of a statue, from the rough block of marble, to the last *ad unguem* finish; which is all that is done by the master hand.[61] The previous labour is merely mechanical, and may be done by a common workman from the model of the sculptor.

The *Venus and Adonis* is full of simplicity, grace, and tenderness.

The *Cupid and Psyche* is a charming composition, but Psyche's hair looks as if it had been dressed by a French friseur.

There is much to admire in the group of *The Graces*; – but there is also much of that finical prettiness of which I complain. They are three pretty simpletons, – with the *niminy-piminy* airs of a fashionable boarding school; there is *silliness* without *simplicity*; – and no two qualities can be more opposite.

Again – there is a trickery and quackery in the finishing of Canova's

---

[61] [Literally, 'to the fingernail'.]

15. Antonio Canova, *Naiad*, back view, drawn by G. Tognoli and engraved by Domenico Marchetti, in *Recueil de statues, groupes, bustes, mausolées, colosses et monumens de tout genre*. © The British Library Board (Tab.488.c.). 37.4 x 53.0 cm

statues, which is below the dignity of a sculptor. The marble is not left in its natural state, – but it must be stained and polished to aid the effect. The other sculptors laugh at this, and well they may; – for these adventitious graces soon fade away, and are beside the purpose of sculpture, whose end was, and is, to represent *form* alone.

January 10th. With the most lively recollection of Canova, I went this morning to examine the *Studio* of Thorwaldson, a Danish sculptor; – whose works are much more to my fancy. There is a freshness and originality in his designs, guided by the purest taste. What can be more elegant and beautiful than his Basso-Relievo of *Night*? His *Venus victrix* approaches nearer than any modern statue, to the Venus de Medicis. There is a Shepherd too, which is a delightful specimen of simplicity and nature; – and the charm of these statues is, that while they emulate, they have not borrowed any thing from the works of the ancients.

A bust of Lord Byron – a good likeness.

January 11th. Removed from the Via degli otto Cantoni, to the Piazza Mignanelli. The fatigue of mounting 104 steps after a morning's

16. *Hermaphrodite*, in Domenico de Rossi, *Raccolta di statue antiche e moderne*, illustrated by Pavolo Alessandro Maffei (Rome: Stamperia della Pace, 1704), Plate LXXVIII, engraved by Claude Randon. © The British Library Board (688.i.9.). 32.2 x 21.5 cm. The sculpture, with the mattress by Gianlorenzo Bernini, shown in the engraving, is now in the Louvre, Paris

excursion, was intolerable; – to say nothing of the fish-stalls, and the other noises of the Corso; amongst which, I was not a little surprised by a daily morning serenade from the odious squeaking bag-pipe. Who could have expected to meet this instrument so far from Scotland? – and yet it is indigenous in this land of music, that is, in the more southern part of it, – in Calabria.

Walked on the Pincian Hill; where the French constructed an excellent promenade. Here all the beauty and fashion of Rome resort, when the weather is fine, to parade, either in their equipages, or on foot, and discuss the gossip and tittle-tattle of the town.

The day was beautiful, and the elastic purity of the air has given me an agreeable foretaste of the charms of an Italian spring. Pauline, the Princess Borghese, was on the walk, with a bevy of admirers; – as smart and pretty a little bantam figure, as can be imagined. She bears a strong resemblance to her brother Napoleon; and her genius seems also to partake of the same character and to scorn the restrictions of ordinary rules.

The symmetry of her figure is very striking, and she once sat, if that be the phrase, to Canova; who modelled her statue as a *Venus victrix* lying on a couch. This statue is now in the Borghese palace, but is kept under lock and key, and cannot be seen without a special order from Pauline herself.

[Charlotte Eaton,] *Rome in the Nineteenth Century*, 3 vols (Edinburgh and London: Archibald Constable & Co. and Hurst, Robinson, & Co., 1820), vol. 3, pp. 295–300

In the bewitching grace and softness of feminine beauty, and the playful innocence of childhood, Canova excels all others – and even himself; for in the heroic style he certainly does not soar so high. His heroes either border on effeminacy, like his Perseus; or fly into extravagance, like his Hercules. Yet, with all their faults, his works in this style are conceptions of true genius. The idea is bold and grand; but we feel that he has overshot his mark. He has got out of Nature, in attempting to rise above it, – and the eye that has been accustomed to the chaste design and correct forms of ancient art, must be hurt with their glaring defects.

Indeed, it is unreasonable to suppose, that any one artist, of whatever powers, should excel in departments so opposite. One might as well expect that Michael Angelo, – whose genius, by the way, is the very Antipodes of that of Canova, – should have produced *his* smiling Hebes, voluptuous Venuses, and dancing Nymphs, – that Albano should have pourtrayed the gloomy anchorites and martyrdoms of Caravaggio and Spagnoletti, – Salvator Rosa painted the warm sunshines of Cuyp, – or Pindar written the epic poems of Homer, – as that Canova, who can call forth at will the most bewitching forms of female beauty and grace, should excel in an Ajax or a Hercules.

Canova's sepulchral monuments, too, seem to me to have a heaviness and want of interest. We feel they have been a labour to his fancy, and they are rather a toil to us: – For whether Italy weeps over the tomb of Alfieri, – Rome writes on a tablet, – Padua's castellated head meditates, over nothing, – or Religion looks clumsy on the tomb of Rezzonico, – we turn wearied from their contemplation, and from the expression of the unmeaning lisp of admiration which habit or politeness draws forth, – to the bright and immortal creations of his genius, – to his Hebes, his Venuses, his dancing Nymphs, his infant Loves, and his laughing Graces.

Of these, his Hebe, which has been four times repeated with variations, is, perhaps, the most universally admired. I cannot, however, approve of the gold necklace with which the last is adorned; not even the sanction of antiquity can ever reconcile me to decorations so unsuited to sculpture. We know that the practice of some of the greatest masters of Greece may be adduced, not only for necklaces, and ear-rings, and ornaments of all kinds, in gold and precious stones, – but for painted cheeks. If this was done, however, in the vain attempt to create a nearer approach to living nature, the objects of sculpture seem to have been strangely mistaken and debased. Most certainly they do not consist in the close imitation of life; for, in that case, a common raree-show of waxwork, would exceed the finest sculpture of Phidias. Upon what principle this custom can be reconciled to true taste, I am at a loss to understand. To me it seems about as bad as the Gothic custom of investing painted heads with real crowns.

The Venus coming out of the Bath,* in all its fourfold repetitions, varies, in some points, from the original; and the last, destined for Lord Lansdowne, and perhaps the most beautiful of them all, is, in fact, a new statue.

But Canova's own favourite is the Venus Victorious, under which the beautified portrait of the Principessa Borghese is represented; and this, I think, I before told you, is withheld from view by its possessor.[62]

Perhaps the most beautiful of all his works, – the Venus and Adonis,† – was finished at the age of six-and-thirty. This exquisite groupe, in my opinion, far surpasses the Mars and Venus, which he is now doing for the Prince Regent. It was intended to represent Peace and War, but it is not sufficiently chaste or severe for such a subject; the expression is too voluptuous, a fault, by the way, with which the works of this great artist are sometimes chargeable. Yet

---

* Originally done for the gallery of Florence, when it was robbed of the Venus de Medicis, and now in the Palazzo Pitti.
[62] [See Eaton, *Rome in the Nineteenth Century*, vol. 3, p. 47.]
† It is in the palace of the Marchese Berio, at Naples.

it is a beautiful groupe, and, if considered merely as Venus hanging on the enamoured God of War, the expression is appropriate and faultless. As yet, it has not advanced beyond the model, and there seems little prospect of its being soon finished. Three blocks of marble have already failed, after the labour was considerably advanced, owing to the blemishes in the heart of them, and the fourth is about to be tried.

The beautiful figure of the reclining Nymph, half-raising herself to listen to the lyre of the sweet little Love at her feet, is on the point of being dispatched to the Prince Regent, to whom it was ceded by Lord Cawdor.

The groupe of the Graces, the beauty of which is the object of universal admiration here, is also destined for our country, and will adorn Woburn Abbey. Beautiful as it is, I own it struck me as being rather *manieré*, especially in the attitude and face of the central figure, which is chargeable with somewhat of affectation, – somewhat of studied Opera-house airs, and *put-on* sweetness of countenance. But I criticize with reluctance a work, which, whatever may be its faults, has rarely been equalled in modern art, and the progress of which I have long watched with unspeakable interest and delight. It is only a few days since I saw the finishing strokes given to it by the hand of Canova.

Perhaps you may have no very clear idea of the progress of a sculptor in his work; at least, I find that many of my countrymen, whom I have introduced to Canova's studio, had previously supposed that his custom was to fall upon a block of marble, and chisel away till he made it into a statue. Forgive me for the improbable supposition, that you should be in such an error; but let me explain, that a sculptor begins upon much more ductile materials than marble. He forms his model in clay, and this is entirely the work of his own hands; but before he begins, the statue is perfectly *ideato*, – the visionary figure is before him.

When finished, a cast is taken from it by his assistants, which is dotted over with black points at regular intervals, to guide the workmen. From this model they begin to work, and having reduced the block of marble into form, and made it a rough-hewn statue, the sculptor himself resumes his labours. The exterior surface, as it were, is his to form and perfect, and the last finishing touches he generally gives by candle-light. It is afterwards polished with pumice-stone.

This is the invariable process. Many are the delightful hours I have spent with Canova, both when he has been employed in modelling and chiselling; and few are the companions whose society will be enjoyed with such interest, or remembered with such regret.

Lady Morgan [Sydney Morgan, née Owenson], *Italy*, 2 vols (London: Henry Colburn, 1821), vol. 2, pp. 227–30

'Rome,' says Evelyn, 'is most tempting for a great person or a wanton purse;' a truth particularly felt in visiting the *studii*, or workshops of sculptors and painters, by those who are not *great persons*, and have not a *wanton purse*.[63] Rome is indeed, at this moment, the great studio of the world; and this is the aspect in which it is most delightful to consider her. The congress of talent assembled from all nations of the earth, to promote the arts, is well worth all other congresses; and Genius sending forth her sons from the frozen regions of the Baltic, or the sunny vallies of the dew-dripping South, affords a far more gracious aspect of society, than those portentous meetings of sovereigns, in which the interest of a few takes precedence of the welfare of all; and which are no less fatal to the liberties of the nations they represent, than of those whom they assemble to crush.

Amidst the rubbish, ruins, and fragments, which fill up the court and avenues of the palace of the Barberini, lie some of the most distinguished studii of Rome; some, I believe, occupying the very outhouses raised for the workmen who built that ponderous edifice in former ages, when the Coliseum was plundered for its erection. Among these the workshop of the CAVALIERE THORWALDSON is the most attractive, though the quick demand for his exquisite productions leaves but few of his works on hand. His basso-rilievos are his finest efforts; particularly his splendid model of the Triumph of Alexander, bespoke by Napoleon for the façade of the Quirinal, whose own triumphs were at an end before the work was finished. The heads, and, above all, that of the conqueror himself, taken from his bust in the Capitol, are most striking. A plaster cast of this basso relievo was put up in the Quirinal, and a copy in marble was, I believe, purchased by Monsieur Sommariva, of Paris, decidedly the most munificent patron of the arts in Europe.*

In the studio of RADOLF SCHADOW, a German sculptor, we were struck by his '*filatrice*,' which, among other merits, has that of extreme originality, not being in the least borrowed from the antique. It is the figure of a beautiful girl in the act of spinning. It is full of movement and life; and the attitude with one hand elevated above the head, while the eye regards the motion of

---

[63] [John Evelyn, *The Diary of John Evelyn*, edited by E.S. de Beer, 6 vols (Oxford: Oxford University Press, 1955), vol. 2, p. 4. (Evelyn is writing here not of Rome but of the temptations to expense provoked by the beauties of his father's estate at Wotton, in Surrey.)

* The collection of Mons. Sommariva at Paris has already been mentioned in the Author's work on France. We found this gentleman in Rome and Naples, as busy in purchasing statues, pictures, and busts, as if he were about to found, not to complete a collection. We sometimes accompanied him to the studio of his friend Canova, and witnessed his anxiety to rival potentates in the good graces of the genius of sculpture. I believe he has succeeded in carrying off Canova's favourite '*nymph*' [not the *Chloris* encountered by Matthews], who had more competitors, when we were at Rome, for her possession, than any living beauty in Europe.

the simple spindle near the ground, is extremely picturesque and varied. The golden thread seemed to vibrate to the touch of her tremulous finger.

In the studio of FABRICE we saw also another deviation from the calm motionless dignity of the antique; a Venus, trying in painful curiosity, the point of an arrow (with which she has been wounded), while an *espiègle* little Love is struggling to get it out of her hands. This charming group was done for the Prince Esterhazy, whose orders are to be seen executing by almost every artist in Italy.

But there was one studio which we frequently visited, to which curiosity alone did not lead us; where we often sought the man more than the artist, and where the sublimest of all the arts, illustrated by its noblest productions, were not the sole inducements of our visits – the studio of Canova.*

It is always delightful to oppose the calumnies which invidious dulness heaps on the head of genius, by adducing living proofs of the union of the highest order of talent with the most elevated virtue. The life of Canova is perfectly in point with this purpose. From the first of his brilliant career, his family benefited by his exertions; as he proceeded in life and fame, the sphere of his benevolence was extended with his means; and when, on the completion of his ungracious mission to Paris†, the Pope bestowed on him an annual revenue of three thousand piastres, he assigned a part of his increased income to the maintenance of the families of decayed artists.

The studio of Canova is by far the most extensive in Rome; and his most arduous industry can only be estimated by those permitted to wander through his various work-rooms and galleries. Masses of marble, almost mountains, fresh hewn from their native quarries, fill the inferior chambers; others exhibiting the first sketched rudiments of creation succeed; then come the outlined forms starting into being, resembling a metamorphosis of ancient fable, where life has 'half forgot itself to stone.'[64] Further on, are almost living groups of beauties, wits, kings, and pontiffs, with all their

---

* The Marchese Canova and his excellent brother the Abate were among our earliest visitants at Rome; and the pleasure of their society at our fire-side in the prima sera, was among our greatest intellectual enjoyments during our residence in that unintellectual city. Canova has vivacity, much general information, and consequently great conversational powers. His views of society are philosophical, and such as become a genius by no means confined to the art he practises. His appearance and address have all the simplicity of true talent and elevated sentiment; and he is as universally esteemed in his social relations, as he is admired for his art.

† To inspect the packing up of the restored statues. On this occasion he was likewise created Marquis of Ischia, a title which, however, he does not assume. The name of Canova is in itself a patent of nobility, which kings can neither give nor take away, and it will outlive the recollection of any feudal distinctions with which royalty may idly seek to encumber it. It is a foolish vanity in potentates thus to place in parallel and opposition the nobility of social institutions and that of nature. It is applying the touchstone that best detects the baseness of the cheap coin with which they reward alike the services and the servilities of their creatures.

[64] [Adapted from Alexander Pope, 'Eloisa to Abelard', line 24.]

insignia, the wreath, the stylus, the crown, the tiara. In the midst of all, towers a colossal form, which makes the imaged dynasties around it look like pigmies. *Three kings* bespoke this mightiest produce of Canova's immortal chisel, basely emulous to make an idol of him, who had made them — nothing! There is not one royal chapman now to claim the statue, and it lies upon the sculptor's hands. Its sole inscription is, Napoleon!

At the extremity of this suite is the cabinet of the master-genius himself, far from the din and bustle of less inspired workmen; and there was, in our estimation, nothing in Rome more worthy to be seen than Canova himself at work, habited in his nankeen jacket and yellow slippers; his frail and delicate frame energized to Herculean strength; now striking off from the mass, now finishing some trait so delicate as to escape all eyes, save that of Art. When we first visited his studio, he was occupied on his Nymph, which he himself counts a *chef d'œuvre*.[65] Canova was then (1820) passed sixty; but though his health was frail, his enthusiasm was fresh, and his mind vigorous. His whole appearance is nobly expressed in his picture by Sir Thomas Lawrence, which had just been finished when we arrived at Rome.*

---

[65] [Presumably the 'favourite "nymph"' purchased by Sommariva, mentioned in Morgan's footnote above, and not the *Chloris*.]

* The orders of the Italian governments to Canova, during the last twenty years, were munificent. A Theseus was bespoke by the government of Milan at an immense price; three-fourths of which were paid in advance. On the Restoration, the Emperor of Austria paid the remainder, and carried off the statue to *Vienna*. The meanness of these arbitrators of Europe is equal to their dulness and their tyranny. A Perseus also was bespoke by the French Government for Rome; it lay on Canova's hands, until M. Sommariva became its purchaser. When shamed into justice, the Papal government refused to give up a work which was calculated to add new splendour to the Vatican, and paid the sum originally asked for it. Since this period the governments of Italy have ordered nothing from Canova; nor have the cardinals, princes, and nobles of Rome purchased a single picture or statue from any living artist there. The pretty Cupid, in the palace Sciara Colonna, was a present from the painter to the Prince who bears this superb name. It was the only modern picture we remarked in any of the palaces. The saloons of the Duchess of Devonshire were, on the contrary, crowded with recent works. Canova's noble statue of 'Religion,' which would have been so well adapted to St. Peter's, was refused by the government; and he has given it to his native village, Possanio, where he has erected a church, on the plan and size of the portico of the Pantheon, to receive it. It is said that he intended to dedicate this building to God; but the idea was not esteemed orthodox in Rome, and the church remains nameless and undevoted.

Chapter 5

GASTRONOMY, GUSTO AND THE GEOGRAPHY OF THE HAUNTED

'You know not how delicate the imagination becomes by dieting with antiquity day after day.'
Shelley, letter of 1819

'"I feel as though we had shared a meal like this once before, two thousand years ago", she said: "can't you remember?"'
Freud, 'Delusions and Dreams in Jensen's Gradiva' (1907)

'Notwithstanding the universal attractiveness of the subject, there is no class of compositions called eating-songs.'
Leigh Hunt, 'Eating-Songs' (1854)

Travel writing of the late eighteenth and early nineteenth centuries is full of passages that bring gustatory enjoyment into conjunction with other forms of sensory and imaginative gratification – whether deployed as a metaphor or described as part of the actual experience of travelling. The metaphor of taste, establishing a parallel between the exercise of judgement in gastronomic matters and the discerning use of the other senses, allows eating and drinking to play a part in a number of different strategies for appropriating the foreign as a source of pleasure and benefit.[1] As a branch of aesthetic experience, moreover, gastronomy is assigned an imaginative dimension. The three passages at the end of this chapter all pursue the aesthetic and imaginative implications of eating and drinking, and – directly or indirectly – consider the metaphorical or metonymic relation between gastronomy and travel.

Picking out the plums

Gastronomic metaphors are often employed in order to hint that appropriating art, architecture or landscape as a source of pleasure might in fact

---

[1] The preoccupation with this metaphor both in theoretical writings and in poetry, during the eighteenth and early nineteenth centuries, has been explored by Denise Gigante, in *Taste: A Literary History* (New Haven and London: Yale University Press, 2005), and by Jocelyne Kolb, in *The Ambiguity of Taste: Freedom and Food in European Romanticism* (Ann Arbor: University of Michigan Press, 1995).

be as simple as eating and drinking; they can function, in other words, as reassuring digressions to another domain of experience, analogous to the digressions to trivial gossip, or to sexuality, considered in the previous chapter. Adam Walker, after viewing the *Laocoon* at the Vatican, notes enthusiastically: 'Next to this, and the last I could look at, was the Apollo Belvedere; and truly it was a *bon bouche* [sic]!'[2] The Marquis of Normanby uses the same expression to convey the experience of a traveller who has been in Rome long enough to have moved beyond the initial half-crazed excitement that the city prompts, and has gained greater composure and discernment: 'St. Peter's and the Vatican, in short, form not the first attraction to the visitor; they are surveyed at a distance, and reserved for a *bonne bouche*, while the newly arrived flings himself headlong down the Capitoline descent, in search of temples, ruins, columns.'[3]

Piozzi, in Bologna, on her return journey, uses a gastronomic analogy to protect her hyperboles; if her taste for art is an 'appetite', she implies, it must be unaffectedly down-to-earth:

> With regard to pictures however, *l'Appétit vient en mangeant*, as I experienced completely when traversing the Zampieri palace with eagerness that increased at every step. I once more half-worshipped the works of divine Guercino.[4]

On visiting 'the Gallery' (the Uffizi), in Florence, Henry Matthews, making for the room that contains the *Venus de' Medici*, declares: 'Upon the same principle that a child picks out the plums, before he eats the rest of the pudding, – I hurried at once to the Sanctum Sanctorum of this Temple of Taste; – the Tribune.' He concludes his survey of the collection by using this metaphor of juvenile gastronomic impetuousness to emphasize his own powers of discrimination and concision – superior, he implies, to those of visitors who are more dutiful in observing the conventional table manners of sightseeing: 'These are the *plums* of the Gallery; – I leave it to guides and catalogues to discuss the rest of the *pudding*.'[5]

Later in his tour, Matthews is prompted to a further metaphorical assimilation of aesthetic pleasure within the domain of gastronomy by the name of the painter Carlo Dolci. In a diary entry for January 1818, he

---

[2] A[dam] Walker, *Ideas, Suggested on the Spot in a Late Excursion through Flanders, Germany, France, and Italy* (London: J. Robson and J. Johnson, 1790), p. 257.

[3] [Constantine Henry Phipps,] Marquis of Normanby, *The English in Italy*, 3 vols (London, Saunders and Otley 1825), 'The Vatican', pp. 174–197; vol. 2, p. 176.

[4] Hester Lynch Piozzi, *Observations and Reflections Made in the Course of a Journey through France, Italy, and Germany*, 2 vols (London: A. Strahan and T. Cadell, 1789), vol. 2, p. 175; the traveller supplies her own translation: 'Eating increases one's appetite.'

[5] Henry Matthews, *The Diary of an Invalid. Being the Journal of a Tour in Pursuit of Health in Portugal, Italy, Switzerland and France in the Years 1817, 1818 and 1819*, second edition (London: John Murray, 1820), p. 40, p. 45.

remarks: 'Went to Cardinal Fesch's, who has the best and most extensive collection of pictures in Rome', and comments on these works:

> There is just enough of Guido and Carlo Dolci. The pictures of the first have been termed the *honey*, and those of the last may perhaps be called the *treacle* of painting. – Too much saccharine would be cloying.[6]

Aesthetic appetites

As these last passages suggest, gastronomic metaphors often incorporate an ironic awareness of the disparity between the elevated domain of the visual and the more down-to-earth, everyday domain of the gastronomic. The gustatory and gastronomic metaphors employed by Matthews incorporate a sufficient charge of comic incongruity to throw into disorder the assumption that travellers must always strive to devote an unerringly exalted attention to sights and wonders. Lewis Engelbach, in *Naples and the Campagna Felice* (1815), signals a mild but distinct irreverence towards the established pieties when he sets up the drinking of topographically specific wine as one of the responses that must take its place among the expected forms of tribute to one of the sights of the South: 'To dine at the very foot of Vesuvius, and not drink *Lachrime Christi*, would have been worse than being at Rome and not seeing St. Peter's.'[7] Hazlitt, comparing the famous natural cascades at Tivoli and at Terni, concludes by reflecting upon Byron's failure to grasp the 'simple and majestic' character of these falls, when describing them in Canto IV of *Childe Harold's Pilgrimage* (1818); he then shifts abruptly to a work by Byron that he defines as rather less unreservedly committed to the contemplation of the sublime:

> To say the truth, if Lord Byron had put it into *Don Juan* instead of *Childe Harold*, he might have compared the part which her ladyship has chosen to perform on this occasion to an experienced waiter pouring a bottle of ale into a tumbler at a tavern. It has somewhat of the same continued, plump, right-lined descent.[8]

The incongruity between a sublime cascade of water and a humble cascade of ale, here, invites an ironic recognition that taste in the one

---

[6] Matthews, *Diary of an Invalid*, p. 121, p. 122. Matthews is not the only traveller-narrator to be prompted to gastronomic metaphors by the name *Carlo Dolci* or *Dolce*. Anna Jameson declares: 'There is a cloying sweetness in his style, a general want of power which wearies me' (*Diary of an Ennuyée* second edition (London: Henry Colburn), 1826, p. 95).

[7] [Lewis Engelbach,] *Naples and the Campagna Felice. In a Series of Letters Addressed to a Friend in England, in 1802* (London: R. Ackermann, 1815), p. 132.

[8] W[illiam] Hazlitt, *Notes of a Journey through France and Italy* (London: Hunt and Clarke, 1826), p. 328, p. 329. See Lord Byron, *Childe Harold's Pilgrimage*, Canto IV, stanzas 68–72; *The Complete Poetical Works*, edited by Jerome J. McGann, 7 vols (Oxford: Oxford University Press, 1980–92), vol. 2, pp. 147–8.

domain might not in fact be completely dissociated from taste in the other; writings of this period draw on a tradition of philosophical speculation that perceives that the metaphor of taste might bring aesthetic discernment into conjunction with appetite. This tradition attempts to form a concept of taste that is sufficiently refined to exclude such a greedily gustatory element. As Denise Gigante comments on taste and smell: 'The two are thought to convey immediate pleasure or disgust, serving to mediate discrete individuals (if at all) based on bodily instinct without reference to shared ideals.'[9] Nonetheless, the implication of appetite (or even greed) within gastronomic metaphors can prove rhetorically useful: it registers an impulse towards fierce assimilation and appropriation that can be transferred metaphorically onto other modes of sensory experience.

Travellers, then, glimpse the possibilities of appetite as a metaphor that invests the exercise of taste in aesthetic matters with the force and immediacy of such 'bodily instinct'. Matthews's account of picking out the plums in the Uffizi implies that taste in art may be exercised as a series of instantaneous impulses. Hazlitt, at this same gallery, deploys gastronomic metaphors to remark upon the paradoxical 'perfection of vulgarity and refinement together' in Raphael's *Fornarina*, and does so as though he were charting immediate responses of repulsion and relish:

> The Fornarina is a bouncing, buxom, sullen, saucy baker's daughter – but painted, idolized, immortalized by Raphael! Nothing can be more homely and repulsive than the original; you see her bosom swelling like the dough rising in the oven; the tightness of her skin puts you in mind of Trim's story of the sausage-maker's wife – nothing can be more enchanting than the picture – than the care and delight with which the artist has seized the lurking glances of the eye, curved the corners of the mouth, smoothed the forehead, dimpled the chin, rounded the neck, till by innumerable delicate touches, and the 'labour of love,' he has converted a coarse, rude mass into a miracle of art.[10]

In his essay 'On Gusto' (1816), Hazlitt attempts to formulate a concept of taste that incorporates the sensory force of appetite. Concluding his account of the 'luxurious softness and delicacy' of Titian's female figures, he notes that in the works of Van Dyck, which lack gusto, 'the eye does not acquire a taste or appetite for what it sees'. He then explicitly emphasizes that he is using the Italian term *gusto* in order to convey the relation between the literal and figurative referents of the term *taste* (and widen the sensory scope of such a relation): 'In a word, gusto in painting is where the impression made on one sense excites by affinity those of

---

[9] Gigante, *Taste*, p. 3.
[10] Hazlitt, *Notes of a Journey*, p. 262. The earliest instance of *gusto* in the sense of 'relish' listed in the *Oxford English Dictionary* is dated 1647; the earliest example of gusto as 'aesthetic appreciation or perception' cited is 1663.

another.'[11] In his commentary on *La Fornarina* in *Notes of a Journey*, both repulsion and relish are presented as operating according to this model of sensory affinity: the unequivocally gastronomic metaphors that register vulgarity draw attention to the gastronomic appetite entailed in recognizing 'innumerable delicate touches'.

Samuel Rogers, in the final passage below, describing the moment when he succeeds in converting an experience of sparsity and deprivation into one of imaginative repletion, declares: 'I ate with an appetite I had not known before.' His appetite, however, stems not from instinct – the 'scanty fare' before him throws him into 'a splenetic humour' – but from 'poetic visions': contemporary reality dissolves in 'a cloud of smoke' from the hearth, which 'drew the tears into my eyes', and the delights of the view through the window ('a sea sparkling with innumerable brilliants') merge with memories of ancient literature.

Rogers, here, simply by setting the scene as one of eating and drinking, invokes his own reputation as an epicure (noted by Anna Jameson, for example, in one of her allusions to him in Italy), but ironically reverses the more usual plot of using the gustatory sense of *taste* to invigorate aesthetic enjoyment: instead of invoking appetite to reinforce the claim to visual and imaginative appropriation, he charts a narrative in which 'poetic visions' provoke appetite.[12]

Even in this inverted narrative, however, the relish with which the traveller consumes food and wine provides a robustly physical metonym for more nebulous forms of enjoyment. William Stewart Rose, in his *Letters from the North of Italy* (1819), traces out a similar sequence of responses, in which he anticipates imaginative pleasures that will redeem inferior wine by summoning antiquity into a domain of personal immediacy. At Abano, 'at the foot of the Euganean hills', he is lured into an expedition to a nearby town 'at the instance of some persons lodged here like myself, who invited me to make what they called a *baccanàl*'. He explains his motives by invoking a passage from Oliver Goldsmith's *Vicar of Wakefield* (1766), in which a young man is offered, implausibly but alluringly, a part in a venture into the imaginative geography of primitivism. The analogy affirms the compulsiveness of appetite once it has been sharpened by 'classicality':

> As Goldsmith, when the American crimp proposed to him to go as secretary of legation to the Chickasaw Indians, observes, 'that though he knew the fellow lied in his throat, there was something too magnificent in the proposal to be rejected,'

---

[11] William Hazlitt, 'On Gusto', in *Romantic Critical Essays*, edited by David Bromwich (Cambridge: Cambridge University Press, 1987), pp. 96–9; p. 96, p. 97, p. 97.

[12] See Jameson, *Diary of an Ennuyée*, p. 94: 'He talked long, Et *avec beaucoup d'onction* [very unctuously], of ortolans and figs; till methought it was the very poetry of epicurism.'

so, though I believed there was not to be found in the whole plain-country of Padua, a single bottle of wine that could justify the term, was yet too much pleased with the classicality of it not to close with the invitation.[13]

Eating and drinking in ancient places

One of the assumptions traced out within this passage is that drinking, as an activity long associated with poetic inspiration, helps to induce in the traveller the carefree abandonment of literal-mindedness that may prove useful – or necessary – in enjoying the haunted topography of Italy.[14] Joseph Forsyth, at Virgil's Tomb on the outskirts of Naples, indicates that a dismissal of the evidence, in the interest of imaginative satisfaction, is required in order to believe that this is in fact the tomb of Virgil; he then constructs an ironic narrative in which travellers are too awed to compose their own verses on the spot, but, more modestly, express their 'poetic visions' through impassioned drunkenness:

> Visitors of every nation, kings and princes have scratched their names on the stucco of this apocryphal ruin, but the poet's awful name seems to have deterred them from versifying here. I met a party of foreigners who had filled themselves with the God in the vineyard above, and were then reeling down between two precipices to kiss the dust and make further libations to the shade of Virgil.[15]

For Rogers, the erasure of uncertainty as to the resurgence of antiquity is completed as he drinks a glass of wine, which he acquiesces in identifying with the wine most celebrated by Horace; it is this fusion of antiquity and gastronomy, moreover, that inspires him to his culminatory celebration of the pleasures of travel: '"Who," I cried, as I poured out my last glass of Falernian, (for Falernian it was said to be, and in my eyes it ran bright and clear as a topaz-stone) "Who would remain at home, could he do otherwise?"'

Both drinking and eating, at this time, then, are not only adopted as metaphors for aesthetic and imaginative pleasure, and seen as activities that enhance the delights of particular spots: they are, more especially,

---

[13] [William Stewart Rose,] *Letters from the North of Italy*, 2 vols (London: John Murray, 1819) vol. 1, pp. 85–6. See Oliver Goldsmith, *The Vicar of Wakefield*, edited by Stephen Coote (London: Penguin, 1986; first published in 1766), p. 127.

[14] Leigh Hunt, in his preface to *Bacchus in Tuscany, A Dithyrambic Poem, from the Italian of Francesco Redi* (London: 'Printed for John and H.L. Hunt, Tavistock Street', 1825), explains how his first taste of Montepulciano makes it 'impossible to resist' embarking on this translation, and mingles wine and inspiration in explaining how he takes up 'the poet's glass' (p. vi). See Anya Taylor, *Bacchus in Romantic England: Writers and Drink, 1780–1830* (Macmillan: Basingstoke, 1999), for a survey of the range of roles assigned to alcoholic drink in writing (and in everyday life) over this period.

[15] Forsyth, *Remarks on Antiquities, Arts, and Letters during an Excursion in Italy in the Years 1802 and 1803*, first edition (London: T. Cadell and W. Davies, 1813), p. 302.

viewed as modes of enjoyment that play an especially important role in the experience of ancient, haunted places. Charles Dupaty describes a meal in the Temple of the Sibyl at Tivoli, during which a young woman brings him and his companions 'du lait blanc et pur, comme ses belles dents, et des fraises aussi vermeilles que ses jeunes lèvres' ('milk, pure and white as her own fine teeth, together with strawberries, that vied in colour with the natural vermilion of her lips').[16] Shelley, in a letter of 1819 to Thomas Love Peacock, describes an impromptu meal at the Temple of Jupiter at Pompeii: 'Under the colonnade of its portico we sate & pulled out our oranges & figs and bread & [?soil] apples (sorry fare you will say) & rested to eat.'[17] Anna Jameson, in the first of the passages below, gives an immensely detailed account of a picnic at this same town, not only analysing the event itself but also explaining how it might have been better managed.[18] Mariana Starke and her party set out for Pompeii with 'a cold dinner, bread, wine, knives, forks, and glasses': 'We drove to that side of Pompeii which contains the Soldiers' Barracks, where we got out of the carriage, ordering our horses to be put up near the excavated Villa on the opposite side of the Town, and our dinner to be carried to the just-named Villa.'[19] Forsyth, on the cliffs above the Pisciarelli and the ancient Stufe di San Gennaro, in the Campi Phlegraei, remarks, after an observation on the antique uses of the Stufe: 'Here I drank some red wine of volcanic growth, still more delicious than the *lacrime* of Vesuvius.'[20]

In anticipating that Peacock will view his array of foodstuffs as 'sorry fare', Shelley ironically draws attention to its simplicity. Other travellers also describe themselves, in ruins and other sites of memory, enjoying food and drink that can be viewed as the product of nature rather than of cultural elaboration and embellishment. Travel books do in fact sometimes mention that the ancients themselves were not averse to more luxurious delicacies: Henry Swinburne, in his *Travels in the Two Sicilies*

---

16 [Charles Marguerite Jean Baptiste Mercier Dupaty,] *Lettres sur l'Italie, en 1785*, 2 vols (Rome and Paris: de Senne, 1788), vol. 1, p. 256; *Sentimental Letters on Italy*, translated by J. [i.e. Giovanni] Povoleri, 2 vols (London: J. Crowder and J. Bew, 1789), vol. 1, p. 199.
17 *Letters of Percy Bysshe Shelley*, edited by Frederick L. Jones, 2 vols (Oxford: Oxford University Press, 1964), vol. 2, p. 73.
18 See Chloe Chard, 'Picnic at Pompeii: Hyperbole and Digression in the Warm South', in *Antiquity Recovered: The Legacy of Pompeii and Herculaneum*, edited by Victoria Coates and Jon Seidl (Los Angeles: J. Paul Getty Museum, 2007), pp. 115–32, for a discussion of gastronomy and travel that takes this passage as its starting-point.
19 Mariana Starke, *Letters from Italy, between the Years 1792 and 1798, Containing a View of the Revolutions in that Country, from the Capture of Nice by the French Republic to the Expulsion of Pius VI from the Ecclesiastical State*, 2 vols (London: R. Philips, 1800), vol. 2, pp. 97–8. Morgan describes a meal consumed not by herself but by others: she finds in one of the fora at Pompeii 'the workmen seated on blocks of marble or little wheel-barrows: it was their dinner-hour, and they were eating some fruit and bread' (*Italy*, vol. 2, p. 346n).
20 Forsyth, *Remarks on Antiquities, Arts, and Letters*, pp. 304–5.

(1783–85), observes: 'If an antiquary longs for a Roman dish, Sorrento will supply him with the paps of a sow, drest in the antique taste, by the name of Verrina.'²¹ When they visit ancient places, however, travellers usually describe themselves consuming fare that rivals Shelley's 'oranges & figs and bread & [?soil] apples' in simplicity – while, nonetheless, vaguely invoking the sort of food and wine that the ancients might be imagined sampling in their more unpretentious moments. (Both figs and bread are noted by Jameson as among the blackened remains of food from Pompeii found at the Museo Borbonico.)²²

Writers sometimes vaunt the merits of plain fare in haunted places more explicitly. Henry Sass, travelling by sea from Naples to Pozzuoli and Baia, remarks: 'The deliciousness of the air is almost a substitute for food; but many gross mortals are more delighted with the sight of a sumptuous dinner, where they can indulge their real appetites, than with the most lovely scene.' The traveller then explicitly aligns the superior sensibility that prompts an awareness of the beauties of nature with a sense of cultural memory: elaborating on the 'gross mortals' who provide him with such a useful point of contrast, he continues: 'they can have no pleasing association; and where nothing is sown, no harvest can be expected. Hence, in a great measure, arises that general indulgence in sensuality.'²³

Enjoyment of food and drink, then, is disparaged by Sass, but only if it is seen as laden with the luxurious accretions of human culture, distanced from the natural world, and enjoyed with an indifference to 'pleasing association'. At Cuma, on the same day, Sass is happy to proclaim his enjoyment of a simple gastronomic pleasure, suffused with the memory of Horace's poetry: 'On this coast we drank of the Falernian wine; and, although I do not suppose it was so good as anciently, yet it was very pleasant to the taste.'²⁴ Jameson, at Pompeii, pursues a similar line of argument: she rejects food and drink that is redolent of luxury and excess and voices a preference for more simple items, which, in her view, offer a more efficacious strategy for deriving pleasure from the haunted surroundings. In addition to the 'more substantial cates' on offer is an item that seems to summon up local and classical associations: 'we had oysters from Lake Lucrine (or Acheron), and classically excellent they were'. The 'London bottled porter, and half a dozen different kinds of wine', however, mark a

---

[21] Henry Swinburne, *Travels in the Two Sicilies, in the Years 1777, 1778, 1779, and 1780*, 2 vols (London: P. Elmsly, 1783–85), vol. 1, p. 117.

[22] [Jameson,] *Diary of an Ennuyée*, p. 259.

[23] Henry Sass, *A Journey to Rome and Naples, performed in 1817; giving an Account of the Present State of Society in Italy, and containing Observations on the Fine Arts* (London: Longman, Hurst, Rees, Orme and Brown, 1818), pp. 213–14, p. 214.

[24] Sass, *Journey to Rome and Naples*, p. 222.

departure from the local and the natural. In a more thoughtfully planned picnic, the participants would sit down 'on the platform of the old Greek Temple . . . or, if the heat were too powerful, under the shade of the hill near it', and would consume relatively simple fare: 'There we would make our cheerful and elegant repast, on bread and fruits, and perhaps a bottle of Malvoisie or Champagne.'

For Sass, the rejection of over-elaborate food is accompanied not only by an awareness of the pleasures of association but also by a reference to 'the harmony of nature'.[25] Jameson, too, places every possible emphasis on the aesthetic delights of the natural world, and their value in enhancing 'cheerful and elegant' gastronomy. Her picnic would, she specifies, be deferred 'a fortnight later, or till the vines were in leaf'. It would be followed by 'a minute examination of the principal objects of interest and curiosity', and then by a journey back to Naples in which the natural world forges an easy continuity between antiquity and the present:

> We would wait till the shadows of evening had begun to steal over the scene, purpling the mountains and the sea; we would linger there to enjoy all the splendours of an Italian sunset; and then, with minds softened and elevated by the loveliness and solemnity of the scenes around, we would get into our carriage, and drive back to Naples beneath the bright full moon; and, by the way, we would 'talk the flowing heart,' and make our recollections of the olden time, our deep impressions of the past, heighten our enjoyment of the present.

Eating and drinking in a simple yet pleasing manner, then, supplies a strategy for feeling at one with the natural world; nature, in turn, in its southern vitality, hauls the ancient past into the sensory immediacy of the present. In other words, food and wine, when aligned with nature rather than culture, supply reassuringly material, concrete metonyms for the more nebulous aesthetic delights of the surroundings, which themselves, as enduring elements within the topography, metonymically erase distinctions between past and present. The natural scenery that is invoked is itself often of a kind that tends towards visual indeterminacy, and so metaphorically endorses this erasure of chronological distinctions: Jameson's ideal picnic, as described in the passage just quoted, culminates in a scene in which visual differentiation is diminished by 'the shadows of evening', which cast a purple tinge over mountains and sea alike. Shelley, immediately after his simple meal at Pompeii, describes the scene around the portico in which he sits down to eat as one in which the blue sea reflects the purple of the sky, and the mountains echo the colour of the sea:

> Above & between the multitudinous shafts of the [?sunshiny] columns, was seen the blue sea reflecting the purple heaven of noon above it, & supporting as it were

---

[25] Sass, *Journey to Rome and Naples*, p. 213.

on its line the dark lofty mountains of Sorrento, of a blue inexpressibly deep, & tinged towards their summits with streaks of new-fallen snow.[26]

The past then manifests itself within this landscape:

> This scene was what the Greeks beheld. (Pompeii you know was a Greek city.) They lived in harmony with nature, & the interstices of their incomparable columns, were portals as it were to admit the spirit of beauty which animates this glorious universe to visit those whom it inspired.'[27]

As Shelley moves on to the tombs beyond the eastern gate of the city, he charts out a plot in which nature reanimates memories of antiquity:

> These tombs were the most impressive things of all. The wild woods surround them on either side and along the broad stones of the paved road which divides them, you hear the late leaves of autumn shiver & rustle in the stream of the inconstant wind as it were like the step of ghosts.[28]

For Sass, in his sea journey from Naples, the joys of 'pleasing association' are enhanced by the power of an unruffled sea to induce a sense of undisrupted visual continuity: 'The water was so smooth that we imperceptibly glided on, and, but for the objects on shore, might have supposed ourselves stationary.'[29]

Drinking with the ancients

The second passage below, from Eustace's *Tour Through Italy* (1813), hovers on the edge of similar continuities between nature, the ancient world and gustatory pleasure. The visual delights of natural luxuriance – the 'softness and richness' of the landscape – lead the traveller to reflect on the verses of 'the ancient poets' upon this region and its 'delicious wines'. Rather than investing the contemporary versions of these wines with a pleasure fortified by such literary mediation, however, as Rogers does when drinking his last glass of Falernian, Eustace observes: 'It has often been asked why Italy does not now produce wines so excellent, and in such variety as anciently.'

The traveller, then, seems to settle for a plot that might be termed *deteriorationist*. He nonetheless rejects the two main explanations for vinous deterioration – a change in climate, or a neglect in cultivating the vine. For a moment, it seems as though he is deploying a strategy familiar from accounts of works of art: expectation, he suggests, has been raised so high that it must necessarily be disappointed: 'Accustomed from our infancy

---

[26] Shelley, *Letters*, vol. 2, p. 73.
[27] Shelley, *Letters*, vol. 2, p. 73.
[28] Shelley, *Letters*, vol. 2, p. 74.
[29] Sass, *Journey to Rome and Naples*, p. 213 (partially quoted above, p. 26).

to hear the wines of Italy and Greece extolled to the skies by the ancient poets, we expect to find them singularly delicious.'[30]

After various further deliberations, however, Eustace suggests not only that wine in Italy has deteriorated, but that it had already begun to do so in antiquity, despite its 'primary importance' in the social and intellectual life of the ancients. In apparent endorsement of this analysis, he offers an account of the half-finished canal, 'one of the extravagant whims of Nero', which diminished the fertility of the land on which the famous Caecuban wine was produced.

Having apparently resolved the question that he has posed, Eustace then adopts a rather different approach, suggesting that modern Italy could well produce wine equal to that of antiquity. As though scenting the danger of becoming a mere purveyor of 'shew-knowledge', as Shelley terms him, he comments cautiously: 'As it is not intended to expand a few cursory remarks into a dissertation, it may finally be observed that several of the wines celebrated in ancient times still retain, at least, some share of their ancient reputation.'[31] After noting the esteem in which diverse wines are held, he offers an enthusiastic endorsement of Lachryma Christi ('a rich and delicious wine'). The quotation from Horace that follows acquires, in this context, an air of conclusiveness, according the wines of antiquity a culminatory place within his list of those of the present, and so allowing a narrative of continuity to displace that of deterioration.

As the traveller marks the end of his digression, and returns to the topic of his journey to Naples, he affirms that the topography of the haunted is a place of sensory pleasure: he experiences 'night in all its charms; bright, serene, and odiferous'.[32]

A contemporary of Eustace's, through the ingenuity that he displays in attempting to elude pedantry, registers all the more strongly an awareness that wine may draw travellers into 'shew-knowledge', and (again, in Shelley's words) away from an awareness of the topography of the haunted as an 'inexhaustible mine of thought and feeling'.[33] When J. M.

---

[30] Hazlitt, for example, employing this strategy in his *Notes of a Journey through France and Italy* (London: Hunt and Clarke, 1826), implies that the general acclaim of the *Venus de' Medici* ineluctably induces reservations in the traveller: 'I do not know what to say of the Venus, nor is it necessary to say much where all the world have already formed an opinion for themselves.' He then proceeds to utter a string of criticisms, finally demoting the Venus to the status of mere 'ornamental art' (p. 259, p. 261).

[31] See Shelley, *Letters*, vol. 2, p. 89.

[32] As Gigante notes, in a passage partially quoted above, taste and smell are consistently seen as allied senses, more conspicuously 'bound up with the chemical physiology of the body' than sight and hearing (*Taste*, p. 3).

[33] Shelley, *Letters*, vol. 2, p. 89.

Le Riche, in his *Antiquités des environs de Naples, et dissertations qui y sont relatives*, introduces a discussion of ancient methods of storing wine into a tour of Pompeii, he does so by using an open-air 'collation' near a cellar containing amphorae as the starting-point for a conversation in which a spirited young woman elicits from a scholarly abbé some information about the uses of such vessels:

> Après une légère collation à laquelle tous les voyageurs avaient pris part, Mademoiselle Hortense, c'est le nom de la nièce du Général, se tournant en riant vers l'abbé, lui dit: mais M. l'abbé, croyez-vous qu'avec vos amphores, l'on pouvait conserver le vin aussi bien et aussi long-tems que dans nos bouteilles?[34]
>
> After a light collation in which all the travellers participated, Mademoiselle Hortense – that is the name of the general's niece – turning laughingly towards the abbé, said to him: but, Monsieur l'abbé, do you believe that it is possible to keep wine in your amphorae as well and as long as in our bottles?

The abbé, vaunting the merits of the wine once stored within these receptacles, concludes suavely by expressing his hope that his questioner will no longer be 'anti-amphoriste' ('anti-amphorist').[35]

Colour and luminosity in landscape and wine

Eustace, in attempting to combine scholarly reflection with sensory immediacy, introduces his speculations on wine with an account of colour and light ('Evening now far advanced, shed a purple tint over the sides and summits of the mountains, that gave at once a softness and richness to the picture, and contrasted finely with the darkness of the plains below, and the light colors of a few thin clouds flitting above'). Allusions to light and colour (as distinct from references to effects of light and shade) become more frequent from around the end of the eighteenth century onwards. Jameson, returning to Naples after the excessively luxurious picnic at Pompeii, is struck by the colouring of the scene:

> I saw the sun sink behind Capri, which appeared by some optical illusion like a glorious crimson transparency suspended above the horizon: the sky, the earth, the sea, were flushed with the richest rose colour, which gradually softened and darkened into purple.

Striking colour and luminosity are often introduced as attributes of scenes in which grapes or foodstuffs are cultivated. Colour, in such passages, is linked metonymically to the allure that these natural products will themselves exercise: since it is a quality traditionally associated with

---

[34] J. M. Le Riche, *Antiquités des environs de Naples, et dissertations qui y sont relatives* (Naples: Imprimerie française, 1820), p. 31.
[35] Le Riche, *Antiquités*, p. 31.

superficial seductiveness in painting (as implied in Matthews's reference to the 'glowing beauties' of Titian, and his doubt as to whether 'the Venetian painters ever give us more than the *bodies*', in his account of the Palazzo Borghese, in Chapter 3), colouring can readily be defined as appealing to the senses through an invitation to immediate relish that is analogous to the allure exercised by food and wine.[36] For Forsyth, travelling southwards towards Rome from Montefiascone and Viterbo, the 'glow' of a scene of *vendemmia* anticipates the effulgence of the wine, while also typifying the liveliness of the grape-harvesters, which itself revives the ancient past:

> The vintage was in full glow. Men, women, children, asses, all were variously engaged in the work. I remarked in the scene a prodigality and negligence which I never saw in France. The grapes dropped unheeded from the panniers, and hundreds were left unclipt on the vines. The vintagers poured on us as we passed the richest ribaldry of the Italian language, and seemed to claim from Horace's old *vindemiator* a prescriptive right to abuse the traveller.[37]

Hugh William Williams, describing the 'golden treasure' of the Indian corn alongside the road from Pisa to Leghorn (Livorno), explicitly emphasizes the role of 'briliancy' of colour in the visual enthralment induced by the Italian landscape; he then at once moves on to the vines from which wine will be made:

> The brilliancy of the maize subdued the other hues of nature, and suggested hints of splendid harmony, shewing that colour, when well arranged, is often more agreeable to the eye than when aërial tones prevail. The full and *gem-like* brilliancy of Italian landscape, in the autumnal season, must captivate the dullest eye.
> Our road was bordered with festoons of vine, rich with clustering grapes. Under this voluptuous drapery the mendicants would take their stations; yet, strange to say! would leave the fruit untouched.[38]

Rogers, at Terracina, locates luminosity both in landscape ('a sea sparkling with innumerable brilliants') and in wine; as the memory of Horace's Falernian wells up within it, the latter acquires the additional allure of colour: 'in my eyes it ran bright and clear as a topaz-stone.' Hazlitt, in his account of crossing the Alps, included in Chapter 2, is

---

[36] Matthews, *Diary of an Invalid*, p. 165; the Venetian school, as noted in this context above (p. 135 n. 31), was associated with seductive use of colour. Jacqueline Lichtenstein, in *La couleur éloquente: rhétorique et peinture à l'âge classique* (Paris: Flammarion, 1999[1989]), charts the longstanding association of colour with the persuasiveness of rhetoric rather than with the abstract reasoning of philosophy; this work has been translated by Emily McVarish as *The Eloquence of Colour: Rhetoric and Painting in the French Classical Age* (Berkeley: University of California Press, 1993).

[37] Forsyth, *Remarks on Antiquities, Arts and Letters*, pp. 131–2.

[38] H[ugh] W[illiam] Williams, *Travels in Italy, Greece, and the Ionian Islands. In a Series of Letters, Descriptive of Manners, Scenery, and the Fine Arts*, 2 vols (Edinburgh: A. Constable & Co., 1820), vol. I, pp. 195–6.

preoccupied with these same visual qualities in wine, and elides them with the landscape metonymically, as the source of light, and therefore of colour as well, is revealed to come from the 'boundless wastes' outside the 'stone-hovel'. A reference to its appealing smell links such qualities to the unmediated force of appetite: 'I shall not soon forget the rich ruby colour of the wine, as the sun shone upon it through a low glazed window that looked out on the boundless wastes around, nor its grateful spicy smell as we sat around it.'[39]

One of the most famous elisions between colour, gustatory pleasure and the enthralment of the South is in the second stanza of Keats's 'Ode to a Nightingale', in which the speaker, exclaiming 'O, for a draught of vintage!', and musing that such wine would taste of 'Dance, and Provençal song, and sunburnt mirth!', invokes the Fountain of Hippocrene, sacred to the Muses (and therefore a source of poetic inspiration); the 'true' Hippocrene, however, is described in terms that (whatever the claims of scholars that the water of this fountain was violet-coloured) are strongly suggestive of wine rather than water, and so displace the headiness of the one onto the other:

> O, for a beaker full of the warm South,
>   Full of the true, the blushful Hippocrene,
>   With beaded bubbles winking at the brim,
>   And purple-stainèd mouth.[40]

'For a while at least all effort is over'

One way of viewing both the preoccupation with colour and the interest in eating in the open air (and particularly in ancient places) is as a result of the formation of a new concept of the pleasure of travel, which is invoked alongside the concept of pleasure mingled with benefit, but which nevertheless includes forms of gratification that might previously have been defined as frivolous. After analysing his emotions during his meal, and affirming his new-found relish for foreign travel, Rogers sets out to justify this relish; in doing so, he argues that the pursuit of pleasure and 'profit' may be compatible with more carefree approaches to enjoying the foreign.

In formulating this argument, Rogers repeatedly refers to the 'Preface' in Sterne's *Sentimental Journey*, in which the traveller-narrator, Yorick, sits down in 'an old Desobligeant' ('A chaise, so called in France, from its

---

[39] Hazlitt, *Notes of a Journey*, p. 203.
[40] John Keats, 'Ode to a Nightingale', stanza 2, lines 5–8. John Barnard, in his notes to *John Keats: The Complete Poems*, second edition (Harmondsworth: Penguin, 1977), registers uncertainty as to whether 'blushful' refers to wine or to 'violet-coloured' water (p. 655, n. 16).

holding but one person', he explains in a footnote) in the courtyard of an inn at Calais: 'being determined to write my journey, I took out my pen and ink, and wrote the preface to it in the *Disobligeant* [*sic*].'[41] Rogers adopts this same on-the-spot approach to reflecting on the topic in hand: 'opening my journal-book and dipping my pen in my ink-horn, I determined, as far as I could, to justify myself and my countrymen in wandering over the face of the earth.' He invokes Yorick's preface from the outset, moreover, by situating himself within one of the categories of traveller that is listed in it: 'Splenetic Travellers'.[42]

Rogers then, however, explains that, on our travels, 'we improve and imperceptibly'; we find that 'seas and mountains are no longer our boundaries', and 'our benevolence extends itself with our knowledge'. In taking this buoyant view, he dissociates himself from Yorick, who, with ironic perversity, insists that nature has placed severe restrictions upon the little 'imperfect power of spreading our happiness sometimes beyond *her* limits' that we possess: 'It must have been observed by many a peripatetic philosopher, That nature has set up by her own unquestionable authority certain boundaries and fences to circumscribe the discontent of man.'[43]

Rogers also diverges from another section of Yorick's preface, in which wine, far from merging easily with 'poetic visions' to supply a hedonistic contentment, epitomizes the dangerous and unpredictable effects of travelling. After offering a catalogue of travellers, categorized according to their motives and dispositions, Yorick reflects that his reader, 'if he has been a traveller himself . . . may be able to determine his own rank and place in the catalogue – it will be one step towards knowing himself; as it is great odds, but he retains some tincture and resemblance, of what he imbibed or carried out, to the present hour'. The metaphor of imbibing is then extended into an epic simile, in which the uncertainties of travel conjure up a vision of the naked, vulnerable, drunken Noah:

> The man who first transplanted the grape of Burgundy to the Cape of Good Hope (observe he was a Dutch man) never dreamt of drinking the same wine at the Cape, that the same grape produced upon the French mountains – he was too phlegmatic for that – but undoubtedly he expected to drink some sort of vinous liquor; but whether good, bad, or indifferent – he knew enough of this world to know, that it did not depend upon his choice, but that what is generally called *chance* was to decide his success: however, he hoped for the best; and in these hopes, by an intemperate confidence in the fortitude of his head, and the depth

---

[41] Laurence Sterne, *'A Sentimental Journey' with 'The Journal to Eliza' and 'A Political Romance'*, ed. Ian Jack (Oxford: Oxford University Press, 1991; first published in 1768), p. 8, p. 8n, p. 9.
[42] Sterne, *Sentimental Journey*, p. 11.
[43] Sterne, *Sentimental Journey*, p. 9.

of his discretion, *Mynheer* might possibly overset both in his new vineyard; and by discovering his nakedness, become a laughing-stock to his people.

Even so it fares with the poor Traveller, sailing and posting through the politer kingdoms of the globe in pursuit of knowledge and improvements.[44]

Rogers, in contrast, implicitly classifies his imaginative transformation of an unpromising meal as an instance of the power of travel to restore 'that taste for natural and simple pleasures, so remarkable in early life'. While other remedies for inanition may sweep us into a state in which we 'rush on danger, and even on death', travel is free from such dangers: 'in travelling we multiply events, and innocently.'

In defining travel in this way, Rogers retains not only the link between pleasure and benefit ('we forget the profit in the pleasure') but also the concept of the Grand Tour as an activity in which the traveller returns to his or her native country, enriched by the experience of the foreign ('must we not return better citizens than we went?'). In suggesting that travel restores elements of the 'golden time' of childhood, however, he also opens up the possibility of a rather different view: that it offers an escape from the everyday cares and responsibilities that render us incapable of childish joy (or, as Rogers puts it, make us 'weary and sick at heart'). Such an urge to embrace irresponsible pleasures is innocent because it is temporary: '*for a while at least* all effort is over' (emphasis added).

Hazlitt, in his essay 'On Going a Journey', deploys a similar concept of travel as an escape from everyday cares (and, in fact, takes it further, to suggest an escape from the burden of identity: 'Oh! . . . to be known by no other title than *the Gentleman in the parlour*!'). Foreign travel, in particular, interrupts both everyday existence and an everyday sense of self:

> There is undoubtedly a sensation in travelling into foreign parts that is to be had nowhere else: but it is more pleasing at the time than lasting. It is too remote from our habitual associations to be a common topic of discourse or reference, and, like a dream or another state of existence, does not piece into our daily modes of life. It is an animated but a momentary hallucination.[45]

In classifying the pleasures of travel as temporary, travellers gain access to a new option: they can define these pleasures as transporting without conceding that the experience of gratification entails any permanent loss of stability or identity. The concept of provisional escape, in other words, serves the needs of the tourist, striving to keep danger at bay. One of the concepts that most strongly affirms the possibility of a risk-free hedonism in writings of this period is that of the *dolce far niente* – a form of happy

---

[44] Sterne, *Sentimental Journey*, p. 11, pp. 11–12.
[45] William Hazlitt, 'On Going a Journey', in *The Essays of William Hazlitt: A Selection*, introduced by Catherine Macdonald Maclean (London: Macdonald, 1949), pp. 29–40; p. 34, p. 39.

indolence that stops short of outright enervation. Stendhal, in *Rome, Naples et Florence* (1817/1826), explicitly sets the concept in opposition to English industriousness:

> Par ces mots célèbres, *dolce far niente*, entendez toujours le plaisir de rêver voluptueusement aux impressions qui remplissent son cœur. Otez le *loisir* à l'Italie, donnez-lui le travail anglais, et vous lui ravissez la moitié de son bonheur.[46]

> By these well-known words, *dolce far niente*, you must understand the pleasure of dreaming voluptuously, in response to the impressions that fill your heart. Take *leisure* away from Italy, give it the English concept of work, and you take away half of its happiness.

Such voluptuous reveries are, travellers assume, delights that they may themselves enjoy quite innocently, since an escape from care is appropriate to their own experience of travel as leisure: a temporary freedom for everyday responsibility. Jameson, in a passage already quoted in Chapter 3, declares: 'All my activity of mind, all my faculties of thought and feeling, and suffering, seemed lost and swallowed up in an indolent delicious reverie, a sort of vague and languid enjoyment, the true *"dolce far niente"* of this enchanting climate.'[47]

Pleasant sensations in a delicious climate

Dolce, of course, is a word that evokes gastronomic gratification; it is precisely because gustatory pleasure is so instinctive that, like the allurements of colour, it supplies a useful metaphor for delights that retain a certain childlike innocence. The concept of travel as temporary abandonment of 'effort' that is formed in travel writing of this period makes it easy to construct continuities between the pleasures of gastronomy and those of travel itself.

Gastronomic pleasure, moreover, also readily serves as a metonym for the delights of Italy: eating and drinking in that country provide an affirmation that the traveller is seizing the forms of rapture and enchantment specific to the region south of the Alps. Two final commentaries emphasize how gastronomic references and metaphors can be allotted the role of intensely invoking the pleasures of Italy.

In *Rome, Naples et Florence*, Stendhal describes the yearly trapping of thrushes 'au *roccolo*' (in a net), and subsequent eating of them, as 'un des plus vifs plaisirs de la Lombardie' ('one of the greatest pleasures of Lombardy'). The whole gastronomic ritual acquires an innocence from

---

[46] Stendhal [Henri-Marie Beyle], *Rome, Naples et Florence*, edited by Pierre Brunel (Paris: Gallimard, 1987; first edition published in 1817, revised edition in 1826), p. 188.
[47] [Jameson,] *Diary of an Ennuyée*, p. 262.

its rustic simplicity. The songbirds are a part of the natural world; the dish that incorporates them is therefore close to this world. (Any feeling that their contribution to the delights of nature might make the trapping of them seem like a despoliation is absent from this passage.) The polenta on which they are served is, moreover, Stendhal specifies, one of the staple foods of the Lombard peasantry. The trapping of the birds entails an excursion into the 'air délicieux du matin' ('delicious morning air') that is described in terms of the emotion of joy – the most simple and childlike form of pleasure, and in this case invested with yet greater simplicity, since it is 'un accès de joie *animale*' ('an access of *animal* joy'). In the evening, eating the birds at supper, the traveller yet again experiences joy, and compares his feelings to the intense pleasures of animals. The receptiveness of women to such pleasures is implicitly invoked as further proof of the spontaneous, instinctual character of this upsurge of 'joie *animale*':

> Les dames raffolent des *uzei colla polenta*. On prend au filet, à la fin de l'automne, une immense quantité de petits oiseaux (*uzei*) qu'on sert en rôti sur une pâte jaune faite au moment même avec de la farine de maïs et de l'eau chaude. Cette *polenta* est pendant toute l'année la nourriture du paysan lombard. J'ai passé les plus agréables matinées au *roccolo* de M. Cavalletti, à Monticello, avec trois prêtres. Cet air délicieux du matin donne un accès de joie *animale*. Le soir, les délices et la joie du souper avec les *uccelletti*, la *polenta* et l'*entrain* général, semblent reculer les bornes de l'existence du côté des plaisirs si vifs de la bête.[48]

> The ladies go mad about *uzei colla polenta*. In late autumn, the Lombards trap immense numbers of little birds (*uzei*) in a net, and serve them grilled, on a yellow porridge made there and then with maize flour and hot water. This *polenta* is the food of the Lombard peasant throughout the year. I have spent the most agreeable mornings at the *roccolo* of Monsieur Cavalletti, in Monticello, with three priests. This delicious morning air induces an access of *animal* joy. In the evening, the delights and the joy of the supper with the *uccelletti*, the *polenta* and the general high spirits, seem to roll back the bounds of existence and bring us closer to the pleasures felt so forcefully by animals.

Stendhal's use of the term *délices*, translated here as *delights*, emphasizes the elision between the pleasures of the table and those of the countryside, and recalls the expression *les délices de l'Italie*, deployed as the title of an early eighteenth-century travel book by Alexandre de Rogissart; aspects of the Italian climate and natural world are often described as 'delicious'

---

[48] Stendhal, *Rome, Naples et Florence*, p. 195. The gastronomic metaphor implicit in *délices* (translated here as *delights*) is suggested by Randle Cotgrave's inclusion of 'dainties' among the translations of the term, in *A Dictionarie of the French and English Tongues*, introduced by William S. Woods (Columbia, South Carolina: University of South Carolina Press, 1950; facsimile of the first edition of 1611).

or 'délicieux' – as the morning air is here.⁴⁹ (Sass, for example, in his description of an 'excursion' by sea from Naples, quoted above, declares: 'The deliciousness of the air is almost a substitute for food.')⁵⁰

To emphasize the strength of such pleasures yet more hyperbolically, Stendhal summons up the image of a puritanical Englishman, incapable of such transports, and typifies this 'odd character' by reference to the hapless Eustace: 'Je voudrais voir un méthodiste anglais transporté au milieu d'une telle ivresse; il éclaterait en injures ou irait se pendre (voir Eustace parlant de la joie italienne)'⁵¹ ('I should like to see an English Methodist transported into such a state of intoxication: he would burst into insults or would go and hang himself (see Eustace speaking of Italian joy)'.

Sydney Morgan is more deliberative in her attitude to pleasure in Bologna: she lists 'sumptuous dinners' among the forms of enjoyment supplied by the thoughtful hospitality of the Bolognese, together with well-planned sightseeing ('every facility was afforded us of seeing what was best deserving of attention; and ... in no one instance were we left to the trite and commonplace information of a valet-de-place'). The traveller then, however, invests the city with pleasures of a distinctly sensory character, allowing the dinners to prompt a metaphor of dining that casts aspersions on the English in Italy (Morgan defines herself as Anglo-Irish), for sticking too closely to the map:

> A celebrated modern French pilgrim went 'to Jerusalem in search of *pleasant sensations*:' I should say, to judge by my own experience, it would not be necessary to travel further than Bologna. English travellers, however, who travel as they eat, *par la carte*, simply pass through Bologna on their way to the great cities.⁵²

The pursuit of 'pleasant sensations', ostensibly cited as a piece of self-advertising rhetorical flamboyance, is nonetheless endorsed when transferred to a more modest adventurousness in Italy.

---

49 Alexandre de Rogissart, *Les delices de l'Italie: contenant une description exacte du païs, des principales villes, de toutes les antiquitez, & de toutes les raretez qui s'y trouvent*, 4 vols (Paris: Michel Clousier, 1707; first published in 1706 [?]). The Library of Congress Online Catalog lists an edition of 1743, suggesting that the book continued to be read long after its initial appearance.
50 Sass, *Journey to Rome and Naples*, p. 213; see also p. 177 ('the deliciousness of the climate'), [Jameson,] *Diary of an Ennuyée*, p. 239 ('delicious weather', 'this delicious land'), p. 294 ('these rich delicious skies'), and Eaton, *Rome in the Nineteenth Century*, vol. 3, p. 419 ('one of those delicious evenings'). All these additional examples are in passages included in Chapter 1.
51 Stendhal, *Rome, Naples et Florence*, pp. 195–6. (Eustace was in fact a Roman Catholic priest, not a Methodist.)
52 Morgan, *Italy*, vol. 1, p. 300n. The celebrated modern French pilgrim' is presumably Chateaubriand, although I have been unable to find this precise form of words anywhere in his *Itinéraire de Paris à Jérusalem, et de Jérusalem à Paris* (1811).

[Anna Jameson,] *Diary of an Ennuyée* (London: Henry Colburn, 1826), pp. 245–8

Jameson observes: 'Our excursion to Pompeii yesterday, was "a Pic-nic party of pleasure," *à l'Anglaise*'; she mentions her low expectations of such an occasion, and admits that 'the day, however, turned out more pleasant than I expected' (pp. 241–2). After an account of viewing wall-paintings in a newly excavated building and a general account of the streets and houses, she describes in the following extract the gastronomic components of this 'party of pleasure'. (Jameson's *Diary* includes another account of a picnic, in the grounds of the Villa Pamphili, in Rome (pp. 279–81); here, too, she discerns 'too many luxuries' – not to mention 'too many servants, (who on these occasions are always *de trop*)' (p. 280).)

Hurried on by a hungry, noisy, merry party, we at length reached the Caserna, (the ancient barracks, or as Forsyth will have it, the Prætorium).[53] The central court of this building has been converted into a garden; and here, under a weeping willow, our dinner table was spread. Where Englishmen are, there will be good cheer if possible; and our banquet was in truth most luxurious. Besides more substantial cates, we had oysters from Lake Lucrine, (or Acheron), and classically excellent they were; London bottled porter, and half a dozen different kinds of wine. Our dinner went off most gaily, but no order was kept afterwards: the purpose of our expedition seemed to be forgotten in general mirth: many witty things were said and done, and many merry ones, and not a few silly ones. We visited the beautiful public walk and the platform of the old temple of Hercules: I call it *old* because it was a ruin when Pompeii was entire. The Temple of Isis, the Theatres, the Forum, the Basilica, the Amphitheatre, which is in a perfect state of preservation, and more elyptical in form than any of those I have yet seen, and the School of Eloquence, where R** mounted the rostrum and gave us an oration extempore; equally pithy, classical and comical. About sun-set we got into the carriages and returned to Naples.

Of all the heavenly days we have had since we came to Naples, this has been the most heavenly; and of all the lovely scenes I have beheld in Italy, what I saw to-day has most enchanted my senses and imagination. The view from the eminence on which the old temple stood, and which was anciently the public promenade, was splendidly beautiful: the whole landscape was at one time overflowed with light and sunshine; and appeared as if seen through an impalpable but dazzling veil. Towards evening the outlines became more distinct: the little white towns perched upon the hills, the

---

[53] See Forsyth, *Remarks on Antiquities, Arts and Letters*, p. 330.

gentle sea, the fairy island of Rivegliano with its old tower, the smoking crater of Vesuvius, the bold forms of Mount Lactarius and Cape Minerva, stood out full and clear under the cloudless sky; and as we returned, I saw the sun sink behind Capri, which appeared by some optical illusion like a glorious crimson transparency suspended above the horizon: the sky, the earth, the sea, were flushed with the richest rose colour, which gradually softened and darkened into purple: the short twilight faded away, and the full moon, rising over Vesuvius, lighted up the scenery with a softer radiance.

Thus ended a day which was not without its pleasures: – yet had I planned a party of pleasure to Pompeii, methinks I could have managed better. *Par exemple,* I would have deferred it a fortnight later, or till the vines were in leaf; I would have chosen for my companions two or at most three persons whom I could name, whose cultivated minds and happy tempers would have heightened their own enjoyment and mine. After spending a few hours in taking a general view of the whole city, we would have sat down on the platform of the old Greek Temple which commands a view of the mountains and the bay; or, if the heat were too powerful, under the shade of the hill near it. There we would make our cheerful and elegant repast, on bread and fruits, and perhaps a bottle of Malvoisie or Champagne: the rest of the day should be devoted to a minute examination of the principal objects of interest and curiosity: we would wait till the shadows of evening had begun to steal over the scene, purpling the mountains and the sea; we would linger there to enjoy all the splendours of an Italian sunset; and then, with minds softened and elevated by the loveliness and solemnity of the scenes around, we would get into our carriage, and drive back to Naples beneath the bright full moon; and, by the way, we would 'talk the flowing heart,'[54] and make our recollections of the olden time, our deep impressions of the past, heighten our enjoyment of the present; and this would be indeed a day of *pleasure*, of such pleasure as I am capable of feeling – of imparting – of remembering with unmixed delight. Such was *not* yesterday.

John Chetwode Eustace, *A Tour through Italy*, 3 vols (London: J. Mawman, 1813–19), vol. 1, pp. 481–5

We were now engaged in the defiles of *Mount Massicus*, which communicate with those of the *Callicula*, a mountain covered with forests and crowned with *Calvi*, the ancient *Cales*. From these defiles we emerged by a road cut through the rock above Francolisi, and as we looked down beheld the plains of *Campania* spread before us, bordered by the *Apennines* with the craggy point of *Ischia* towering to the sky on one side, and in the centre *Vesuvius*, calmly lifting

---

[54] [Jameson is perhaps adapting Alexander Pope, 'The First Satire of the Second Book of Horace, Imitated', line 65: 'My head and heart thus flowing thro' my quill'.]

his double summit wreathed with smoke. Evening now far advanced, shed a purple tint over the sides and summits of the mountains, that gave at once a softness and richness to the picture, and contrasted finely with the darkness of the plains below, and the light colors of a few thin clouds flitting above.

From *Francolini* we traversed the *Falernus Ager*, which is the tract enclosed between the sea, *Mount Massicus* and *Callicula*, and the river *Vulturnus*; a territory so much celebrated by the ancient poets, and so well known to the classical reader for its delicious wines. It has often been asked why Italy does not now produce wines so excellent, and in such variety as anciently; and it has been as often answered either that the climate has changed, or that the cultivation of the grape has been neglected, and the vines allowed to degenerate for want of skill and attention. As for the first of these reasons, we find nothing in ancient authors that can furnish the least reason to suppose that any such revolution has happened. The productions of the soil are the same, and appear at the same stated periods; the seasons correspond exactly with the descriptions of the poets; the air is in general genial and serene, though chilled occasionally (at least in many provinces) with hard wintry frosts, and sometimes disturbed by sudden unseasonable storms full as grand and as mischievous as that described by Virgil.* Neglect and ignorance are reasons more plausible, but will not perhaps on examination be found much more satisfactory. Arts essential to the existence of man, when once known are never forgotten, and articles so necessary as bread and wine cannot possibly be entirely neglected. The science of tillage passes from father to son, and cannot be obliterated unless the whole mass of population in a country be at once destroyed, and a link struck out of the chain of human generations. Moreover the mode of gathering and pressing the grape; of boiling and storing the wine is nearly the same now as anciently. Besides from the reasons given above it would follow, that the culture of the vine was lost all over Italy, Greece, and Sicily, and that the vine itself had degenerated in all the countries that lie south of the Alps, howsoever favored in other respects by nature. In fact very few of the numberless wines produced in these auspicious climates are palatable to an English or a French traveller, who is apt to find in them either a lusciousness or a raciness, or an inexpressible something that disgusts him, and is not always removed even by familiarity. Nor ought this circumstance to surprize us. Accustomed from our infancy to hear the wines of Italy and Greece extolled to the skies by the ancient poets, we expect to find them singularly delicious while we forget that the goodness of wine depends upon taste, and that our taste has been formed, I had nearly said vitiated, by wines of a flavor very different from that of the classic grape. If the Italian wines therefore are not in so much repute now as they were

---

* Georg. I. [*Georgics*, 1.311–34.]

formerly, it is to be attributed not so much to the degeneracy of the vine, as to the change of taste not only in Transalpine countries but even in Italy itself. The modern Italians are extremely sober; they drink wine as Englishmen drink small beer, not to flatter the palate but to quench the thirst; provided it be neither new, flat, nor unwholesome, it answers their purpose, and they require from it nothing more. Very little attention is therefore paid in the cultivation of the vine, to the quality or perfection, but merely to the quantity of the produce. Not so the ancients: they were fond of convivial enjoyments: they loved wine, and considered it not only as a gratification to the palate, but as a means of intellectual enjoyment, and a vehicle of conversation. To heighten its flavor therefore, to bring it to full maturity by age, in short, to improve it by every method imaginable, was with them an object of primary importance; nor can it occasion surprize that in circumstances so favorable, the vine should flourish. Yet with all this encouragement the two most celebrated wines in Italy, the Cæcuban and the Falernian, had lost much of their excellency and reputation in Pliny's time; the former in consequence of a canal drawn across the vale of Amyclæ by the Emperor Nero, and the latter from its very celebrity, which occasioned so great a demand, that the cultivators unable to resist the temptation, turned their attention from the quality to the quantity.[55] This cause of decline is indeed considered as common to both these species of wine; but in the former it was only an accessary [sic], in the latter a principal agent.

The canal alluded to, was one of the extravagant whims of Nero, who had resolved to open an inland communication between *Ostia* and the *Lake Avernus*, by a navigable canal which might afford all the pleasures, without any of the inconveniences of a voyage in the usual manner. This work was begun but never finished; and it is probable that the *Lago Fundano* or *Amyclano*, which was to have formed part of the projected canal, was lengthened and extended across the little plain to the very foot of *Mount Cæcubus*; thus depriving the flats of a considerable part of that moisture which perhaps caused their fertility. The Cæcuban wine so much celebrated was produced, according to Pliny, in the poplar groves that rose in the marshes on the bay of Amyclæ. That same author gives a long list of Italian wines, all good though of very different degrees of excellence, and I have no doubt that modern Italy, if the cultivation of the vine had the same encouragement now as anciently, would furnish a catalogue equal to it both in excellence and variety. As it is not intended to expand a few cursory remarks into a dissertation, it may finally be observed that several of the wines celebrated in ancient times still retain, at least, some share of their ancient reputation. Thus a wine produced in the very extremity of the

---

[55] [Pliny, *Natural History*, 14.8.61–2.]

Adriatic Gulph, on the banks of the Timavus*, and in the vicinity of *Aquileia*, is still in as great request at *Trieste* as it was formerly in Rome; as is the *Rhetian* wine so much extolled by Virgil at *Venice* and *Verona*. The wines of *Luna* and *Florence* are even now much esteemed all over the north of Italy, as are those of the *Alban Mount*, including *Frescati* and *Gensano*, in Rome. The vines that flourish on the sides and around the base of Vesuvius still continue to furnish a rich and delicious wine, well known to all travellers, and to most readers under the appellation of Lachryma Christi. To conclude, Horace has comprised with his usual neatness the four principal wines of Italy, all the produce of the coast which we have just traversed, in the following stanza:

> Cæcubum et prelo domitam Caleno
> Tu bibes uvam, mea nec Falernæ
> Temperant vites, neque Formiani
> Pocula colles.[56]
>
> 1.20

Before we arrived at *Capua* night had set in, but it was night in all its charms; bright, serene, and odiferous. The only object that could then strike our eyes or excite our curiosity was the luciola, a bright insect, many of which were flying about in every direction like sparks of fire, casting a vivid light around them, and seeming to threaten the waving corn over which they flitted with a conflagration. We entered Naples at a late hour, and drove to the Gran Bretagna, an excellent inn on the sea shore, and close to the royal garden.

Samuel Rogers, *Italy, a Poem* (London: T. Cadell and E. Moxon, [1822–28] 1830), pp. 169–73

FOREIGN TRAVEL

It was in a splenetic humour that I sate me down to my scanty fare at TERRACINA; and how long I should have contemplated the lean thrushes in array before me, I cannot say, if a cloud of smoke, that drew the tears into my eyes, had not burst from the green and leafy boughs on the hearth-stone. 'Why,' I exclaimed, starting up from the table, 'why did I leave

---

* This wine was called Pucinum. The place now bears the name of *Castel Duino*, and corresponds with the description given of it by Pliny, *saxeo colle, maritimo afflatu*. [– A rocky hill, exposed to the sea-breezes. – Nat. Hist.] Lib. xiv. cap. vi. [See Pliny, *Natural History*, 14.8.60: the translation and extra references are added in later editions.]

[56] [Horace, *Odes*, 1.20.9–12. In the sixth edition of Eustace's *Tour* (vol. 2, p. 327), this translation (omitting the Calenian wine mentioned in the original) is added in a footnote: 'From the Cæcubian vintage prest / For you shall flow the racy wine; / But ah! My meagre cup's unblest / With the rich Formian or Falernian vine / *Francis*.']

my own chimney-corner? – But am I not on the road to BRUNDISIUM? And are not these the very calamities that befel HORACE and VIRGIL, and MÆCENAS, and PLOTIUS, and VARIUS? HORACE laughed at them – Then why should not I?[57] HORACE resolved to turn them to account; and VIRGIL – cannot we hear him observing, that to remember them will, by and by, be a pleasure?'[58] My soliloquy reconciled me at once to my fate; and when; for the twentieth time, I had looked through the window on a sea sparkling with innumerable brilliants, a sea on which the heroes of the Odyssey and the Eneid had sailed, I sat down as to a splendid banquet. My thrushes had the flavour of ortolans; and I ate with an appetite I had not known before. 'Who,' I cried, as I poured out my last glass of Falernian,* (for Falernian it was said to be, and in my eyes it ran bright and clear as a topaz-stone) 'Who would remain at home, could he do otherwise? Who would submit to tread that dull, but daily round; his hours forgotten as soon as spent?' and, opening my journal-book and dipping my pen in my ink-horn, I determined, as far as I could, to justify myself and my countrymen in wandering over the face of the earth. 'It may serve me,' said I, 'as a remedy in some future fit of the spleen.'

Ours is a nation of travellers;† and no wonder, when the elements, air, water, and fire, attend at our bidding, to transport us from shore to shore; when the ship rushes into the deep, her track the foam as of some mighty torrent; and, in three hours or less, we stand gazing and gazed at among a foreign people. None want an excuse. If rich, they go to enjoy; if poor, to retrench; if sick, to recover; if studious, to learn; if learned, to relax from their studies. But whatever they may say and whatever they may believe, they go for the most part on the same errand; nor will those who reflect, think that errand an idle one.

---

57 [Horace, *Satires*, 1.5 ('A Journey to Brundisium').]
58 [Virgil, *Aeneid*, 1.203.]
* We were now within a few hours of the Campania Felix. On the colour and flavour of Falernian consult Galen and Dioscorides. [Aelius Galenus – or Claudius Galenus – and Pedanius Dioscorides, ancient writers whose works were concerned with medical and related matters.]
† As indeed it always was, contributing those of every degree, from a *milord* with his suite to him whose only attendant is his shadow. Coryate in 1608 performed his journey on foot; and, returning, hung up his shoes in his village-church as an ex-voto. Goldsmith, a century and a half afterwards, followed in nearly the same path; playing a tune on his flute to procure admittance, whenever he approached a cottage at night-fall. [See Thomas Coryate, *Coryats Crudities. Hastily gobled up in five moneths travells in France, Savoy, Italy, Rhetia commonly called the Grisons Country, Helvetia alias Switzerland, some parts of High Germany and the Netherlands* (London: printed by W[illiam] S[tansby for the author], 1611). The story of Oliver Goldsmith travelling on foot, on his return journey from Italy, is recounted in Thomas Percy's prefatory 'account of his life and writings' in Oliver Goldsmith, *The Miscellaneous Works*, 4 vols (London: J. Johnson, 1801), vol. 1, pp. 34–6.]

Almost all men are over-anxious. No sooner do they enter the world, than they lose that taste for natural and simple pleasures, so remarkable in early life. Every hour do they ask themselves what progress they have made in the pursuit of wealth or honour; and on they go as their fathers went before them, till, weary and sick at heart, they look back with a sigh of regret to the golden time of their childhood.

Now travel, and foreign travel more particularly, restores to us in a great degree what we have lost. When the anchor is heaved, we double down the leaf; and for a while at least all effort is over. The old cares are left clustering round the old objects; and at every step, as we proceed, the slightest circumstance amuses and interests. All is new and strange.* We surrender ourselves, and feel once again as children. Like them, we enjoy eagerly; like them, when we fret, we fret only for the moment; and here indeed the resemblance is very remarkable; for, if a journey has its pains as well as its pleasures (and there is nothing unmixed in this world) the pains are no sooner over than they are forgotten, while the pleasures live long in the memory.

Nor is it surely without another advantage. If life be short, not so to many of us are its days and its hours. When the blood slumbers in the veins, how often do we wish that the earth would turn faster on its axis, that the sun would rise and set before it does; and, to escape from the weight of time, how many follies, how many crimes are committed! Men rush on danger, and even on death. Intrigue, play, foreign and domestic broil, such are their resources; and, when these things fail, they destroy themselves.

Now in travelling we multiply events, and innocently. We set out, as it were, on our adventures; and many are those that occur to us, morning, noon, and night. The day we come to a place which we have long heard and read of, and in ITALY we do so continually, it is an era in our lives; and from that moment the very name calls up a picture. How delightfully too does the knowledge flow in upon us, and how fast!.† Would he who sat in a corner of his library, poring over books and maps, learn more or so much in the time, as he who, with his eyes and his heart open, is receiving

---

* We cross a narrow sea; we land on a shore which we have contemplated from our own; and we awake, as it were, in another planet. The very child that lisps there, lisps in words which we have yet to learn.

Nor is it less interesting, if less striking, to observe the gradations in language, and feature, and character, as we travel on from kingdom to kingdom. The French peasant becomes more and more Italian as we approach Italy, and a Spaniard as we approach Spain. [This footnote is absent in the 1830 edition, but present in later editions.]

† To judge at once of a nation, we have only to throw our eyes on the markets and on the fields. If the markets are well-supplied, the fields well-cultivated, all is right. If otherwise, we may say, and say truly, these people are barbarous or oppressed.

impressions all day long from the things themselves?* How accurately do they arrange themselves in our memory, towns, rivers, mountains; and in what living colours do we recall the dresses, manners, and customs of the people! Our sight is the noblest of all the senses.[59] 'It fills the mind with most ideas, converses with its objects at the greatest distance, and continues longest in action without being tired.'[60] Our sight is on the alert when we travel; and its exercise is then so delightful, that we forget the profit in the pleasure.

Like a river, that gathers, that refines as it runs, like a spring that takes its course through some rich vein of mineral, we improve and imperceptibly – nor in the head only, but in the heart. Our prejudices leave us, one by one. Seas and mountains are no longer our boundaries. We learn to love, and esteem, and admire beyond them. Our benevolence extends itself with our knowledge. And must we not return better citizens than we went? For the more we become acquainted with the institutions of other countries, the more highly must we value our own.

---

* Assuredly not, if the last has laid a proper foundation. Knowledge makes knowledge as money makes money, nor ever perhaps so fast as on a journey.
[59] [John Donne, Sermon 23.]
[60] [Joseph Addison, *Spectator*, Essay no.411 (dated 21 June 1712, no. 2 in the sequence 'The Pleasures of the Imagination'); see Richard Steele and Joseph Addison, *Selections from the Tatler and the Spectator*, edited by Angus Ross (London: Penguin, 1988), p. 368.]

Bibliography

Primary texts written before 1840 (and selected sources cited in notes)
Where two editions are listed, the reference is to the earlier edition unless otherwise stated.

Addison, Joseph, *Remarks on Several Parts of Italy, in the Years 1701, 1702, 1703* (London: Jacob Tonson, 1705)

Anson, George, *A Voyage round the World in the Years MDCCXL, I, II, III, IV*, compiled by Richard Walter (London: W. Bowyer and J. Nichols, 1776)

Baretti, Joseph [Giuseppe], *An Account of the Manners and Customs of Italy; with Observations on the Mistakes of Some Travellers, with Regard to that Country*, second edition, 2 vols (London: T. Davies, L. Davis and C. Rymers, 1768)

Beckford, William, *Biographical Memoirs of Extraordinary Painters* (London: William Clarke, [1780] 1824)

Beckford, William, *Dreams, Waking Thoughts and Incidents* (1783), in *The Travel Diaries of William Beckford of Fonthill*, edited by Guy Chapman, 2 vols (London: Constable and Houghton and Mifflin, 1928), vol.1, pp.1–310

Bell, John, *Observations on Italy. By the late John Bell, Fellow of the Royal College of Surgeons, Edinburgh, &c* (Edinburgh and London: William Blackwood and T. Cadell, 1825)

Boigne, [Charlotte-Louise-Éléonore-Adélaïde] de, *Mémoires de la Comtesse de Boigne*, edited by Charles Nicollaud, 4 vols (Paris: Plon-Nourrit, 1907)

Brosses, Charles de, *Lettres familières*, edited by Giuseppina Cafasso and Letizia Norci Cagiano de Azevedo, Mémoires et documents sur Rome et l'Italie Méridionale, Nouvelle Série, 4, 3 vols, continuous pagination (Naples: Centre Jean Bérard, 1991)

Browne, Sir Thomas, *Christian Morals*, 'published from the Original and Correct Manuscript of the Author' by John Jeffery (London and Cambridge: Cambridge University Press, Knapton and Morphew, 1716)

Brydone, P[atrick], *A Tour through Sicily and Malta. In a Series of Letters to William Beckford, Esq. of Somerly in Suffolk*, 'A New Edition', 2 vols (London: W. Strahan and T. Cadell, [1773] 1775)

Burke, Edmund, *A Philosophical Enquiry into the Origin of our Ideas of the Sublime and Beautiful*, edited by James Boulton (Oxford: Blackwell, 1987)

Byron [George Noël Gordon, Lord], *Byron's Letters and Journals*, edited by Leslie A. Marchand, 13 vols (London: Murray, 1973–94)

Byron [George Noël Gordon, Lord], Lord, *The Complete Poetical Works*, edited by Jerome J. McGann, 7 vols (Oxford: Oxford University Press, 1980–92)

Carver, Jonathan, *Jonathan Carver's Travels through America, 1766–1768; An Eighteenth-Century Explorer's Account of Uncharted America*, edited by Norman Gelb (New York and Chichester: Wiley, [1778] 1993)

Cecconi, Leonardo, *Storia di Palestrina, città del prisco Lazio* (Ascoli: 'Per Nicco a Ricci Stampator pubblico', 1756)

Cellini, Benvenuto, *Vita di Benvenuto Cellini scritta da lui medesimo*, transcribed and edited by Giuseppe Molini, 2 vols (Florence: 'tipograifa all'insegna di Dante', 1832)

Cellini, Benvenuto, *The Life of Benvenuto Cellini*, translated by John Addington Symonds, second edition, 2 vols (London: John C. Nimmo, 1888)

Chateaubriand, [François René de] *Itinéraire de Paris à Jérusalem, et de Jérusalem à Paris*, edited by Émile Malakis, 2 vols (Baltimore and London: Johns Hopkins University Press, [1811] 1941)

Chateauvieux, Frédéric Lullin de, *Lettres écrites d'Italie en 1812 et 13, à M. Charles Pictet*, 2 vols (Paris and Geneva: chez J.J. Paschoud, 1816)

Cochin, Charles Nicolas, *Voyage d'Italie: ou, recueil des notes sur les ouvrages de peinture et de sculpture, qu'on voit dans les principales villes d'Italie*, 3 vols (Paris: 'Ch. Ant. Jombert', 1758)

Coleridge, S[amuel] T[aylor], 'On the Principles of Genial Criticism concerning the Fine Arts, More Especially those of Statuary and Painting, Deduced from the Laws and Motions which Guide the True Artist in the Production of his Works', in *Biographia Literaria, with his Aesthetical Essays*, edited by J. Shawcross, 2 vols (Oxford: Clarendon Press, 1907), vol. 2, pp.219–43

Coleridge, Samuel Taylor, *Coleridge's Miscellaneous Criticism*, edited by Thomas Middleton Raysor (London: Constable, 1936)

Coryate, Thomas, *Coryats Crudities. Hastily gobled up in five moneths travells in France, Savoy, Italy, Rhetia commonly called the Grisons Country, Helvetia alias Switzerland, some parts of High Germany and the Netherlands. Newly digested in the hungry aire of ODCOMBE in the County of Somerset, and now dispersed to the nourishment of the travelling members of this kingdome* (London: printed by W[illiam] S[tansby for the author], 1611)

Cotgrave, Randle, *A Dictionarie of the French and English Tongues*, introduced by William S. Woods (Comumbia, South Carolina: University of South Carolina Press, 1950; facsimile of the first edition of 1611)

Drummond, Alexander ('His Majesty's Consul at Aleppo'), *Travels through Different Cities of Germany, Italy, Greece, and Several Parts of Asia, as far as the Banks of the Euphrates: In a Series of Letters. Containing an Account of what is most remarkable in their Present State, as well as in their Monuments of Antiquity* (London: W. Strahan, 'for the Author', 1754)

[Dupaty, Charles Marguerite Jean Baptiste Mercier,] *Lettres sur l'Italie, en 1785*, 2 vols (Rome and Paris: de Senne, 1788)

Dupaty, [Charles Marguerite Jean Baptiste Mercier,] *Sentimental Letters on Italy*, translated by J. [i.e. Giovanni] Povoleri, 2 vols (London: printed for the translator by J. Crowder, and sold by J. Bew, 1789)

Eaton, Charlotte, *Rome in the Nineteenth Century; Containing a Complete Account of the Ruins of the Ancient City, the Remains of the Middle Ages, and the Monuments of Modern Times. With Remarks on the Fine Arts, on the State of Society, and on the Religious Ceremonies, Manners, and Customs, of the Modern Romans. In a Series of Letters Written during a Residence at Rome, in the Years

1817 and 1818, 3 vols (Edinburgh and London: Archibald Constable & Co. and Hurst, Robinson, & Co., 1820)

Elliott, Sir Gilbert, *Life and Letters of Sir Gilbert Elliot, First Earl of Minto, from 1751 to 1806*, edited by the Countess of Minto, 3 vols (London: Longmans, Green, 1874)

[Engelbach, Lewis,] *Naples and the Campagna Felice. In a Series of Letters Addressed to a Friend in England, in 1802* (London: R. Ackermann, 1815)

Eustace, The Rev. John Chetwode, *A Tour through Italy, Exhibiting a View of its Scenery, its Antiquities, and its Monument; Particularly as they are Objects of Classical Interest and Elucidation: with an account of the present state of its cities and towns; and occasional observations on the recent spoliations of the French*, 3 vols (London: J. Mawman, 1813–19). Vol. 3 consists of Sir R[ichard] Colt Hoare's 'A Classical Tour through Italy and Sicily; tending to illustrate some districts which have not been described by Mr. Eustace in his classical tour'. (On the page preceding the title page, Eustace's travel narrative is titled *A Classical Tour through Italy*, and this title, adopted in later editions, is the one by which contemporaries usually refer to the work.)

Eustace, The Rev. John Chetwode, Eustace, John Chetwode, *A Classical Tour through Italy An. MDCCCII*, sixth edition, 4 vols (London: J. Mawman, 1821)

Evelyn, John, *The Diary of John Evelyn*, edited by E.S. de Beer, 6 vols (Oxford: Oxford University Press, 1955)

Fontanier, Pierre, *Les Figures du discours* (Paris: Flammarion, [1821–27] 1977)

Forsyth, Joseph, *Remarks on Antiquities, Arts, and Letters during an Excursion in Italy in the Years 1802 and 1803*, first edition (London: T. Cadell and W. Davies, 1813)

Forsyth, Joseph, *Remarks on Antiquities, Arts, and Letters during an Excursion in Italy in the Years 1802 and 1803*, second edition (London: John Murray, 1816). Some but not all copies of this edition include an 'Advertisement' in which the author's brother, Isaac Forsyth, gives an account of his brother's capture by the French on his return journey, and subsequent imprisonment.

Galiffe, James Aug., 'of Geneva', *Italy and its Inhabitants: An Account of a Tour in that Country in 1816 and 1817: Containing a View of Characters, Manners, Customs, Governments, Antiquities, Literature, Dialects, Theatres, and the Fine Arts; with some Remarks on the Origin of Rome and of the Latin Language*, 2 vols (London: John Murray, 1820)

Galt, John, *The Life and Studies of Benjamin West, Esq.*, 2 vols (London: T. Cadell and W. Davies, 1816–20)

Gell, Sir William, and John P. Gandy, *Pompeiana. The Topography, Edifices, and Ornaments of Pompeii*, new edition, 2 vols (London: Rodwell and Martin, 1824)

Gibbon [Edward], *Gibbon's Decline and Fall of the Roman Empire*, introduced by Christopher Dawson, 6 vols (London and New York: Dent and Dutton, 1954)

Goldsmith, Oliver, *An History of the Earth, and Animated Nature*, 8 vols (London: J. Nourse, 1774)

Goldsmith, Oliver, *The Miscellaneous Works. . . A new edition. . . To which is prefixed some account of his life and writings [by Thomas Percy], 4 vols (London: J. Johnson, 1801)

Goldsmith, Oliver, *The Vicar of Wakefield*, edited by Stephen Coote (London: Penguin, [1766] 1986)

Graham, Maria, *Three Months Passed in the Mountains East of Rome, during the Year 1819* (London: Longman, Hurst, Rees, Orme and Brown; Edinburgh: A. Constable & Co., 1820)

Graham, Maria, *Three Months Passed in the Mountains East of Rome, during the Year 1819*, second edition (London: Longman, Hurst, Rees, Orme and Brown; Edinburgh: A. Constable & Co., 1821)

Gray, Robert, *Letters during the Course of a Tour through Germany, Switzerland and Italy, in the Years MDCCXCI, and MDCCXCII. With Reflections on the Manners, Literature and Religion of these Countries* (London: F. & C. Rivington, 1794)

Greatheed, B[ertie], R[obert] Merry, W[illiam] Parsons and Mrs. [Hester Lynch] Piozzi, *The Florence Miscellany* (Florence: G. Cam, 1785)

Guinan-Laoureins, J.B. [Jean Baptiste Reinolds], *Tableau de Rome vers la fin de 1814* (Brussels: Imprimerie de Weissenbruch, 1816)

Hamilton, Sir William, *Observations on Mount Vesuvius, Mount Etna, and Other Volcanos: in a Series of Letters, Addressed to the Royal Society* (London: T. Cadell, 1772)

Hawkesworth, John, *An Account of the Voyages Undertaken by Order of his Present Majesty for Making Discoveries in the Southern Hemisphere, and Successively Performed by Commodore Byron, Captain Wallis, Captain Cartaret, and Captain Cook, in the Dolphin, the Swallow, and the Endeavour: Drawn up from the Journals which were kept by the Several Commanders, and from the Papers of Joseph Banks, Esq.*, 3 vols (London: W. Strahan and T. Cadell, 1773)

Hazlitt, William, *Criticisms on Art and Sketches of the Picture Galleries of England*, edited by W[illiam] Carew Hazlitt, 2 vols (London: 1843–44)

Hazlitt, William 'English Students at Rome', in *Essays on the Fine Arts*, edited by W[illiam] Carew Hazlitt (London: Reeves and Turner, 1873), 321–33

Hazlitt, W[illiam], *Notes of a Journey through France and Italy* (London: Hunt and Clarke, 1826)

Hazlitt, William, 'On Going a Journey' [1822], in *The Essays of William Hazlitt: A Selection*, introduced by Catherine Macdonald Maclean (London: Macdonald, 1949), 29–40

Hazlitt, William, 'On Gusto' [1816], in *Romantic Critical Essays*, edited by David Bromwich (Cambridge: Cambridge University Press, 1987), 96–9

Hazlitt, William, 'On Wit and Humour' [1818], in *Lectures on the English Comic Writers* (Oxford: Oxford University Press, 1943), 1–35

Hobhouse, John [Cam], *Historical Illustrations of the Fourth Canto of Childe Harold: containing dissertations on the ruins of Rome, and an essay on Italian literature* (London: John Murray, 1818)

Hunt, Leigh, *Bacchus in Tuscany, A Dithyrambic Poem, from the Italian of Francesco Redi, with Notes Original and Select* (London: 'Printed for John and H.L. Hunt, Tavistock Street', 1825)

[Jameson, Anna,] *Diary of an Ennuyée*, second edition (London: Henry Colburn, 1826); first published in 1826

Johnson, James, *Change of Air; or, the Pursuit of Health; an Autumnal Excursion through France, Switzerland and Italy, in the Year 1829, with Observations and Reflections on the Moral, Physical, and Medical Influence of Travelling-Exercise, Change of Scene, Foreign Skies, and Voluntary Expatriation*, third edition (London: S. Highley, 1831)

Keats, John, *The Complete Poems*, second edition, edited by John Barnard (Harmondsworth: Penguin, 1977)

[Lalande, Joseph Jérôme le Français de,] *Voyage d'un Françaid en Italie, fait dans les années 1765 et 1766*, 8 vols (Venice and Paris: chez Desaint, 1769)

Lassels, Richard, *The Voyage of Italy; or, A Compleat Journey through Italy*, edited by S. W[ilson], 2 parts (Paris: V. du Moutier, 1670)

[Le Riche, J.M.] *Antiquités des environs de Naples, et dissertations qui y sont relatives, par M. J.L.R.* (Naples: Imprimerie française, 1820)

Longinus, *Dionysius Longinus on the Sublime: translated from the Greek, with Notes and Observations, and Some Account of the Life, writings, and Character of the Author*, translated by William Smith, fourth edition (London: E. Johnson, 1770)

MacCulloch, John, *On Malaria: an Essay on the Production and Propagation of this Poison, and on the Nature and Localities of the Places by which it is Produced; with an Examination of the Diseases Caused by it, and of the Means of Preventing or Diminishing them, both at Home and in the Naval and Military Service* (London: Longman, Rees, Orme, Brown and Green, 1827)

Marmontel, [Jean-François,] 'Alcibiade, ou le Moi' in *Contes Moraux*, 'nouvelle édition, corrigée et augmentée', 3 vols (Paris: chez Merlin, 1770), vol. 1, pp. 1–34

Matthews, Henry, *The Diary of an Invalid. Being the Journal of a Tour in Pursuit of Health in Portugal, Italy, Switzerland and France in the Years 1817, 1818 and 1819*, second edition (London: John Murray, 1820)

Maupertuis, [Pierre Louis Moreau de,] *La Figure de la Terre déterminée par les observations de Messieurs De Maupertuis, Clairaut, Camus, Le Monnier de l'Académie Royale des Sciences, et de M. l'Abbé Outhier, Correspondant de la même Académie, accompagnés de M. Celsius, Professeur d'Astronomie à Upsal: faites par ordre du Roy au Cercle Polaire* (Amsterdam: chez Jean Catuffe, 1738)

Maupertuis, [Pierre Louis Moreau] de, *La Figure de la terre, déterminée par les observations de messieurs de Maupertuis, Clairaut, Camus, Le Monnier, de l'Académie Royale des Sciences, et de M. l'Abbé Outhier, correspondant de la même Académie, accompagnés de M. Celsius, Professeur d'Astronomie à Upsal, faites par ordre du roy au Cercle Polaire* (Paris: Imprimerie royale, 1738)

Maupertuis, [Pierre Louis Moreau] de, *The Figure of the Earth, Determined from Observations Made by Order of the French King, at the Polar Circle, By Messrs de Maupertuis, Camus, Clairaut, Le Monnier, Members of the Royal Academy of Sciences; the Abbé Outhier, Correspondant of the Academy; and Mr. Celsius, Professor of Astronomy at Upsal, translated from the French of M. de Maupertuis* (London: T. Cox, 1738)

Middleton, Conyers, *A Letter from Rome, Shewing an Exact Conformity between Popery and Paganism: or, the Religion of the Present Romans to be Derived entirely from that of their Heathen Ancestors* (London: W. Innys, 1729)

[Miller, Anne, Lady,] *Letters from Italy, Describing the Manners, Customs, Antiquities, Paintings, &c. of that Country, in the Years MDCCLXX and*

MDCCLXXI, to a Friend Residing in France. By an English Woman, 3 vols (London: Edward and Charles Dilly, 1776)
[Montagu, Lady Mary Wortley,] *Letters of the Right Honourable Lady M—y W---y M----e: Written during her Travels in Europe, Asia and Africa, to Persons of Distinction, Men of Letters, &c. in Different Parts of Europe*, 4 vols (London: T. Becket and P.A. de Hondt, 1763–67)
Montesquieu [Charles Louis de Secondat, Baron de], *De l'esprit des lois*, edited by Victor Goldschmidt, 2 vols (Paris: Flammarion, [1748] 1979)
Montesquieu [Charles Louis de Secondat, Baron de], 'Essai sur le goût, dans les choses de la nature et de l'art. Fragment imparfait trouvé parmi les papiers de feu M. le Président de Montesquieu', in Alexander Gerard, *Essai sur le goût, augmenté de trois dissertations sur le même sujet, par Messieurs de Voltaire, d'Alembert et de Montesquieu*, translated by 'M.E***' [M.-A. Eidous] (Paris: chez Delalain, and Dijon, chez la Veuve Coignard and Louis Frantin, 1766), 265–306
Montesquieu [Charles Louis,] Monsieur de Secondat, Baron de, *The Spirit of Laws*, translated by Thomas Nugent, 2 vols (London: J. Nourse and P. Vaillant, 1750)
Moore, John, *A View of Society and Manners in Italy, with Anecdotes Relating to some Eminent Characters*, second edition, 2 vols (London: W. Strahan and T. Cadell, 1781)
Morgan, Lady [Sydney Morgan, née Owenson], *Italy*, 2 vols (London: Henry Colburn, 1821)
Morgan, Lady [Sydney Morgan, née Owenson], *The Life and Times of Salvador Rosa*, 2 vols (London: Henry Colburn, 1824)
Normanby, [Constantine Henry Phipps,] Marquis of, *The English in Italy*, 3 vols (London: Saunders and Otley, 1825)
[Parsons, William,] *A Poetical Tour, in the Years 1784, 1785, and 1786. By a Member of the Arcadian Soceity at Rome* (London: 'printed at the Logographic Press, for J. Robson, and W. Clarke', 1787)
Peacock, Thomas Love, *'Nightmare Abbey'; 'Crotchet Castle'*, edited by Raymond Wright (Penguin: Harmondsworth, 1969)
Piozzi, Hester Lynch, *Observations and Reflections Made in the Course of a Journey through France, Italy, and Germany*, 2 vols (London: A. Strahan and T. Cadell, 1789)
Piozzi, Hester Lynch, *The Piozzi Letters: Correspondence of Hester Lynch Piozzi, 1784–1821 (formerly Mrs. Thrale)*, edited by Edward A. Bloom and Lillian D. Bloom, 6 vols (Newark, London and Toronto: University of Delaware Press and Associated University Presses, 1989–96)
Pommereul, [François René Jean, Baron] de, *Campagne du Général Buonaparte en Italic, pendant les années IVe et Ve de la République Français, par un officier général* (Paris: 'chez Plassan, chez Bernard', 1797)
Radcliffe, Ann, *A Sicilian Romance*, edited by Alison Milbank (Oxford: Oxford University Press, 1993)
Reynolds, Frances, *Enquiry concerning the Principles of Taste, and the Origin of our Ideas of Beauty* (London: Baker and Galabin, 1785)
Reynolds, Sir Joshua, *Discourses on Art*, edited by Robert R. Wark (New Haven and London: Yale University Press, 1975); delivered between 1769 and 1790
Richardson, John, *A Dissertation on the Languages, Literature, and Manners of*

Eastern Nations. Originally Prefixed to a Dictionary Persian, Arabic, and English (Oxford: Clarendon Press, 1777)

Rogers, Samuel, *Italy, a Poem* (London: T. Cadell and E. Moxon, [1822–28] 1830)

Rogissart, Alexandre de, *Les delices de l'Italie: contenant une description exacte du païs, des principales villes, de toutes les antiquitez, & de toutes les raretez qui s'y trouvent: ouvrage enrichi d'un tres-grand nombre de figures en taille-douce*, 4 vols (Paris: Michel Clousier, [1706?] 1707)

[Rose, William Stewart, (identified by the letters W.S.R. at the end of the Introduction),] *Letters from the North of Italy, addressed to Henry Hallam, Esq.*, 2 vols (London: John Murray, 1819)

Sade, Marquis de [Donatien Alphonse François de Sade], *Voyage d'Italie*, Bibliothèque Sade, edited by Maurice Lever, 4 parts, 7 vols (Paris: Fayard, 1993–95), part 3

Sass, Henry, *A Journey to Rome and Naples, performed in 1817; giving an Account of the Present State of Society in Italy, and containing Observations on the Fine Arts* (London: Longman, Hurst, Rees, Orme and Brown, 1818)

Schlegel, Friedrich von, *Über die Sprache und Weisheit der Indier* (Heidelberg: Mohr und Zimmer, 1808)

Shelley, Mary, *The Journals of Mary Shelley, 1814–1844*, edited by Paula R. Feldman and Diana Scott-Kilvert, 2 vols (Oxford: Oxford University Press, 1987)

Shelley, Percy Bysshe, *The Letters of Percy Bysshe Shelley*, edited by Frederick L. Jones, 2 vols (Oxford: Oxford University Press, 1964)

Sherlock, Martin, *Letters from an English Traveller, Translated from the French Original Printed at Geneva. With Notes* (London: J. Nichols, T. Cadell and N. Conant, 1780)

[Sherlock, Martin,] *Lettres d'un voyageur anglois* ('à Londres', [Geneva?]: privately printed, 1779)

Sherlock, Martin, *New Letters from an English Traveller. Written originally in French . . . and now translated into English by the Author* (London: J. Nichols, T. Cadell, P. Elmsly, H. Payne and N. Conant, 1781)

Sherlock, M[artin] *Nouvelles Lettres d'un Voyageur Anglois*, second edition (London and Paris: Esprit and La Veuve Duchesne, 1780)

Simond, Louis, *A Tour in Italy and Sicily* (London: Longman, Orme, Brown and Green, 1828)

Simond, Louis, *Voyage en Italie et en Sicile*, 2 vols (Paris: A. Sautelet et compagnie, 1828)

Smith, Sir James Edward, *Memoir and Correspondence of the Late Sir James Edward Smith, M.D.*, edited by Lady [Pleasance] Smith, 2 vols (London: Longman, Rees, Orme, Brown, Green and Longman, 1832)

Smith, Sir James Edward, *A Sketch of a Tour on the Continent, in the Years 1786 and 1787*, 3 vols (London: B. and J. White, 1793)

Smollett, Tobias, *Travels through France and Italy*, edited by Frank Felsenstein (Oxford: Oxford University Press, [1766] 1981)

Staël, Madame de [Anne Louise Germaine de Staël-Holstein], *Corinne, ou l'Italie*, edited by Claudine Herrmann, 2 vols (Paris: Éditions des Femmes, [1807] 1979)

Starke, Mariana, *Letters from Italy, between the Years 1792 and 1798, Containing a View of the Revolutions in that Country, from the Capture of Nice by the French

Republic to the Expulsion of Pius VI from the Ecclesiastical State, 2 vols (London: R. Philips, 1800)

Steele, Richard, and Joseph Addison, *Selections from the Tatler and the Spectator*, edited by Angus Ross (London: Penguin, 1988)

Stendhal [Henri-Marie Beyle], *Promenades dans Rome*, in *Voyages en Italie*, edited by V. del Litto, Bibliothèque de la Pléiade (Paris: Gallimard, [1830] 1973), 593–1291

Stendhal [Henri-Marie Beyle], *Rome, Naples et Florence*, edited by Pierre Brunel (Paris: Gallimard, [1817/1826] 1987)

Sterne, Laurence, *'A Sentimental Journey' with 'The Journal to Eliza' and 'A Political Romance'*, edited by Ian Jack (Oxford: Oxford University Press, [1768] 1991)

Sterne, Laurence, *The Life and Opinions of Tristram Shandy, Gentleman*, edited by Graham Petrie (Harmondsworth: Penguin, [1759–66] 1976)

Swinburne, Henry, *Travels in the Two Sicilies, in the Years 1777, 1778, 1779, and 1780*, 2 vols (London: P. Elmsly, 1783–85)

Temple, Lancelot [John Armstrong], *[A] Short Ramble through Some Parts of France and Italy* (London: T. Cadell, 1771)

Trench, Melesina Chevenix St George, *Journal Kept during a Visit to Germany in 1799, 1800*, edited by the Dean of Westminster (London: Savil and Edwards, printers, 1861)

Ulloa, Antonio de, *Relación histórica del viage a la América meridional, hecho de orden de S. Mag., para medir algunos grados de Meridiano terrestre, con otras varias observaciones astronomicas y phisicas*, 4 vols (Madrid: Antonio Maria, 1748)

Vacca, Flaminio, 'Memorie di varie antichità trovate in diverse luoghi della città di Roma scritte da Flaminio Vacca nell'Anno 1594', in Antonio Nibby, *Roma Antico di Famiano Nardini, riscontrata, ed accresciuta delle ultime scoperte, con note ed osservazioni critico antiquarie*, fourth edition, 4 vols (Rome, 'Nella Stamperia de Roma', [1665], 1818–20), vol. 4, pp. 1–50 (paginated as separate text)

Varro [Marcus Terentius], *On the Latin Language*, with an English translation by Roland G. Kent, 2 vols (Cambridge, Massachusetts: Harvard University Press [1951])

Vasari, Giorgio, *Le Vite de' più eccellenti pittori scultori e archittettori, nelle redazioni del 1550 e 1568*, edited by Rosanna Bettarini and Paola Barocchi, 6 vols (Florence, Studio per edizioni scelte [Sansoni], 1966–99)

Vasari, Giorgio, *The Lives of the Painters, Sculptors, and Architects*, translated by A.B. Hinds, 4 vols (London and New York: Dent and Dutton, 1950)

Vigée-Lebrun, [Elisabeth,], *Souvenirs de MadameVigée-Lebrun*, 2 vols (Paris: Charpentier, [1835–37] 1891)

Walker, A[dam], *Ideas, Suggested on the Spot in a Late Excursion through Flanders, Germany, France, and Italy* (London: J. Robson and J. Johnson, 1790)

Walpole, [Horace], *The Works of Horatio Walpole, Earl of Orford*, 5 vols (London: G.G. and J. Robinson and J. Edwards, 1798)

Walpole, Horace, *The Yale Edition of Horace Walpole's Correspondence*, edited by W.S. Lewis, 40 vols (London and New Haven: Yale University Press, 1937–83)

[Watkins, Thomas], *Travels through Switzerland, Italy, Sicily, the Greek Islands to*

Constantinople; through Part of Greece, Ragusa, and the Dalmatian Isles; in a Series of Letters to Pennoyre Watkins, Esq., from Thomas Watkins, A.M. F.R.S. in the Years 1787, 1788, 1789, second edition, 2 vols (London: J. Owen, [1792] 1794)

Webb, Daniel, *An Inquiry into the Beauties of Painting; and into the Merits of the most Celebrated Painters, Ancient and Modern* (London: R. and J. Dodsley, 1760)

Williams, H[ugh] W[illiam], *Travels in Italy, Greece, and the Ionian Islands. In a Series of Letters, Descriptive of Manners, Scenery, and the Fine Arts*, 2 vols (Edinburgh: A. Constable & Co., 1820)

Winckelmann, Johann Joachim, *Historie de l'art chez les anciens*, translated by Hendrik Jansen, 2 vols, (Paris: 'chez l'auteur: Barrois l'aîné', 1790–an X/1803)

Wollstonecraft, Mary, *Letters Written during a Short Residence in Sweden, Norway, and Denmark* [1796], in Mary Wollstonecraft and William Godwin, *'A Short Residence in Sweden, Norway and Denmark' and 'Memoirs of the Author of "The Rights of Woman"'*, edited by Richard Holmes (London: Penguin, 1987)

Young, Arthur, *Travels during the Years 1787, 1788, and 1789; Undertaken More Particularly with a View of Ascertaining the Cultivation, Wealth, Resources, and National Prosperity of the Kingdom of France*, 2 vols, second edition (London and Bury St Edmunds: J. Rackham, 1794); first volume originally published in 1792.

Primary texts written after 1840

Auden, W.H. and Louis MacNeice, *Letters from Iceland* (London: Faber and Faber, [1937] 1985)

Bowen, Elizabeth, *A Time in Rome* (London: Longmans, 1960)

Conrad, Joseph *'Heart of Darkness' with 'The Congo Diary'*, edited by Robert Hampson (London: Penguin, 2000)

Douglas, Norman, *Fountains in the Sand* (Oxford: Oxford University Press, [1912] 1986)

Freud, Sigmund, 'A Disturbance of Memory on the Acropolis' [1936; first English translation 1941], in *The Pelican Freud Library* (Harmondsworth: Penguin, 1973–), translated under the general editorship of James Strachey, vol. 2, edited by Angela Richards, 443–56

Freud, Sigmund, *The Interpretation of Dreams*, The Pelican Freud Library (Harmondsworth: Penguin, 1973–), translated by James Strachey, edited by James Strachey and Alan Tyson, revised by Angela Richards, vol. 4

Huxley, Aldous, 'The Pierian Spring', in *Along the Road: Notes and Essays of a Tourist* (London: Chatto and Windus, 1925), 190–201

James, Henry, *Italian Hours*, edited by John Auchard (University Park, Pennsylvania: Pennsylvania State University Press, [1909] 1992)

James, Henry, *The Portrait of a Lady* (Penguin: Harmondsworth, [1881] 1971)

Parker, Dorothy, *The Collected Dorothy Parker*, with an introduction by Brendan Gill (London: Penguin, 2001)

Waugh, Evelyn, *Labels: A Mediterranean Journal* (Harmondsworth: Penguin, [1930] 1985)

Wharton, Edith, 'False Dawn (The Forties)', in *Old New York* (New York: Simon and Schuster, [1924] 1995)

Secondary works

Andrews, Malcolm, 'Dickens, Turner and the Picturesque', in *Imagining Italy: Victorian Writers and Travellers*, edited by Catherine Waters, Michael Hollington and John Jordan (Newcastle-upon-Tyne: Cambridge Scholars Publishing, 2010), 177–94

Balfour, Ian, 'Torso: (The) Sublime Sex, Beautiful Bodies, and the Matter of the Text', *Eighteenth-Century Studies*, 39:3 (2006), 323–36

Bann, Stephen, 'Le peuple romain', in *Maestà di Roma: d'Ingres à Degas; les artistes français à Rome*, exhibition catalogue (Rome: Electa, 2003), pp.244–8

Barrell, John, 'The Dangerous Goddess: Masculinity, Prestige and the Aesthetic in Early Eighteenth-Century Britain', in *The Birth of Pandora and the Division of Knowledge* (Basingstoke: Macmillan, 1992), 63–87

Bataille, Georges, 'L'expérience intérieure', in *Œuvres complètes*, edited by Michel Foucault, 12 vols (Paris: Gallimard, 1970–88), vol.5, 7–181

Benedict, Barbara M., *Curiosity: A Cultural History of Early Modern Inquiry* (Chicago and London: University of Chicago Press, 2001)

Chambers, Ross, *Loiterature* (Lincoln, Nebraska, and London: University of Nebraska Press, 1999)

Chard, Chloe, 'Crossing Boundaries and Exceeding Limits: Destabilization, Tourism and the Sublime', in *Transports: Travel, Pleasure and Imaginative Geography, 1600–1830*, edited by Chloe Chard and Helen Langdon (New Haven and London: Yale University Press, 1996), 117–49

Chard, Chloe, 'Effeminacy, Pleasure and the Classical Body', in *Femininity and Masculinity in Eighteenth-Century Art and Culture*, edited by Gill Perry and Michael Rossington (Manchester and New York: Manchester University Press, 1994), 142–61

Chard, Chloe, 'Lassitude and Revival in the Warm South: Relaxing and Exciting Travel, 1750–1830', in *Pathologies of Travel*, edited by George Revill and Richard Wrigley (Amsterdam and Alberta, Georgia: Rodopi, 2000), 175–205

Chard, Chloe, 'Nakedness and Tourism: Classical Sculpture and the Imaginative Geography of the Grand Tour', *Oxford Art Journal*, 18:1 (1995), 14–28

Chard, Chloe, 'Picnic at Pompeii: Hyperbole and Digression in the Warm South', in *Antiquity Recovered: The Legacy of Pompeii and Herculaneum*, edited by Victoria C. Gardner Coates and Jon L. Seydl (Los Angeles: J. Paul Getty Museum, 2007), 115–32

Chard, Chloe, *Pleasure and Guilt on the Grand Tour: Travel Writing and Imaginative Geography, 1600–1830* (Manchester and New York: Manchester University Press, 1999)

Chard, Chloe, 'Scholarship and Sensibility: Anna Jameson and Sydney Morgan in Siren Land', in *Women, Scholarship and Criticism: Gender and Knowledge c.1790–1900*, edited by Joan Bellamy, Anne Laurence and Gill Perry (Manchester and New York: Manchester University Press, 2000), 58–75

Conrad, Peter, *Shandyism: The Character of Romantic Irony* (Oxford: Blackwell, 1978)
Douglas, Mary, 'The Social Control of Cognition: Some Factors in Joke Perception', *Man: The Journal of the Royal Anthropological Institute*, new series, 5 (1968), 361–76
Findlen, Paula, 'Becoming a Scientist: Gender and Knowledge in Enlightenment Italy', *Science in Context*, 16 (2003), 59–88
Fineman, Joel, '"The Pas de Calais": Freud, the Transference and the Sense of Woman's Humor', in *On Puns: The Foundation of Letters*, edited by Jonathan Culler (Oxford: Blackwell, 1988), 100–14
Freud, Sigmund, 'Beyond the Pleasure Principle', in *The Pelican Freud Library* (Harmondsworth: Penguin, 1973–), translated under the general editorship of James Strachey, vol. 11, edited by Angela Richards, 269–338
Freud, Sigmund, *Jokes and Their Relation to the Unconscious*, translated and edited by James Strachey and revised by Angela Richards, *The Pelican Freud Library*, (Harmondsworth: Penguin, 1973–), vol. 6
Freud, Sigmund, 'On Humour' (1927), in *Art and Literature*, translated under the general editorship of James Strachey, edited by Albert Dickson, *The Pelican Freud Library* (Harmondsworth: Penguin, 1973–), vol. 11, 425–33
Fried, Michael, *Absorption and Theatricality: Painting and Beholder in the Age of Diderot*, (Berkeley and Los Angeles: University of California Press, 1980)
Gigante, Denise, *Taste: A Literary History* (New Haven and London: Yale University Press, 2005)
Haskell, Francis, *Rediscoveries in Art: Some Aspects of Taste, Fashion and Collecting in England and France* (London: Phaidon, 1976)
Honour, Hugh, 'Canova's Studio Practice – I: The Early Years', *The Burlington Magazine*, 114:828 (1972), 146–59
Honour, Hugh, 'Canova's Studio Practice – II: 1792–1822', *The Burlington Magazine*, 114:829 (1972), 214–29
Kofman, Sarah, *Pourquoi rit-on? Freud et le mot d'esprit* (Paris: Galilée, 1986)
Kolb, Jocelyne, *The Ambiguity of Taste: Freedom and Food in European Romanticism* (Ann Arbor: University of Michigan Press, 1995)
Lamb, Jonathan, *Preserving the Self in the South Seas, 1680–1840* (Chicago and London: University of Chicago Press, 2001)
Leask, Nigel, *Curiosity and the Aesthetics of Travel Writing, 1770–1840: 'from an antique land'* (Oxford: Oxford University Press, 2002)
Lichtenstein, Jacqueline, *La couleur éloquente: rhétorique et peinture à l'âge classique* (Paris: Flammarion, 1999)
Low, Barbara, *Psycho-Analysis: A Brief Account of the Freudian Theory* (London: George Allen and Unwin Ltd, 1920)
McCalman, Iain (general editor), *An Oxford Companion to the Romantic Age: British Culture 1776–1832* (Oxford: Oxford University Press, 1999)
MacCannell, Dean, *The Tourist: A New Theory of the Leisure Class* (New York: Schocken Books, 1976)
McFarland, Thomas, *Romanticism and the Forms of Ruin: Wordsworth, Coleridge, and Modalities of Fragmentation* (Princeton: Princeton University Press, 1981)
Reddy, William M., *The Navigation of Feeling: A Framework for the History of Emotions* (Cambridge: Cambridge University Press, 2001)

Redford, Bruce, *Dilettanti: The Antic and the Antique in Eighteenth-Century England* (Los Angeles: The J. Paul Getty Museum and the Getty Research Institute, 2008)

Schaffer, E.S., '"To Remind us of China" – William Beckford, Mental Traveller on the Grand Tour: The Construction of Significance in Landscape', in *Transports: Travel, Pleasure and Imaginative Geography, 1600–1830*, edited by Chloe Chard and Helen Langdon (New Haven and London: Yale University Press, 1996), 207–42

Schor, Naomi, *Reading in Detail: Aesthetics and the Feminine* (New York and London: Methuen, 1987)

Siegel, Jonah, *Haunted Museum: Longing, Travel and the Art-Romance Tradition* (Princeton: Princeton University Press, 2005)

Stewart, Susan, *On Longing: Narratives of the Miniature, the Gigantic, the Souvenir, the Collection* (Durham and London: Duke University Press, 1993)

Taylor, Anya, *Bacchus in Romantic England: Writers and Drink, 1780–1830* (Basingstoke: Macmillan, 1999)

Thomas, Nicholas, 'Licensed Curiosity: Cook's Pacific Voyages', in *The Cultures of Collecting*, edited by John Elsner and Roger Cardinal (London: Reaktion Books, 1994), 116–36

Wrigley, Richard, 'Pathological Topographies and Cultural Itineraries: Mapping "Mal'aria in Eighteenth- and Nineteenth-Century Rome', in *Pathologies of Travel*, edited by George Revill and Richard Wrigley (Amsterdam and Alberta, GA: Rodopi, 2000), 207–28

Index

References to the readings (but not to quotations in the introductory sections) are in bold. Brief quotations from Shakespeare and the Bible are not indexed.

Addison, Joseph,
   Cato, **58**
   Remarks on Several Parts of Italy, 18, 19
   Spectator, Essay no. 411, **241**
affectation, risk of, 26, 30, 40, 84, 161
   countered by digression, 31
   and female travellers, 17
   and pedantry, 18–19
air
   bad, **127, 132, 136, 153**
      see also malaria
   and effects of atmosphere and light, **57**, 88–9, **98–9, 101–2, 103, 234–5**
   pleasurable effects of, **117–18**, 222, **233**
   purity of, on Mount Etna, **104–5**
   of Rome, and inspiration, 201
   see also travel, and 'change of air'
Albano, Francesco, **209**
Alboin, King of the Lombards, **96**
Alfieri, Vittorio, 70
Alps, the, 103
   compared with Apennines, 44
   language demanded or excited by, 23, 33, 81–2, **98–9**, 174
   politics and nature on, 91–2, **94–6**
   and rustic domesticity, 79–80, **99**
   sublimity of, 33, 47, 76–7, **93–4, 100–2**
   storms and natural turmoil on, **92, 93–4, 103**
   traversal of, 14, 29, 33, 76–84, **86–102**, 227–8
   see also Cenis, Mount; sublime, the
alterity, 23, 24, 27–9, 35, 43, 64–6, 82
Anson, George, Admiral, *A Voyage round the* World, 43, **54**
anxiety, and travel *see* unease, and travel
Apennines, the, 136–7, 235
   compared with the Alps, 44
   'the Mountains East of Rome', 28 n.61, 31, 143–8, **151–8**
Apollo Belvedere, 16, 25, 164, *165* (Figure 5), 181, **185**, 203
Armstrong, John *see* Temple, Lancelot
art
   and acquisitiveness, 204–5
   anxieties of commenting on, 161–2
   and the female spectator, 18, 160, 163–84, **185–9**, 196–9, 200, **205–7**
   and gossip, 193–6, 204
   and the Grand Tour, 14, 159
   and laughter, 161–84, **184–9**
   and life, 193–6
   and 'odd' spectators, 160, 161–84, **184–9**
   as process, 22, 192–3, **211**

viewed in studios, 22, **136**, 160, 189–205, **205–14**, *190* (Figure 11)
and sexuality, 164–84, **185–9**, **205–6**
see also hyperbole, and art; pleasure, and art; responsiveness, emotional, to art; responsiveness, physical, to art
artists
  and their models, 138, 140, **150**
  as sights, 201–2
  as travellers, 83, **99**, 140, 142, **149**, 201–4, **212**
  see also art, viewed in studios; Rome, sculpture studios in
association, poetic and historical, pleasures of, 3, 42 n.8, 51, 57, 68, 219–24, 236
Auden, W.H., *Letters from Iceland*, 30

Banks, Sir Joseph, **52**
banditti
  dress and appearance of, 146, *152* (Figure 4)
  and drinking, penchant for, 140, 147, **149**, **154**
  mediated by art and literature, 139–42
  peasants searching for, *151* (Figure 3), **157**
  on road from Rome to Naples, 12, 124, 125n, **136–7**, 138–43, **148–51**, **154**
  as sights, 147
  wives and mistresses of, 138, 140, 146, **150**
  see also Apennines, Monti Sabini; light and shade, effects of, and banditti; Rosa, Salvator, and banditti
Bassano, Leandro, *Raising of Lazarus*, 23–4
bathos, 23, 84–6
  in commentary on art, 181
  and food, 62–3, 85, **105**, 143, **150**, **189**

and the sublime, 84–6, **105**, **106**, **108–9**
  see also art, and laughter
beautiful, the, 113–14, 174
Beckford, William
  Biographical Memoirs of Extraordinary Painters, 141
  Dreams, Waking Thoughts and Incidents, 35, 112 n.2
Bell, John, *Observations on Italy*, 29
Bernini, Gianlorenzo
  Charity, **184–5**
  Ecstasy of St Teresa, 181
  mattress for classical *Hermaphrodite*, *208* (Figure 16)
  Santa Bibbiana, 162
Blanc, Mont, 44, 174
Boccaccio, Giovanni, *Decameron*, **102**
Boigne, Charlotte-Louise-Éléonore-Adélaïde de, *Mémoires*, 194 n.43
Bologna, 47, 216
Bonaparte, Lucien, 142, **149–50**
Borghese, Paolina, 194–6, *194* (Figure 12), *195* (Figure 13), 201, **209**, **210**
boundaries,
  dissolution of, 114–15
  traversal of, 12, 20, 77, 120 *see also* Alps, the, traversal of; banditti, on the road from Rome to Naples
  and destabilization, 14
  and digression, 35
Bowen, Elizabeth, *A Time in Rome*, 30
Brosses, Charles de, *Lettres familières*, 181
Browne, Sir Thomas, *Christian Morals*, **55**
Brydone, Patrick, *A Tour through Sicily and Malta*, **54–5**, 75, 83, 84–5, **102–5**
Burke, Edmund, *Philosophical Enquiry*, 76–7, 113–14
Byron, George Gordon Noel (Baron Byron)
  Alpine journal, 23, 174
  The Bride of Abydos, 127 n.22

Byron, George Gordon Noel (Baron Byron) (*cont.*)
  Childe Harold's Pilgrimage, 31, 44, 61, 62 n.50, 79, 163, 202–3, 204, 217
  Bust of, by Thorvaldsen, **207**
  Don Juan, 217
  letters of, 14 n.22, 181
  Manfred, 61
  'The Curse of Minerva', 62, **72**

Canova, Antonio, **186**, 204
  as a foreigner in Rome, 201–2
  Recueil de statues, *167* (Figure 6), *168* (Figure 7), *194* (Figure 12), *195* (Figure 13), *206* (Figure 14), *207* (Figure 15)
  portrait of, by Sir Thomas Lawrence, **214**
  sculptures of
    Chloris (*Naiad*, 'reclining Nymph'), 197, **205–6**, *206* (Figure 14), *207* (Figure 15), 210
    Cupid and Psyche, **198**, **205**, 206
    Daedalus and Icarus, **205**
    Hebe, 210
    Hercules and Lychas, **205**, **209**
    Magdalene, 193
    Mars and Venus, **210–11**
    Napoleon, 193, **214**
    Nymph (bought by Sommariva), **198**, 212, 214
    Perseus, **209**, 214n
    Religion, 214n
    sepulchral monuments of, **210**
    Theseus, 214n
    The Three Graces, 166–71, *167* (Figure 6), *168* (Figure 7), 191, 192, **206**, 210
    Venere Vincitrice (with Paolina Borghese as model), *194* (Figure 12), *195* (Figure 13), 201, **209**, 210
    Venus and Adonis, **205**, **206**, 210
    Venus Coming out of the Bath, 204, 210
  studio of, in Rome, 190, 191–3, 193, 196–9, 200, **205–7**, **209–11**, 212n, 213–14
Capua, 15, 29, **238**
Caravaggio, Michelangelo Merisi da, **209**
Carver, Jonathan, *Travels through America*, 35
Cecconi, Leonardo, *Storia di Palestrina*, **153n**
Cellini, Benvenuto, *Vita*, **90**
Cenis, Mount, **88**, **90**, **91**, **92**, **93**, **95**, **98**, **100**, **102**
Chateaubriand, François René de, **233**
  Itinéraire, 5–6, 15
Chateauvieux, Frédéric Lullin de, *Lettres écrites d'Italie*, **155n**
Cicero, Marcus Tullius, **118**
Cochin, Charles Nicolas, *Voyage d'Italie*, 8–9
Coleridge, Samuel Taylor
  'On the Principles of Genial Criticism', 174
  'Wit and Humour', 196
colour,
  blue of sea and skies, the, 45, 49, 56
  of clothing, **100**, 146, **151**
  and effects of light, 72, 223–4, 226–8, **234–5**
  and jewellery, in sculpture, **210**
  in landscape, 55, 86, **101**, 223–4, 226–8, **234–6**
  and pleasure, 226–31
  in wine, 80, 99, 226–8
  in Venetian painting, **135 n.31**, 227
connoisseurs, as 'odd' travellers, 161–2
Conrad, Joseph, *Heart of Darkness*, 65–6
consumerism, and art, 204–5
Cook, James, Captain, 36
Corradini, Antonio, *Veiled Christ*, 159 n.1
Cornwall, Barry, *Marcian Colonna*, 67
Coryate, Thomas, *Coryats Crudities*, **239n**

Cowper, William, *The Task* (adapted by an *improvvisatore*), 60
curiosity, 13

danger, **1**, **2–3**, 21, 110–58
  and banditti, 137–48, **148–58**
  and crossing boundaries, 14
  dissipates torpor, 141, 149
  and dirt, 63–4
  and disease, 120–4, **124–37**
  and enervation, 12, 15, 110–15, **115–20**, **127**
  flirting with, 13–14, 63, **85**
  and pleasure, 12–14
  and the sublime, **89**, 93
  and travel, 44–5, **54–5**, 229–30
  see also boundaries, traversal of; destabilization
Derry, Frederick Augustus Hervey, Bishop of, and Earl of Bristol, **107**
destabilization, **1**, 5–15, 29, 110–58, 203–4
  and enervation, 110–15, **115–20**
  and the sublime, 14, 75–7, **93–4**, **102**
  and tourism, 14–15, 115
  see also boundaries, traversal of; danger; haunted, the; ruins, ancient
digression, 31–7, 81
  and art criticism, 179–84, **186–9**, **193**
  and the first-person travel narrative, 31–4
  to gastronomy, 216
  and hyperbole, 31, 81
  and sentimentalism, 32–4, 41, 85–6
  topographical, **2**, 34–7, 43–4, **54**, 64–6, 77–8, **87**, **88**, **89**, **90**, **103**, **127**, 142, 145, 150, **155–6**, **158**
dirt, 4, 19, 43, 53, 63–6, 67, 71–2, **124**
  rubbish and ruins, 192, **212**
disease, 120–24, **124–36**
  see also malaria
disorder, and digression, 34, 182–4

Dolce, Carlo (also Dolci), 216–17
dolce far niente, the, 115, **120**, 230–31
Domenichino (Domenico Zampieri)
  Diana and her Nymphs, 8, 124, **134**, **135** (Figure 2), 181–2
  frescoes in San Andrea della Valle, 11
  Sibyl, **134**
  St Jerome, mosaic copy of, **185**
Donne, John, Sermon 23, **241 n.57**
Douglas, Norman, *Fountains in the Sand*, 28
drinking
  in ancient or evocative places, 80, 96, 99, 217, 220–4, **234–5**, **239**
  as a metaphor for destabilization, 229–30
Dryden, John, 'Of the Pythagorean Philosophy', **56 n.42**
Dupaty, Charles, *Lettres sur l'Italie*, translated as *Sentimental Letters on Italy*, 7, 26, 35–6, 110–11, 112, 113–15, **116–19**, 197, 221

eating
  in ancient or evocative places, 80, 220–4, **234–5**, **238–9**
  see also food; gastronomy
Eaton, Charlotte, *Rome in the Nineteenth Century*, 24, 25, 27, 43, 61–6, **71–2**, **72–4**, 191–3, 195, 201–2, 203, 233 n.50, **209–11**
Elliott, Sir Gilbert, *Life and Letters*, 194 n.43
enervation, in the warm South, 12, 15, 110–15, **115–20**, **127**
Englelbach, Lewis, *Naples and the Campagna Felice*, 34, 174–8, *175* (Figure 9), *176* (Figure 10), 179–80, **187–9**, 217
ennui, 83, **129**, **132**
  see also Jameson, Anna, *Diary of an Ennuyée*
Etna, Mount, 25, 50, **54–5**, 84–5, **102–5**

Eustace, John Chetwode, *Tour through Italy*, 11, 18–19, 30–31, **124n, 146 n.55**, 199, 224–5, 226, 233, **235–8**
Evelyn, John, *Diary*, 90, 205, **211**

'Fabrice' (Giuseppe De Fabris), studio of, in Rome, **213**
Farnese Hercules, 171–3, *172* (Figure 8), 179, **186**
fatigue
  and sightseeing, 1, 7–12, 14–15
  and travel, **130, 149, 207–9**
  see also languor; lassitude
feminine, the *see* Grand Tour, the, and gender
Florence
  English society in, **131–2**
  sights of
    Santa Croce, 47
    Uffizi ('the Gallery'), 160, 216, 218
Fontanier, Pierre, *Les figures du discours*, 29–30
food
  and bathos, 62–3, 85, **105**, 143, **150, 189**
  in cultural comparisons, 40
  and natural simplicity, 221–3
  see also eating; gastronomy
Forsyth, Joseph, *Remarks on Antiquities, Arts, and Letters*, 7 n.6, 14 n.22, 18, 20 n.35, 21, 25, 25–6, 60–61, **68**, 114, **119**, 148, 201, 203, 220, 221, 227
Freud, Sigmund
  Beyond the Pleasure Principle, 114 n.6
  'A Disturbance of Memory on the Acropolis', 50, 139
  'On Humour', 82–3
  The Interpretation of Dreams, 139 n.39
  Jokes and Their Relation to the Unconscious, 164

Galiffe, James, *Italy and its Inhabitants*, 10, 12, 26–7, 30, 31–2, 160–1, 195 n.44

Galt, John, *The Life and Studies of Benjamin West*, 161 n.5
gastronomy, 215–33, **233–41**
  and aesthetic taste, 26, 215–20
  and antiquity, 219, 220–6, **234–41**
  gastronomic metaphors, 215–20
    'delicate', 219
    'delicious', 51, **56, 57, 68, 131**, 222, 232–3
    '*dolce*', 216–17, 231
    see also pleasure, 'intoxication'; taste
  and natural simplicity, 221–3, 230, 231–3, **234–5**
  and rustic domesticity, 79–80, **99**
  see also, drinking; eating; food; taste; wine
Gell, Sir William, *Pompeiana*, 120
Gesner, Salomon, 'The First Navigator', **69**
Gibbon, Edward, *Decline and Fall of the Roman Empire*, 145, **153n, 155**
Gibson, John
  Psyche borne away by the Zephyrs, 193, 204–5
  studio of, in Rome, 193
Goethe, Johann Wolfgang von, 'Song of Mignon', from *Wilhelm Meisters Lehrjahre*, **56 n.41**
Goldsmith, Oliver, **239n**
  An History of the Earth, **88 n.18**
  'The Hermit', **106**
  The Vicar of Wakefield, 219
Gothic novel, 1, **97, 139–42**
'Gothic' view of Italy, 20, 37
Graham, Maria, *Three Months Passed in the Mountains East of Rome*, 138, 140, 143–7, **151–8**
  'Peasants in Search of Banditti' (illlustration to), *151* (Figure 3)
  'Station of the Brigands near Guadagnola' (illustration to), *152* (Figure 4)

Grand Tour, the
  concept of, 1, 9–11, 12, 13, 23, 77, 82, 131, 230
  and gender, 9, 15–18, 44–5, **55**
  itinerary of, 9–10, 12, 32, 77
  see also art, and the Grand Tour; pleasure, and benefit; travel
Gray, Robert, *Letters during the Course of a Tour*, 28
Gray, Thomas, 'Alliance of Education and Government', 144, **152**
Greatheed, Bertie, et al.,*The Florence Miscellany*, **88n**
Guercino (Giovanni Francesco Barbieri), 61, 216
guide books, and the genres of travel writing, 31
Guido *see* Reni, Guido
Guinan-Laoureins, J.B. (Jean Baptiste Reinolds), *Tableau de Rome*, 169

Hamilton, Emma, 182 n.28, 194, 201
Hamilton, Sir William, **106**, 194 n.43
  Observations on Mount Vesuvius, Mount Etna, and Other Volcanoes, 107 n.43
Hannibal,
  on the Alps, 78, 79, **90**, **96**
  in Capua, 15, 29
haunted, the, 15, 17, 18, 19, 62–3, **74**, 221
Hawkesworth, John, *An Account of the Voyages... in the Southern Hemisphere*, **52 n.33**
Hazlitt, William
  'English Students at Rome', 121, 203–4
  Notes of a Journey, 12, 28 n.61, 42 n.9, 78–9, 79–84, **97–102**, 138–9, 140, 141, 142–3, **148–51**, 162, 217–18, 219, 227–8
  'On Gusto', 218–19
  'On Wit and Humour', 82, 161
  Hermaphrodite, 197, *208* (Figure 16), **205**

Hobhouse, John Cam
  footnotes to Byron's *Childe Harold*, 31
  Historical Illustrations, 31 n.68
Hogarth, William, *Strolling Actresses Dressing in a Barn*, 182
Homer, **209**, **239**
  Odyssey, **3n**, 112, **115**
Honoratus, Marcus Servius,
  commentaries on Virgil, 126 n.21
Horace (Quintus Horatius Flaccus), **124**, **136**, 220, 222, 225, 227, **235 n.53**, **238**, **239**
horror, 1, **4**, 65, 76, 138
  see also Gothic novel, the; romance; 'romantic'
Hunt, Leigh, *Bacchus in Tuscany*, 220 n.14
Huxley, Aldous, *Along the Road*, 66
hyperbole, 23–7, 29–31, 84
  and alterity, 23, 24
  and art, 23–4, 24–5, 25, 160–1
  and bathos, 84–6
  and digression, 31, 81
  failures in, 23, 81–2, **98–9**, 174
  of incomparability, 192, **214**
  of indescribability, 24–7, **152–3**, 192, **211**
  and indeterminacy, 25–6
  and irony, 36
  and litotes, 29
  and the sublime, 33, 77–8
  risks of, 43–4, 84, 161
  and topographical digression, 35–7
  of unrepresentability, 24–7
  and the unforgettable, 26–7, 80
  see also responsiveness, emotional; responsiveness, physical

improvisation, 201
  and process, incompletion and vitality, 22–3, 60–1, **68–70**
indeterminacy, 113–15, 116–19, 223–4
  and hyperbole, 25–6
indolence, 111–15, **115–20**, 230–31
  see also dolce far niente, the; South, the ('the warm South'), pleasures of

irony, 17, 36, 41, 42, 62–3, 84–6, **102–9**
  see also digression, and sentimentalism
Italians, the
  degradation of, **67**
  rising towards the condition of art, 80, **99**, 147–8, **150**
  sobriety of, **237**
  sympathetic identification with, 59–60
  travelling in England, 64–5
Italy
  haunted character of, 62
  political vicissitudes of, 21–2, 58–60, **67**
  viewed from Alps, 79, **93**, **96**

James, Henry
  Italian Hours, 147–8
  Portrait of a Lady, 199–200
Jameson, Anna, *Diary of an Ennuyée*, 6, 7–8, 16, 19, 22, 24, 26, 27, 31, 36, 40, 42 n.8, 44–5, 45–51, **55–6**, 58–61, 61–2, 66, **67–70**, 75, 111, 115, **119–20**, 159 n.1, 160, 193, 194 n.43, 202–3, 204–5, 217 n.6, 219, 221, 222–3, 226, 231, 233 n.50, **234–5**
Johnson, James, *Change of Air*, 15
Juvenal (Decimus Iunius Iuvenalis), *Satires*, 137 n.36

Kauffman, Angelica, as foreigner in Rome, 201
Keats, John, 'Ode to a Nightingale', 228

Laboureur, Maximilen (sculptor), *Hope*, 124, **136**
Lalande, Joseph Jérôme le Français de, *Voyage d'un Français en Italie*, **91**
languor, 6, 111–12, **119–20**, 123, **128**, **129–30**, **132**, **133**, 231
  see also lassitude
Laocoon, 216

Lassels, Richard, *The Voyage of Italy*, 16
lassitude, 12, 47
  see also languor
laughter
  and anxiety or unease, 82–4, 198–9
  and art, viewing of, 161–84
  and disorder, 196
  and 'odd' travellers, 81–4, **98–100**, 161–84, **184–9**
  and unease, 82–4
Lawrence, Sir Thomas, portrait of Canova, **214**
lazzaroni, **52**, **57**, **119**, 146
Le Riche, J.M., *Antiquités des environs de Naples*, 225–6
light and shade, effects of, **4–5**
  and banditti, 140–2
limits, impatience of, 49–51
  see also boundaries, traversal of
litotes, 11, 27–9, 63
Longinus, Dionysius, *Peri Hypsous*, 50–1, 76, 114 n.5
luxuriance, in landscape, 124, **137**, 224

MacCulloch, John, *On Malaria*, 121
malaria
  12, 120–2, 124, **125**, **127**, **136**, **138**, **155**
manliness *see* Grand Tour, the, and gender
Marmontel, Jean-François, *Contes Moraux*, 123, **128**
Martens, Hans Ditlef Christian, *Pope Leo XII visits Thorwaldsen's Studios*, 190 (Figure 11)
masculinity *see* Grand Tour, the, and gender
Matthews, Henry, *Diary of an Invalid*, 5, 25, 28–9, 49, 62–3, 78, 123, 124, **134–7**, 146–7, 164–6, 169, 170, 171, 175, 178, 180–1, 184, **185–6**, 190, 192, 196–9, 200, **205–9**, 216–17, 218, 227
Maupertuis, Pierre Louis Moreau de *La Figure de la terre*, 36, 77–8, **89**

Michelangelo, **209**
Middleton, Conyers, *Letter from Rome*, 10
Miller, Anne, Lady, *Letters from Italy*, 171–3
Milton, John
  'L'Allegro', **100**
  Paradise Lost, 42, 53, 90, **92**, **94**, **95**, **96**
Montagu, Lady Mary Wortley, *Letters*, **90**
Montesquieu, Charles Louis de Secondat, Baron de
  De l'esprit des lois, 111–12, 114
  'Essai sur le goût', 163 n.8
moonlight, viewing sights by, 61–3, 72–4, **132**, 223
Moore, John, **69**
  View of Society and Manners in Italy, 28, 162, 171–3, 179, 180, 184, **186**
Moore, Thomas
  'Love's Young Dream', **129**
Morgan, Sydney, Lady [Sydney Owenson]
  reputation for fearlessness, 22, **67**
  Italy, **1–5**, 8, 13–14, 15, 18–19, 21, 28 n.61, 35, 37, 77, 78, 79, 80, 85, **90–6**, **107–9**, 120, **124–5**, 191, 192, 198, 202, 205, **212–14**, 221 n.19, 233
    Sir Thomas Morgan's appendix to, 121–2
  Life and Times of Salvator Rosa, 142

Naples, 238
  animation of, 11–12, **57–8**, 112, **119**
  arrival in, 235, **238**
  climate of, **119–20**, 127
  compared with England, 45, **56**
  compared with Rome, 10–12, 19–20
  degraded condition of inhabitants, 51, 57
  environs of, **1–5**, 116–19
    Baia, 3n, 4, 26, 117, 222
    Capri, 24, 235
    Herculaneum, 1, 4
    Pompeii, **4**, **124**, 221–4, **234–5**
    see also Vesuvius, Mount
  and itinerary of Grand Tour, 12, 16
  manners in, 28, 36–7, 42–3, **52–4**, 56–7
  natural drama of, 1–5, 12, 21, 56, 57
  as place of repose, **1–2**, 7
  and pleasure, 10–12, 20, 45, 56, **57–8**
  responses to, 1–2, 6–7, 49–51
  road to, from Rome, 47, 124, **124–5**, **136–7**, 137–43, **148–51**, 154
  sights of
    Santa Chiara, 37
    Virgil's Tomb, 220
  and topographical digression, 36–7
  violence in, **54**
  see also lazzaroni; Pontine Marshes; South, the ('the warm South'), pleasures of
Napoleon, 78–9, **90**, **94**, **96**, **97–8**, 196, **209**, **212**
Nirvana principle, the, 114
Normanby, Constantine Henry Phipps, Marquis of, *The English in Italy*, 17, 63 n.52, 122–4, **126–34**, 216
novel, the, and genres of travel writing, 32

Parker, Dorothy, 'The Artist's Reward', 174
Peacock, Thomas Love, 221
  Crotchet Castle, 195
  Nightmare Abbey, 15
pedantry, rejection of, 18–20
people, the ('il popolo'), 20, **119**, 146–8, **150–1**, *151* (Figure 3)
  see also banditti; improvisation; lazzaroni; Rome, *rioni* (quarters) of, Trastevere, and the *trasteverini*
Peresio, Giovanni Camillo, *Il Maggio Romanesco*, **153n**
Petrarch (Francesco Petrarca), **153n**
  'Canzoniere "Che debb'io far?"', **67**

Petrarch (Francesco Petrarca) (*cont.*)
  Rerum Senilium Libri (*Letters of Old Age*), **127n**
picturesque, the, 24, **137**
  and dirt, 66
  and 'il popolo', 146–8
Pignotti, Lorenzo, **96n**
Piozzi, Hester Lynch (Mrs. Thrale, née Salusbury)
  journal, 41
  Observations and Reflections, 23–4, 24–5, 26, 28, 35, 40–1, 42–5, 48–9, 51, **52–4**, 61, 76–7, 77–8, 85, **86–9**, **105–7**, 161, 181–2, 216
pleasure, **103**, **104**, **105**, 151, 225
  and art, 160
  and benefit, 13, 23, 228, 230, **240–1**
  in cultural comparisons, 40–3, **53–4**, 56, 231–4
  and danger, 12–14, 121, **115–16**, **118–19**, 151
  and enthralment, 41–3
  and excitement, 45, 56, **128–9**, **132–3**, 216
  failures in, 39–40
  gastronomic, 215–33, **234–41**
  and gender, 10, 16, 17, 44–5
  innocent and irresponsible, 230–3, **240–1**
  'intoxication', 10, 79, 80, **102**, 233
  and the Grand Tour, 10–11, 13, 39–40
  multisensory, 225
  and the sublime, 77, **88**, 114–15
  and tourism, 14, 58–9
  the 'triste plaisir' of travel, 5–6, 123, 147
  in the warm South, *see* South, the ('the warm South'), pleasures of
  see also dolce far niente, the; laughter
Pliny (Gaius Plinius Secundus), *Natural History*, **237**
Pommereul, François René Jean, Baron de, *Campagne du Général Buonaparte en Italie*, **94n**

Pontine Marshes, 120–1, **136**
  see also Naples, road to, from Rome
Pope, Alexander
  'Eloisa to Abelard', **213 n.64**
  'Epistle to Dr Arbuthnot', **109**
  Essay on Criticism, 97
  'The First Satire of the Second Book of Horace, Imitated', **235 n.52**
Porta, Guglielmo della, *Justice*, **184–5**
Poussin, Nicolas, as foreigner in Rome, 201
preterition, trope of, 27, 58, **67–8**
process, 20–3, 26, 60–1
  and art, 22, 192–3, **211**
  and Italian politics, 21–2
  and improvisation, 22–3
  and nature, 20–1, 26
Propertius, Sextus, 110, **118**

Radcliffe, Ann, *A Sicilian Romance*, 140–2
Raphael (Raffaele Sanzio), 80, **99**, 161
  Deposition, **134**
  Entombment, 181
  La Fornarina, 24, 218, 219
  precursors of, 20
  St John the Baptist, 162
  Transfiguration, 33
    Mosaic copy of, **185**
  Virgin with Donor (*Madonna di Foligno*), 181
Reni, Guido, 217
  St Michael the Archangel, mosaic copy of, **185**
responsiveness
  emotional, 17, 19
    to art, 159, 160–1, 182
    and female travellers, 18
    and sentimentalism, 32
  physical, 124, **133**
    to art, 159
restlessness, 1, 5–7, 35, 44, **131**
Reynolds, Frances, *Enquiry*, 76
Richardson, John, *A Dissertation on the Languages, Literature, and Manners of Eastern Nations*, 145, **158**

road-building, 78–9, 86, **94–5**, **100**
Rogers, Samuel, *Italy*, 219, 220, 227, 228–30, **238–41**
Rogissart, Alexandre de, *Les délices de l'Italie*, 232–3
Roman Catholicism, 11, 43, **52–4**
romance, 40, 62–3, 173, **186**
Romano, Giulio, works of, in Mantua, 24
'romantic', 42 n.8, 139–42, 143, **149**, **150**
Romanticism, 17–18, 20–3
Rome,
  art in, vast quantities of, 8–11, 204
  artists in, 201–4
    see also sculpture studios in
  arrival in, 33, 122–3, 124
  and authority, 11, 20
  contrasted with Naples, 10–12, 19–20
  dirt and rubbish in, 63–6, 71–2, 192, **212**
  environs of
    the Campagna, 120, **151–3**, 155
    Tivoli, 25, 144, 157, 217, 221
  fatigue induced by, 8–11
  grandeur of, 11, **133**
    see also seriousness of
  and hyperbole, 30
  noise of, 209
  rioni (quarters) of, Trastevere, and the trasteverini, 146, 147
  sculpture studios in, 22, **136**, 160, 189–214, *190* (Figure 11), **205–14**
  seriousness of, 10–12, 19, 112, 199–200
  sightseeing in, 49
  sights of, 19, 181
    Capitoline Museum, 61
    Coliseum, 19, 27, **71**, **72–4**, **212**
    by moonlight, 61–3, **72–4**
    Fountain of Egeria, 40
    Palatine, the, **72–4**, **133**
    Pantheon, 39, 40, 63–6, **71–2**
    Roman Forum, the, 24, **74**
    St Peter's, 8, 35, 36, **53**, 162–3, **184–5**, **214n**, 216, 217
  Tomb of the Horatii and Curatii, 40
  Vatican, the, **44**, 160–1, 164–6, **185–6**, 197, 199, 203, 216
Rosa, Salvator, **3n**, 141–2, **209**
Rose, William Stewart, *Letters from the North of Italy*, 219–20
Rossi, Domenico de, *Raccolta di statue*, *208* (Figure 16)
Rowe, Nicholas, *Jane Shore*, 42, **53**
Rowlandson, Thomas, Don Luigi meets Donna Anna in the Museum', *175* (Figure 9)
ruins, ancient, 15, 21, 125
  in the Bay of Naples, **117–18**
  in Rome, 11, 192, **212**, 216
  and the haunted, 62, **74**
  and solitude, 133
  over-valued, 19
  and weeds, 62
  see also Rome, sights of

Sade, Donatien Alphonse François de, *Voyage d'Italie*, 162
Sass, Henry, *Journey to Rome and Naples*, 25, 26, 51–2, **56–8**, 120 n.13, 222, 223, 224, **233**
Schadow, Rudolph, *Filatrice*, **212–13**
Schlegel, Friedrich von, *Über die Sprache und Weisheit der Indier*, 145, **158**
Scott, Sir Walter, 150
  Rob Roy, 79, **97 n.34**
  Waverley, 156
sculpture,
  classical and neo-classical, 3–40, 41, 164–73, *165* (Figure 5), *167* (Figure 6), *168* (Figure 7), *172* (Figure 8), **185–6**, 189–205, *190* (Figure 11), *194* (Figure 12), *195* (Figure 13), *206* (Figure 14), *207* (Figure 15), *208* (Figure 16), **205–14**
  colour and jewellery in, **210**
  and process, 22, 192–3, **211**
  viewed by torchlight, 61, **185**

sculpture, (cont.)
  viewed in studios, 124, 189–205, **205–214**
Seneca, Lucius Annaeus, **118**
sentimentalism, 17–18, 24, 29, 32–4, 41–3, 46
  see also Sterne, Laurence, *A Sentimental Journey*
Shakespeare, William, references to (excluding brief quotations), 184
  The Winter's Tale, **145**
Shelley, Mary, journal of, 45
Shelley, Percy Bysshe, letters of, 19, 62 n.50, 221, 223–4, 225
Sherlock, Martin
  Lettres d'un voyageur anglois, translated as *Letters from an English Traveller*, 36, 162–3, **184–5**
  Nouvelles lettres d'un voyageur anglois, 34, **54 n.37**
sights
  and intensity, 63, 85
  and 'markers', 25
  in Naples, paucity of, **1–2**, 7
  in Rome, proliferation of, 2, 8–9
sightseeing, 233
  and digression, disruptive effect of, 32, 85–6
  and fatigue, **1**, 7–12, 14–15
  and sequential progression, 31
  see also sculpture, viewed in studios; sculpture, viewed by torchlight; Naples, sights of; Rome, sights of; tourism
Simond, Louis, *Voyage en Italie et en Sicile*, translated as *A Tour in Italy and Sicily*, 36–7
Sirens, the, 112–13, **115–16**
sirocco, the, 122, **127**
Smith, Sir James Edward,
  Memoir, 10, 12, 19
  A Sketch of a Tour on the Continent, 54 n.37
Smollett, Tobias, *Travels through France and Italy*, 39, 63–4

solitude
  and framing, 63
  and the haunted, 62–3, **73–4**
  and solemnity, **132**
  and travel, 5, 123, **128–31**, 133–4
Sommariva, Gianbattista (art collector), 198, **212**
South, the ('the warm South')
  allure of, 6–7, 20
  benefits of, delusory, **126–7**, **133–4**
  and the cold North, 10, 45, 49
  effeminacy and effemination in, 15, 110–15, **115–19**
  enervation in, 12, 114–15, **119–20**
  and indeterminacy, 26, 223–4, **235**
  pleasures of, 51, **56**, 57–8, 110–15, 115–20, 222–4, 231–3, **234–5**
  anticipated on the Alps, 20, 79–80, **96** see also dolce far niente, the; laughter
  vitality and vivacity of, **2–3**, 22, 112
Spagnoletto, Lo (Jusepe de Ribera), **209**
Spence, Joseph, *Polymetis*, 165 (Figure 5), *172* (Figure 8)
Staël, Germaine de,
  Corinne, 5, 6, 22, 32, 42n.8, 46, 112, 121, **124 n**, 123, 147, 200, 201
  translation of Goethe's 'Song of Mignon', **56**
Starke, Mariana, *Letters from Italy*, 221
Stendhal (Henri Beyle)
  De l'amour, 20 n.35
  Promenades dans Rome, 8, 11, 166–71, 175, 178, 180, 181, 184, 190–1, 193
  Rome, Naples et Florence, 20 n.35, 231–3
Sterne, Laurence
  A Sentimental Journey, 32–4, 39, 41–2, 59, **67**, **68**, 79–80, 81–2, 85–6, 228–30, **238–41**
  Tristram Shandy, 41
sublime, the
  on the Alps, 33, 47, 76–7, **93–4**, **100–2**

and bathos, 84–6, **105**, **106**, **108–9**
and the beautiful, 113–14, 174
and danger, **89**
and destabilization, 14, 75, 77, **93–4**, **101–2**
and hyperbole, 33
and impatience of limits, 49–51, 77–80
and indeterminacy, 26, 113–15, **116–19**
and infinitude, 26, 49–51, **55–6**, 75, 114
and language, 26–7, 81–2, **87**, **98–9**
and pleasure, **88**
and self-affirmation, 75, 76, 79, 160–1, 203
and terror, **2n**, 26–7, **88**
and transcendence, **104–5**
Swinburne, Henry, *Travels in the Two Sicilies*, 24, 112–13, **115–16**, 221–2

Tahiti ('Otaheite'), 28, 36–7, 41, **52**
  see also digression, topographical
taste
  changes in, 20
  and gastronomy, 26, 215–20
  the 'man of taste', authority of, 16–17, 160, 182
  metaphor of, 215, 217–19
Temple, Lancelot [John Armstrong], *Short Ramble*, 16, 17 n.29, 39–40
Terni, cascade (and inn) at, 26, 27, 31, 88 n.19, 217
Terracina, 6–7, 124, **136–7**, **238–9**
terror, 1, **4**, 76, **103**
  and the sublime, **88**
Thomson, James, *The Seasons*, 87, 88
Thorvaldsen, Bertel, **185**
  as foreigner in Rome, 201–2
  studio of, in Rome, 190–1, *190* (Figure 11), 192, **207**, **212**
  works of,
    Lord Byron, bust of, **207**
    Night (bas-relief), **207**

Shepherd, **207**
Triumph of Alexander, **212**
Venus Victrix, **207**
Tibullus, Albius, **117**
Titian (Tiziano Vecelli), 134–5, 218, 227
  Venus Blinding Cupid's Eyes, 181
tourism
  as approach to the foreign, 14, 58–9, **67–8**, 115, 230
  'behind-the-scenes', and studio visits, 191
  and exclusion of encounters with human beings, 14, 58–60
  and framing, 61–2, 63
  and 'markers', 25
  and pleasure, 58, 230
  the term *tourist*, 14 n.22
  see also sightseeing
transgression *see* boundaries, traversal of
travel
  as an adventure of the self, 13, 203–4
  and anxiety and unease, 83, 84
  and 'change of air', 122–4, **126–34**
  effects of, 43–5
  and gender, 44–5, **55**
  and personal need, 45–51
  and revival, 124, **128–9**, 133
  and unease, 82–4
  see also destabilization; Grand Tour, the; pleasure; tourism
travellers
  behaviour of, in the warm South, 15, 112
  drinking and reeling, 220
  English, **131**, 138, 142, **150**, **239–40**
  female, **125**, 163–84, 171–3, 174, **185–9**
  odd, 81–4, 98–100, 161–84, **184–9**
    see also art, and the female spectator; art, and 'odd' spectators; artists, as travellers
  as sights, 201–4
travelling, on foot, **98–100**

travel writing,
  and autobiography, 48–9
  genres of, 31
  language of *see* digression;
    hyperbole; litotes;
    preterition
  and the novel, 32
  see also guide books
Trench, Melesina Chevenix St
  George, journal of, 182
  n.28
Tresham, Henry, *The Ascent of
  Vesuvius*, 108 (Figure 1)

Ulloa, Antonio de, travel writings
  of, 44
unease, and travel, 83–4, 129, 161–2

Vacca, Flaminio, 'Memorie di Varie
  antichità', **153n**
Van Dyck, Sir Anthony (also, for
  example, Van Dyke), 218
Varro, Marcus Terentius, *De Lingua
  Latina*, **95n**
Vasari, Giorgio,*Vite*, **134 n.30**,
  178–9
Venice, 26, 28, 47, 130
Venus de' Medici, 160, **185**, **207**, 210
  n.62, 216
  criticized, 28 n.61, 39–40
  eludes description, 25
Vesuvius, Mount, 4, 35, 51, **57**, 85,
  108 (Figure 1), 139, **148**,
  217, 221, **234**, **235**, **238**
  crater of, 18, **106–7**, **107–9**
  eruptions of, 2, **4n**, 5, 26–7, 55–6,
  104, **105–9**
Vigée-Lebrun, Elisabeth, *Souvenirs*,
  194 n.43
Vinci, Leonardo da, *Christ Disputing
  with the Doctors*, 181
Virgil (Publius Vergilius Maro), 220,
  238, **239**
  Aeneid
    associations with, 3
  Eclogues, **188 n.34**
  Georgics, **236**
Voltaire, François-Marie Arouet de,
  La Henriade, **56 n.41**

Walker, Adam, *Ideas, Suggested on the
  Spot*, 216
Walpole, Horace, letters of, **90**, **91**,
  92, 194 n.43
Watkins, Thomas, *Travels*, 25
Waugh, Evelyn, *Labels*, 26
Webb, Daniel, *An Inquiry into the
  Beauties of Painting*, 182
  n.29
Weeping Dacia, the, 41
West, Benjamin, 161 n.5
Wharton, Edith, 'False Dawn', 20
  n.35
Williams, Hugh William, *Travels in
  Italy*, 227
Winckelmann, Johann Joachim,
  *Geschichte der Kunst des
  Alterthums*, 173
wine,
  ancient and modern, 224–6,
    235–8
  and the ancients, 65, **236–8**
  anticipating the pleasures of Italy,
    79–80, **96**, **99**, 227–8
  Caecuban, 225, **237–8**
  colour and luminosity of, **99**,
    226–8, **239**
  and destabilization, 229–30
  Falernian, 220, 222, 224, 227,
    237–8, **239**
  Lachryma Christi, **107**, 217, 221,
    238
  and luxury, **234**
  and poetic inspiration, 220
  suitable for drinking at Pompeii,
    223, **235**
  see also gastronomy; South, 'the
    warm South'
Wollstonecraft, Mary, *Letters Written
  during a Short Residence
  in Sweden, Norway, and
  Denmark*, 46
women
  excluded from sights, **125**
  as sights, 32–3
Wordsworth, William, 'Peter Bell',
  111, **119**
Wright, Joseph, *Maria, from Sterne*,
  41

EU authorised representative for GPSR:
Easy Access System Europe, Mustamäe tee 50,
10621 Tallinn, Estonia
gpsr.requests@easproject.com

www.ingramcontent.com/pod-product-compliance
Lightning Source LLC
Chambersburg PA
CBHW071405300426
44114CB00016B/2186